AT&T

AT&T COMPUTER SOFTWARE CATALOG
MS-DOS Software for the AT&T PC 6300 and PC 6300 PLUS

Winter 1986

Prentice-Hall
A Division of Simon & Schuster, Inc.
Englewood Cliffs, New Jersey 07632

ISBN 0-8359-9278-0
Select Code No: 311-021

The *AT&T COMPUTER SOFTWARE CATALOG—MS-DOS Software for the AT&T PC 6300 and PC 6300 PLUS* is produced by AT&T Information Systems, Inc., and is published two times a year.

Editor in Chief: Jean Kytt Marcus
Editor: Joy McGann Faxon
Associate Editor: Elisabet Starr Winquist
Manuscript Entry: Christine Victoria Eastman
Sharon Aldrich
Staff Associate: Lisa S. French
Technical Consultant: Harrel Wright
UNIX Software Review Technician: Laura Shaw Lenhart

Publisher:
Prentice-Hall
A Division of Simon & Schuster, Inc.
Englewood Cliffs, NJ 07632

Project Manager: Pamela C. Jacoby
Production Supervision: Ann L. Mohan
Cover Design: Joyce Thompson
Photography: Mike Mitchell

IMPORTANT NOTE TO USERS

Descriptions and other information related to each software product contained in this *Catalog* have been furnished by its respective vendor or supplier. While every reasonable effort has been made to ensure the accuracy of all information in this *Catalog*, AT&T Information Systems, Inc. and Prentice-Hall do not guarantee the accuracy of any statements made within the descriptions and do not assume, and hereby expressly and absolutely disclaim, any liability to any party for any loss or damage caused by errors or ommissions or statements of any kind in the *AT&T Computer Software Catalog*, its updates, supplements or special editions, whether such errors are omissions or statements resulting from negligence, accident or any other cause. Neither AT&T Information Systems, Inc. nor Prentice-Hall expressly or implicitly guarantees any compatibility of the software products listed herein. Neither AT&T Information Systems, Inc. nor Prentice-Hall endorses, warrants, represents or recommends any of the products or services described in the *AT&T Computer Software Catalog* or their vendors and suppliers.

Data entry and editorial development for the *AT&T Computer Software Catalog* performed on the AT&T 3B20 computer.

From an electronically transmitted manuscript, the page proofs for this catalog were composed on a TYXSET 1000 System by TYX Corporation in Reston, Virginia, and output using a Canon LBP-CX Laser Beam Printer. The camera-ready copy was also composed on a TYXSET 1000 System and output using a Mergenthaler 101.

10 9 8 7 6 5 4 3 2 1

Printed in the United States of America

CONTENTS

PREFACE TO THE SECOND EDITION

The *AT&T Computer Software Catalog* is a thorough, up-to-date reference manual of software products that have been reviewed or certified for compatiblity with AT&T's computers. The second edition, which has been reformatted and expanded to two volumes to accommodate new software entries since the first edition, presents information concerning application categories, computer requirements, detailed product descriptions, ordering, and more.

The *AT&T Computer Software Catalog* plays a significant role by providing all Independent Software Vendors distributing *UNIX* System V and/or *MS*-DOS software the opportunity to inform the marketplace of their software products by listing those products in the *Catalog*.

The *AT&T Computer Software Catalog—UNIX System V Software for the AT&T 3B2/3B5/3B20 and UNIX PC* best serves the *UNIX* community and marketplace by providing accurate and complete descriptions of software products for *UNIX System V* that have been reviewed and/or certified for compatibility with AT&T's 3B family of computers and the *UNIX* PC. *MS*-DOS software referenced in the companion volume, *AT&T Computer Software Catalog—MS-*DOS *Software for the AT&T PC 6300 and PC 6300 PLUS*, has been reviewed and/or certified for compatibility with the two named personal computers. By listing only software that is known to be compatible, the *AT&T Computer Software Catalog* can help each reader make informed decisions when purchasing both hardware and software.

The *Catalog* refrains from endorsing any of the referenced software products. Evaluating software is subjective and makes sense only when taking into account the specific needs and skill level of the user. Each user has unique requirements and preferences and thus should seek the advice of a local AT&T authorized dealer or Account Executive to determine what products best suit the application.

TRADEMARK ACKNOWLEDGMENTS

Registered trademarks and trademarks will be italicized throughout the *AT&T Computer Software Catalog*.

Accord is a trademark of Global Information Systems Technology, Inc.
ACES is a trademark of Fifth Generation Technologies, Inc.
Administrative Software is a trademark of Conetic Systems, Inc.
ADRSII is a registered trademark of International Business Machines Corporation
Advanced DB Master is a trademark of DB Master Associates
Advanced Trace86 is a trademark of Morgan Computing Company, Inc.
AEPEX is a trademark of Timberline Systems, Inc.
ANDROMEDA is a trademark of California Automation, Inc.
APL*PLUS is a registered trademark of STSC, Inc.
ARC is a trademark of Armor Systems, Inc.
Armor Systems, Inc., is a trademark of Armor Systems, Inc.
Ashton-Tate is a trademark of Ashton-Tate
AST-3780 is a trademark of AST Research
AST-BSC is a trademark of AST Research
Basic Four is a registered trademark of MAI Basic Four, Inc.
BASIC/FOUR is a registered trademark of MAI Basic Four, Inc.
BBx is a trademark of BASIS, Inc.
BERMAN TECHNOLOGIES is a trademark of Berman Technologies
BLAST is a registered trademark of Communications Research Group
BRANCH STORE RETAILING is a trademark of TRAC LINE Software, Inc.
BROKER'S HELPER is a trademark of North American Software, Inc.
Business Basic Extended is a trademark of BASIS, Inc.
BYTECRAFT is a trademark of Bytecraft, Inc.
C*I*P is atrademark of Concentric Data Systems, Inc.
C-ISAM is a trademark of Relational Database Systems, Inc.
Calcomp is a registered trademark of Calcomp, Inc.
CARES is a trademark of Fifth Generation Technologies, Inc.
CBASIC is a trademark of Digital Research, Inc.
Cdex is a trademark of Cdex Corporation
CHART-MASTER is a registered trademark of Decision Resources
Client Arranger is a trademark of Creative Solutions, Inc.
Collect is a trademark of MicroPride, Inc.
CompuServe is a registered trademark of CompuServe
Computer Action Learning is a registered trademark of Computer Action Learning
Conetic Systems is a trademark of Conetic Systems, Inc.
Consolidation Module is a trademark of Chang Labs
Copylink is a trademark of U.S. Digital Corporation
Cornerstone is a trademark of Infocom, Inc.
CorrectStar is a trademark of MicroPro International Corporation
CP/M is a registered trademark of Digital Research, Inc.
CP/M-86 is a registered trademark of Digital Research, Inc.
CROSS SELL MANAGER is a trademark of Berman Technologies
CUSTOMER INQUIRY WORKBENCH is a registered trademark of ProfitKey International
D.A.T.A. is a trademark of TOM Software, Inc.
DataFlex is a trademark of DataAccess Corporation
DataGrabber is a trademark of Decision Resources
Datamension Corporation is a trademark of Datamension Corporation
DataZoom is a trademark of PowerBase Systems, Inc.
DAVID is a registered trademark of KJ Software, Inc.
Dayflo is a trademark of Dayflo, Inc.
dBASE is a registered trademark of Ashton-Tate
dBASE II is a registered trademark of Ashton-Tate
dBASE III is a trademark of Ashton-Tate
DEC is a trademark of Digital Equipment Corporation
DIAGRAM-MASTER is a trademark of Decision Resources
DIBOL is a registered trademark of Digital Equipment Corporation
DIF is a registered trademark of Software Arts, Inc.
Digital Research C is a trademark of Digital Research, Inc.
Digital Research is a registered trademark of Digital Research, Inc.
Dimension is a registered trademark of AT&T
DISPATCHER'S WORKBENCH is a registered trademark of ProfitKey International
DISTRIBUTING is a trademark of TRAC LINE Software, Inc.
DMP 29 is a trademark of Houston Instruments, Inc.
DMP 41 is a trademark of Houston Instruments, Inc.
DR Draw is a trademark of Digital Research, Inc.
DR Graph is a trademark of Digital Research, Inc.
DR. LOGO is a trademark of Digital Research, Inc.
dWINDOW is a trademark of Liberty Bell Systems
E-Z PC is a trademark of EZ PC, Inc.
EASY REFERENCE is a trademark of Morgan Computing Company, Inc.
EasyGantt is a trademark of Morgan Computing Company, Inc.
EasyWriter is a trademark of Informational Unlimited Software
ENABLE is a trademark of The Software Group
ENGINEER'S WORKBENCH is a registered trademark of ProfitKey International
EPSON is a registered trademark of Epson America, Inc.
Epson FX-100 is a trademark of Epson America, Inc.
Epson FX-80 is a trademark of Epson America, Inc.
ESTIMATOR'S WORKBENCH is a registered trademark of ProfitKey International
Ethernet is a trademark of Xerox Corporation
EXCALIBUR PLUS is a registered trademark of Armor Systems, Inc.
EXEC*U*STAT is a registered trademark of EXEC*U*STAT
Expert Advisor is a registered trademark of Management Support Technology, Inc.
Expert Manager is a registered trademark of Management Support Technology, Inc.
FGT is a trademark of Fifth Generation Technologies, Inc.
filePro is a registered trademark of The Small Computer Company
Files & Folders is a trademark of Starcom Computer Corporation
Financial Navigator is a trademark of MoneyCare, Inc.
FlashCalc is a trademark of Paladin Software Corporation
FLEXSYSTEM is a trademark of International Small Business Computers, Inc.
FOCUS is a trademark of Information Builders, Inc.
FORMIX is a trademark of Master Computer Systems, Inc.
Friday! is a trademark of Ashton-Tate
Frieze is a trademark of ZSOFT Corporation
FX-MX Epson 130 is a trademark of Epson America, Inc.
FX-MX Epson 80 is a trademark of Epson America, Inc.

G & G 1040 is a trademark of G & G Software, Inc.
G & G GL is a trademark of G & G Software, Inc.
Gantt-Pack is a registered trademark of Gantt Systems, Inc.
Gould is a trademark of Gould, Inc.
Grafpoint is a trademark of Grafpoint
GraphPlan is a trademark of Chang Labs
GRAPHWRITER is a trademark of Graphic Communications, Inc.
GW is a trademark of Microsoft Corporation
HAI*LINE is a trademark of Holland Automation International
H-BOMM is a trademark of Helmsman Systems, Inc.
H-BUY is a trademark of Helmsman Systems, Inc.
H-CHAMP is a trademark of Helmsman Systems, Inc.
H-MAKE is a trademark of Helmsman Systems, Inc.
H-MRP is a trademark of Helmsman Systems, Inc.
H-PLAN/M is a trademark of Helmsman Systems, Inc.
H-STORE is a trademark of Helmsman Systems, Inc.
Hayes is a registered trademark of Hayes Microcomputer Products, Inc.
Hewlett-Packard is a registered trademark of the Hewlett-Packard Company
Higgins is a trademark of Conetic Systems, Inc.
HP 7400 is a registered trademark of the Hewlett-Packard Company
IBM is a registered trademark of International Business Machines Corporation
IBX is a registered trademark of Intecom Corporation
Infocom is a trademark of Infocom, Inc.
INFORMIX is a registered trademark of Relational Database Systems, Inc.
Innovative is a trademark of Innovative Software, Inc.
K-Graph is a trademark of Micro Data Base Systems, Inc.
K-Mouse is a trademark of Micro Data Base Systems, Inc.
K-Paint is a trademark of Micro Data Base Systems, Inc.
K-Report is a trademark of Micro Data Base Systems, Inc.
K-Text is a trademark of Micro Data Base Systems, Inc.
KINGDOM is a trademark of Seismic Micro-Technology
Knoware is a trademark of Knoware Learning Systems, Inc.
KnowledgeMan is a registered trademark of Micro Data Base Systems, Inc.
Laser Jet is a trademark of the Hewlett-Packard Company
LATTICE is a registered trademark of Lattice, Inc.
Leading Edge is a trademark of Leading Edge Products, Inc.
LEVEL II COBOL is a trademark of Micro Focus, Inc.
Lifetree Software, Inc. is a trademark of Lifetree Software, Inc.
Link Module is a trademark of Chang Labs
LOTUS is a registered trademark of Lotus Development Corporation
LQ 1500 is a trademark of Epson Corporation
MAI is a registered trademark of MAI Basic Four, Inc.
MailMerge is a registered trademark of MicroPro International Corporation
MAINSTAY is a trademark of Mainstay Software Corporation
Master Membership Profile is a registered trademark of Membership Services, Inc.
METAFILE is a registered trademark of Metafile Information Systems, Inc.
MASTER SCHEDULER'S WORKBENCH is a registered trademark of ProfitKey International
MASTER WORKS is a registered trademark of Management Support Technology, Inc.
MEDALLION is a trademark of Timberline Systems, Inc.
Medi-Span is a registered trademark of Medi-Span, Inc.
MemoPlan is a trademark of Chang Labs
MICRO CONTROL is a trademark of International Management Reporting Services, Inc.
MICROCA$H is a registered trademark of Future Technologies International, Inc.
MicroPlan is a trademark of Chang Labs
Microsoft is a registered trademark of Microsoft Corporation
MicroTEX is a trademark of Addison-Wesley Publishing Company, Inc.
MP/M-86 is a trademark of Digital Research, Inc.
MS is a registered trademark of Microsoft Corporation
MultiMate is a trademark of Multimate International Corporation
Multiplan is a registered trademark of Microsoft Corporation
Multiscreen is a trademark of The Santa Cruz Operation, Inc.
NetWare is a registered trademark of Novell, Inc.
Noted Author Series is a registered trademark of KJ Software, Inc.
Novell is a registered trademark of Novell, Inc.
NWA STATPAK is a trademark of Northwest Analytical, Inc.
OfficeLink is a trademark of Office Solutions, Inc.
OfficeSpeller is a trademark of Office Solutions, Inc.
OfficeWriter is a trademark of Office Solutions, Inc.
Open Access is a registered trademark of Software Products International, Inc.
Open Systems is a trademark of Open Systems, Inc.
ORDER ENTRY WORKBENCH is a registered trademark of ProfitKey International
Overhead Express is a trademark of BPS
Paladin is a trademark of Paladin Software Corporation
Pascal/MT+ is a trademark of Digital Research, Inc.
PC MANAGER is a trademark of Tymon, Inc.
PC Paintbrush is a trademark of Z-Soft Corporation
PC-Interface is a trademark of Locus Computing Corporation
PC/FOCUS is a registered trademark of Information Builders, Inc.
PCAT is a trademark of Arlington Software and Systems Corporation
PCnet is a trademark of Orchid Technology
PeachCalc is a trademark of Peachtree Software
PeachText is a registered trademark of Peachtree Software, Inc.
Peachtree Software is a registered trademark of Peachtree Software, Inc.
pfs is a registered trademark of Software Publishing Corporation
PL/1 is a trademark of Digital Research, Inc.
PLACEMENT POWER is a trademark of Resource Control Systems Corporation
PLANNER'S WORKBENCH is a registered trademark of ProfitKey International
Polaroid is a trademark of Polaroid Corporation
POSCOM is a trademark of New Systems, Inc.
Power-base is a trademark of PowerBase Systems, Inc.
PowerLinks is a trademark of PowerBase Systems, Inc.
Professional BASIC is a trademark of Morgan Computing Company, Inc.
Punctuation + Style is a trademark of Oasis Systems
PURCHASING WORKBENCH is a registered trademark of ProfitKey International
Q-ONE is a registered trademark of Quadratron Systems, Inc.
Quickstart is a trademark of Paladin Software Corporation
Rags to Riches is a trademark of Chang Labs
RAMIS is a registered trademark of Mathematics Products Group
RealWorld is a trademark of RealWorld Corporation
REBOS is a registered trademark of Clover Data Systems, Inc.
RELAY is a trademark of VM Personal Computing
Report Manager is a registered trademark of Datamension Corporation
Reportflo is a trademark of Dayflo, Inc.
RETAILING is a trademark of TRAC LINE Software, Inc.
RM/COBOL is a trademark of Ryan-McFarland Corporation
SAS is a registered trademark of SAS Institute, Inc.
SCHEDULER'S WORKBENCH is a registered trademark of ProfitKey International
Seamless Integration is a trademark of Samna Corporation
Sideways is a trademark of Funk Software, Inc.
SIGN-MASTER is a registered trademark of Decision Resources
SIMCOM is a trademark of New Systems, Inc.
SOFTBOL is a registered trademark of Omtool, Inc.
Solomon III is a trademark of TLB, Inc.
SPEED is a trademark of TOM Software, Inc.
Spellbinder is a registered trademark of Lexisoft, Inc.
Spellbinder Scientific is a registered trademark of Lexisoft, Inc.
SPORTSLOG is a trademark of Cyndek, Inc.
StarIndex is a trademark of MicroPro International Corporation
STATGRAPHICS is a registered trademark of Statistical Graphics Corporation
STONEWARE is a registered trademark of DB Master, Inc.
Sumagraphics is a registered trademark of Sumagraphics Corporation
SUPER SEARCH is a trademark of Research Control Systems Corporation
SuperCalc is a registered trademark of Computer Associates International, Inc., Micro Products Division
SuperSoft is a trademark of SuperSoft, Inc.
SuperWriter is a registered trademark of Computer Associates International, Inc., Micro Products Division
SURFAS is a trademark of Geophysical Techniques, Inc.
Symphony is a registered trademark of Lotus Development Corporation
T3 is a trademark of Triad Computing, Inc.
TASCOM is a trademark of New Systems, Inc.
TED is a registered trademark of Morgan Computing Company, Inc.
Tektronix is a trademark of Tektronix Corporation
TenCORE is a trademark of Computer Teaching Corporation
TerminALL is a trademark of TOPIC Systems, Inc.
TEX is a trademark of American Mathematical Society
TextMerge is a trademark of Lifetree Software, Inc.
TGRAF is a trademark of Grafpoint
The 1040 Solution is a trademark of Creative Solutions, Inc.
THE ART OF NEGOTIATING is a registered trademark of Gerard I. Nierenberg
THE BENCHMARK is a registered trademark of Benchmark/Metasoft, Inc.
THE WORD PLUS is a trademark of Oasis Systems
The Write-Up Solution is a trademark of Creative Solutions, Inc.
Timberline is a registered trademark of Timberline Systems, Inc.
TOMBASIC is a trademark of TOM Software, Inc.
TOPFILE is a trademark of TOPIC Systems, Inc.
TOPIC is a registered trademark of TOPIC Systems, Inc.
TOPOIL is a trademark of TOPIC Systems, Inc.
TRAC LINE INTEGRATED ACCOUNTING is a trademark of TRAC LINE Software, Inc.
TRAC LINE is a registered trademark of TRAC LINE Software, Inc.
TRAK is a trademark of GP Systems Corporation
Trigger is a trademark of Thoughtware, Inc.

True BASIC is a trademark of True BASIC, Inc.
Truevision is a trademark of AT&T
Uro-Diagnostic System is a trademark of Eris Medical Technology
VERTICAL SOFTWARE SERIES is a trademark of TRAC LINE Software, Inc.
Visi-On Applications Manager is a trademark of Paladin Software Corporation
Visi-On Calc is a trademark of Paladin Software Corporation
Visi-On Graph is a trademark of Paladin Software Corporation
Visi-On is a trademark of Paladin Software Corporation
Visi-On Presentations is a trademark of Paladin Software Corporation
Visi-On Word is a trademark of Paladin Software Corporation
VisiCalc is a trademark of Software Arts, Inc.
Volkswriter Deluxe is a trademark of Lifetree Software, Inc.
Volkswriter is a registered trademark of Lifetree Software, Inc.
Volkswriter Scientific is a trademark of Lifetree Software, Inc.
VT is a trademark of Digital Equipment Corporation
Wang is a registered trademark of Wang Laboratories, Inc.
Winchester disk is a registered trademark of Lanier Business Products
Word Base Manager is a trademark of Samna Corporation
WORDSCOPE is a registered trademark of Computer Action Learning, Inc.
WordStar is a registered trademark of MicroPro International Corporation
Wordvision is a registered trademark of Bruce & James, Program Publishers, Inc.
XENIX is a registered trademark of Microsoft Corporation
1-2-3 is a trademark of Lotus Development Corporation
20/20 is a trademark of Access Technology, Inc.
3Com is a registered trademark of 3Com Corporation
4-POINT GRAPHICS is a trademark of International Microcomputer Software, Inc.

INTRODUCTION

NOTES TO READERS

The name and address of the distributor of the product(s) are provided on each listing page to assist the reader in obtaining additional information about the product(s). AT&T cannot guarantee the accuracy of the prices quoted in the *AT&T Computer Software Catalog*, as these may have fluctuated since publication. Anyone interested in purchasing a package should contact the vendor through the address provided to check current pricing. Although most companies are eager to respond to your requests, AT&T cannot take responsibility for their failure to do so. Should you have trouble contacting any of these companies, please let us know by contacting us at:

AT&T Computer Software Catalog
AT&T Information Systems
1776 On the Green
Morristown, New Jersey 07960

The *AT&T Computer Software Catalog* is intended to be comprehensive, accurate, and current, but also practical to use and accessible. We welcome your comments, criticisms, and suggestions for improvement.

NOTES TO SOFTWARE VENDORS

Thank You

AT&T thanks all those companies listed for their support in the production of this *Catalog*. Your participation enables AT&T to satisfy the needs of individuals, businesses, and other institutions that use both the *UNIX* System V operating system and *MS*-DOS.

To Other UNIX System V and MS-DOS Independent Software Vendors

If your product was not listed in this edition of the *AT&T Computer Software Catalog*, we're sorry we missed you. To participate in the Summer 1986 edition of the *Catalog*, *UNIX* System V Vendors should complete the *Software Product Data Sheet* on page 445 of this book (permission is granted to photocopy it). Send this product information directly to:

Vendor Involvement Program
AT&T Information Systems, Inc.
One Speedwell Avenue
Room 744W
Morristown, New Jersey 07960

AT&T does not have an internal program to review submitted *MS*-DOS software for use with our machines; however, we do accept such reviews from several respected, independent testing laboratories for listing in our *Catalog*. Vendors of *MS*-DOS software are asked to contact us at the following address or telephone number for a list of testing facilities now reviewing software on AT&T PC hardware according to testing criteria established by AT&T:

AT&T Software Catalog Program
AT&T Information Systems
1776 On the Green
Morristown, New Jersey 07960

(201) 898-6170

HOW TO USE THE *AT&T COMPUTER SOFTWARE CATALOG* *MS-DOS SOFTWARE for the AT&T PC 6300 and PC 6300 PLUS*

The *AT&T Computer Software Catalog* is a software product reference manual for the AT&T PC 6300 AND PC 6300 PLUS. The *Catalog* is divided into ten sections or categories of software products. These categories are:

1. Communications
2. Database Management Systems
3. Education/Training
4. General Business Applications
5. Graphics
6. Industry/Vertical
7. Integrated
8. Spreadsheets
9. Systems Programming
10. Word Processors

Appendices of hardware adjuncts follow the sections listed above.

Within each of these categories the *AT&T Computer Software Catalog* is organized alphabetically by the name of the company that produced the program. The *Catalog* provides the following information for each software product:

1. Company
2. Product
3. Category
4. AT&T Computers Supported
5. Media
6. Description
7. Language
8. Requirements
9. Support
10. Retail Price
11. Distributor

Indexes are provided at the back of this *Catalog* to assist the reader in locating software listings.

HOW TO ORDER THE *AT&T COMPUTER SOFTWARE CATALOG* *MS-DOS SOFTWARE for the AT&T PC 6300 and PC 6300 PLUS*

To purchase the *AT&T COMPUTER SOFTWARE CATALOG*, call or write to:

The AT&T Customer Information Center
2855 North Franklin Road
Indianapolis, IN 46219

1-800-432-6600 (within the U.S.)
1-317-352-8557 (outside the U.S., except Canada)

Telex: 5101009077

For Canadian Residents Only:

1-800-255-1242

Please include the select code for this document (see copyright page). Also include your shipping address and payment by major credit card or check payable to AT&T Technologies. AT&T publishes a companion volume referencing *UNIX* System V software for AT&T's *UNIX*-based computers.
The *AT&T COMPUTER SOFTWARE CATALOG—UNIX System V Software for the AT&T 3B2/3B5/3B20 Computers and UNIX PC* (Select Code 311-020) can be ordered through the AT&T Customer Information Center as well.

SPECIAL NOTE FOR CANADIAN CUSTOMERS:

Canadian customers wishing to purchase third-party software referenced in this *Catalog* should call the distributor directly. Prices are quoted in U.S. dollars and are subject to applicable duties and taxes, as well as price differences due to exchange rate fluctuations.

For inquiries about products distributed through AT&T, contact the nearest AT&T Canada, Inc. Branch Office. For your convenience, a list of branch locations follows:

AT&T Canada, Inc. (Headquarters)
Toronto, Ontario
(416) 449-4300

AT&T Canada, Inc.
Ottawa, Ontario
(613) 238-7641

AT&T Canada, Inc.
Montreal, Quebec
(514) 876-1444

AT&T Canada, Inc.
Vancouver, British Columbia
(604) 689-8911

AT&T PC 6300 AND PC 6300 PLUS SOFTWARE

The AT&T PC 6300 and AT&T PC 6300 PLUS software products in this *Catalog* have been certified and/or reviewed by AT&T or an AT&T-authorized testing laboratory. AT&T **certified** software will be designated with the notation "This product has been certified" at the bottom of the listing page. **Certified** software products referenced in the *Catalog* have met rigorous software certification criteria established by AT&T.

Reviewed software acceptance testing is designed with the user in mind. It stresses the application at the unit and system levels, addressing reliability, ease of use, quality of documentation, and functionality, as well as other aspects necessary to qualify for inclusion in the *AT&T Computer Software Catalog*. The acceptance review is structured to ensure that the product performs as specified and is not intended to be a rigorous, comprehensive, or destructive analysis.

All referenced software is compatible with the AT&T PC 6300 and may be compatible with the recently announced AT&T PC 6300 PLUS as well. As we were not able to complete our compatibility review for all listed third-party software on the PC 6300 PLUS due to publication deadlines, only those packages that were actually tested on the PC 6300 PLUS have been designated accordingly. Listings of PC 6300 software that have been determined to work with the PC 6300 PLUS are shown with the following logo:

6300 PLUS

Company:
AT&T

Product:
AT&T 4410 Terminal Emulation*

Category:
Communications

Computer:
AT&T PC 6300

Media:
Diskette

Language:
C

Requirements:
MS-DOS 2.0
128 KB RAM

Support:
This product is fully supported by AT&T Information Systems and carries a 90-day warranty on the media. Remote nationwide customer service hotline is provided Monday through Friday between the hours of 8:00 a.m. and 5:00 p.m. local time. Installation, additional hotline coverage, and extended maintenance agreements are also available.

Retail Price:
$100

Distributor:
AT&T (800) 247-1212
or call your local AT&T authorized dealer or Account Executive.

***This product has been certified by AT&T.**

Description:

4410 Terminal Emulation enables the AT&T PC 6300 to function as an AT&T 4410 asynchronous terminal. The 4410 is an ANSI 3.64 terminal designed for applications involving extensive interaction with a host. Like the 4410 terminal, eight-user program function keys are provided. Data can be transmitted at rates up to 9600 bps. The Emulator allows for communication with any computer equipped to interface with ASCII based asynchronous displays. *MS*-DOS files can be sent to a host computer and files can be received and stored from a host computer.

With the 4410 communications program, the concurrent context switch software allows users to easily switch back and forth between the communications program and a loaded application. Additionally, processing can go on in both programs concurrently. Switch and *PC-Interface* software.

Company:
AT&T

Product:
AT&T 513 Terminal Emulation*

Category:
Communications

Computer: AT&T PC 6300

Media: Diskette

Language:
C

Requirements:
MS-DOS 2.11
128 KB RAM

Support:
This product is fully supported by AT&T Information Systems and carries a 90-day warranty on the media. Remote nationwide customer service hotline is provided Monday through Friday between the hours of 8:00 a.m. and 5:00 p.m. local time. Installation, additional hotline coverage, and extended maintenance agreements are also available.

Retail Price:
On request

Distributor:
AT&T (800) 247-1212
or call your local AT&T authorized dealer or Account Executive.

***This product has been certified by AT&T.**

Description:

The 513 Terminal Emulator software allows the AT&T PC 6300 to act like an asynchronous AT&T 513 terminal. It provides smart terminal capabilities, such as local and full screen editing, and programmable function keys. Additionally, the software supports a file-transfer capability allowing the user to transmit both ASCII and Binary files to or from another PC or host.

With the 513 communications program, the concurrent Context Switch software allows the user to easily switch back and forth between the communications program and a loaded PC application. Additionally, processing can go on in both programs concurrently.

Company:
AT&T

Product:
AT&T Communications Manager*

Category:
Communications

Computer:
AT&T PC 6300

Media:
Diskette

Language:
C

Requirements:
128 KB RAM
256 KB with AT&T Context Switch

Support:
This product is fully supported by AT&T Information Systems and carries a 90-day warranty on the media. Remote nationwide customer service hotline is provided Monday through Friday between the hours of 8:00 a.m. and 5:00 p.m. local time. Installation, additional hotline coverage, and extended maintenance agreements are also available.

Retail Price:
$599

Distributor:
AT&T (800) 247-1212 or call your local AT&T authorized dealer or Account Executive.

***This product has been certified by AT&T.**

Description:

The AT&T Communications Manager expansion card plugs into one slot of the AT&T PC 6300. The Communications Manager has a built-in 300/1200 baud modem. In addition, this expansion card has an on-board speaker for call progress monitoring. The Communications modular jack interfaces, which supports RJ11, RJ12, and RJ13 interfaces. The telephones supported by the Communications Manager hardware are 500-type (rotary dialers), 2500-type (TOUCH-TONE dialers) and key telephones with appropriate adapter. Also included with the Communications Manager packages are two 7-foot modular phone cords.

Company:
AT&T

Product:
Concurrent Context Switch*

Category:
Communications

Computer:
AT&T PC 6300

Media:
Diskette

Language:
C

Requirements:
MS-DOS 2.11
256 KB RAM
2 floppy disk drives

Support:
This product is fully supported by AT&T Information Systems and carries a 90-day warranty on the media. Remote nationwide customer service hotline is provided Monday through Friday between the hours of 8:00 a.m. and 5:00 p.m. local time. Installation, additional hotline coverage, and extended maintenance agreements are also available.

Retail Price:
$100

Distributor:
AT&T (800) 247-1212
or call your local AT&T authorized dealer or Account Executive.

***This product has been certified by AT&T.**

Description:

Concurrent Context Switch is a software package that enables the user to quickly and easily switch back and forth between concurrent foreground and background tasks on the AT&T PC and a remote host computer. It is designed for use with an AT&T Terminal Emulation program such as the 4410 Terminal Emulation or the 513 Terminal Emulation.

Company:
AT&T

Product:
PC-Interface*

Category:
Communications

Computer:	**Media:**
AT&T PC 6300	Diskette

Language:
C, Intel. 86. Assembler Binary

Requirements:
20 KB RAM memory on the AT&T PC 6300
3B2 hardware with 3B2 *PC-Interface* software
Ethernet capability is required for the PC 6300

Support:
This product is fully supported by AT&T Information Systems and carries a 90-day warranty on the media. Remote nationwide customer service hotline is provided Monday through Friday between the hours of 8:00 a.m. and 5:00 p.m. local time. Installation, additional hotline coverage, and extended maintenance agreements are also available. User's/Administrator's documentation is provided.

Retail Price:
$100

Distributor:
AT&T (800) 247-1212
or call your local AT&T authorized dealer or Account Executive.

***This product has been certified by AT&T.**

Description:

The *PC-Interface* software package supports transparent file sharing and command execution for the 3B2 and Personal Computers running under *MS*-DOS 2.X. The organization and structure of the files are managed by the 3B2; they are native *UNIX* system files and directories. However, applications resident on the personal computer view those files as if they were local files to the PC. The 3B2 file system appears to the 3B2 to be an additional disk volume. PC users may select the appropriate protection requirements for their data. Users can take advantage of the many *MS*-DOS programs available. *PC-Interface* also supports remote printing. *PC-Interface* is available on RS-232 or *Ethernet*.

Company:
AT&T and AST Research

Product:
AST 3780*

Category:
Communications

Computer: AT&T PC 6300

Media: Diskette

Language:
AST Proprietary Language

Requirements:
128 KB RAM

Support:
This product is fully supported by AT&T Information Systems and carries a 90-day warranty on the media. Remote nationwide customer service hotline is provided Monday through Friday between the hours of 8:00 a.m. and 5:00 p.m. local time. Installation, additional hotline coverage, and extended maintenance agreements are also available.

Retail Price:
$310 CC-432
Advanced Communications Board
$585 software only

Distributor:
AT&T (800) 247-1212
or call your local AT&T authorized dealer or Account Executive.

***This product has been certified by AT&T.**

Description:

AST-3780 is a complete software and hardware package which emulates all common BISYNC RJE Workstations (2780, 3780, 2770, & 3741). The board is designed to capture the full power of any computer supporting the BISYNC, point-to-point communications protocol.

AST-3780 allows the user to transfer program, data, or text files between the AT&T Personal Computer and a host computer system at high (up to 19.2 K baud) speeds. All messages are automatically checked for possible data transmission or reception errors and are corrected as necessary without operator intervention. The data may then be used as input to a program running on the Personal Computer, or output from the PC may be sent to the host system. More advanced features include:

- Unattended operation
- Back-to-back mode
- Hold-scroll
- Device independence

Company:
AT&T and AST Research

Product:
AST-BSC*

Category:
Communications

Computer: AT&T PC 6300

Media: Diskette

Language:
AST Proprietary Language

Requirements:
128 KB RAM
CC432 Advanced Communications Board
Synchronous modem for distances of more than 50 feet

Support:
This product is fully supported by AT&T Information Systems and carries a 90-day warranty on the media. Remote nationwide customer service hotline is provided Monday through Friday between the hours of 8:00 a.m. and 5:00 p.m. local time. Installation, additional hotline coverage, and extended maintenance agreements are also available.

Retail Price:
$310 CC-432
Advanced Communications Board
$385 software only

Distributor:
AT&T (800) 247-1212
or call your local AT&T authorized dealer or Account Executive.

***This product has been certified by AT&T.**

Description:

AST-BSC is a complete software and hardware package allowing connection of the AT&T Personal Computer to a mainframe system. It provides for interactive remote communication in a 3270 environment using the BISYNC communication protocol.

AST-BSC allows the emulation of a 3276/3274 remote control unit, a 3278-1/3279-2A terminal, and a 3278 type printer. With *AST-BSC*, the PC is connected to the host system via synchronous modems running up to 9600 baud, over switched or nonswitched facilities. Beyond the standard 3270 functions, *AST-BSC* provides several enhancements to better utilize your PC:

- Host sessions remain active while in DOS
- Printer output can be directed to "Disk" file
- 3270 key mapping (configurable)
- Numeric keypad support

OPTIONS:

- Optional 3780 RJE terminal emulation
- 3270 interactive file transfer
- Optional ASCII terminal and PC clustering

Company:
AT&T and AST Research

Product:
AST-SNA*

Category:
Communications

Computer: AT&T PC 6300

Media: Diskette

Language:
AST Proprietary Language

Requirements:
128 KB RAM
CC-432 Advanced Communications Board
Synchronous modem for distances of more than 50 feet

Support:
This product is fully supported by AT&T Information Systems and carries a 90-day warranty on the media. Remote nationwide customer service hotline is provided Monday through Friday between the hours of 8:00 a.m. and 5:00 p.m. local time. Installation, additional hotline coverage, and extended maintenance agreements are also available.

Retail Price:
$310 CC-432
Advanced Communications Board
$585 software only

Distributor:
AT&T (800) 247-1212
or call your local AT&T authorized dealer or Account Executive.

***This product has been certified by AT&T.**

Description:

AST-SNA is a complete software and hardware package allowing connection of the AT&T Personal Computer to a mainframe system. It provides for interactive remote communication in a 3270 SNA environment using the SDLC protocol.

AST-SNA allows the emulation of a 3276/3274 remote control unit, a 3278-2/3279-2A terminal, and a 3287 type printer. With *AST-SNA*, the PC is connected to the host system via synchronous modems running up to 9600 baud, over switched or nonswitched facilities. Beyond the standard 3270 functions, *AST-SNA* provides several enhancements to better utilize your PC:

- Host sessions remain active while in DOS
- Printer output can be directed to a "Disk" file
- 3270 key mapping (configurable)
- Numeric keypad support

OPTIONS:

- 3270 interactive file transfer
- Optional 3770 RJE terminal emulation
- Optional ASCII terminal and PC clustering

Company:
AT&T and AST Research

Product:
AST-PCOX*

Category:
Communications

Computer: AT&T PC 6300

Media: Diskette

Language:
AST Proprietary Language

Requirements:
128 KB RAM
AST-PCOX Communications Board

Support:
This product is fully supported by AT&T Information Systems and carries a 90-day warranty on the media. Remote nationwide customer service hotline is provided Monday through Friday between the hours of 8:00 a.m. and 5:00 p.m. local time. Installation, additional hotline coverage, and extended maintenance agreements are also available.

Retail Price:
$1,145 for software and hardware

Distributor:
AT&T (800) 247-1212
or call your local AT&T authorized dealer or Account Executive.

***This product has been certified by AT&T.**

Description:

The *AST-PCOX* consists of a circuit board, which plugs into an empty expansion slot of the AT&T PC 6300, and emulation software. The board has a coaxial connector on it, which allows for local hookup to a 3274 or 3276 control unit. The control unit can be either local or remote from the mainframe. To the control unit the PC looks like a 3270 terminal. All that is necessary is that the 3274 control unit be configured to specify the types of terminals or printers attached to it.

With the *PCOX* installed in the PC there is no change required to the host or PC software, regardless of operating system, access method, or application. The control program software operates in resident mode; this means the PC can be utilized for other DOS application processing as well. Once you have loaded the emulation software into the PC you can use a "hot" key to go back and forth to DOS. Beyond the standard 3270 PC functions, *AST-PCOX* supports:

- Screen prints
- Screen save to disk
- Screen control application program interface
- Foreign keyboard support
- File transfer in interactive or batch mode

Company:
AT&T and Computerized Office Services, Inc.

Product:
AT&T Tango*

Category:
Communications

Computer:	**Media:**
AT&T PC 6300	Diskette

Language:
C (90%) + 8088 Assembler (10%)

Requirements:
128 KB RAM

Support:
This product is fully supported by AT&T Information Systems and carries a 90-day warranty on the media. Remote nationwide customer service hotline is provided Monday through Friday between the hours of 8:00 a.m. and 5:00 p.m. local time. Installation, additional hotline coverage, and extended maintenance agreements are also available.

Retail Price:
$195

Distributor:
AT&T (800) 247-1212 or call your local AT&T authorized dealer or Account Executive.

***This product has been certified by AT&T.**

Description:

Tango is communication software that connects the AT&T PC 6300 with computers running on the *UNIX* Operating System. Features include:

- Execution of *MS*-DOS commands and programs on PC 6300 under control of *UNIX* System hosts
- File transfer using standard error correction protocols with automatic conversion between *UNIX* System and *MS*-DOS file formats
- Terminal emulation of *DEC*, *IBM*, and *TEKTRONIX* (full graphics capabilities) terminals selectable from *UNIX* System host

Tango utilizes a standard RS-232 serial port on the PC 6300 and connects to the *UNIX* System computer via modem or direct connection.

Company:
Communications Research Group

Product:
***BLAST* (BLocked ASynchronous Transmission)**

Category:
Communications

Computer:
AT&T PC 6300

Media:
Diskette

Language:
C

Requirements:
64 KB RAM
RS-232 serial port
5 1/4" disk drive

Support:
Full support by telephone (504) 923-0888

Retail Price:
$250–$395

Distributor:
Communications Research Group
8939 Jefferson Highway
Baton Rouge, LA 70809
Tel: (504) 923-0888

Description:

BLAST is a family of communications software products currently available on more than 120 different micro, mini, and mainframe computers.

The basic function of *BLAST* is error-free file transfer. Any version of *BLAST* can transfer a binary or text file error-free to any other version of *BLAST*. In addition, *BLAST* has auxiliary communications features such as terminal mode, text file upload and capture, and autodial modem support.

BLAST software uses the standard asynchronous serial ports found on most computers, so no additional computer hardware is required.

The protocol used by *BLAST* has an advanced, full duplex, sliding-window design that operates efficiently over noisy telephone lines, and circuits subject to propagation delay such as satellite links and network virtual circuits (LANs, Packet Network, PBXs).

BLAST versions are available for most AT&T computers as well as many other major vendors' computers.

Company:

Grafpoint

Product:

***TGRAF*-05 4105 Emulation**

Category:

Communications

Computer:	**Media:**
AT&T PC 6300 **AT&T PC 6300 PLUS**	Diskette

6300 PLUS

Language:
Assembly

Requirements:
128 KB RAM
One floppy disk
Printer and display enhancement board optional
Asynchronous communications port

Support:
Free telephone support (408) 249-7951
Software updates

Retail Price:
$495

Distributor:
Grafpoint
4340 Stevens Creek Blvd. # 280
San Jose, CA 95129
Tel: (408) 249-7951

Description:

High speed *Tektronix 4105* and Digital Equipment Corporation *VT100* emulation. Stores pictures locally on disk and produces color or black and white hardcopy on a variety of printers.

Company:
The IMS Group, Inc.

Product:
Telecommunications Manager

Category:
Communications

Computer: AT&T PC 6300

Media: Diskette

Language:
dBASE II

Requirements:
256 KB RAM
10 MB hard disk
MS-DOS version 2.0+

Support:
User manual
Two hours training
Hotline (512) 494-9542
Enhancements to software package provided for the first year

Retail Price:
$2,500
$350/month lease with support

Distributor:
The IMS Group, Inc.
975 W. Bitters Rd.
Suite 204B
San Antonio, TX 78216
Tel: (512) 494-9542

Description:

Telecommunications Manager provides cable management facility, hardware inventory, vendor work order, and electronic memo. It also publishes internal directory, vendor rate analysis, and internal cost allocation for computer and telephone systems management.

Company:
InfoCenter Software, Inc.

Product:
iLINK Version 2.0

Category:
Communications

Computer: AT&T PC 6300

Media: Diskette

Language:
Compiled BASIC

Requirements:
128 KB RAM
A monochrome or color monitor
The PC iLINK program diskette
Any communications package which allows the transfer of ASCII files between micro and mainframe computers
A log-on ID for access to VM/CMS or MVS/TSO on the mainframe
iLINK installed on the mainframe

Support:
iLINK customers are supplied with on-site support from technical representatives as well as a hotline to answer any questions

Retail Price:
$450

Distributor:
InfoCenter Software, Inc.
171 Main St.
P.O. Box 878
New Paltz, NY 12561
Tel: (914) 255-8925

Description:

There now exists the ability to effectively and inexpensively link the environment of mainframes to the personal computers of the knowledge worker with iLINK. iLINK allows the transfer of data between most Information Center fourth generation language DBM's running under VM/CMS or MVS/TSO (such as *RAMIS*, *SAS*, *FOCUS*, *ADRSII*, and others) and any of over 150 personal computer spreadsheet or database packages, including *LOTUS 1-2-3*, *dBASE* and *SuperCalc* products. As the only generic link, iLINK enables the knowledge worker to access all of the principle databases, whether mainframe or PC.

The user-friendly menus, extensive on-line help messages, and a complete and well organized user's manual make iLINK a product which can be used by those persons who do not have a great deal of computer experience. The knowledge worker, led by iLINK, can easily master the uploading, downloading, or crossloading of data. Furthermore, an automatic procedure can be designed so that a knowledge worker can extract data from the mainframe and move these down to a PC with a single command.

iLINK works with any communications package which has file transfer capability and, because it rests on top of the existing system, iLINK will not bypass existing security. By eliminating errors and time spent on reentering data, the iLINK program offers users substantial productivity improvement and cost savings. iLINK also allows customers to use existing computer hardware and software to the fullest potential.

Company:

Intercomputer Communications Corp. (ICC)

Product:

Terminal Emulation and File Transfers-TO BURROUGHS, SPERRY, HONEYWELL, and *DEC* MAINFRAMES–Supported by a single communication card, ICC Intercom 1000

Category:

Communications

Computer:	**Media:**
AT&T PC 6300	Diskette

Language:

Assembler and other

Requirements:

One floppy disk drive
256 KB RAM
Intercom 1,000 Communications Card (optional)

Support:

One year free phone support by ICC
30-day evaluation period

Retail Price:

$245—$895 for emulation and/or file transfer system, depending on mainframe type.

Distributor:

Intercomputer Communications Corp. (ICC)
3195 Linwood Ave.
Cincinnati, OH 45208
Tel: (513) 321-3199

Description:

The ICC hardware and software products interconnect AT&T PC 6300 microcomputers with all BURROUGHS, SPERRY, HONEYWELL, and *DEC* mainframes. Some of the key features which will vary by mainframe type, include:

- Supports all *MS*-DOS operating system machines and features instant toggling between full terminal emulation and DOS use with no loss of processing.
- Allows two-way transfer of editor files and automatic reformatting.
- Allows forms storage at the micro.
- Is menu-driven for ease of use.
- Allows advanced file transfers (printer backup and flat files) and automatically reformats them for micro use.
- The INTERCOM 1,000 card supports TDI (direct connect) or RS-232 communications (synch or asynch). It also allows concatenation and provides a serial port.
- Terminal emulation and advanced file transfers are part of a full family of interconnecting products from ICC that include database extraction, virtual disk file sharing, and a LAN gateway which is planned to be introduced in the future.

An April, 1985 review of ICC products by *Data Decisions* found the products to be:

- "a very proficient product"
- "able to make Burroughs to PC communications a reality, and does it very capably"

ICC plans to introduce in 1986, *IBM*, 3270/3780 emulation and file transfer capability, with one firmware card supporting emulation to *IBM*, BURROUGHS, SPERRY, HONEYWELL, and *DEC* mainframes.

Company:
Quadratron Systems, Inc.

Product:
Q-MAIL

Category:
Communications

Computer:
AT&T PC 6300

Media:
Diskette

Language:
C

Requirements:
Any terminal;
Any printer

Support:
User manual
Reference guides
Demonstration guides
Quick reference cards
Installation guides
Hotline support (OEM's only)
Training (OEM's only)
On-line help (818) 789-8588

Retail Price:
$155

Distributor:
Essex Office Systems
333 North Fairfax St.
Alexandria, VA 22341
Tel: (703) 549-9240

Description:

Q-MAIL, electronic mail program, can be used for sending notes and documents to various users on the same system or across systems automatically. It uses the *Q-ONE* word processor to create messages, but it will easily interface with other types of editors as well. Features include an undelete "waste-basket" function, in and out basket, and certified and classified mail.

Company:
TOPIC Systems, Inc.

Product:
***TerminALL* Release 2.0**

Category:
Communications

Computer:
AT&T PC 6300
AT&T PC 6300 PLUS

Media:
Diskette

6300 PLUS

Language:
C

Requirements:
256 KB RAM and user-furnished *MS*-DOS (2.11 or later)
One 320 5 1/4" floppy disk drive (minimum)
Asynchronous modem

Support:
Manual with technical appendix
Telephone support, (914) 471-1363
Full warranty for software, 90 days for media

Retail Price:
$195; with CONTEXT SWITCH $295

Distributor:
TOPIC Systems, Inc.
P.O. Box 5279
Poughkeepsie, NY 12602
Tel: (914) 471-1363

Description:

TerminALL is a versatile and effective asynchronous communications controller which allows up to 26 user-defined communications services, databases, and host computers to be menu-selected with automatic setting of communications and interface parameters.

Provides emulation of popular ASCII terminals with baud rates to 9600.

Provides user-defined function strings activated by single keystroke which can include dialup and sign-on sequences, etc.

Supports transmission from disk file, and reception to any combination of video, disk file and printer. Furnished with full-screen Video File Editor to create files for transmission and for editing of received files.

Provides off-line print from file support.

Supports a variety of user-selected National Character Sets.

TerminALL provides an excellent interface between the PC 6300 (and compatibles) and *UNIX* systems.

Optional CONTEXT SWITCH is available matching *TerminALL* to provide for *TerminALL* and user-provided application program to co-exist with ability to switch between *TerminALL* and application program. In AUTOANSWER mode and CONTEXT SWITCH, incoming call is automatically answered and switch performed to service the call.

Emulation of ADDS REGENT 40 to interface with AT&T Technologies ENERGY COMMUNICATIONS SYSTEM ADJUNCT, allowing the PC 6300 to be utilized as the terminal, is included. With use of the CONTEXT SWITCH option, the ENERGY SYSTEM can always be connected while the operating engineer can be executing other software with the ability to switch back and forth.

Company:
U.S. Digital Corporation

Product:
***Copylink* Version 2.41**

Category:
Communications

Computer:
AT&T PC 6300

Media:
Diskette

Language:
Assembler

Requirements:
128 KB RAM
RS-232/modem

Support:
Factory Telephone, (503) 654-0668

Retail Price:
$99.95

Distributor:
U.S. Digital Corporation
5687-H S.E. International Way
Portland, OR 97222
Tel: (503) 654-0668

Description:

Copylink is a sophisticated communications program for microcomputers. Extremely flexible as well as easy to use. Comparable to programs that cost twice as much, described by *Microcomputing Magazine* as "the best communications software value on the market today...." *Copylink* is two programs in one:

Copylink is a 300/1200 baud modem control program that comes preset to communicate with all the popular databases, bulletin boards, and timesharing systems. It can also be used to send electronic mail in a store-and-forward fashion or in a real-time mode with automatic answerback capability. Communications parameters can be reset at any time within the operation of the program and customized to accommodate several different network configurations. *Copylink* can emulate LSI ADM3A or *VT*100 terminals. *Copylink* easily downloads or uploads files to/from any mainframe that communicates with ASCII terminals. *Copylink* supports automatic dialing and redialing from an unlimited directory of names and numbers. In fact, for most users the only command normally used is the "call" command (i.e., CALL JOE). *Copylink* can be set up to automatically logon, print out the contents of a mailbox, send a message, logoff, and disconnect the phone line. It will automatically save files and disconnect the line if the user forgets to do so before exiting the program. Automatic single-keystroke functions can also be set up. The files on a *Copylink*-equipped PC can be accessed by another remote system in an unattended mode. Works with all 103 or 212A, as well as *Hayes*-compatible modems.

Copylink is also an XMODEM-compatible file transfer program which runs on over 35 different micros running *CP/M* or *MS*-DOS; supporting hard-wired file transfer rates up to 19,200 baud with sophisticated error checking. It is extremely easy to use, as the user only has to type "S" to send a single file, multiple files, or wildcard file assignments. The receiving system has only to type "R." It can transfer more than a disk-full of data (prompts the operator to change disks).

Company:
VM Personal Computing

Product:
RELAY

Category:
Communications

Computer:	**Media:**
AT&T PC 6300	Diskette
6300 PLUS **AT&T PC 6300 PLUS**	

Language:
Macro Assembler

Requirements:
128 KB RAM
Asynchronous communications
Adapter, any asynchronous modem

Support:
Printed tutorial for first-time users
Full reference manual
Periodic product upgrades
Free fixes for "bugs"
90-day diskette warranty (203) 798-7364

Retail Price:
$149

Distributor:
Manufacturers Representative
Western Technology Brokers
104 West 74th St.
New York, NY 10023
Tel: (212) 580-1500

Description:

RELAY is a most powerful, yet easy to use, asynchronous micro to micro and micro mainframe communications software product.

RELAY is the only communications product that provides the user with concurrent operations. This capability allows the user to send and receive files, exchange messages, and run other programs all at the same time.

RELAY is fully menu-driven and has a complete built-in context sensitive help system to provide the user with answers to any *RELAY* questions at any time.

RELAY emulates a variety of terminals, including TTY, which provides access to bulletin boards and all of the popular information services as well as *VT-100* & *VT*-52 emulation to enable the user to connect with a variety of mini-computers.

RELAY transfers both text and binary files and supports many of the popular protocols as well as *RELAY's* own unique 100% error free bidirectional protocol.

RELAY comes with its own mainframe-like Full Screen Editor. The *RELAY* Editor allows the user to edit files while communicating with another PC or Host. Users may utilize the Editor and *RELAY's* intelligent script language to create scripts which will automate repetitive procedures like logging on or provide host session management.

RELAY is the micro member of a family of micro to mainframe communication software products. When an *IBM* VM or TSO mainframe is running is able to up load or down load any type of file or data error-free. If the *IBM* VM Host is also running with the *RELAY* 3270 software product then the PC 6300 will emulate a 3270 type terminal. This is all accomplished with standard inexpensive voice grade dial up asynchronous modems or by a direct asynchronous connection to the host. No longer does 3270 type emulation require the expense of Irma type coax products, synchronous modems or protocol converters. *RELAY'S* general highlights are:

- Concurrent operations—ie:

  Sends and receives in both directions at the same time

  Edit a file while sending and receiving and printing

  Terminal session while sending, receiving and running another program all concurrently

(Continued on next page)

Description: ***(Continued)***

Complete mainframe support—including:

> *RELAY/VM*, *RELAY/TSO*, *RELAY/*3270 *IBM* mainframe software
>
> *VT-100*, *VT*-52, and other Terminal Emulations
>
> 3270 Terminal Emulation without the extra expense of additional Hardware (ie WITHOUT IRMA, PCOX coax type Boards, $1,000 synchronous modems or protocol converters on the host)

- Menu Driven for beginners (and Experts)
- Extensive context sensitive Program Help
- Talks To Other Programs
- Wake up and connect unattended on a particular date and time
- Unattend Operation with Password Protection
- Unlimited Phone Directory
- Use all the new features of the new Superset Smart Modems

Company:
AT&T

Product:
AT&T Video Data Catalog*

Category:
Database Management Systems

Computer:	**Media:**
AT&T PC 6300	Diskette

Language:
C

Requirements:
Hard disk; 512 KB RAM recommended
An NTSC Composite Video Monitor or an Analog RGB Monitor for displaying color video images
An AT&T *Truevision* Image Capture Board (ICB) for capturing video images
An AT&T *Truevision* Video Display Adapter Board (VDA) for displaying video images
Any standard modem, for the Network Video Data Catalog, or for transmitting video or picture files to a remote site using Local Video Data Catalog
Standard video input source for image creation (keep in mind that some sources do not produce composite video output. These sources may require a conversion). You may use any of the following: color video camera, video cassette recorder, television signal, or video disc player.

Support:
This product is fully supported by AT&T Information Systems and carries a 90-day warranty on the media. Remote nationwide customer service hotline is provided Monday through Friday between the hours of 8:00 a.m. and 5:00 p.m. local time. Installation, additional hotline coverage, and extended maintenance agreements are also available.

Retail Price:
$695

Distributor:
AT&T (800) 247-1212
or call your local AT&T authorized dealer or Account Executive.

***This product has been certified by AT&T.**

Description:

AT&T Video Data Catalog combines personal computer and networking capabilities to support business applications with state-of-the-art technology that can capture video images and display them with textual data to an analog color monitor attached to a PC. AT&T Video Data Catalog runs on an AT&T PC 6300 and can be used with the AT&T network or in a standalone mode.

AT&T Video Data Catalog consists of menu-driven programs that enable users to define, create, update, and search databases and display video pictures and associated text that have been captured and sorted on their personal computer.

The package includes a terminal emulator software module that allows a supplier's customer to browse through a supplier's video catalog, his or her own PC, and generate purchase orders.

Supporting the video feature, of the product are two PC expansion boards; the AT&T *Truevision* Visual Display Adapter and the AT&T *Truevision* Image Capture Board.

Product documentation addresses software and hardware installation, database definition, creation, updating and searching, and the capture, refining, storing and retrieval of video images.

Company:
AT&T and Ashton-Tate

Product:
dBASE II*

Category:
Database Management Systems

Computer: **AT&T PC 6300**

Media: Diskette

Language:
C

Requirements:
128 KB RAM

Support:
This product is fully supported by AT&T Information Systems and carries a 90-day warranty on the media. Remote nationwide customer service hotline is provided Monday through Friday between the hours of 8:00 a.m. and 5:00 p.m. local time. Installation, additional hotline coverage, and extended maintenance agreements are also available.

Retail Price:
$420

Distributor:
AT&T (800) 247-1212
or call your local AT&T authorized dealer or Account Executive.

***This product has been certified by AT&T.**

Description:

The core of Ashton-Tate's product line, *dBASE II*, is the world's largest-selling database management system for microcomputers.

dBASE II is a relational database management system. It includes an on-disk tutorial with 10 lessons to introduce the beginner to some of the many uses for *dBASE II*. *dBASE II* is highly adaptable to almost any data storage and retrieval task.

Through the use of the *dBASE* programming language it is possible to design reports which use existing forms, such as invoices and checks. The *dBASE* language is based on easy-to-understand English language commands such as CREATE, APPEND, and MODIFY. The only limitation to users for this package is the programmer's imagination.

dBASE II can be used for everything from simple tasks, such as mailing lists and inventories, to sophisticated financial applications. *dBASE* allows a great deal of flexibility: when changes are needed the user can modify the program without having to reenter data, and, conversely, the user can change data without changing the program.

dBASE II can handle data from other programs, or create files that other programs can use. A *dBASE II* database can contain up to 65,535 records and up to 32 fields per record.

Company:
AT&T and Ashton-Tate

Product:
dBASE III*

Category:
Database Management Systems

Computer: AT&T PC 6300

Media: Diskette

Language:
C, Assembly

Requirements:
256 KB dual floppy drives

Support:
This product is fully supported by AT&T Information Systems and carries a 90-day warranty on the media. Remote nationwide customer service hotline is provided Monday through Friday between the hours of 8:00 a.m. and 5:00 p.m. local time. Installation, additional hotline coverage, and extended maintenance agreements are also available.

Retail Price:
$695

Distributor:
AT&T (800) 247-1212
or call your local AT&T authorized dealer or Account Executive.

***This product has been certified by AT&T.**

Description:

dBASE III is a powerful database management system for an AT&T Computer. *dBASE III* can handle over a billion records per file, limited only by the user's computer system. Up to ten files can remain open, for sophisticated application programs. When the user has two related files, information can be accessed based upon data in the other.

dBASE III handles procedures, parameter passing and automatic variable. *dBASE III* uses powerful yet simple commands. The new assist mode allows invoice users the power and flexibility of a menu driven interface.

Company:
AT&T and Ashton-Tate

Product:
Friday!*

Category:
Database Management Systems

Computer: **AT&T PC 6300**

Media: Diskette

Language:
C

Requirements:
128 KB RAM

Support:
This product is fully supported by AT&T Information Systems and carries a 90-day warranty on the media. Remote nationwide customer service hotline is provided Monday through Friday between the hours of 8:00 a.m. and 5:00 p.m. local time. Installation, additional hotline coverage, and extended maintenance agreements are also available.

Retail Price:
$295

Distributor:
AT&T (800) 247-1212
or call your local AT&T authorized dealer or Account Executive.

***This product has been certified by AT&T.**

Description:

Friday! is an easy-to-use, menu driven file management system for people who do not need a full production, relational database. *Friday!* files are compatible with *dBASE II* and can be automatically converted to *dBASE III*, allowing users to upgrade to the more powerful products in the *dBASE* line if their information management needs become more complex.

Company:
AT&T and Relational Database Systems, Inc.

Product:
File-it!*

Category:
Database Management Systems

Computer:	**Media:**
AT&T PC 6300	Diskette

Language:
C

Requirements:
256 KB RAM for *MS*-DOS systems
Video display terminal
Serial or parallel printer for reporting capabilities

Support:
This product is fully supported by AT&T Information Systems and carries a 90-day warranty on the media. Remote nationwide customer service hotline is provided Monday through Friday between the hours of 8:00 a.m. and 5:00 p.m. local time. Installation, additional hotline coverage, and extended maintenance agreements are also available. A User's Guide is provided with the software.

Retail Price:
$295

Distributor:
AT&T (800) 247-1212
or call or call your local AT&T authorized dealer or Account Executive.

***This product has been certified by AT&T.**

Description:

The *File-it!* file manager allows a computer novice to maintain, modify, add to, and retrieve vital information easily and efficiently.

File-it! provides a self-contained and fully interactive environment which lets a computer novice construct a file in minutes. Once the required fields are described to *File-it!*, a default form is automatically created.

This form can be used for data entry and inquiry purposes immediately, or modified to simulate existing paper forms. Display and input fields, blank lines, and text displays can be moved, added, or deleted with a few simple keystrokes.

At any point in the system a single keystroke displays a help screen. This screen provides extensive reference information and procedure instructions relative to the work in process.

When the file is queried, *File-it!* retrieves only the information that is relevant to the user's request. Information can be selected based on one or more specific values, a range of values, or a value that closely approximates the specified value.

File-it! builds true *C-ISAM* files. It is, therefore, compatible at the file level with all systems and applications software that use RDS' *C-ISAM* and *INFORMIX*.

File-it! is ideal for key accounts lists, mailing lists, phone lists, financial records, and more.

Company:
AT&T and Relational Database Systems, Inc.

Product:
INFORMIX*

Category:
Database Management Systems

Computer:	**Media:**
AT&T PC 6300 6300 PLUS **AT&T PC 6300 PLUS**	Diskette

Language:
C

Requirements:
256 KB RAM for *MS*-DOS systems
Video display terminal
Serial or parallel printer for reporting capabilities

Support:
This product is fully supported by AT&T Information Systems and carries a 90-day warranty on the media. Remote nationwide customer service hotline is provided Monday through Friday between the hours of 8:00 a.m. and 5:00 p.m. local time. Installation, additional hotline coverage, and extended maintenance agreements are also available. A User's Guide is provided with the software.

Retail Price:
$795

Distributor:
AT&T (800) 247-1212
or call or call your local AT&T authorized dealer or Account Executive.

***This product has been certified by AT&T.**

Description:

INFORMIX is a relational database management system that provides comprehensive tools for application development, as well as the utilities required to create and maintain databases. A menu creation facility allows user customization of *INFORMIX*'s menu-driven environment. Through interactive screens, single or multilevel menus can be created quickly and easily.

Custom screen generation, data entry, and query-by-forms capabilities form an integral part of *INFORMIX*. A screen can display and update fields from multiple database files. Queries based on specific values, ranges of values, inequalities, or wildcard designations, are easily performed with a minimum of keystrokes.

INFORMIX's powerful, interactive query language can be used to extract information in the most relevant fashion, create and store the results of arithmetic, logical or aggregate operations, and perform global data management functions. With *INFORMIX*'s nonprocedural report writing language, nontechnical personnel can extract, manipulate, format, and display data from one or multiple files.

A C language interface provides a library of C routines that perform database operations. These routines can be incorporated into any C program through simple call statements that set up and perform queries.

INFORMIX is ideal for applications such as: accounting, document control, inventory control, MRP, and order entry.

Company:
Benchmark/Metasoft, Inc.

Product:
***THE BENCHMARK* Data Manager**

Category:
Database Management Systems

Computer:
AT&T PC 6300

Media:
Diskette

Language:
Assembly

Requirements:
256 KB RAM

Support:
Telephone support (800) 621-1908

Retail Price:
$295

Distributor:
Benchmark/Metasoft, Inc.
6509 W. Frye Rd., Suite 12
Chandler, AZ 85224
Tel: (602) 961-0003

Description:

The Data Manager is a versatile and practical database program for storing business and technical information. The user customizes forms for storing data and then uses these forms to build databases. Forms and databases can be edited quickly and easily. The Data Manager also allows for merging and printing databases and is integrated with both the Word Processor and the Graphics Package.

Company:

Concentric Data Systems, Inc.

Product:

C*I*P (Concentric Information Processor)

Category:

Database Management Systems

Computer:	**Media:**
AT&T PC 6300 **AT&T PC 6300 PLUS**	Diskette

6300 PLUS

Language:

BCL

Requirements:

192 KB RAM
Color display optional
Printer recommended but not required
MS-DOS releases 1.1, 2.0, 2.1, 3.0, or 3.1

Support:

Dealers: Toll-free telephone support plus a large variety of Technical Notes for commonly asked questions.
Training available
Users: Telephone support between the hours of 9:00 a.m. and 5:00 p.m. Eastern time
90-day warranty on disks
Product updates for registered users

Retail Price:

$295

Distributor:

Concentric Data Systems, Inc.
18 Lyman St.
Westboro, MA 01581
Tel: (617) 366-1122
(800) 325-9035

Description:

C.I.P is a full-featured file management product for the AT&T PC 6300 and compatibles. *C.I.P* incorporates a myriad of features while still being easy to learn, use and remember.

C.I.P features the first visual report writer for database products. *C.I.P*'s report writer allows the user to create presentation quality custom reports in a fraction of the time required using other products. Fields are positioned interactively on-screen, as they will appear in the finished report.

C.I.P uses sophisticated techniques to create files that are extremely compact and yet allows rapid, random access of any record from any size file in seconds (file size limited to 65,000 bytes). Any or all fields can be keys or indexes.

C.I.P has extensive arithmetic capabilities for calculations within records and on reports. Date calculations are fully supported, including the computation of past and future dates, as well as the difference between any two dates (in days, weeks, months, or years). With these features, *C.I.P* can be used for a wide variety of business applications that other products are unable to handle.

With *C.I.P*, forms, reports, and even files can be changed without copying or re-entering data. Such restructuring allows the user to concentrate on immediate needs without fear that he or she will have to start from scratch if the needs change.

C.I.P can import and export data to and from other products including *dBASE II*, *dBASE III*, *pfs* and *Lotus 1-2-3*. Formats include DIF, ASCII, delimited ASCII, and labeled ASCII. With the *C.I.P* MERGE utility, form letters can be prepared easily using most popular word processors.

Company:

Conetic Systems, Inc.

Product:

C/TOOLS Database Application Generation System

Category:

Database Management Systems

Computer:	**Media:**
AT&T PC 6300	Diskette

Language:

C

Requirements:
256 KB RAM and hard disk

Support:
3-day training course $495
Phone support (415) 430-8875
Support contracts available
Newsletter
On site

Retail Price:
$795 (w/o utilities)

Distributor:

Conetic Systems, Inc.
1470 Doolittle Drive
San Leandro, CA 94577
Tel: (415) 430-8875

Description:

C/TOOLS is a fully integrated relational type database system and fourth generation application generation system. C/TOOLS provide a visually driven and interactive system that provides a consistent interface for the creation of the four key elements of a database application: data files, data entry screens, reports and menus.

The record management system supports nine data types and three file types: hashed, ISAM and sequential files. Field length and record limit are virtually unlimited. Up to 128 indexes of up to eight fields each may be declared. Fields used in keys may be stored in any order in the record and need not be of the same data type. Records may be accessed on key value, partial key value or any single or multiple field patterns. Metacharacter searches are also supported. Primary and secondary key declarations may be updated, changed or deleted. Multiple data files may be opened to the limit allowed by the operating system. Record locking is provided. To access the data files, data input and retrieval screens are created interactively on the terminal in a free format environment. Literal text and data fields may be placed anywhere on the screen. They may be changed at any time. Automatic editing of fields insures entry of correct data types and lengths with automatic formatting for money, date and time data type. Fields can be declared as mandatory input fields, entry fields, display only or invisible fields. Initial values and default values may be specified. The calculated fields features are extensive and powerful. Algebraic, exponential and all other C language arithmetic operations are supported. A calculated field can be specified as a screen only field and/or as an actual field in a data file. Dissimilar data types (i.e. money and integer) may be calculated. The C/TOOLS also allow you to move to different data entry screens, query or add a record, and move back to your current screen at the same place you left it. For very specialized requirements not covered by these powerful features, C edit routines may be written for any field.

The report writer produces screen displayed or hard copy documents from the data files. The report writer is screen oriented for exceptional ease of use. The user simply lays out the report format on the screen in the way he or she wants the report to appear. Multi-tiered sorting, subtotals and totals are some of the features that can be tapped. The screen generated report format is translated into a file of report writer text. For very complex reports, this text file may be edited to whatever extent is necessary. Powerful operators are available for arithmetic computations, variable and proce-

(Continued on next page)

Description: ***(Continued)***

dure declarations and formatting. Data files may be updated using the report writer. Primary and secondary indexes defined for the data files are used by the report writer to provide quick report writer output.

To tie the whole system together, a screen oriented menu generator allows for development of single or multiple column menus for control of the developed applications without reduction in power or flexibility. Any sequence of commands associated with the choice selected can be executed including calling other menus.

The C/TOOLS provide the means to bring up database applications in an environment that allows a dramatic reduction in development time and maintenance time. The product has been used by companies in the Fortune 500 category for very sophisticated applications as well as by individuals with simple database requirements. The C/TOOLS database and application generation system was used to develop the powerful, fully integrated Conetic Systems accounting system, the C/BOOKS.

Company:
Conetic Systems, Inc.

Product:
***Higgins Administrative Software* Version 1.0**

Category:
Database Management Systems

Computer:	**Media:**
6300 PLUS **AT&T PC 6300** **AT&T PC 6300 PLUS**	Diskette

Language:
C

Requirements:
256 KB RAM
Color display optional

Support:
Dealer support hotline
End user hotline

Retail Price:
$395

Distributor:
Conetic Systems, Inc.
1470 Doolittle Drive
San Leandro, CA 94577
Tel: (415) 430-8875

Description:

Higgins is a new class of office automation software: an information retrieval system which interactively manages everything from daily schedules to task lists for project completion to automatically filling out expense reports.

Higgins is an interactive administrative assistant built on a natural language relational database management system that is also available from Conetic Systems (C/Systems and C/TOOLS). The main modules of Higgins consist of Time Manager, Directory, To-Do List, Personal File system, and Expense Report. *Higgins* also has an autodialer with routing capabilities, a scratch pad for quick notes, a timer and a calculator.

Higgins allows complete interaction among all of its modules. Working from a central directory, the user can cross-index; search on user-assigned keywords; track expenses by date, by client, by event, or by project; and search his or her calendar by date, event, or client. With *Higgins* the user may assign a priority number to any task. Then, using the retrieval capabilities, the user can demand a report of a given period's appointments subdivided by priority, keyword, association, client, or project. *Higgins* prints out reports in a variety of formats combining a calendar and a To-Do log with a phone list of all of the people to be seen during a specific period.

Higgins is interactive with other DOS-based programs for the personal computer. The users run any other program from within *Higgins* and returns automatically to the *Higgins* main menu, where the other program files, letters, and spreadsheets may be indexed and tracked as easily as the things maintained under *Higgins*'s own umbrella.

Higgins Version 1.0 is compatible with later versions and with a variety of local area networks.

Company:
DataAccess Corporation

Product:
***DataFlex* Version 2.0E**

Category:
Database Management Systems

Computer:	**Media:**
AT&T PC 6300 6300 PLUS **AT&T PC 6300 PLUS**	Diskette

Language:
Pascal MT+

Requirements:
192-256 KB RAM
600 K disk or hard disk

Support:
Support provided locally through distributors and dealers
Intermediate and advanced level hands on training classes, each of 3 days duration

Retail Price:
16-bit single user–$995

Distributor:

DataAccess Corporation
8525 S.W. 129 Terrace
Miami, FL 33156-6565
Tel: (305) 238-0012

Description:

DataFlex is a comprehensive transportable application development database software system. It provides the combined functions of a programming language, a true relational database management system, an "image" oriented screen forms processor, report generator, query, and a full set of powerful utilities. *DataFlex* has features ranging from automatic file definition and code generation to on-line multikey ISAM and user-definable macros. *DataFlex* based applications are fast, reliable, and totally transportable across processors and a variety of operating systems and local area networks.

DataFlex can be an effective tool for system users at different levels of sophistication and experience. Professional programmers and application developers can completely replace programming languages such as BASIC or Pascal with *DataFlex*. It has all of the features of these conventional development tools with the advantages of an integral database management system and on-line multikey ISAM. Developers can also reduce programming time and enhance productivity by using *DataFlex* pre-programmed screen and report handling macros.

Microcomputer users in a business environment can derive far more utility from their systems by using *DataFlex*'s easy-to-use report and screen/forms code generators. Complete programs can be created automatically by *DataFlex* without ever writing a single command or line of code. Programs created in this fashion can be compiled and used immediately or modified to perform special functions according to the user's requirements. Query, one of *DataFlex*'s utilities, can be used to extract information from a database and report it to the screen, a printer, or a disk file for use with word processing, spreadsheets, or other programs.

Applications developed with *DataFlex* are completely computer independent. Compiled *DataFlex* programs, referred to as "configurations," can be transported to any system that is supported with a *DataFlex* "Runtime" module. The runtime module is system specific and can execute any *DataFlex* configuration. This structure allows software developers to create application programs that are not limited to a particular computer or operating system. System users are thus provided with a broader range of product choices which they can run if *DataFlex* is installed on their system.

The user has a uniquely protected software investment if applications are used or developed with *DataFlex*. Since data and applications can be transported across different computers, the user can freely migrate programs and information if the system

(Continued on next page)

Description: ***(Continued)***

should be enlarged or changed. If *DataFlex* has been used to implement databases and applications in the *CP/M* environment, the entire system can be easily migrated to *MS*-DOS without even a recompilation! Any investment that the business may have made in developing its applications is completely protected, as is the investment in employee training and familiarity that users will have developed using the *DataFlex* software.

Company:
DayFlo, Inc.

Product:
DayFlo

Category:
Database Management Systems

Computer:	**Media:**
AT&T PC 6300 **AT&T PC 6300 PLUS**	Diskette

6300 PLUS

Language:
C

Requirements:
320 KB RAM

Support:
Technical support (714) 476-3044
Training
Sales support (714) 476-3044

Retail Price:
$495

Distributor:
DayFlo, Inc.
2500 Michelson Drive
Bldg. # 425
Irvine, CA 92715
Tel: (714) 476-3044

Description:

DayFlo is a free-form text database designed to let you manage both structured and text information in a powerful, but easy-to-use manner. *DayFlo* combines the data storage and retrieval capabilities of a database with the text handling capabilities of a word processor. You can use *DayFlo* to track clients and key accounts, manage projects, handle office correspondence, and more. *Dayflo* can be used in such vertical applications as Executive Search, Litigation Support, Personnel Management, Library Management, etc.

Company:
DayFlo, Inc.

Product:
ReportFlo

Category:
Database Management Systems

Computer: **AT&T PC 6300**

Media: Diskette

Language:
C

Requirements:
384 KB RAM

Support:
Technical support (714) 476-3044
Sales support (714) 476-3044
Training

Retail Price:
$195

Distributor:
DayFlo, Inc.
2500 Michelson Ave.
Bldg. # 425
Irvine, CA 92715
Tel: (714) 476-3044

Description:

ReportFlo is the powerful report writer creating professional reports, lists, tables, letters, and documents from records stored in *DayFlo*. *ReportFlo* is flexible and can incorporate both text and columnar tables in the same document. *ReportFlo* has calculation and formula capabilities as well as totals, counts, and averages. *ReportFlo* also enhances the word processing functionality of *Dayflo* by offering such features as document titles, headers, footers, page numbering, mail merge capabilities, and more.

Company:

Dun & Bradstreet Plan Services

Product:

The Personal Connection–Client Information System

Category:

Database Management Systems

Computer:	**Media:**
AT&T PC 6300	Diskette

Language:

Compiled BASIC

Requirements:

128 KB RAM
Compilers
Peripherals

Support:

Full documentation is included in price
Toll-free telephone number available for support
Nationwide–(800) 447-0683
Illinois only–(800) 322-4578

Retail Price:

$345

Distributor:

Dun & Bradstreet Plan Services
4517 North Sterling Ave.
Peoria, IL 61615
Tel: (309) 688-4095

Description:

The Client Information System is a complete database system that is used to maintain pertinent information on clients and prospects. CIS is also a very powerful marketing and follow-up tool that gives the user complete flexibility in qualifying prospects.

Codes used to categorize clients are defined by the user. Using these codes, the user can quickly and easily "pull" from the client data files all clients meeting specific criteria. The list of selected clients can be printed or sent to a disk file to be merged with a letter using a word processor.

Complete client information on up to 1200 individuals can be maintained using the CIS system. (Maximum number of clients depends upon hardware configuration.) Information on any client can be found in less than two seconds.

CIS also has telephone dialing capability when used with a *Hayes* Smartmodem.

Company:
Dun & Bradstreet Plan Services

Product:
The Personal Connection–Estate Inventory

Category:
Database Management Systems

Computer:	**Media:**
AT&T PC 6300	Diskette

Language:
Compiled BASIC

Requirements:
128 KB RAM

Support:
Full documentation is included in price
Toll-free telephone number available for support
Nationwide–(800) 447-0683
Illinois only–(800) 322-4578

Retail Price:
$235

Distributor:
Dun & Bradstreet Plan Services
4517 North Sterling Ave.
Peoria, IL 61615
Tel: (309) 688-4095

Description:

Estate Inventory is a database program which provides a permanent record of every asset in your client's estate. Up to 240 separate properties may be listed showing the description, market value, basis, debt ownership, annual debt, reduction, annual income potential, growth rate, and maintenance cost. Estate Inventory provides both a total estate valuation and personal financial statement, as well as a cash flow analysis by item. It also incorporates a password security system to maintain confidentiality.

Company:
Dun & Bradstreet Plan Services

Product:
The Personal Connection–Estate Plan

Category:
Database Management Systems

Computer:	**Media:**
AT&T PC 6300	Diskette

Language:
Word Processing Overlay

Requirements:
Word Processor

Support:
Full documentation is included in price
Toll-free telephone number available for support
Nationwide–(800) 447-0683
Illinois only–(800) 322-4578

Retail Price:
$75

Distributor:
Dun & Bradstreet Plan Services
4517 North Sterling Ave.
Peoria, IL 61615
Tel: (309) 688-4095

Description:

Estate Plan is a modern database system which provides a permanent record of all the information that would be needed in connection with the settlement of your client's estate.

The information begins with a listing of the people to be contacted (i.e., family members, advisors, clergy, etc.) and then continues with the funeral arrangements, location of important documents, list of advisors, business continuation agreement, estimated settlement costs, donor card for anatomical gifts, directive to physicians for elimination of life support systems in the event of a terminal illness, and finally, an obituary for the newspaper.

The program provides a hard copy printout for the client and his advisors as well as a permanent record on diskette. Each information item is numbered to assist in quickly making updates and changes.

EP is a word processing "overlay" program and must be used in conjunction with a word processing program such as *WordStar* or *Volkswriter*.

Company:
Infocom, Inc.

Product:
***Cornerstone* Release 5.1**

Category:
Database Management Systems

Computer:	**Media:**
AT&T PC 6300 **AT&T PC 6300 PLUS**	Diskette

6300 PLUS

Language:
Proprietary

Requirements:
256 KB RAM
Two floppy disk drives recommended
512 KB and hard disk

Support:
Technical hotline (617) 576-3190
Dealer hotline 1-800-654-4481

Retail Price:
$495

Distributor:
Infocom, Inc.
125 Cambridge Park Drive
Cambridge, MA 02140
Tel: 1-800-654-4481

Description:

Cornerstone is a powerful, full-featured relational database system, designed to help nonprogrammers manage information. *Cornerstone* can assist in solving an entire range of information management problems faced each working day, from mailing lists and sales tracking to personnel management and resource planning. *Cornerstone* offers the following features:

- Powerful context-specific help. Explains available commands, most recent error messages, and even allowable data values
- Menu-driven command structure. Commands entered by typing or choosing from the menu. Menus can be hidden for sophisticated users
- Interactive report writer. Allows different formats to be used for entering, viewing, and selecting records
- Any field can be indexed at any time (enhances the speed of sorting and selecting data)
- Thorough data checking. Includes minimum and maximum values, unique values, mandatory fields, and automatic filling in of fields
- On-Disk Tutorial, Beginner's Guide, and Owners' Handbook
- Advanced database structures including multi-valued fields and subrecords
- Complex selection (search) criteria are storable for repeated use
- *Cornerstone* reads files in *dBASE II* and *PFS* formats and exchanges information with *Lotus 1-2-3* and *WordStar*

Specifications include:

- 8,000,000 characters per file
- 120 files per database
- 255 saved formats per file
- 160 fields per record
- Any and all fields can be indexed
- Each field may have multiple values (up to 255)
- 4,000 characters per record, expandable by sub-records. Each subrecord may contain up to 4,000 characters

(Continued on next page)

Description: ***(Continued)***

- All records of variable length

The Beginner's Guide and On-Screen Tutorial teach the user the basics of building and using a database. A customized keyboard template clearly labels the functions of each function key, and Help and Option keys provide immediate assistance to the user who is uncertain of what to do next.

Cornerstone also offers menus, prompts, and questions to guide the user through the entire operation of building the database.

Company:
Information Builders

Product:
PC/FOCUS

Category:
Database Management Systems

Computer: AT&T PC 6300

Media: Diskette

Language:
Fourth Generation Language

Requirements:
512 KB RAM
10 MB hard disk

Support:
90-day hotline (212) 736-6130
Extended maintenance service

Retail Price:
$1,595

Distributor:
Information Builders
1250 Broadway
New York, NY 10001
Tel: (212) 736-4433

Description:

PC/FOCUS is a complete database and application development system. It contains all of the components for its mainframe counterpart *FOCUS*, plus several new functions: an integrated full-screen editor and a communication program for file transfers. *PC/FOCUS* is a complete environment for developing local PC applications and for reporting from files downloaded from the mainframe. It also provides a distributed processing environment where database transactions are entered, validated, and formatted locally, then sent to the mainframe for processing. Additionally, *PC/FOCUS* enables you to prototype and test mainframe *FOCUS* procedures without consuming mainframe computer resources. Once developed, the procedures can be sent to the mainframe for production execution.

Company:
Innovative Software

Product:
The Smart Data Manager 2.0

Category:
Database Management Systems

Computer:	**Media:**
AT&T PC 6300	Diskette

Language:
C

Requirements:
256 KB RAM
Two floppy or one floppy + hard disk
MS DOS 2.0 or higher

Support:
Example files and on-screen tutorials
Quick key reference guide
Registered SMART owners
Support hotline
Ongoing updates

Retail Price:
$495

Distributor:

Innovative Software
9300 W. 110 St., Suite 380
Overland Park, KS 66204
Tel: (913) 383-1089

Description:

The Smart Data Manager is a product that can be operated by its own menus, custom-defined menus or a built-in command language. With a capacity of 1,000,000 records per file and 255 fields per record, it has the full power to handle large complex applications. Moreover, separate files can be viewed through multiple windows for easy data queries and updates; complex calculations and multiple file interactions can be performed within a file, between files and in report and form generation; and full relational file capabilities permit the contents of one file to affect the contents of another.

Additional features include up to 10 "screen views" of a file; as many as 15 pages per "screen view;" and security password entry at both the screen and file levels to protect proprietary data and end user applications.

HIGHLIGHTS

- One of the largest databases available.
- Password protection at both file and screen levels.
- Custom designed data entry screens.
- Custom designed menus.
- Graphic character sets for incorporating custom designed lines and boxes.
- Designated "read only" and "must enter" data entry field.
- Character and numerical range verification for data entry.
- Calculation capabilities: math, trigonometric, statistical, financial, date and time.
- Decision-making capabilities select, lookup, case, if/then/else, and/or, boolean, choose.
- Text manipulation capabilities: repeat, midstring, concatenate.
- Full-screen formula editor.
- Browse: scroll through entire files or subsets of file on-screen.
- Linked-window scrolling.
- File summarizations in table format for sending to spreadsheet.
- Relational file data transfers, lookups, transactions, and new file creation based on the contents of two other files.

(Continued on next page)

Description: ***(Continued)***

- Number of files open at one time only limited by RAM.
- Complex file sorts, queries and searches.
- Report generating to screen, printer and disk.
- Custom applications development with "Project Processing" and the Smart Programming Language.

SPECIFICATIONS

- 1,000,000 records per file.
- 255 fields per record.
- 1000 characters per field.
- 4096 characters per record.
- 25 on-screen windows.
- 15 key fields maintained for sorting.
- 15 minor fields per key field.
- 10 screen views per file.
- 15 pages per screen view.
- 8 field types: date, time, Social Security number, phone numeric, alphanumeric, counter, inverted name.

Company:
Membership Services, Inc.

Product:
Master Membership Profile

Category:
Database Management Systems

Computer:	**Media:**
AT&T PC 6300 6300 PLUS **AT&T PC 6300 PLUS**	Diskette

Language:
dBASE II COMPILED

Requirements:
128 KB RAM

Support:
Toll-free telephone support (800) 527-9919 ext. 0581
Texas WATS (800) 442-7950 ext. 0581
User newsletter
Software updates are available
Training seminars are regularly scheduled

Retail Price:
$1,000

Distributor:
Membership Services, Inc.
P.O. Box 152130
Irving, TX 75061
Tel: (214) 438-0581

Description:

The *Master Membership Profile* is a state-of-the-art data management system designed to help the user use church members' records, not just keep them. All functions are menu-driven to provide easy access to all the information needed to carry out church programs. The user can select, sort, or arrange names or other information in a variety of ways. The computer can also use word processing and the information in *Master Membership Profile* to format personal letters. The *Master Membership Profile* provides the flexibility of at least 13 usable output formats including mailing labels, church directories, cards, listings, offering envelopes, and pledge cards.

Company:
Metafile Information Systems, Inc.

Product:
METAFILE

Category:
Database Management Systems

Computer:	**Media:**
AT&T PC 6300 **AT&T PC 6300 PLUS**	Diskette

6300 PLUS

Language:
Assembler

Requirements:
128 KB RAM
Color display optional
One diskette drive and one additional drive, hard disk storage device
Parallel or serial printer
One serial RS-232 communication port
Hard disks
RAM disks
Printers
Spoolers
Modems
Supports up to a maximum of 640 KB RAM

Support:
Each Metafile, Inc. location holds monthly classes taught by data processing professionals. Metafile Information Systems, Inc. software support programs offer a complete network of services including:

- Telephone support
- Hardware and software maintenance
- Technical support
- Marketing support
- Consulting services

Retail Price:
$995

Distributor:
Metafile Information Systems, Inc.
401 Sixteenth St.
Rochester, MN 55904
Tel: (312) 724-0310

Description:

METAFILE is a fully integrated application environment combining a fourth generation language, report generation, text processing, and file record and screen management. This environment provides the ideal setting for the development of user-specified applications.

All facilities are easily accessed through a hierarchical menu structure, beginning with the *METATFILE* Assistant. From the Assistant, the user or developer can choose to view a directory, check on the current status of the *METAFILE* environment, and select from a list of all available commands in the program. Any menu can be bypassed by direct entry of commands.

The programming language brings together all of the components of *METAFILE*. This powerful, fourth generation language allows an application developer to exercise as much power over the system as required. The language has a rich supply of procedure control commands, handy built-in functions, arithmetic and string operators, and complete access to the interactive command set.

The report generation facilities are complete with menus, on-line prompting, and ad hoc reporting. Simple commands like SORT, LIST, and FIND produce professional looking reports.

The text editor has many of the features of a stand-alone word processing package and is especially useful when coupled with the features of the database. As a developer is preparing text, data calculations can be easily merged to produce customized output. A special lookaside feature allows the user to concurrently perform operations on a smaller portion of the screen without disturbing the operation being worked on in the main display area.

The database manager qualifies and sorts records and provides rapid access through indexing. Up to five databases can be active at one time. Data integrity is ensured in applications by describing the elements that comprise the database, such as length type (character, date, or numeric), position , default value, or ranges. The developer can specify data entry forms or use the default data entry screens.

Other features include networking support, open architecture, and PC to PC communications via telephone lines.

Three versions of *METAFILE* are available to run database applications: the full *METAFILE* system, Runtime, and Runtime Plus.

Company:
Oracle Corporation

Product:
***ORACLE* Version 4.1.X**

Category:
Database Management Systems

Computer:	**Media:**
AT&T PC 6300	Diskette

Language:
SQL

Requirements:
1 MB RAM recommended
Peripherals—required hard disk
Compilers—none required but Oracle Corp. supports various compilers

Support:
Training included in purchase price. Otherwise, classes available at additional charge. Support is available for approximately 10 percent of purchase price.

Retail Price:
$1,000

Distributor:

Oracle Corporation
2710 Sand Hill Rd.
Menlo Park, CA 94025
Tel: (415) 854-7350

Description:

The *ORACLE* relational database management system, which runs on micro, mini, and mainframe computers, includes a growing set of application tools for application generation, report writing, color graphics, spreadsheet, and network communications.

ORACLE also includes SQL data language, a nonprocedural language. SQL utilizes commands for data query, definition, control, and manipulation. Statements may be entered either through a terminal interface or embedded in programming languages such as C, COBOL, FORTRAN, Pascal, BASIC, *PL/1*, or ASSEMBLER through a host language interface. The interactive application facility includes an interactive application generator for building applications with no programming and an interactive application processor for processing applications at the terminal level. A report generator is provided for the development of formatted reports, with interweaving of database information and additional textual information into a single report, letter, or document. Facilities include data compression, compressed indexes, data clustering, virtual buffer paging, concurrent access, and multiple database activity through 100% reentrant code. Data protection, security, recovery, and restart functions are also supported.

Company:
P2/i, Inc.

Product:
Business Card System

Category:
Database Management Systems

Computer: AT&T PC 6300

Media: Diskette

Language:
MAI Business BASIC/Micro (BB/M)

Requirements:
128 KB RAM
Runtime version of BB/M included

Support:
Phone-in support for dealers only, (505) 822-8585
Product upgrades available
Dealer training available

Retail Price:
$195

Distributor:
P2/i, Inc.
A Division of Arinco Computer System
1704 Moon N.E., #7
Albuquerque, NM 87112
Tel: (505) 822-8585

P2/i, Inc. is an authorized Value Added Reseller for AT&T Computers.

Description:

The P2/i Business Card System provides fingertip storage and retrieval of product and/or service information normally lost in stacks of business cards. After information is entered into the system, individual cards may be recalled by product, company, or the person's name. Additionally, information regarding telephone or in-person meetings can be stored with memorandums indicating the associated action required and its date. As action-needed dates become current, the system will remind the user to check the file.

Company:
P2/i, Inc.

Product:
Opinion Survey Data Analysis System

Category:
Database Management Systems

Computer:
AT&T PC 6300

Media:
Diskette

Language:
MAI BASIC

Requirements:
256 KB RAM
Two floppy disks, with minimum configuration

Support:
90-day warranty
Post-warranty support policies
Call P2/i for details (505) 822-8585

Retail Price:
$1,495

Distributor:
P2/i, Inc.
A Division of Arinco Computer Systems
1704 Moon N.E., #7
Albuquerque, NM 87112
Tel: (505) 822-8585

P/2i, Inc. is an authorized Value Added Reseller for AT&T Computers.

Description:

A sophisticated tool for creating custom surveys, the Opinion Survey Data Analysis System has been designed to provide a fast, easy way of accumulating and analyzing survey data. It may be used as an on-line data capture system and as a batch processing system.

Company:
PowerBase Systems, Inc.

Product:
Power-base

Category:
Database Management Systems

Computer:	**Media:**
AT&T PC 6300 6300 PLUS **AT&T PC 6300 PLUS**	Diskette

Language:
C and Assembler

Requirements:
320 KB RAM
MS-DOS (2.0 or later)
Two disk drives storing at least 320 KB each (double-sided floppy or hard disk)
Optional printer

Support:
Warranty
$95 Maintenance Agreement (enclosed in 2.1)
Free updates released for one year
Customer Support department and hot line
Fix-Disk service
Dealer referral service

Retail Price:
$595 (includes two *Power-base* Application Series templates)

Distributor:
PowerBase Systems, Inc.
12 West 37th St.
New York, NY 10018
Tel: (212) 947-7214

Description:

Power-Base is a fully menu-driven multifile database management system. In 1985, for the second consecutive year, *Power-base* received the highest overall rating of all relational DBMSs evaluated by *Software Digest.* Among *Power-base's* top-rated features are: *DataZoom*, which permits instant access to related information in other files: *PowerLinks*, built-in data transfer links between *Power-base* and other popular software programs (*Lotus 1-2-3*, *Symphony*, *MultiMate*, *VisiCalc*, *WordStar/MailMerge*, *dBASE II*, *pfs:file*, etc.) and ASCII files; customized multifile/multisort reporting; "*Query-By-Example*", wild card random searches; data entry support for 13 foreign languages (selected as one of 30 nation/language options); relational fields (Look-ups, Functions); user-designed mailing label generator; global replaces and recalculations; table validations and a wide range of Entry Rules. Inclusive in the price of *Power-base* 2.1 is a choice of two templates from the new *Power-base* Application Series. The currently available business application templates I3 Analysis, Sales Prospect Tracking, Order Processing/Invoicing, Inventory Control, Human Resource Management and Association Management. A LAN version of *Power-base*, using *3Com*'s networking technology, was released in late Summer, 1985.

Company:
The Small Computer Company, Inc.

Product:
***filePro* 16**

Category:
Database Management Systems

Computer:	**Media:**
6300 PLUS **AT&T PC 6300** **AT&T PC 6300 PLUS**	Diskette

Language:
C

Requirements:
256 KB RAM
Printer
Hard disk

Support:
3 months' free telephone support with purchase
Thereafter $100/six months
$175/year
Newsletter
On-site training by request

Retail Price:
$495

Distributor:
The Small Computer Company, Inc.
230 West 41st St., 12th Floor
New York, NY 10036
Tel: (212) 398-9290

Description:

The *MS*-DOS *filePro* 16 allows the user to create a sophisticated, data-independent integrated business system. Its capacities include 999 fields per record; 4,608 characters per record; 16,000,000 records per file; 12 indexes per file; and 24 digits per numeric field. It is menu-driven and features modular design. It has a full-screen facility for creating custom screen and report layouts. Ten files are usable concurrently. This application also provides built-in field types (error checking), user-defined field types, user-defined menus, conditional math, data protection, and password security.

Professional support, including custom programming, is available from authors.

Company:
The Small Computer Company, Inc.

Product:
***filePro* 16 Plus**

Category:
Database Management Systems

Computer:
AT&T PC 6300

Media:
Diskette

Language:
C

Requirements:
384 KB RAM
Printer

Support:
3 months' free telephone support with purchase
Thereafter $100/six months
$175/year
Newsletter
On-site training by request

Retail Price:
$495–$990

Distributor:

The Small Computer Company, Inc.
230 West 41st St., 12th Floor
New York, NY 10036
Tel: (212) 398-9290

Description:

filePro 16 Plus, an advanced version of *filePro* 16, allows the user to create a sophisticated, data-independent integrated business system. It features modular design; a built-in processing-table debugger; "when" processing, which lets the user send information to other files while in update mode; on-line posting; and automatically balanced indexes. It allows the users to set one-to-many relationships, for more versatile lookups. Capacities include 999 fields per record; 16,384 characters per record; 16,000,000 records per file; 12 indexes per file; and 24 digits per numeric field. The application is menu-driven and features a full-screen facility for creating custom screen and report layouts; 10 files usable concurrently; built-in field types (error checking); user-defined field types; user-defined menus; conditional math; data protection; and password security.

Professional support, including custom programming, is available from authors.

Company:
Starcom Computer Corporation

Product:
Files & Folders

Category:
Database Management Systems

Computer:	**Media:**
AT&T PC 6300	Diskette

Language:
Written in Pascal, C, and 8086 Assembly. Runs as an executable program.

Requirements:
190 KB RAM free (256 KB)

Support:
Telephone support 8:00 a.m. to 5:00 p.m. (206) 881-2828. Training through distributors/dealers/manufacturers reps. Limited warranty to original licensee: That diskettes(s) on which program is recorded be free from defects in materials and workmanship under normal use and service for a period of 90 days from the date of delivery, provided customer has returned the registration card delivered with the licensed program.

Retail Price:
$495

Distributor:

Starcom Computer Corporation
15446 Bel-Red Rd., Suite 340
Redmond, WA 98052
Tel: (206) 881-2828

Description:

Files & Folders is a relational database offering flexible and sophisticated data management capabilities for non-technical computer users. It is an easy-to-use system that offers the power and flexibility to organize data as simple as mailing lists and as complex as full accounting business systems such as A/R, A/P, G/L, and inventory control.

The entire program is function-key menu driven. The use of softkeys displayed on the bottom of the screen gives the operator all of the choices, eliminating the need to memorize commands. Help screens are always available.

Folder layouts are dynamic and free form. Custom business forms can easily be created on the screen. Folder layout can also be revised at any time without having to re-enter data. The "EXPAND" feature allows three-dimensional viewing of related folders instantly.

Information reporting is simple and fast. List & Sort lets the user extract information immediately, sort it, do calculations, and print the results, or transfer the information to allow integration with other programs such as word processors or spreadsheets.

The built-in report writer allows creating and saving complex reports in minutes without having to develop cumbersome command structures.

Files & Folders provides multifile relational database power in an easy-to-use format that sets new standards in bringing complex capabilities within reach of the typical PC user.

Company:
Stoneware

Product:
Advanced DB Master

Category:
Database Management Systems

Computer:	**Media:**
AT&T PC 6300 6300 PLUS **AT&T PC 6300 PLUS**	Diskette

Language:
Pascal

Requirements:
256 KB RAM (512 recommended)
Two floppy disk drives or compatible hard disk
Printer required for reports (serial or parallel)

Support:
Free technical phone support (415) 454-6500
The User's Manual includes a 250 page step-by-step tutorial
Sample files
File planning worksheets

Retail Price:
$495

Distributor:
Stoneware
50 Belvedere St.
San Rafael, CA 94901
Tel: (415) 454-6500

Description:

Advanced DB Master is a database management system designed specifically for business and professional users who want performance without programming. *Advanced DB Master* lets a user store, search, reorganize, and calculate information and then print out fully customized reports. The program uses menu options and screen prompts. Its easy-to-use features include: table look-ups, text merge, field validation, browse audit trail, keystroke macros. *Advanced DB Master* allows users to exchange data with other programs, such as *dBASE II*, *Lotus 1-2-3*, other *DB Master* files, and other computers. It can store up to 16 MB of information and is the only leading information management system that allows files to span across more than one diskette (up to 44 floppy diskettes per file). Program includes hard disk capability, a user's guide, program diskettes, an application template diskette with four sample files, and a reference wall chart. For customer convenience, *Advanced DB Master* 2.1 is not copy-protected.

Company:
TOM Software, Inc.

Product:
***EZ-SPEED* Records Management System**

Category:
Database Management Systems

Computer: AT&T PC 6300

Media: Diskette

Language:
TOMBASIC

Requirements:
TOMBASIC

Support:
Training and technical support provided by the local licensed consultant
Fees depend on the consultant and the type of service provided

Retail Price:
$800–$3,500 depending on the hardware

Distributor:
TOM Software, Inc.
127 S.W. 156th Ave.
P.O. Box 66596
Seattle, WA 98166
Tel: (206) 246-7022

TOM Software, Inc. is an authorized Value Added Reseller for AT&T Computers.

Description:

EZ-SPEED is a series of programs designed to help someone with no programming experience do what it usually takes a programmer to do–create computer files and design reports. Virtually any type of information from a catalog-type file can be stored in the computer–lists of customers, vendors, sales leads, equipment, inventory, or any other records presently maintained by hand. As computer files are designed, *EZ-SPEED* guides the user with on-screen questions and fill-in-the-blank displays. With a single keystroke, the user can ask the system to display "HELP" operating instructions at any time during the design process. A special report generator function helps design reports using any file in the system. Because the report generator can handle mathematical operations, it is a powerful tool for management reporting. If *EZ-SPEED* is part of a system that includes *SPEED* I accounting modules, the user can draw upon data from any file and include it in a report. *EZ-SPEED* also interfaces with the TOM word processing system, *D.A.T.A.* 3500, for automatic letter generation.

Company:
Cdex Corporation

Product:
Cdex* Training for *dBASE II

Category:
Education/Training

Computer:	**Media:**
AT&T PC 6300 6300 PLUS **AT&T PC 6300 PLUS**	Diskette

Language:
Cdex Authoring System–XPL

Requirements:
40-or 80-column, color or monochrome monitor
1 disk drive
128 KB RAM

Support:
Technical support hotline: (800) 982-1213
California: (415) 964-7600
90-day warranty
After 90 days, disks are available for $10 each with return of damaged disk

Retail Price:
$99.95

Distributor:
Cdex Corporation
1885 Lundy Ave.
San Jose, CA 95131
Tel: (800) 982-1213

Description:

Provides comprehensive training for new and experienced users of *dBASE II*. Two interactive tutorial disks and reference guide are included. Learn to create, design, and maintain customized database systems using *dBASE II*.

Company:
Cdex Corporation

Product:
Managing Your Business w/*Lotus 1-2-3*

Category:
Education/Training

Computer:
AT&T PC 6300

Media:
Diskette

Language:
Cdex Authoring System–XPL

Requirements:
1 disk drive
128 KB RAM
80-column display, color or monochrome

Support:
Technical support hotline (800) 982-1213
90-day warranty

Retail Price:
$149.95

Distributor:
Cdex Corporation
1885 Lundy Ave.
San Jose, CA 95131
Tel: (800) 982-1213

Description:

User will learn to use *Lotus 1-2-3* to measure business success and profitability. Teaches important business indicators and provides tools to help analyze them: Return on Sales, Asset Turnover, Financial Leverage. Tutorial disk and templates disk, ten template worksheets, and reference guide are included. The ten templates are:

- Sales History and Forecast
- Product Margin Analysis and Forecast
- Department Expense Budget
- Profit and Loss Statement
- Cash Flow Projection
- Materials Requirements Plan
- Accounts Receivable Record and Analysis
- Accounts Payable Record and Analysis
- Balance Sheet
- *Cdex* Profit Model

Company:
Comprehensive Software

Product:
Introduction to Databases

Category:
Education/Training

Computer:
6300 PLUS
AT&T PC 6300
AT&T PC 6300 PLUS

Media:
Diskette

Language:
C

Requirements:
128 KB RAM
Monitor
1 floppy disk

Support:
Replacement copies for registered end users at $10 additional charge
Support number (213) 214-1461

Retail Price:
$59.95

Distributor:
Comprehensive Software
2316 Artesia Blvd., Suite G
Redondo Beach, CA 90278
Tel: (213) 214-1461

Description:

Introduction to Databases is designed to lead the user through the maze of database software–before a few hundred dollars are spent on the wrong package. It educates the user on the importance of databases, their use, and which ones are appropriate, and even helps determine whether one is needed at all.

Company:
Comprehensive Software

Product:
Introduction to the Operating System

Category:
Education/Training

Computer:	**Media:**
AT&T PC 6300 **AT&T PC 6300 PLUS**	Diskette

6300 PLUS

Language:
BASIC

Requirements:
128 KB RAM
Monitor
1 disk drive

Support:
Replacement copies for registered end users at $10 additional charge
Support number (213) 214-1461

Retail Price:
$59.95

Distributor:
Comprehensive Software
2316 Artesia Blvd., Suite G
Redondo Beach, CA 90278
Tel: (213) 214-1461

Description:

Introduction to the Operating System unravels the mysteries of the DOS operating system and shows the user how to put it to work. You'll learn about commands, how to store and retrieve information, and much more.

Company:
Comprehensive Software

Product:
Introduction to Personal Computing

Category:
Education/Training

Computer:	**Media:**
AT&T PC 6300 **AT&T PC 6300 PLUS**	Diskette

6300 PLUS

Language:
C

Requirements:
128 KB RAM
Color or monochrome display
Floppy disk

Support:
Replacement copies for registered end users at $10 additional charge
Support number (213) 214-1461

Retail Price:
$59.95

Distributor:
Comprehensive Software
2316 Artesia Blvd., Suite G
Redondo Beach, CA 90278
Tel: (217) 352-1165

Description:

Using a step-by-step instruction manual and a friendly, interactive teaching technique, Introduction to Personal Computing brings your AT&T PC 6300 to life. Complete with illustrations, animation, and sound.

Company:

Global Information Systems Technology, Inc.

Product:

Accord

Category:

Education/Training

Computer:	**Media:**
AT&T PC 6300	Diskette

Language:

Tutor, C, Nonprogrammer Development Tools For Courseware

Requirements:

256 KB RAM for command subset
512 KB RAM for full language support

Support:

90 days; 5 one-week courses
Software support line
Post-warranty maintenance
Customer vendor's site

Retail Price:

$600

Distributor:

Global Information Systems Technology, Inc.
201 W. Springfield, Suite 700
Champaign, IL 61820
Tel: RPI I-CALL-BACK

Global Information Systems Technology, Inc. is an authorized Value Added Reseller for AT&T Computers.

Description:

Accord is a graphic-interactive courseware authoring and delivery system for computer-based training (CBT). *Accord* operates in both *UNIX* System V and *MS*-DOS environments and is compatible with office automation.

Accord consists of four components: menu-oriented Authoring aids, English-like TUTOR CBT language compiler and runtime system, subroutine library, and CMI/router (computer-managed instruction). *Accord* is a multilevel authoring system which even allows inclusion of courses written in other languages such as C, FORTRAN, PASCAL, and others. Courseware is binary-compatible between delivery systems and can utilize equipment normally found in the automated office—such as terminals, PC's, and multiuser *UNIX* system computers. Training and normal work can coexist at the workplace, eliminating the need for travel or separate dedicated training systems.

Accord authoring systems are available on *UNIX* system computers such as the 3B2/300, 3B2/400, 3B15, and 3B20. Courses or training are delivered in any of three ways: standalone using the AT&T PC 6300; via terminals attached to the *UNIX* system host; or distributed processing using PC 6300 workstations in conjunction with *PC-Interface*.

A variety of workstations can be accommodated: ANSI alphanumeric terminals, 4010-compatible graphic terminals, color or monochrome graphic PC's, up to CAD/CAM high resolution displays. Additionally, the PC 6300 workstation can support: mouse, touch, and bitpad pointing devices; video image capture; and videodisk, either separate screen or graphic overlay. Networks can use RS-232, STARLAN, or *Ethernet* connections.

Global Information Systems Technology, Inc., is a value-added reseller for AT&T Information Systems. All *Accord* packages are available as turn-key systems. License structures suitable for course publishing are available.

Company:
Knoware Learning Systems, Inc.

Product:
Knoware

Category:
Education/Training

Computer:	**Media:**
AT&T PC 6300	Diskette

Language:
COMPILED C

Requirements:
128 KB RAM
MS-DOS

Support:
Telephone support at hotline: (800) THE-KNOW available Monday through Friday from 9:00 a.m. to 5:00 p.m. E.S.T.

Retail Price:
$149

Distributor:
Knoware Learning Systems, Inc.
219 Vassar St.
Cambridge, MA 02139
Tel: (617) 576-3821

Description:

Knoware version 2.0 is a software starter set and educational software program that teaches computer literacy to first time users. Its format is a learning adventure that brings novices to an effective level of proficiency and confidence. The user climbs to the top of the corporate ladder by applying computer skills to each job along the way. These skills are acquired from hands-on experience with a database management program, a spreadsheet, a word processor, a business graphics program, and four financial applications.

Knoware differs from other educational programs in that it comes with actual functional applications that can be used independently of the learning adventure. Within a few hours, the user can be writing letters and memos, maintaining lists, managing budgets, preparing graphic presentations, and making investment decisions. The user gets hundreds of dollars worth of applications at a fraction of the cost.

Knoware uses colorful graphics and a step-by-step approach to make the educational process enjoyable and to reduce computer phobia. The program includes disks and a brief set of instructions for use. *Knoware* also includes a workbook (optional to the program's operation) that allows the user to get to deeper and deeper levels of expertise with each application. Sturdy plastic clamshell packaging allows for browsability. One of several enhancements to the 2.0 version is the inclusion of a printing utility for each of the applications.

Company:
Knoware Learning Systems, Inc.

Product:
Knowonder

Category:
Education/Training

Computer: AT&T PC 6300

Media: Diskette

Language:
COMPILED C

Requirements:
128 KB RAM
MS-DOS

Support:
Telephone support at hotline: (800) THE-KNOW available Monday through Friday from 9:00 a.m. to 5:00 p.m. E.S.T.

Retail Price:
$95

Distributor:
Knoware Learning Systems, Inc.
219 Vassar St.
Cambridge, MA 02139
Tel: (617) 576-3821

Description:

Knowonder is the latest addition to the *Knoware* family of software starter sets. It is a fantasy learning adventure for the young and young-at-heart! *Knowonder* uses outstanding graphics and functional software applications to guide the user to become ruler of the magical kingdom of Erawonk. Its adventure format appeals to novices who are ready to combine substantial learning with entertainment.

Adventurers enter the land of Erawonk, meet a wonderful wizard, and attempt, by learning five of the most commonly used computer applications, to become ruler of the kingdom. These applications include: Logo, word processing, database management, spreadsheets, and a calendar/planner. Using *Knowonder*, the user can become familiar with these applications in a short time, and understanding them offers a head start on the road to using the computer to its maximum potential. The program does not require a manual, although the *Knowonder* workbook assists the user in achieving more sophisticated levels of knowledge.

Knowonder provides the user with an operational applications software for programming in Logo, doing word processing, using a spreadsheet, and scheduling with a calendar/planner–hundreds of dollars worth of software at a fraction of the cost.

Company:
Total Learning Systems, Inc.

Product:
TLS-A Total Learning System for *MS*-DOS

Category:
Education/Training

Computer:	**Media:**
6300 PLUS **AT&T PC 6300** **AT&T PC 6300 PLUS**	Diskette

Language:
BASIC–Presented in compiled BASIC. Disk does not require operator to have BASIC loaded for operation.

Requirements:
128 KB RAM
One double-sided, double-density drive
MS-DOS version 2.0–3.1

Support:
Telephone: (305) 771-2100 8:30 a.m. to 5:30 p.m. EST

Retail Price:
$49.95

Distributor:
Total Learning Systems, Inc.
2005 W. Cypress Creek Rd. #4
Ft. Lauderdale, FL 33309
Tel: (305) 771-2100

Description:

TLS is a computer-aided instruction in computer operation and *MS*-DOS use. It provides skill-based training selectable for hard disk, single, or two drives; color/monochrome, sound; beginning or advanced selections. Reference guide is included for start-up instructions and review of individual topics.

Once training is completed, operator may select "Summary Level" to review specific topics.

Company:
Armor Systems, Inc.

Product:
***EXCALIBUR PLUS* Accounts Payable**

Category:
General Business Applications

Computer:	**Media:**
AT&T PC 6300	Diskette

Language:
Armor's own proprietary command language, *ARC*

Requirements:
128 KB RAM
10 MB hard disk

Support:
Available via dealer network and corporate direct
Corporate and regional dealer training
Optional end user support contract with Armor Headquarters' Technical Support personnel

Retail Price:
$695

Distributor:

Armor Systems, Inc.
324 N. Orlando Ave.
Maitland, FL 32751
Tel: (305) 629-0753

Description:

The *EXCALIBUR PLUS* Accounting Software Package is comprised of 12 fully integrated modules. The software has vertical market applicability to over 190 different industries.

Accounts Payable:

Allows you to post invoices with multiple distribution, to disburse payments where necessary, and to select debit and credit chart of accounts numbers while posting. The system enables you to query the status of any vendor, and will display account aging on your screen. The AP module provides a detailed audit trail of invoice posting activity and payment disbursement activity. It also allows automatic disbursement of invoices.

All *EXCALIBUR PLUS* modules will operate independently. However, it is suggested that the Accounts Receivable and Inventory modules be used in conjunction with the Billing, Order Entry and Point-of-Sale modules.

Company:
Armor Systems, Inc.

Product:
***EXCALIBUR PLUS* Accounts Receivable**

Category:
General Business Applications

Computer:	**Media:**
AT&T PC 6300	Diskette

Language:
Armor's own proprietary command language, *ARC*

Requirements:
128 KB RAM
10 MB hard disk

Support:
Available via dealer network and corporate direct
Corporate and regional dealer training
Optional end user support contract with Armor Headquarters' Technical Support personnel

Retail Price:
$695

Distributor:

Armor Systems, Inc.
324 N. Orlando Ave.
Maitland, FL 32751
Tel: (305) 629-0753

Description:

The *EXCALIBUR PLUS* Accounting Software Package is comprised of 12 fully integrated modules. The software has vertical market applicability to over 190 different industries.

Accounts Receivable:

Maintains customers on balance forward, straight balance forward, or open invoice method. The module prepares individual aging brackets, individual or group statements, and performs regular "budget" invoicing, with or without tax or service charges, for any number of customers. The AR module tracks sales and cash by salesman, preparing a commission statement (at a separate commission rate, if necessary) for each. Invoices can be aged on the due date or the date they were entered, and all customer data is easily accessible for quick review. The AR module maintains separate credit card handling and budget payment schedules for each customer.

All *EXCALIBUR PLUS* modules will operate independently. However, it is suggested that the Accounts Receivable and Inventory modules be used in conjunction with the Billing, Order Entry and Point-of-Sale modules.

Company:
Armor Systems, Inc.

Product:
***EXCALIBUR PLUS* Billing**

Category:
General Business Applications

Computer:	**Media:**
AT&T PC 6300	Diskette

Language:
Armor's own proprietary command language, *ARC*

Requirements:
128 KB RAM
10 MB hard disk

Support:
Available via dealer network and corporate direct
Corporate and regional dealer training
Optional end user support contract with Armor Headquarters' Technical Support personnel

Retail Price:
$695

Distributor:
Armor Systems, Inc.
324 N. Orlando Ave.
Maitland, FL 32751
Tel: (305) 629-0753

Description:

The *EXCALIBUR PLUS* Accounting Software Package is comprised of 12 fully integrated modules. The software has vertical market applicability to over 190 different industries.

Billing:

Prepares invoices with or without interaction from the Order Entry module—all with automatic price computation for inventory and noninventory items, and discounts and sales tax by line item. Invoices may be stored, recalled for corrections, and printed on stock paper or pre-printed forms. Inventory allocations, sales history, and audit analysis reports are prepared automatically by the system, as are UPS charges, where applicable. Messages may be printed on invoices if desired, and any back orders corresponding to that invoice are also displayed.

All *EXCALIBUR PLUS* modules will operate independently. However, it is suggested that the Accounts Receivable and Inventory modules be used in conjunction with the Billing, Order Entry and Point-of-Sale modules.

Company:

Armor Systems, Inc.

Product:

***EXCALIBUR PLUS* Customer Information/ Database Management**

Category:

General Business Applications

Computer:	**Media:**
AT&T PC 6300	Diskette

Language:

Armor's own proprietary command language, *ARC*

Requirements:

128 KB RAM
10 MB hard disk

Support:

Available via dealer network and corporate direct
Corporate and regional dealer training
Optional end user support contract with Armor Headquarters' Technical Support personnel

Retail Price:

$395

Distributor:

Armor Systems, Inc.
324 N. Orlando Ave.
Maitland, FL 32751
Tel: (305) 629-0753

Description:

The *EXCALIBUR PLUS* Accounting Software Package is comprised of 12 fully integrated modules. The software has vertical market applicability to over 190 different industries.

Customer Information/Database Management:

Manipulates 18 user-defined fields for recording and storing customer data. The fields may be sorted in any order, and printed as a customer listing or on mailing labels.

All *EXCALIBUR PLUS* modules will operate independently. However, it is suggested that the Accounts Receivable and Inventory modules be used in conjunction with the Billing, Order Entry and Point-of-Sale modules.

Company:
Armor Systems, Inc.

Product:
***EXCALIBUR PLUS* Fixed Assets**

Category:
General Business Applications

Computer:	**Media:**
AT&T PC 6300	Diskette

Language:
Armor's own proprietary command language, *ARC*

Requirements:
128 KB RAM
10 MB hard disk

Support:
Available via dealer network and corporate direct
Corporate and regional dealer training
Optional end user support contract with Armor Headquarters' Technical Support personnel

Retail Price:
$395

Distributor:
Armor Systems, Inc.
324 N. Orlando Ave.
Maitland, FL 32751
Tel: (305) 629-0753

Description:

The *EXCALIBUR PLUS* Accounting Software Package is comprised of 12 fully integrated modules. The software has vertical market applicability to over 190 different industries.

Fixed Assets:
Allows you to select any of six methods of computing depreciation, including the ACRS (Accelerated Cost Recovery System). This system handles both calendar and fiscal year operation, with three different first-year conventions, and offers three declining balance methods. Depreciation may be computed by more than one method per asset.

All *EXCALIBUR PLUS* modules will operate independently. However, it is suggested that the Accounts Receivable and Inventory modules be used in conjunction with the Billing, Order Entry and Point-of-Sale modules.

Company:
Armor Systems, Inc.

Product:
***EXCALIBUR PLUS* General Ledger**

Category:
General Business Applications

Computer:
AT&T PC 6300

Media:
Diskette

Language:
Armor's own proprietary command language, *ARC*

Requirements:
128 KB RAM
10 MB hard disk

Support:
Available via dealer network and corporate direct
Corporate and regional dealer training
Optional end user support contract with Armor Headquarters' Technical Support personnel

Retail Price:
$695

Distributor:
Armor Systems, Inc.
324 N. Orlando Ave.
Maitland, FL 32751
Tel: (305) 629-0753

Description:

The *EXCALIBUR PLUS* Accounting Software Package is comprised of 12 fully integrated modules. The software has vertical market applicability to over 190 different industries.

General Ledger:

Allows you to store the present and past year's data for comparison, and to build new company files or consolidate old ones at any time. It handles a virtually unlimited amount of 7-digit chart of accounts numbers with up to 1200 subaccounts for each. The module manipulates 1200 separate departments and prints profit and loss statements for each. The GL module prints a net change analysis for all balance sheet accounts. Other GL features include an "after-the-fact" payroll feature, allowing you to set up and maintain employee records, post payroll checks, and generate W-2 forms and 1099's. A separate "rapid distribution" program with unlimited column spreadsheet is included along with an amortization/payment schedule.

All *EXCALIBUR PLUS* modules will operate independently. However, it is suggested that the Accounts Receivable and Inventory modules be used in conjunction with the Billing, Order Entry and Point-of-Sale modules.

Company:
Armor Systems, Inc.

Product:
***EXCALIBUR PLUS* Inventory Control**

Category:
General Business Applications

Computer:	**Media:**
AT&T PC 6300	Diskette

Language:
Armor's own proprietary command language, *ARC*

Requirements:
128 KB RAM
10 MB hard disk

Support:
Available via dealer network and corporate direct
Corporate and regional dealer training
Optional end user support contract with Armor Headquarters' Technical Support personnel

Retail Price:
$695

Distributor:
Armor Systems, Inc.
324 N. Orlando Ave.
Maitland, FL 32751
Tel: (305) 629-0753

Description:

The *EXCALIBUR PLUS* Accounting Software Package is comprised of 12 fully integrated modules. The software has vertical market applicability to over 190 different industries.

Inventory Control:

Records and tracks items with explosion parts up to 255 levels deep. Items allocated or backordered in other modules are tracked in detail. The system handles floor plan activity and stores customer and salesperson data needed for serial-numbered items. You can assign a maximum 21-character alphanumeric part number, and a 15-digit group/alternate part number to any inventory item. You can also record up to 255 prices per item, control them, and have the system automatically compute them by your markup percent. Cross-referencing items by superseded or preceded item numbers is a simple, three-step process, as is assigning substitute item numbers or deleting items (with or without explosion of parts). Inventory items may be recorded by LIFO, FIFO, or the average cost method.

All *EXCALIBUR PLUS* modules will operate independently. However, it is suggested that the Accounts Receivable and Inventory modules be used in conjunction with the Billing, Order Entry and Point-of-Sale modules.

Company:
Armor Systems, Inc.

Product:
***EXCALIBUR PLUS* Job Cost/Work in Process**

Category:
General Business Applications

Computer:	**Media:**
AT&T PC 6300	Diskette

Language:
Armor's own proprietary command language, *ARC*

Requirements:
128 KB RAM
10 MB hard disk

Support:
Available via dealer network and corporate direct
Corporate and regional dealer training
Optional end user support contract with Armor Headquarters' Technical Support personnel

Retail Price:
$695

Distributor:

Armor Systems, Inc.
324 N. Orlando Ave.
Maitland, FL 32751
Tel: (305) 629-0753

Description:

The *EXCALIBUR PLUS* Accounting Software Package is comprised of 12 fully integrated modules. The software has vertical market applicability to over 190 different industries.

Job Cost/Work in Process:
Allows you to complete and print work order estimates, and turn them into actual work orders whenever necessary. You can set up a virtually unlimited number of functions for each work order, with cost, overhead, and billing charge computed for each function. Billing may be computed on a full or partial basis by estimate, actual cost, or cost plus percent. The system prints variance reports comparing estimate and actual work orders for projected gain or loss by function. Work orders may be assigned job numbers, and then the system will print data for all work orders within a job.

All *EXCALIBUR PLUS* modules will operate independently. However, it is suggested that the Accounts Receivable and Inventory modules be used in conjunction with the Billing, Order Entry and Point-of-Sale modules.

Company:
Armor Systems, Inc.

Product:
***EXCALIBUR PLUS* Order Entry**

Category:
General Business Applications

Computer:	**Media:**
AT&T PC 6300	Diskette

Language:
Armor's own proprietary command language, *ARC*

Requirements:
128 KB RAM
10 MB hard disk

Support:
Available via dealer network and corporate direct
Corporate and regional dealer training
Optional end user support contract with Armor Headquarters' Technical Support personnel

Retail Price:
$695

Distributor:
Armor Systems, Inc.
324 N. Orlando Ave.
Maitland, FL 32751
Tel: (305) 629-0753

Description:

The *EXCALIBUR PLUS* Accounting Software Package is comprised of 12 fully integrated modules. The software has vertical market applicability to over 190 different industries.

Order Entry:
Displays customer's aged balance due on the screen as your operator prepares an order. The system makes it easy to recall orders for corrections, print picking tickets for new orders, and find out what raw materials are needed to complete a given assembly. Inventory item status is also displayed as that item is posted to order. Order Entry prints order analysis reports by customer, group of customers, item and/or date. Expired orders are easily deleted from the system. In this case, the system prints a notice to send to the customer whose order has expired.

All *EXCALIBUR PLUS* modules will operate independently. However, it is suggested that the Accounts Receivable and Inventory modules be used in conjunction with the Billing, Order Entry and Point-of-Sale modules.

Company:
Armor Systems, Inc.

Product:
***EXCALIBUR PLUS* Payroll**

Category:
General Business Applications

Computer:	**Media:**
AT&T PC 6300	Diskette

Language:
Armor's own proprietary command language, *ARC*

Requirements:
128 KB RAM
10 MB hard disk

Support:
Available via dealer network and corporate direct
Corporate and regional dealer training
Optional end user support contract with Armor Headquarters' Technical Support personnel

Retail Price:
$695

Distributor:

Armor Systems, Inc.
324 N. Orlando Ave.
Maitland, FL 32751
Tel: (305) 629-0753

Description:

The *EXCALIBUR PLUS* Accounting Software Package is comprised of 12 fully integrated modules. The software has vertical market applicability to over 190 different industries.

Payroll:

Handles hourly, salaried, commissioned, contract, and tipped employees. Earnings may be distributed by the hour or fractional hour, to an unlimited number of cost centers. Union dues, Worker's Compensation, federal and state payroll tax, and payroll checks can be automatically computed (payroll checks allow automatic override of any field). The payroll module can automatically post time cards for payroll computation.

All *EXCALIBUR PLUS* modules will operate independently. However, it is suggested that the Accounts Receivable and Inventory modules be used in conjunction with the Billing, Order Entry and Point-of-Sale modules.

Company:
Armor Systems, Inc.

Product:
***EXCALIBUR PLUS* Point-of-Sale**

Category:
General Business Applications

Computer:	**Media:**
AT&T PC 6300	Diskette

Language:
Armor's own proprietary command language, *ARC*

Requirements:
128 KB RAM
10 MB hard disk

Support:
Available via dealer network and corporate direct
Corporate and regional dealer training
Optional end user support contract with Armor Headquarters' Technical Support personnel

Retail Price:
$695

Distributor:
Armor Systems, Inc.
324 N. Orlando Ave.
Maitland, FL 32751
Tel: (305) 629-0753

Description:

The *EXCALIBUR PLUS* Accounting Software Package is comprised of 12 fully integrated modules. The software has vertical market applicability to over 190 different industries.

Point-of-Sale:

Directly activates a cash drawer attached to a personal computer, or can stand alone with a manually-operated cash register system. It produces invoices for both the cash and charge customer–either a narrow, cash register-style invoice (receipt) or a traditional wide invoice. Invoices may be stored and recalled later to be corrected before printing. The system records and tracks lost sales, prints picking tickets before the corresponding invoices are completed, and handles noninventory (preset) items. Each sale may be assigned to a sales clerk. The module displays any item's inventory status on the screen, and all entries are stored for a detailed sales summary report, including cash sales. A warning is displayed if any customer has exceeded his/her credit limit.

All *EXCALIBUR PLUS* modules will operate independently. However, it is suggested that the Accounts Receivable and Inventory modules be used in conjunction with the Billing, Order Entry and Point-of-Sale modules.

Company:

Armor Systems, Inc.

Product:

***EXCALIBUR PLUS* Purchase Orders**

Category:

General Business Applications

Computer:	**Media:**
AT&T PC 6300	Diskette

Language:

Armor's own proprietary command language, *ARC*

Requirements:

128 KB RAM
10 MB hard disk

Support:

Available via dealer network and corporate direct
Corporate and regional dealer training
Optional end user support contract with Armor Headquarters' Technical Support personnel

Retail Price:

$695

Distributor:

Armor Systems, Inc.
324 N. Orlando Ave.
Maitland, FL 32751
Tel: (305) 629-0753

Description:

The *EXCALIBUR PLUS* Accounting Software Package is comprised of 12 fully integrated modules. The software has vertical market applicability to over 190 different industries.

Purchase Orders:

Enables you to create, change, view, or delete purchase orders and their accompanying detail. The module posts all data specified, and transfers data to the Inventory module, affecting quantity on hand, average cost, FIFO or LIFO costs, and quantity on order. You have the ability to print a selected roster of drop/ship addresses in label or list form. It allows you to order inventory and noninventory items. The module handles scheduled ordering and can automatically generate purchase orders based on the inventory-below-minimum amount set up in the Inventory module.

All *EXCALIBUR PLUS* modules will operate independently. However, it is suggested that the Accounts Receivable and Inventory modules be used in conjunction with the Billing, Order Entry and Point-of-Sale modules.

Company:
AT&T

Product:
AT&T Mortgage Line*

Category:
General Business Applications

Computer:	**Media:**
AT&T PC 6300	Diskette

Language:
COBOL

Requirements:
256 KB RAM
10 MB internal hard disk
Printer AT&T 455 (requires *Centronics* parallel interface, 25-pin)
Modem: 2212C/FDX

Support:
This product is fully supported by AT&T Information Systems and carries a 90-day warranty on the media. Remote nationwide customer service hotline is provided Monday through Friday between the hours of 8:00 a.m. and 5:00 p.m. local time. Installation, additional hotline coverage, and extended maintenance agreements are also available.

Retail Price:
$3,600

Distributor:
AT&T (800) 247-1212
or call your local AT&T authorized dealer or Account Executive.

***This product has been certified by AT&T.**

Description:

AT&T Mortgage Line offers users the ability to automate all aspects of the mortgage process, from prequalification to closing. The system was designed for ease of use and has the flexibility to process most loans offered in today's market.

As loan and borrowed data are entered into the system, they are checked for errors and stored in a loan file where they may be updated at any time, from initial application through final approval. All calculations, such as prepaid finance charges, total principal and interest over the life of the loan, insurance premiums, annual percentage rates, loan-to-value ratios and escrow amounts, are performed automatically. Various types of mortgage plans can be calculated easily to offer customers the ability to select the plan most appropriate for them.

All document printing is done on standard industry forms, such as FNMA 1003/FHLMC 65.

However, a built-in report generator also lets users customize their own forms; for example, closing documents status and exception reports can be generated on demand. Pipeline and management reports can be easily produced since the system maintains a complete inventory of committed and uncommitted loans.

The system can also be tied to AT&T's Mortgage Service Network to link remote offices, mainframes, and service bureaus. The network can also be used to solicit information on available mortgage monies from the money lenders themselves.

AT&T Mortgage Line offers a total solution; developed by mortgage lenders for mortgage lenders, it can provide organization with today's tools for streamlining the mortgage process, making their operations more productive and profitable.

Company:
AT&T and American Business Systems, Inc.

Product:
AT&T Business Accounting System*

Category:
General Business Applications

Computer: AT&T PC 6300
Media: Diskette

Language:
RM/COBOL

Requirements:
128 KB minimum internal memory with hard disk unit
RM/COBOL Runtime–AT&T PC compatible version
Color monitor (if special color features unique to this version are desired)

Support:
This product is fully supported by AT&T Information Systems and carries a 90-day warranty on the media. Remote nationwide customer service hotline is provided Monday through Friday between the hours of 8:00 a.m. and 5:00 p.m. local time. Installation, additional hotline coverage, and extended maintenance agreements are also available.

In addition, there are several accounting primers, user and installation guides specially designed to help the end-user set-up and operate the BUSINESS ACCOUNTING SYSTEM efficiently and effectively.

Retail Price:
All Five Modules $2,325
Accounts Payable $ 500
Accounts Receivable $ 500
Payroll $ 600
Order/Inventory $ 600
General Ledger $ 500

Distributor:
AT&T (800) 247-1212
or call your local AT&T authorized dealer or Account Executive.

***This product has been certified by AT&T.**

Description:

AT&T BUSINESS ACCOUNTING SYSTEM software is a series of applications designed to provide a complete accounting system for firms with up to one billion dollars in assets. The System consists of five modules: ORDER AND INVENTORY MANAGEMENT, ACCOUNTS RECEIVABLE, ACCOUNTS PAYABLE, PAYROLL, and GENERAL LEDGER. Each package can be used as a standalone application or several packages can be integrated together.

All five modules of the AT&T BUSINESS ACCOUNTING SYSTEM have been independently reviewed, tested and verified by PEAT, MARWICK, MITCHELL and COMPANY, Certified Public Accountants. The AT&T Business Accounting System, Version 3.04, has been found to conform with the features and operations outlined in the product's description, to provide reasonable processing control and audit trails, and, if properly used, to facilitate the preparation of meaningful business data. The features of each package consist of the following:

ORDER AND INVENTORY MANAGEMENT:

Tracks incoming orders, adjusts inventory levels, and handles order processing. It supports five price breaks and three base price methodologies (quantity, units, dollar break), produces invoices, tracks back orders, provides the last three purchases for average cost reporting, and updates AT&T ACCOUNTS RECEIVABLE and GENERAL LEDGER Modules.

ACCOUNTS RECEIVABLE:

This module supports intermixed files of customers with balance forward and open items. It can handle up to 85 different taxing authorities and provides four ways of handling cash receipts. It supports five aged balances per customer. This package can be integrated with the AT&T GENERAL LEDGER Module.

ACCOUNTS PAYABLE:

This module supports cash or accrual based accounts and payments from multiple banks and checking accounts, writes checks, computes vendor discounts and produces seven major reports. This package can be integrated with the AT&T GENERAL LEDGER Module.

(Continued on next page)

Description: ***(Continued)***

PAYROLL:

Tracks deductions by month-to-date, quarter-to-date and year-to-date. It will provide for up to 99 user defined earning categories and up to 20 taxing authorities in addition to all of the states. This package can be integrated with the AT&T GENERAL LEDGER Module.

GENERAL LEDGER:

This Module supports 2-5-2 numbering, 12 or 13 business periods, and up to 99 companies with up to 100 departments per company. All transaction data can be trial posted with cost of goods, taxes and net income computed. A report writer prepares financial reports such as profit and loss statements, balance sheets, and sources and uses of funds statements. Up to ten report formats and available to the user. Data is received from all other AT&T packages.

Each of AT&T BUSINESS ACCOUNTING SYSTEM Modules is discussed more fully in the following pages.

Company:

AT&T and American Business Systems, Inc.

Product:

AT&T Business Accounting System–ACCOUNTS PAYABLE MODULE*

Category:

General Business Applications

Computer:	**Media:**
AT&T PC 6300	Diskette

Language:
RM/COBOL

Requirements:
128 K minimum internal memory with hard disk unit
RM/COBOL Runtime–AT&T PC compatible version
Color monitor (if special color features unique to this version are desired)

Support:
This product is fully supported by AT&T Information Systems and carries a 90-day warranty on the media. Remote nationwide customer service hotline is provided Monday through Friday between the hours of 8:00 a.m. and 5:00 p.m. local time. Installation, additional hotline coverage, and extended maintenance agreements are also available.

In addition, there are several accounting primers, user and installation guides specially designed to help the end-user set-up and operate the BUSINESS ACCOUNTING SYSTEM efficiently and effectively.

Retail Price:
$500 (if purchased separately)

Distributor:

AT&T (800) 247-1212
or call your local AT&T authorized dealer or Account Executive.

***This product has been certified by AT&T.**

Description:

The AT&T ACCOUNTS PAYABLE Module allows businesses to track and control information about money they owe. By providing accurate, timely payables information, this module helps businesses operate more efficiently. The ACCOUNTS PAYABLE Module produces comprehensive financial management reports and provides a complete audit trail of all transactions. Like other modules in the AT&T BUSINESS ACCOUNTING SYSTEM the ACCOUNTS PAYABLE Module can stand alone or interface with the AT&T GENERAL LEDGER Module.

FEATURES:

- Supports both cash and accrual accounting
- Supports computer-generated checks, as well as manual checks and partial payments
- Uses four types of payment status: "Pay when due," "Prepaid," "take discount," and "on hold"
- Prepares Automatic Vouchers to pay recurring expenses, such as rent and equipment leases
- Processes vouchers, adjustments to posted vouchers, automatic payments, and both manual and partial payments
- Maintains vendor purchase history
- Defines accounts for up to 99 companies
- Automatically computes and takes vendor discounts
- Handles multiple banks and bank accounts
- Maintains a list of all vendors used by each company
- Supports multiple, user-defined aging categories
- Automatically "flags" unusually large vendor invoices
- Allows the deferral of payments on specified vouchers to a later date
- Uses Inquiry and Display options to let the user view reference and transaction data on screen
- Incorporates a multilevel Password feature that controls employee access to every ACCOUNTS PAYABLE function
- Directly updates the GENERAL LEDGER Module

(Continued on next page)

Description: ***(Continued)***

The AT&T ACCOUNTS PAYABLE Module prepares the following reports, lists, directories and checks for each company's use:

- ACCOUNTS PAYABLE Title Listing
- ACCOUNTS PAYABLE Title Trace Report
- Bank Edit Report
- Bank Trace Report
- Vendor Directory
- Vendor List
- Vendor Trace Report
- Automatic Voucher Edit Report
- Automatic Voucher Trace Report
- Automatic Voucher Posting Report
- New Payables Voucher Edit Report
- New Payables Voucher Posting Report
- Adjustment Edit Report
- Adjustment Posting Report
- Manual/Partial Payment Edit Report
- Manual/Partial Payment Posting Report
- Voucher Hold Report
- Cash Requirements Report
- Check Register
- Aged Payable Report
- Account Distribution Report
- Vendor History Report
- Voucher Journal Report
- Adjustment Journal Report
- Check Journal
- Checks
- Transaction Report
- ACCOUNTS PAYABLE GENERAL LEDGER Merge Report

Company:

AT&T and American Business Systems, Inc.

Product:

AT&T Business Accounting System–ACCOUNTS RECEIVABLE MODULE*

Category:

General Business Applications

Computer:	**Media:**
AT&T PC 6300	Diskette

Language:

RM/COBOL

Requirements:

128 KB minimum internal memory with hard disk unit

RM/COBOL Runtime–AT&T PC compatible version

Color monitor (if special color features unique to this version are desired)

Support:

This product is fully supported by AT&T Information Systems and carries a 90-day warranty on the media. Remote nationwide customer service hotline is provided Monday through Friday between the hours of 8:00 a.m. and 5:00 p.m. local time. Installation, additional hotline coverage, and extended maintenance agreements are also available.

In addition, there are several accounting primers, user and installation guides specially designed to help the end-user set-up and operate the BUSINESS ACCOUNTING SYSTEM efficiently and effectively.

Retail Price:

$500 (if purchased separately)

Distributor:

AT&T (800) 247-1212

or call your local AT&T authorized dealer or Account Executive.

***This product has been certified by AT&T.**

Description:

The AT&T ACCOUNTS RECEIVABLE Module allows businesses to track and control information related to money owed to them. By providing accurate, timely receivables information, this module helps businesses operate more efficiently. The AT&T ACCOUNTS RECEIVABLE Module produces comprehensive financial management reports and provides a complete audit trail of all transactions. Like all other AT&T BUSINESS ACCOUNTING SYSTEM Modules, the ACCOUNTS PAYABLE Module can stand alone or integrate with the AT&T GENERAL LEDGER Module.

FEATURES:

- Supports both open items and balance forward customers
- Defines accounts for up to 99 companies
- Allows specification of finance charge percentages and aging periods
- Provides easy transaction entry for customer invoices, adjustments to customer accounts, payments from customers and debit and credit memos
- Maintains complete customer profiles
- Includes flexible payment entry to pay the invoice on account through a specified date, and to pay finance charges; the system also allocates discounts allowed and applies credits
- Prints complete customer statements that show all transactions and running balances
- Optionally prints two-line messages to customers on statements
- Prepares and prints numerous, useful reports, such as the ACCOUNT RECEIVABLE Distributions to the GENERAL LEDGER Report and the Credit History Report
- Displays major reports directly on screen
- Uses Inquiry and Display options to let the user view reference and transaction data on screen
- Incorporates a multilevel Password feature that controls employee access to every ACCOUNTS RECEIVABLE function
- Directly updates the AT&T GENERAL LEDGER Module

(Continued on next page)

Description: ***(Continued)***

The AT&T ACCOUNTS RECEIVABLE Module prepares the following reports, journals, lists and statements:

- Customer List
- Customer Directory
- Customer Trace Report
- Credit History Report-All Customers
- Credit History Report-Credit Balances Only
- Credit History Report-Delinquent Accounts
- Credit History Report-Totals by Aging Categories
- ACCOUNTS RECEIVABLE Account Title Listing Report
- ACCOUNTS RECEIVABLE Account Title Trace Report
- Sales Tax Report
- Sales Edit Report
- Sales Post Report
- Adjustment Edit Report
- Adjustment Post Report
- Cash Receipts Edit Report
- Cash Receipts Post Report
- Debit/Credit Memos Edit Report
- Debit/Credit Memos Post Report
- Post Finance Charges Report
- Customer Statements
- Sales Journal
- Cash Journal
- Credit Memo/Debit Memo Journal
- Adjustment Journal
- Aged Trial Balance Report
- Account Distribution Report
- Cash Sheets
- Sales Tax/Finance Charge Trace Report
- ACCOUNTS RECEIVABLE GENERAL LEDGER Merge Report

Company:

AT&T and American Business Systems, Inc.

Product:

AT&T Business Accounting System–GENERAL LEDGER MODULE*

Category:

General Business Applications

Computer:	**Media:**
AT&T PC 6300	Diskette

Language:
RM/COBOL

Requirements:
128 KB minimum internal memory with hard disk unit
RM/COBOL Runtime–AT&T PC compatible version
Color monitor (if special color features unique to this version are desired)

Support:
This product is fully supported by AT&T Information Systems and carries a 90-day warranty on the media. Remote nationwide customer service hotline is provided Monday through Friday between the hours of 8:00 a.m. and 5:00 p.m. local time. Installation, additional hotline coverage, and extended maintenance agreements are also available.

In addition, there are several accounting primers, user and installation guides specially designed to help the end-user set-up and operate the BUSINESS ACCOUNTING SYSTEM efficiently and effectively.

Retail Price:
$500 (if purchased separately)

Distributor:
AT&T (800) 247-1212
or call your local AT&T authorized dealer or Account Executive.

***This product has been certified by AT&T.**

Description:

The AT&T GENERAL LEDGER Module is a comprehensive system that automates the accounting procedures for typical businesses. It can stand alone to handle traditional accounting needs and provide a wide range of financial reports. It can also interface with other AT&T BUSINESS ACCOUNTING SYSTEM Modules to accommodate detailed transactions and reports from specific applications, such as ACCOUNTS RECEIVABLE, ACCOUNTS PAYABLE, or PAYROLL.

FEATURES:

- Allows posting of current month even before closing previous months.
- Support 12 or 13 accounting periods.
- Handles multiple companies, as well as multiple profit center within a company.
- Allows addition of transactions to previously closed periods and propagates the effect of these transactions through the fiscal year.
- Uses flexible 2-5-2 account numbering structure to track activity in profit centers and in departments.
- Uses inquiry and display options to let you view transaction data directly on screen.
- Includes a menu-driven, user-defined Report Writer for preparing special financial statements.
- Prepares both consolidating and consolidated reports.
- Prepares up to 15 Journals for recording transactions, including General, Cash Receipts, Cash Disbursements, Sales and Payroll journals.
- Maintains data from the previous year, the current year, and from budget projections for tracking and comparison purposes.
- Provides complete, detailed audit trails of all transactions.
- Incorporates a multilevel Password feature that controls employee access to every GENERAL LEDGER Module function.
- Receives and stores data from other AT&T BUSINESS ACCOUNTING SYSTEM Modules.

The AT&T GENERAL LEDGER Module prepares the following reports, journals and reference lists:

(Continued on next page)

Description: ***(Continued)***

- Department List
- Journal Titles List
- Chart of Accounts
- Title Trace Report
- Last Year/Budget Trace Report
- Transaction Report
- General Ledger Trial Post Report
- Trial Balance Report
- Up to 15 User-defined Journals
- Working Trial Balance Report
- Schedule of Accounts Payable Report
- List of Accounts Payable Report
- Up to 99 User-defined Reports, including:
  - –Profit and Loss Statement
  - –Balance Sheet
  - –Sources and Uses of Funds Statement

Company:

AT&T and American Business Systems, Inc.

Product:

AT&T Business Accounting System–ORDER/INVENTORY MANAGEMENT MODULE*

Category:

General Business Applications

Computer:	**Media:**
AT&T PC 6300	Diskette

Language:
RM/COBOL

Requirements:
128 KB minimum internal memory with hard disk unit
RM/COBOL Runtime–AT&T PC compatible version
Color monitor (if special color features unique to this version are desired)

Support:
This product is fully supported by AT&T Information Systems and carries a 90-day warranty on the media. Remote nationwide customer service hotline is provided Monday through Friday between the hours of 8:00 a.m. and 5:00 p.m. local time. Installation, additional hotline coverage, and extended maintenance agreements are also available.

In addition, there are several accounting primers, user and installation guides specially designed to help the end-user set-up and operate the BUSINESS ACCOUNTING SYSTEM efficiently and effectively.

Retail Price:
$600 (if purchased separately)

Distributor:
AT&T (800) 247-1212
or call your local AT&T authorized dealer or Account Executive.

***This product has been certified by AT&T.**

Description:

The AT&T ORDER/INVENTORY MANAGEMENT Module is a complete package for managing incoming orders and monitoring product inventory. It provides a total management system for sales activities and results in reduced inventory levels through a sophisticated inventory tracking and purchasing system. It can stand alone or interface with other AT&T BUSINESS ACCOUNTING SYSTEM Modules, including ACCOUNTS RECEIVABLE and GENERAL LEDGER, to provide an unparalleled revenue management system.

FEATURES:

- Supports ship to, bill to, and drop ship address
- Uses a 9-character alphanumeric product number
- Supports a variety of customer, product and order discount structures
- Handles cash, C.O.D., open account and counter orders
- Includes a Purchase Order subsystem
- Prints all Invoices
- Automatically computes tax amounts for customers and for products
- Isolates orders that exceed credit limits
- Tracks last 12 months of product sales in units and in dollar amounts
- Allows for quick, accurate repricing based on product range or product class
- Supports average cost and last three levels of purchase history for LIFO/FIFO inventory valuations
- Allows five price breaks per product, plus three pricing options per break, including dollar break, quantity break, and Unit of Measure
- Automatically tracks product on hand, on order and backorder by customer, on hold, and on order from a vendor
- Incorporates a multilevel Password feature that controls employee access to every ORDER/INVENTORY Module function
- Directly updates both ACCOUNTS RECEIVABLE and GENERAL LEDGER Modules

The AT&T ORDER/INVENTORY MANAGEMENT Module prepares the following reports, forms, and reference lists for your company's use:

(Continued on next page)

Description: ***(Continued)***

- Picking slips
- Invoices
- Invoice Register
- Transaction Balance Report
- Order Releases Report
- Open Order Report by Order
- Back Order Report by Customer
- New Order Report by Customer
- Order History Report
- Credit Memo Report
- Credit Hold Report
- Stock Status Report
- Minimum On-Hand Report
- Catalog Report by Product Name
- Catalog Report by Product Number
- Gross Return Report
- Product History Report
- Product List
- Product Trace Report
- Purchase Order Receipts Report
- Inventory Valuation Report
- Price List
- Product Repricing Trace Report
- Year-To-Date Customer Sales Report
- Monthly Sales by Salesperson Report
- Monthly Sales by Inside Salesperson Report
- Year-To-Date Sales by Salesperson Report
- ACCOUNTS RECEIVABLE Account Title Listing
- ACCOUNTS RECEIVABLE Title Trace Report
- Sales Tax/Finance Charge Trace Report
- Sales Tax Report
- Customer List
- Customer Directory
- Stock Status Report by Product Name
- Stock Status Report by Product Number
- Vendor Pricing Report
- ACCOUNTS RECEIVABLE Merge Report
- GENERAL LEDGER Merge Report

Company:
AT&T and American Business Systems, Inc.

Product:
AT&T Business Accounting System–PAYROLL MODULE*

Category:
General Business Applications

Computer:	**Media:**
AT&T PC 6300	Diskette

Language:
RM/COBOL

Requirements:
128 KB minimum internal memory with hard disk unit
RM/COBOL Runtime–AT&T PC 6300 compatible version
Color monitor (if special color features unique to this version are desired)

Support:
This product is fully supported by AT&T Information Systems and carries a 90-day warranty on the media. Remote nationwide customer service hotline is provided Monday through Friday between the hours of 8:00 a.m. and 5:00 p.m. local time. Installation, additional hotline coverage, and extended maintenance agreements are also available.

In addition, there are several accounting primers, user and installation guides specially designed to help the end user set up and operate the BUSINESS ACCOUNTING SYSTEM efficiently and effectively.

Retail Price:
$600 (if purchased separately)

Distributor:
AT&T (800) 247-1212
or call your local AT&T authorized dealer or Account Executive.

***This product has been certified by AT&T.**

Description:

The AT&T PAYROLL module is a personnel management system designed to expedite the most time-consuming aspects of business: processing payrolls, withholding taxes, and maintaining accurate employee information. Like the other AT&T BUSINESS ACCOUNTING SYSTEM modules, PAYROLL can standalone or interface with the AT&T GENERAL LEDGER module.

FEATURES:

- Supports multiple companies
- Processes payrolls: weekly, biweekly, semi-monthly, monthly, or quarterly
- Supports up to 99 user-defined earning categories, including salaried, hourly and piecework
- Produces separate checks for each earning category
- Supports numerous taxing authorities, including all 50 states and major metropolitan districts
- Automatically calculates income taxes, FICA, and up to 99 user-defined withholding deduction amounts
- Prints payroll checks, W-2s, State Quarterly Earnings Report, and many more reports
- Supports direct deposits
- Provides complete, detailed audit trails
- Handles multiple unions
- Supports an earnings adjustment factor
- Maintains personnel and demographic data, including salary histories, home addresses and family records
- Incorporates a multilevel Password feature that controls employee access to every PAYROLL module function

The AT&T PAYROLL Module prepares the following reports and reference lists:

- Employee Attendance List
- Manual Check List
- Attendance Report
- Payroll Checks
- Check Register
- Check Register Report

(Continued on next page)

Description: ***(Continued)***

- Gross Pay Analysis Report
- Payroll Register
- Employee Time Sheet
- Direct Deposit Report
- Department Report
- Gross Pay Analysis by Quarter Report
- Quarterly Earnings Report
- State Quarterly Earnings Report
- State Monthly Earnings Report
- Employee Earnings Report
- Employee Deduction Report
- Union Deduction Report
- Seniority Report
- W-2 Wage and Tax Statements
- Employee Report
- Employee Pay Code Report
- Employee Trace Report
- Employee Pay Trace Report
- Personnel Report
- Personnel Trace Report
- Pay Code Title Report
- Pay Code Trace Report
- Tax Authority Title Report
- Tax Authority Trace Report
- Payroll Account Title Listing
- Payroll Title Trace Report
- Deduction Title
- Deduction Trace Report
- GENERAL LEDGER Merge Report

Company:
Bobby J. Hall & Associates

Product:
Accounts Payable Module

Category:
General Business Applications

Computer:	**Media:**
AT&T PC 6300	Diskette

Language:
Compiled BASIC

Requirements:
256 KB RAM
Printer
Dual diskette drives or one diskette drive and a fixed disk

Support:
Dealer support
Direct telephone support line, (601) 684-8394
90-day warranty with software
Detailed user manual including a step-by-step sample problem

Retail Price:
$475

Distributor:
Bobby J. Hall & Associates
P.O. Box 646
McComb, MS 39648
Tel: (601) 684-6402

Description:

The Accounts Payable Module allows entry and modifications of vendor data, invoicing, credits, etc; writes checks and payment of invoices; prints journals; and posts to General Ledger. Features of the package include versatile payment cycle selections including:

- Invoice number, date, dollar amount, and all open invoices.
- Check reconciliation provided in General Ledger Print report.
- Vendor report shows invoices by vendor with dollar amount owed and due dates.
- Vendor report shows total outstanding, total purchases year-to-date, and total purchases last year.
- Vendor inquiry shows total current and year-to-date.
- Interfaces to General Ledger.

Company:
Bobby J. Hall & Associates

Product:
Accounts Receivable Module

Category:
General Business Applications

Computer:	**Media:**
AT&T PC 6300	Diskette

Language:
Compiled BASIC

Requirements:
256 KB RAM
Printer
Dual diskette drives or one diskette drive and a fixed disk

Support:
Dealer support
Direct telephone support line, (601) 684-8394
90-day warranty with software
Detailed user manual including a step-by-step sample problem

Retail Price:
$475

Distributor:
Bobby J. Hall & Associates
P.O. Box 646
McComb, MS 39648
Tel: (601) 684-6402

Description:

The Accounts Receivable Module allows entry and modification of customer records, invoice entry, and correction, or records receipt of payment, entry of credit, and automatically posts to General Ledger. You may enter a description of the type of business in which a customer is engaged, and set up the finance and discount terms for a business. In addition, this comprehensive Accounts Receivable Module also allows the businessman to add, update, and print sales representative information. The Accounts Receivable Module provides the capability for tracking monies owed, better control over cash flow, and helps reduce bad debt, all with potentially less clerical effort. Report printing is a feature of this module. 30-, 60-, and 90- day account aging is provided. The module prints statements and a detailed daily sales register. It also interfaces to General Ledger.

Company:
Bobby J. Hall & Associates

Product:
Consolidated Reports

Category:
General Business Applications

Computer: AT&T PC 6300

Media: Diskette

Language:
Compiled BASIC

Requirements:
256 KB RAM
Printer
Dual diskette drive or one diskette drive and a fixed disk

Support:
Dealer support
Direct telephone support line, (601) 684-8394
90-day warranty with software
Detailed user manual including a step-by-step sample problem

Retail Price:
$475

Distributor:
Bobby J. Hall & Associates
P.O. Box 646
McComb, MS 39648
Tel: (601) 684-6402

Description:

The Consolidated Reports package is a support system for the Financial Management Accounting System offered by Bobby J. Hall & Associates that provides a consolidated financial analysis of multiple companies or departments within a company. All available programs, sorts, and procedures can be selected from menus. The Consolidated Reports package makes use of data previously recorded on your General Ledger data diskettes and your Management Reports program diskettes. Entries made through other modules are automatically transferred to the correct files without operator intervention. This module is easy to use by someone not experienced in data processing or accounting. Prints include a consolidated P & L, Balance Sheet, and numerous management reports.

Company:
Bobby J. Hall & Associates

Product:
Cost Accounting System

Category:
General Business Applications

Computer: AT&T PC 6300

Media: Diskette

Language:
Compiled BASIC

Requirements:
256 KB RAM
Printer
Dual diskette drives or one diskette drive and a fixed disk

Support:
Dealer support
Direct telephone support line, (601) 684-8394
90-day warranty with software
Detailed user manual including a step-by-step sample problem

Retail Price:
$475

Distributor:
Bobby J. Hall & Associates
P.O. Box 646
McComb, MS 39648
Tel: (601) 684-6402

Description:

The Bobby J. Hall & Associates Cost Accounting System is designed to combine all the transactions entered in the General Ledger by selected cost account numbers to permit a broad range of accounting across General Ledger chart numbers, time, and companies. Multiple cost codes may be combined to permit a wide range of cost accounting. The programs are menu-driven for ease by the end-user. Careful construction of the cost code will permit a breakdown by enterprise, job, activity, and/or location. Numerous printed reports are available.

Company:
Bobby J. Hall & Associates

Product:
Depreciation Analysis Module

Category:
General Business Applications

Computer:
AT&T PC 6300

Media:
Diskette

Language:
Compiled BASIC

Requirements:
256 KB RAM
Printer
Dual diskette drives or one diskette drive and a fixed disk

Support:
Dealer support
Direct telephone support line, (601) 684-8394
90-day warranty with software
Detailed user manual including a step-by-step sample problem

Retail Price:
$475

Distributor:
Bobby J. Hall & Associates
P.O. Box 646
McComb, MS 39648
Tel: (601) 684-6402

Description:

The straight line and accelerated cost recovery system of the Depreciation Analysis Module provides a means of developing a depreciation schedule of real and personal property including livestock and buildings. Input, updating, and report printing are features of this module. The depreciation analysis has several important features; it is based upon classes (livestock, equipment, buildings); it performs "What If" calculations without data file updates; provides a Depreciation Schedule report; and uses either the accelerated cost recovery system of depreciation or the straight line method of depreciation. It also allows for reduced investment credit, and features limited usage of Section 179 deduction.

Company:
Bobby J. Hall & Associates

Product:
General Ledger Module

Category:
General Business Applications

Computer:	**Media:**
AT&T PC 6300	Diskette

Language:
Compiled BASIC

Requirements:
256 KB RAM
Printer
Dual diskette drives or one diskette drive and a fixed disk

Support:
Dealer support
Direct telephone support line, (601) 684-8394
90-day warranty with software
Detailed user manual including a step-by-step sample problem

Retail Price:
$475

Distributor:
Bobby J. Hall & Associates
P.O. Box 646
McComb, MS 39648
Tel: (601) 684-6402

Description:

The General Ledger Module offers the capability of storing up to five years of financial information in the same data file. This module has a Transaction Journal program which allows entry of invoices, sales, deposits, withdrawals, and other transactions. The number of transactions on file and the remaining file capacity as well as the account balance are displayed on the CRT with each account entry. The system will not post unless the account balance is zero (0). All transactions are automatically posted to General Ledger. The General Ledger Print includes the detailed accounting of every transaction during the accounting period with units and quantities. Other reports include Transaction Journal, Balance Sheet, P&L Statement, and Chart of Accounts.

Company:
Bobby J. Hall & Associates

Product:
Management Reports

Category:
General Business Applications

Computer: AT&T PC 6300

Media: Diskette

Language:
Compiled BASIC

Requirements:
256 KB RAM
Printer
Dual diskette drives or one diskette drive and a fixed disk

Support:
Dealer support
Direct telephone support line, (601) 684-8394
90-day warranty with software
Detailed user manual including a step-by-step sample problem

Retail Price:
$475

Distributor:
Bobby J. Hall & Associates
P.O. Box 646
McComb, MS 39648
Tel: (601) 684-6402

Description:

The Management Reports Module provides the user a wide variety of comparative analysis reports. It also includes provisions for budget input and analysis. Highlights include: comparison of year-to-date this year with year-to-date last year; comparison of any month this year with same month last year; displays monthly activity for any General Ledger account; compares budget to actual; plots comparison of any General Ledger activity of this year with last year; adjustment of budget at any time; plot or display of any General Ledger account. Several printed reports are also available.

Company:
Bobby J. Hall & Associates

Product:
Payroll Module

Category:
General Business Applications

Computer: AT&T PC 6300

Media: Diskette

Language:
Compiled BASIC

Requirements:
256 KB RAM
Printer
Dual diskette drives or one diskette drive and a fixed disk

Support:
Dealer support
Direct telephone support line, (601) 684-8394
90-day warranty with software
Detailed user manual including a step-by-step sample problem

Retail Price:
$475

Distributor:
Bobby J. Hall & Associates
P.O. Box 646
McComb, MS 39648
Tel: (601) 684-6402

Description:

The Payroll Module includes programs to enter or modify employee records, enter time, print payroll checks, W-2s, quarterly reports, unemployment reports, and yearly payroll information. It automatically posts to General Ledger. The Payroll Module calculates taxes for federal and up to four state or local taxing districts. It supports combinations of weekly, biweekly, semimonthly, and monthly pay periods for hourly, salaried, and commissioned employees. The input of beginning and ending time can come directly from cards for hourly employees. It provides time-and-one-half overtime multiplier rates (user option); provides for loan (advance) repayment deductions; and interfaces to General Ledger.

Company:

Bytecraft, Inc.

Product:

Teton Accounting Software Series Version 1.6 (all modules combined)

Category:

General Business Applications

Computer:
AT&T PC 6300

Media:
Diskette

Language:
CB86

Requirements:
128 KB RAM
80-column printer with compressed print option or 132-column printer
System sizing routine determines hard disk required

Support:
Optional direct support at $50 per hour by telephone
Sold in five-hour units at $250
Lifetime limited warranty on all products

Retail Price:
$795 single module units
Reduced price in merged module units

Distributor:
Bytecraft, Inc.
701 W. Antler
P.O. Box 1860
Caspar, WY 82602
Tel: (307) 235-6010

Description:

Teton Accounting Software Series is a single-user, modular general accounting package allowing multi-company accounting. It is a double entry, open-item system, using realtime update. The user may specify either cash or accrual. This system consists of General Ledger, Accounts Receivable, and Accounts Payable. The modules work standalone or integrated. Teton Accounting Software Series allows for departments, enterprises, and branches; provides model chart of accounts; offers automatic back-up, restoration, and recovery of damaged data; and features on-line HELP messages for each input field. The package does not allow out-of-balance posting. It provides four-level password protection and a task-oriented user manual. Available also are a sizing routine, tutorial, and worksheets for installation and a self-training workbook.

Company:

Bytecraft, Inc.

Product:

Teton Accounts Payable Accounting Software Module Version 1.6

Category:

General Business Applications

Computer: AT&T PC 6300

Media: Diskette

Language:

CB86

Requirements:

128 KB RAM
80-column printer with compressed print option or 132-column printer
System sizing routine determines hard disk required

Support:

Optional direct support at $50 per hour by phone
Sold in five-hour units at $250
Lifetime limited warranty on all products

Retail Price:

Reduced price in merged module units
$795 single module unit

Distributor:

Bytecraft, Inc.
701 W. Antler
P.O. Box 1860
Caspar, WY 82602
Tel: (307) 235-6010

Description:

Teton Accounts Payable Accounting Software is a single-user, double entry, open-item accounting system, using real time update. It integrates fully with other Teton modules or it may run standalone. User-definable check formatting is offered. Invoices, credit, and debit memos, and checks are retained until purged by the user to the history file. It calculates automatic discounts and penalties, and it permits overrides. Automatic or selective invoice payments are allowed. Vendor history is maintained on year-to-date purchases. The application offers recurring vouchers, manual checks, multiple accounts payable accounts, and multiple checking accounts. It also prints checks and 1099s. Full audit reports are available. Reports include 14 user-requested reports plus full automatic transaction registers. Features include password protection, automatic backup/ restoration, recovery of damaged data files, and on-line HELP messages. It does not allow out-of-balance posting. A task-oriented user manual and installation worksheets are provided. It allows multiple company processing.

Company:
Bytecraft, Inc.

Product:
Teton Accounts Receivable Accounting Software Module Version 1.6

Category:
General Business Applications

Computer:	**Media:**
AT&T PC 6300	Diskette

Language:
CB86

Requirements:
128 KB RAM
80-column printer with compressed print option or 132-column printer
System sizing routine determines hard disk required

Support:
Optional direct support at $50 per hour by phone
Sold in five-hour units at $250
Lifetime limited warranty on all products

Retail Price:
$795 single module units
Reduced price in merged module units

Distributor:
Bytecraft, Inc.
701 W. Antler
P.O. Box 1860
Caspar, WY 82602
Tel: (307) 235-6010

Description:

Teton Accounts Receivable Accounting Software is a single-user, double entry, open-item accounting system, allowing realtime update. It integrates fully with other Teton modules or can run standalone. User-definable six-line message for statements are available. Allows cash or accrual accounting, partial payments, credit and debit memos and automatic billing for recurring invoices and optional interest charges for invoices which are delinquent. This application allows on-screen customer inquiry and provides user-definable tax codes and percentages for up to five authorities. The mini-word processor allows up to six collection or sales letters. Invoices in excess of credit limits are flagged. User-definable defaults minimize keystrokes. A twenty-five character description line for each entry on sales invoices is provided. Optional cycle billing is also offered. Invoices are held on file with full recap of detail. Historical reports are available, as well as four-level password protection, task-oriented user manual, automatic backup, restore and data file recovery, on-line HELP messages and installation worksheets. The package does not allow the system to get out of balance. It allows multicompany processing.

Company:

Bytecraft, Inc.

Product:

Teton General Ledger Accounting Software Module Version 1.6 (general ledger system)

Category:

General Business Applications

Computer:	**Media:**
AT&T PC 6300	Diskette

Language:

CB86

Requirements:

128 KB RAM

80-column printer with compressed print option or 132 column printer

System sizing routine determines hard disk required

Support:

Optional direct support at $50 per hour by phone
Sold in five-hour units at $250
Lifetime limited warranty on all products

Retail Price:

$795 single module units
Reduced price in merged module units

Distributor:

Bytecraft, Inc.
701 W. Antler
P.O. Box 1860
Caspar, WY 82602
Tel: (307) 235-6010

Description:

Teton General Ledger Accounting Software System is a single-user, double entry, open-item accounting system, using realtime update. It integrates fully with other Teton modules or can run standalone. It allows either cash or accrual and provides model chart of accounts. Books are open for the entire fiscal year. The package does not allow out-of-balance posting. However it offers departmental, enterprise, or branch accounting. Previous year comparisons are available on balance sheet and financial statements. The package also allows prior year adjustments while updating current year opening balances automatically. Reports are available in detail or summary form, printed or on screen. User-defined report titles are provided. Reports include trend analysis. The application features password protection and automatic back-up, restore, and recovery of damaged data. Allows multicompany processing. A task-oriented user manual, on-line HELP messages and installation worksheets are available to assist the user.

Company:
Chang Labs

Product:
***Rags to Riches*–Ledger**

Category:
General Business Applications

Computer:
AT&T PC 6300

Media:
Diskette

Language:
CB86

Requirements:
128 KB RAM
One disk drive

Support:
Toll-free line for dealer and end user support
Nationwide (800) 972-8800
For California (800) 831-8080

Retail Price:
$124.95

Distributor:
Chang Labs
5300 Stevens Creek Blvd.
San Jose, CA 95129
Tel: (408) 246-8020

Description:

Rags to Riches Ledger is a double-entry General Ledger for small businesses. Is RAM-based (requires minimum 128 KB RAM), making it the fastest accounting package available. Integrates on one disk with *Rags to Riches* Receivables (accounts receivable), Payables (accounts payable), and Sales (sales register) modules or stands alone. Has five simple commands–the same five as the other three modules—so when you learn commands for one, you've learned them for all four. Presents three levels of on-screen help for beginner, intermediate, and expert users. Has CALC to simplify calculating discounts, taxes, and surcharges and editor for long memos on accounts and transactions. Provides instant on-screen summaries, so results of each transaction can be seen instantaneously. Tracks cash and credit sales and prints sales journal; tracks cash, check, and credit expenses and prints journals. Accommodates month-end accrual items. Handles posting to multiple accounts. Has transaction search by account. Provides complete audit trails, so you can see detailed chronological history for entire business or particular account. Produces income statement and balance sheet. Provides current, monthly, and yearly totals. Has 27 model charts of accounts of different types of small businesses for easy set-up. Handles up to 96 accounts/1,000 transactions; can be extended up to 5,000 accounts/10,000 transactions with Expansion module that has instant search for accounts (requires minimum 256 KB RAM). Combined Ledger and Expansion called Ledger Plus! Free, limited phone support from Chang Labs.

Company:
Chang Labs

Product:
***Rags to Riches*–Payables**

Category:
General Business Applications

Computer:
AT&T PC 6300

Media:
Diskette

Language:
CB86

Requirements:
128 KB RAM
One disk drive

Support:
Toll-free line for dealer and end user support
Nationwide (800) 972-8800
For California (800) 831-8080

Retail Price:
$124.95

Distributor:
Chang Labs
5300 Stevens Creek Blvd.
San Jose, CA 95129
Tel: (408) 246-8020

Description:

Rags to Riches Payables is an accounts receivable package for small businesses. Is RAM-based, fast (requires minimum 128 KB RAM), and integrates on one disk with *Rags to Riches* Ledger (general ledger), Receivables (accounts receivables), and Sales (sales register) modules or stands alone. Has five simple commands–same five as the other three modules—so when you learn commands for one, you've learned them for all four. Presents three levels of on-screen help–beginner, intermediate, and expert. Has CALC to simplify calculating discounts, taxes, and surcharges and editor for long memos on accounts and transactions. Provides instant on-screen summaries, so results of each transaction can be seen instantaneously. Posts or split-posts invoices by item. Handles discounts, freight, and taxes. Records late charges and early payment discounts. Tracks partial or full payments and deposits. Has optional check printing. Provides instant aging by vendor and on-line vendor follow-up. Prints 30-, 60-, and 90-day aging. Prints one check for multiple invoices. Prints vendor list. Has transaction search by vendor. Handles up to 96 accounts/1,000 transactions; can be extended up to 5,000 accounts/10,000 transactions by adding Expansion module that has instant search by vendor (requires minimum 256 KB RAM). Combined Payables and Expansion called Payables Plus! Free, limited telephone support provided by Chang Labs.

Company:
Chang Labs

Product:
***Rags to Riches*–Receivables**

Category:
General Business Applications

Computer:
AT&T PC 6300

Media:
Diskette

Language:
CB86

Requirements:
128 KB RAM
One disk drive

Support:
Toll-free line for dealer and end user support
Nationwide (800) 972-8800
For California (800) 831-8080

Retail Price:
$124.95

Distributor:
Chang Labs
5300 Stevens Creek Blvd.
San Jose, CA 95129
Tel: (408) 246-8020

Description:

Rags to Riches Receivables is an accounts receivable package for small businesses. Is RAM-based, fast (requires minimum 128 KB RAM), and integrates on one disk with *Rags to Riches* Ledger (general ledger), Payables (accounts payable), and Sales (sales register) modules or stands alone. Has five simple commands–same five as the other three modules—so when you learn commands for one, you've learned them for all four. Presents three levels of on-screen help–beginner, intermediate, and expert. Has CALC to simplify calculating discounts, taxes, and surcharges and has editor for long memos on accounts and transactions. Provides instant on-screen summaries, so results of each transaction can be seen instantaneously. Enters invoices by item. Handles discounts, freight, and taxes. Records late charges and early payment discounts. Accepts partial, over, or full payments. Accepts credits and debits. Prints invoices and statements. Has instant overdue customer list. Shows instant aging by customer. Prints 30-, 60-, and 90-day aging. Has "one-time" billing key. Prints customer list. Has transaction search by customer. Handles up to 96 accounts/1,000 transactions; can be extended up to 5,000 accounts/10,000 transactions by adding Expansion module that has instant search by customer (requires minimum 256 KB RAM). Combined Receivables and Expansion called Receivables Plus! Free, limited telephone support provided by Chang Labs.

Company:
Chang Labs

Product:
***Rags to Riches*–Sales**

Category:
General Business Applications

Computer:	**Media:**
AT&T PC 6300	Diskette

Language:
CB86

Requirements:
128 KB RAM
One disk drive

Support:
Toll-free line for dealer and end user support
Nationwide (800) 972-8800
For California (800) 831-8080

Retail Price:
$99.95

Distributor:
Chang Labs
5300 Stevens Creek Blvd.
San Jose, CA 95129
Tel: (408) 246-8020

Description:

Rags to Riches Sales is a point-of-purchase sales register for small businesses that enables your computer to function with RAM-based speed like a cash register. Consolidates multiple daily sales reports, provides management information and analysis, and merges daily sales reports directly in *Rags to Riches* Ledger (general ledger) for backroom accounting. Integrates on one disk with Ledger, Receivables (accounts receivable), and Payables (accounts payable) modules or stands alone. Has five simple commands–same five as other three modules, so when you learn one, you've learned them all. Presents three levels of on-screen help–beginner, intermediate, and expert. Has CALC to simplify calculating discounts, taxes, surcharges and editor for long memos on accounts and transactions. Provides instant on-screen summaries, so results of each transaction can be seen instantaneously. Tracks items with optional preset price. Computes taxes using two alternative rates. Records sale or refund and prints receipt. Calculates change due. Handles tax-exempt sales. Accepts store or manufacturer coupons, split tender. Tracks sales tax and tips. Tracks loans, pickups, and paidouts. Does simple quotations. Merges data from multiple Sales modules. Provides instant sales analysis by department. Produces instant receipt analysis by type. Provides current, monthly, and yearly totals. Printed reports include sales tax collection, daily sales, cash-in-drawer, sales receipt, end-of-day cash audit, coupon collections, charge purchase journal, refund receipts. Handles up to 96 departments and 96 types of payment; up to 1,000 transactions.

Company:
Computer Action Learning, Inc.

Product:
WORDSCOPE

Category:
General Business Applications

Computer:	**Media:**
6300 PLUS **AT&T PC 6300** **AT&T PC 6300 PLUS**	Diskette

Language:
Compiled Pascal

Requirements:
128 KB RAM

Support:
Diskettes are warranted against defects
Leader's guide
Manual
Exercise books available for group instruction

Retail Price:
$475

Distributor:
Computer Action Learning, Inc.
Harvey Drive, Box X
Summit, NJ 07901
Tel: (201) 273-4829

Description:

WORDSCOPE ...Computer Action Learning is an imaginatively conceived software package which builds the skillful use of business and technical written and spoken language. It is the product of 15 years of data gathered from instructional experience with more than 400 major American corporations and industry associations. The program, through a diagnostic assessment, identifies for users the five major barriers to effective communication.

Once recognized, each barrier becomes the subject of a series of novel, challenging, and entertaining exercise-games through self-paced interaction with the personal computer. The objective of each exercise-game is to demonstrate how the barriers interfere with or destroy good communication and how they can be prevented.

WORDSCOPE provides flexible hours of enjoyable, comprehensive instruction, the satisfaction of achievement, and positive feedback and long-term retention.

Company:
Conetic Systems, Inc.

Product:
C/BOOKS Accounts Payable

Category:
General Business Applications

Computer:	**Media:**
AT&T PC 6300	Diskette

Language:
C

Requirements:
256 KB RAM
Hard disk

Support:
3-day training course $495
Phone support (415) 430-8875
Support contracts available
Newsletter
On site

Retail Price:
G.L., A.R. & A.P. sold as a set only $1,530

Distributor:
Conetic Systems, Inc.
1470 Doolittle Drive
San Leandro, CA 94577
Tel: (415) 430-8875

Description:

Cash management is the most critical area of many businesses. The Accounts Payable system can help manage your cash flow by scheduling pay dates and by keeping track of vendor terms.

The Accounts Payable module is fully integrated with the C/BOOKS accounting system. It is a voucher system containing the same general features as Accounts Receivable. Automatic assignment or manual entry of voucher number. An unlimited number of vendor accounts are allowed and new vendors may be added and existing vendor information updated at any time. Since the voucher date specifies the month in which an expense is accrued, future payable vouchers can be entered at any time. Vouchers can be distributed to an unlimited number of distribution accounts charging their voucher distributions against any accounting subsystem, not just the general ledger. Vendor debit memos are entered on a separate screen with discounts automatically taken and partial payment allowed for any voucher. Cash disbursement allows for the use of multiple bank accounts if desired. The vendor's current balance and date and amount of last payment are on line and available for inquiry at any time. Manual checks may be allowed in addition to computer generated checks. Canceled checks are recorded in a check file to create a bank reconciliation report. Vendor codes are automatically checked against vendor files. The system automatically charges voucher distribution against any accounting subsystem, not just the General Ledger. Discounts are taken automatically. Voucher pay date is selected by user. Partial payment of vouchers may be made. Updating or deletion of voucher and debit memo may be done at any time before payment. The voucher selection routine selects vouchers to be paid. Outstanding vendor credits are automatically applied. Prior to running final checks, the system writes a pre-check list and edits the pre-check list to remove or modify payments if possible before checks are printed. Manual and computer generated checks may be easily voided. Canceled checks are recorded in check file to create the bank reconciliation report. Accounts Payable Reports may be either displayed on the screen or printed. The "Vendor Report" is a listing of vendor names and addresses arranged in vendor number order. The "Vendors by Name Report" is a listing of vendor names and addresses alphabetically by vendor name. "Vendor Balance" is a report that lists all vendors and their current balance. This report also shows the totals of all vendor accounts.

(Continued on next page)

Description: *(Continued)*

The "Aged Accounts Payable Report" shows future, current, over 30-, over 60- and over 90-day aging of outstanding vouchers. The total for each aging category is also shown. The "Vouchers by Vendor Report" lists selected voucher by vendor. Included in this report are vendor code, name, voucher number, date, amount, and pay date. "Voucher by Vendor with Detail" is the same as the previous report except additional information on ledger or journal and account to which the voucher is posted and the debit or credit amount posted is given. "Voucher Detail by Account" is a report that lists selected vouchers by the account to which the voucher is posted. Included are voucher number, date, amount, ledger or journal to which the voucher is posted, debit or credit amount posted to each account, and the total posted to each account. The "Vouchers by Pay Date Report" lists selected vouchers by pay date.

Cash disbursement reports can be either screen displayed or printed. "Cash Disbursements" (pre-check list) lists cash disbursements by bank account and vendor. The "Payable Checks by Vendor Report" lists check issued by payee. The report shows vendor code, name, check number, date, and amount. The "Check Register" lists checks issued in numerical order. Check number, date, payee, and amount are shown. The "Print Checks Report" pays selected vouchers and prints checks and remittance advises. "Bank Statement Reconciliation" for indicated bank account and bank statement date.

Additional reports, screens and data files may be modified using the C/TOOLS of Conetic Systems.

Company:
Conetic Systems, Inc.

Product:
C/BOOKS Accounts Receivable

Category:
General Business Applications

Computer:	**Media:**
AT&T PC 6300	Diskette

Language:
C

Requirements:
256 KB RAM
Hard disk

Support:
3-day training course $495
Phone support (415) 430-8875
Support contracts available
Newsletter
On site

Retail Price:
G.L., A.R. & A.P. sold as set only $1,530

Distributor:
Conetic Systems, Inc.
1470 Doolittle Drive
San Leandro, CA 94577
Tel: (415) 430-8875

Description:

Keeping control of accounts receivable is important to any business. With the Accounts Receivable system your receivables can be managed efficiently.

The accounts receivable module is fully integrated with the C/BOOKS accounting system. It is an open invoice system with no limit on the number of customer accounts. There is no limit on the number of invoice lines for each invoice and each invoice line may be posted to any module of the accounting subsystem. Future invoices can be entered at any time. Customers may be added and existing customer information updated at any time. Customer credits are entered using a separate screen, and credits automatically apply against the customer's invoice when paid. Deferral of credit to future months may be entered if desired. On-line customer inquiry of customer's current balance and date and amount of last payment.

Cash receipt date specifies the month in which receipt is recorded. Cash receipts records customer payments and keeps records of miscellaneous cash receipts. The use of multiple bank accounts is allowed. Application of payments may be to a specific invoice or to a general customer account. The cash receipt date specifies the month in which receipt is recorded. All bank deposits are tracked. The invoice date specifies month in which invoice is accrued, and the customer code is automatically checked against customer file.

Accounts receivable reports may be displayed on the screen or printed. The "Customer Report" is a listing of customer names and addresses arranged in order of customer code. "Customers Alphabetically by Name" is a report that lists customer names and addresses arranged alphabetically by customer name. The "Customer Balance Report" lists all customers and their current balances. The report also shows the total of all customer accounts. The "Aged Accounts Receivable" report shows future, current, over 30-, over 60-, and over 90-day aging of outstanding accounts receivable. A total of each aging category is shown. The "Invoices by Customer Report" lists selected invoices by customer. The report includes customer code, name, invoice number, date, and amount due. The "Invoices by Customer with Detail Report" is the same as previous report except additional information on ledger or journal and the account to which the invoice is posted, and debit or credit amount posted is supplied. The "Inventory Report" lists all inventory products within the file system. Included in this report are product codes, description of the product and current selling price.

(Continued on next page)

Description: ***(Continued)***

Cash receipts reports (screen display or printed) include "Bank Deposits Report" which lists bank code, deposit number, date, date cleared bank, and amount; "Payments by Customer Report" which includes receipt code, date of receipt, bank, customer check number, and amount and "Payments by Customer with Detail Report" which is the same as previous report but also lists journal entry for each cash receipt amount.

Additional reports, screens and data files may be created and existing reports, screens and data files may be modified using the C/TOOLS of Conetic Systems.

Company:
Conetic Systems, Inc.

Product:
C/BOOKS Fixed Assets

Category:
General Business Applications

Computer:	**Media:**
AT&T PC 6300	Diskette

Language:
C

Requirements:
256 KB RAM
Hard disk

Support:
3-day training course $495
Phone support (415) 430-8875
Support contracts available
Newsletter
On site

Retail Price:
$600

Distributor:
Conetic Systems, Inc.
1470 Doolittle Drive
San Leandro, CA 94577
Tel: (415) 430-8875

Description:

The most overlooked part of any accounting system, and the general accounting clerk's biggest headache, is fixed asset management.

The fixed asset program is fully integrated with the entire C/BOOKS accounting system. An unlimited number of fixed assets may be maintained. The fixed asset system records company assets and automatically provides for calculating depreciation. Straight line, double declining balance, sum of the years digits and ACRS recovery system depreciation methods are supported. Assets may be maintained in an inactive file, removed from service or sold and accounted for through the fixed asset system.

Fixed asset reports, either displayed on the screen or printed, may be generated. The "Asset Master Report" lists assets by type with description, purchase date, life of asset, method of depreciation, purchase cost, salvage value, whether new or used, and whether the asset is currently active or inactive. An "Assets with Book Value Report" lists all assets by type, with description, purchase date, original cost, and present book value. "Asset Depreciation Reports" show the amount of calculated depreciation for each asset for a specified period. Also listed is the accumulated depreciation amount and the book value.

Additional reports, screens and data files may be created and existing reports, screens and data files may be modified using the C/TOOLS of Conetic Systems.

Company:
Conetic Systems, Inc.

Product:
C/BOOKS General Ledger

Category:
General Business Applications

Computer:
AT&T PC 6300

Media:
Diskette

Language:
C

Requirements:
256 KB RAM
Hard disk

Support:
3-day training course $495
Phone support (415) 430-8875
Supports contracts available
Newsletter
On site

Retail Price:
G.L., A.R. & A.P. sold as set only $1,530

Distributor:
Conetic Systems, Inc.
1470 Doolittle Drive
San Leandro, CA 94577
Tel: (415) 430-8875

Description:

The C/BOOKS general ledger system is fully integrated with the entire C/BOOKS accounting system. An unlimited number of general ledger accounts are permitted and new accounts may be added at any time. General ledger account balances are available for on-line inquiry at any time. Current balances as well as account balances for all prior periods are maintained. The system allows general journal transaction entry, inquiry, or updating to general ledger accounts or any of the accounting system ledgers or journals. General journal entries are identified as correcting or adjusting entries. Summary information for all transactions posted to each account in a particular ledger during a given accounting period are available for on-line inquiry. A set-up program is provided for user formatting of the balance sheet and income statement.

General ledger reports may be displayed on the screen or printed. The "Ledgers and Journals Report" lists all ledgers and journals being used in the accounting system. The "General Ledger Chart of Accounts Report" is a listing of account numbers and their descriptive titles. A listing of the general journal entries made in a particular accounting period is provided by the "General Journal Entries Report." The "Balance Sheet and Income Statement Format Commands Report" lists commands that were entered to format the balance sheet and income statement.

The "Closing Registers Report" summarizes the activity of each journal for the selected accounting year and period. The "General Ledger Posting Transactions Report" provides a listing of transactions posted to the general ledger. The "Trial Balance Report" shows balances of the general ledger accounts for a particular accounting year and period. The balance sheet and income statements are generated by the "Balance Sheet and Income Statement Report." The "General Ledger Report" lists each general ledger account and shows the beginning balance, current activity and ending balance for the accounting year and period selected. Current balances of all general ledger accounts are provided in the "Current Balance Report."

Additional reports, screens and data files may be created and existing reports, screens and data files may be modified using the C/TOOLS of Conetic Systems.

Company:
Conetic Systems, Inc.

Product:
C/BOOKS Inventory Control

Category:
General Business Applications

Computer:
AT&T PC 6300

Media:
Diskette

Language:
C

Requirements:
256 KB RAM
Hard disk

Support:
3-day training course $495
Phone support (415) 430-8875
Support contracts available
Newsletter
On site

Retail Price:
$600

Distributor:
Conetic Systems, Inc.
1470 Doolittle Drive
San Leandro, CA 94577
Tel: (415) 430-8875

Description:

Keeping track of the inventory for a business can be a time consuming task for the manually bound accounting clerk. The Inventory Control system gives you the tools to manage your inventory levels, and at the same time convert inventory clerks into inventory managers who can assist with the most important aspect of any business cash flow.

The inventory control module is fully integrated with the entire C/BOOKS accounting system. Inventory control allows for tracking an unlimited number of products by category or specific product. Cost of goods account, inventory controlling account, and sales are based on the margin percentage and calculated automatically or may be manually entered. Selling prices which appear as a default value can be entered to the invoice or overridden with a new value. Product records may be flagged as taxable or nontaxable items. The order points and order quantities are used to generate reorder reports. The average cost method of valuing inventory is used.

On-line access to quantities on hand, unit cost and extended value information is available on each product. There is immediate update of product levels upon entering of any transaction. Inventory items can be transferred to other accounting modules such as the job costing module. The balances of products, purchases and sales of each product are maintained in the history file of the products.

Inventory reports may be screen displayed or printed. The "Price List Report" includes all inventory items, or only those categories specified, and their present selling price. The "Inventory Master List Report" lists product descriptions, average unit costs, number price, margin rate, reorder point and quantity, and the total value in inventory for each product. The "Reorder Report" shows the product, average cost, units presently in stock, the reorder point, and the reorder quantity. The "Inventory Activity Report" lists for each inventory item the number of units purchased and cost, the number of units sold and selling price, and the ending inventory balance in units and value. The "Inventory Adjustments Report" shows the manual adjustments that have been made to the inventory level or value. Such adjustments would be the transfer of inventory to a job, or changes in the number of units or value due to physical inventory counts and subsequent changes entered.

Additional reports, screens and data files may be created and existing reports, screens and data files may be modified using the C/TOOLS of Conetic Systems.

Company:
Conetic Systems, Inc.

Product:
C/BOOKS Job Costing

Category:
General Business Applications

Computer:
AT&T PC 6300

Media:
Diskette

Language:
C

Requirements:
256 KB RAM
Hard disk

Support:
3-day training course $495
Phone support (415) 430-8875
Support contracts available
Newsletter
On site

Retail Price:
$600

Distributor:
Conetic Systems, Inc.
1470 Doolittle Drive
San Leandro, CA 94577
Tel: (415) 430-8875

Description:

Businesses which make products to customers' orders or specifications, or which make products in separately identifiable lots or batches, need a fully integrated means of keeping track of the costs of such projects. The Job Costing system gives you the capabilities of tracking such job costs and the management tools to react quickly when costs are out of line with budget estimates.

The job costing module is fully integrated with the entire C/BOOKS accounting system. It allows for unique job identification with each job subdivided into an unlimited number of specific separate tasks. Budget estimates are allowed and cost to date information is accrued. New job profiles may be created using an existing job as a model. Payroll costs may be charged against job activity by using the payroll system. Materials may be charged to the job through the accounts payable vouchers, manual check system or transfer of materials from inventory to the job costing system. Cost of job may be transferred directly to expense accounts or, if desired, to a work in process account while the job is in progress. All jobs are posted to the appropriate expense accounts upon job completion.

Job Costing reports may be either displayed on the screen or printed. The "Job Masters Report" lists all jobs or only specified jobs. Details of the report include the job code, description, activity codes with description for each job, expense accounts charged upon closing of the job, date the job was closed, and the customer. The job cost "Work in Process Journal" lists the job's total expenses by month. Expenses are derived from vouchers, debit memos, inventory transactions, payroll distribution vouchers, etc. The "Job Cost Analysis" listed for each job's activities includes the accumulated costs and labor hours, budget estimates, and variances. "Job Cost with Detail" lists the transactions which make up the accumulated costs, for example, the vouchers, debit memos, payroll vouchers, inventory transactions, and other transactions.

Additional reports, screens and data files may be created and existing reports, screens and data files may be modified using the C/TOOLS of Conetic Systems.

Company:
Conetic Systems, Inc.

Product:
C/BOOKS Payroll

Category:
General Business Applications

Computer:	**Media:**
AT&T PC 6300	Diskette

Language:
C

Requirements:
256 KB RAM
Hard disk

Support:
3-day training course $495
Phone support (415) 430-8875
Support contracts available
Newsletter
On site

Retail Price:
$600

Distributor:
Conetic Systems, Inc.
1470 Doolittle Drive
San Leandro, CA 94577
Tel: (415) 430-8875

Description:

Payroll can be the most time consuming task for any business. The Payroll system gives businesses the flexibility they need to make payroll preparation efficient, fast, and accurate. The Payroll system is fully integrated with the entire C/BOOKS accounting system. It uses the accrual basis of accounting and an unlimited number of employees can be handled. The user may define pay periods such as daily, weekly, semimonthly, monthly, quarterly, annually, etc. for each employee. Tables are provided for the user to define other deductions to the payroll of the individual employee. Instead of keeping easily compromised balances, a history of payroll transactions is kept to determine cumulative figures. These figures are used to generate payroll checks, W-2 forms and reports for preparation of the IRS 941. Computer generated and manual checks are accommodated. The voucher system is used and automatic correction of payroll history occurs if a voucher is changed. The system charges labor to jobs at actual payroll rates, standard labor rates, or a combination of both if used in conjunction with the job costing system. Payroll includes a bank reconciliation program for issued checks.

Payroll reports may be displayed on the screen or printed. Numerous payroll reports are available. The "Employee Master Report" lists all employee names and addresses arranged by employee code. The "Employee Deductions Report" lists payroll information for all employees including pay rates, pay frequencies and deductions. The "Labor Distribution Detail" lists the labor hour distribution by employee including hours worked, actual costs, expense account, charge amount and charge account. The "Payroll Voucher Report" is a listing of selected payroll vouchers which includes employee code, name, starting and ending dates of pay period, gross pay, net pay, etc. "Payroll Vouchers with Detail" are the same as the previous report except additional information on ledger or journal and account to which voucher is posted and the debit or credit amount posted is shown. The "Payroll Register" lists employee payroll and payroll costs for selected pay dates. It also includes employee's gross pay, net pay, and deductions. Summarized on the report are employee deductions as well as employer cost. The "Payroll Register with History" is the same as previous report except quarter-to-date and year-to-date payroll balances are shown for each employee. The "941 Quarterly Tax Report" lists all the necessary information for the 941 quarterly report. The "W-2 Forms Report" prints the W-2 forms

(Continued on next page)

Description: ***(Continued)***

required by the IRS at year end. "Current Payroll Report" lists payroll vouchers that have been selected for payment. From this list you can edit or delete payroll vouchers before actual payment. "Payment Checks by Employee" shows both computer and manual payroll checks issued. The report includes employee name, check number, date and amount. The "Issued Checks by Payee Report" lists all checks issued by payee including both payroll and accounts payable checks. The "Check Register Report" lists all checks issued in check number order. It includes both payroll and accounts payable checks. The "Payroll Checks Report" prints checks for the payment of payroll amounts. "Bank Statement Reconciliation" performs the bank reconciliation for indicated bank account and bank statement date.

Additional reports, screens and data files may be created and existing reports, screens and data files may be modified using the C/TOOLS from Conetic Systems.

Company:

Dun & Bradstreet Plan Services

Product:

The Personal Connection–Business Information System

Category:

General Business Applications

Computer:	**Media:**
AT&T PC 6300	Diskette

Language:

Compiled BASIC

Requirements:

128 KB RAM
2 disk drives

Support:

Full documentation is included in price
Toll-free telephone number available for support
Nationwide–(800) 447-0683
Illinois only–(800) 322-4578

Retail Price:

$345

Distributor:

Dun & Bradstreet Plan Services
4517 North Sterling Ave.
Peoria, IL 61615
Tel: (309) 688-4095

Description:

The Business Information System provides a simple, powerful method of maintaining important information on your business clients and prospects. BIS is also a powerful marketing and prospecting tool that gives the user complete flexibility in qualifying business prospects.

Codes used to classify clients are determined by the user. Prospects can be selected on the basis of over twenty criteria. The list of selected clients can be printed on the screen, on a printer, or to a disk file. The disk file, when combined with a letter, gives you personalized correspondence in a fraction of the time it would take without this powerful marketing and data management program.

Complete business information on up to 1200 clients can be maintained using BIS. Information on any client is available in less than three seconds. (The exact number of clients that can be stored depends upon your hardware configuration.)

BIS also has telephone dialing capability when used in conjunction with the *Hayes* Smartmodem.

Company:
EXEC*U*STAT, Inc.

Product:
EXEC*U*STAT

Category:
General Business Applications

Computer:	**Media:**
AT&T PC 6300	Diskette

Language:
APL

Requirements:
256 KB RAM
Two floppy disk drives or one floppy and hard disk

Color or monochrome monitor

Support:
Warranty
On-site training courses
Technical Help-line available

Retail Price:
$495
Corporate site license & educational discounts are available

Distributor:
EXEC*U*STAT, Inc.
Research Park, 2 Wall St.
Princeton, NJ 08540
Tel: (609) 924-9357

Description:

*EXEC*U*STAT* has been designed to create an interactive data analysis environment which takes advantage of today's microcomputer capabilities. It is ideally suited for individuals who need the speed and power of computers without the costly investment of time to learn the special syntax of the software. The *EXEC*U*STAT* system covers the techniques most used by business statistical analysis, integrated with extensive graphical capabilities and an on-line help facility oriented toward interpretation of statistical output. *EXEC*U*STAT* provides an excellent statistical package for introductory statistical courses. The product could in many cases replace mainframe packages.

*EXEC*U*STAT* includes routines for Basic Plotting, Descriptive Methods, Estimation and Testing, Regression, Forecasting, Time Series Analysis, Financial Analysis Calculation, and several advanced procedures such as Analysis of Variance and NonParametric Statistics. These powerful techniques are invoked by simple menu selections, and while the statistical output is presented on the screen the user can press a single function key to aid and enhance the analysis with a related graphical display. The graphs are available when they are needed, during the analysis process.

Not only are the graphs generated by pressing a single key, but any graph may be edited through interactive cursor movements. Text annotations may be added anywhere on a graph for presentation quality output. Also, any screen can be saved as a disk file for later replay in a slide presentation. Reports may be custom tailored by marking an area on the screen, such as a statistical table, with the cursor, "cutting" it out and pasting it onto one of the pages of the *EXEC*U*STAT* scratchpad.

Graphics may be produced on the screen either in four-color medium resolution or in two-color high resolution. These sharp, custom-tailored displays can be printed by the press of a single key. *EXEC*U*STAT* also operates on many of the popular high-resolution color and monochrome graphic boards along with support for sending the final edited graph to several types of pen plotters. Default options are always generated for axis scaling, titles, color choices, line and point types, shading fill patterns, plot size, and position, although all options may be defined from input panels.

After selecting the desired data variables, *EXEC*U*STAT* leads the way in applying powerful statistical techniques. The variable selection menu dis-

(Continued on next page)

Description: ***(Continued)***

plays only the data appropriate for the current analysis; there is no chance of mistyping an input or making a bad selection. Both selection of observations and data transformations are achieved via menu selections; there is no special syntax or language to learn. A number of different data types are supported, including numeric, fixed decimal, character, date, monthly, and working days.

*EXEC*U*STAT* takes the important step past spreadsheets and data gathering to statistical analysis and graphical displays that not only present the data but provide the valuable insight to answer the questions of Why? How? and What next? The system provides a spreadsheet data editor and also has import facilities for reading data produced by several of the popular PC packages.

Company:

Experience in Software, Inc.

Product:

***THE ART OF NEGOTIATING* Version 1.0**

Category:

General Business Applications

Computer:	**Media:**
AT&T PC 6300 6300 PLUS **AT&T PC 6300 PLUS**	Diskette

Language:

Pascal

Requirements:

256 KB RAM
Two disk drives or a hard disk

Support:

Hotline support Telephone: (405) 644-0694
90-day warranty on disks

Retail Price:

$495

Distributor:

Experience in Software, Inc.
2039 Shattuck Ave., Suite 401
Berkeley, CA 94704
Tel: (415) 644-0694

Description:

This interactive software trains people to negotiate better as they prepare for their own negotiations, whether top-level business deals or personal disputes. The program asks questions and makes suggestions which stimulate the user's awareness of both sides' viewpoints. Then it helps the user develop useful plans of action, including a strategic agenda. The user's information is stored and printed out for easy review. Based on Gerard Nierenberg's *Art of Negotiation* seminar, this software requires no prior computer or negotiating experience.

Company:
Future Technologies International, Inc.

Product:
MICROCA$H

Category:
General Business Applications

Computer:
AT&T PC 6300

Media:
Diskette

Language:
THE ENVIRONMENT

Requirements:
256 KB RAM (minimum)
10 MB hard disk

Support:
Lifetime warranty
1 week training (at FTI or at client site)

Retail Price:
$4,000–$24,000

Distributor:
Future Technologies International, Inc.
40 West Blackwell St.
Dover, NJ 07801
Tel: (201) 328-0730

Description:

MICROCA$H is a microcomputer-based treasury workstation software product. It was designed with the power and sophistication to address the treasury needs of the Fortune 1300. *MICROCA$H* has automated many treasury functions and provides access to current, historical and future (anticipated or scheduled) financial activities and positions for reporting and analysis. *MICROCA$H* is a fully integrated, menu-driven system that utilizes a single source database.

A number of cash management functions can be performed utilizing *MICROCA$H.* They include automatic, unattended reporting service communication for detail debits and credits; bank relationship management including contact names and authorized signers; portfolio management with maturity schedules and strategy analysis; the management of a company's total debt position; initiation of funds transfers with confirmation status; cash forecasting; and the ability to create multiple cash position worksheets through English language commands.

MICROCA$H was the first treasury workstation product to be developed and installed. Since its inception in 1981, *MICROCA$H* has maintained the status of a premier product in the industry.

MICROCA$H is a cost-effective, responsive solution to the problem of cash planning and control.

Company:
Future Technologies International, Inc.

Product:
***MICROCA$H*CENTER**

Category:
General Business Applications

Computer:	**Media:**
AT&T PC 6300	Diskette

Language:
THE ENVIRONMENT

Requirements:
256 KB RAM (minimum)
10 MB hard disk

Support:
Lifetime warranty
2 week training (at FTI or at client site)

Retail Price:
$1,500–$8,750

Distributor:
Future Technologies International, Inc.
40 West Blackwell St.
Dover, NJ 07801
Tel: (201) 328-0730

Description:

The *MICROCA$H*CENTER product is a corporate treasury workstation expressly designed for the corporation with sales ranging from $25 to $200 million. *MICROCA$H*CENTER provides the solution to the treasury needs of today's rapidly emerging corporations. *MICROCA$H*CENTER operates in a menu-driven modular fashion and therefore provides the user with the sophistication and flexibility of today's technology. It also captures the intelligence and user-friendly features of *MICROCA$H*CENTER, FTI's large corporate treasury workstation leader.

MICROCA$H*CENTER, created from the same developmental foundation as *MICROCA$H, provides complete upward compatibility among workstation products. *MICROCA$H*CENTER continues to enjoy and capitalize on the integral capabilities of a single source database and the flexibility of modular enhancements. Automatic communication, bank relationship management, debt and investment management, funds transfer, and cash forecasting are typical features of the system.

Company:
G & G Software, Inc.

Product:
***G&G GL*–A General Ledger Package Version I**

Category:
General Business Applications

Computer:	**Media:**
AT&T PC 6300	Diskette

Language:
Machine Language

Requirements:
128 KB RAM, 16-bit
At least two floppies with 180 KB each
80-column screen
80-column printer

Support:
Manual is included
Office number is available

Retail Price:
$495

Distributor:
G & G Software, Inc.
610 Park Blvd.
Austin, TX 78751
Tel: (512) 458-5760

Description:

G&G GL was written by a certified public accountant for use in an accounting practice that supports an abundance of record keeping for its clients. It is also appropriate for use in any business.

Posting programs (general journal, cash receipts, cash disbursements) require all entries to be in balance. One program provides for making one-sided entries.

Employee payroll records are updated when entries are made to the regular general ledger accounts. (This is sometimes known as "after the fact" payroll entries.) 941 reports are prepared at the end of each quarter and W-2s at the end of the year.

Account numbers for the general ledger accounts are assigned as the user elects. The software supports account number ranges up to 99999.9, although fewer digits may also be used. The chart of accounts for a particular installation is defined by the user. There is no limit on the number of accounts in an installation, as the only limiting factor is the user's disk space.

All output is formatted to fit on 8 1/2 x 11 paper. A fixed asset depreciation module, nine departments, job costing, comparison reports, and budget reports are supported.

Company:
Gantt Systems, Inc.

Product:
***Gantt-Pack* "Work Processor" Version 3.1**

Category:
General Business Applications

Computer:	**Media:**
AT&T PC 6300	Diskette

Language:
Compiled BASIC

Requirements:
256 KB RAM
Two disk drives, (floppy or hard)
132-column printer (standard or compressed mode)

Support:
Full warranty
Telephone (201) 494-7452 and mail support
Training arranged on a consulting basis

Retail Price:
$225

Distributor:

Gantt Systems, Inc.
495 Main St.
Metuchen, NJ 08840
Tel: (201) 494-7452

Description:

The *Gantt-Pack* "Work Processor" is a business planning, scheduling, and project management system that helps users:

- Create a database that details tasks needed to complete a job.
- Change data quickly and easily to reflect schedule changes, added tasks, and completed tasks. Just as a word processor lets you rearrange text effortlessly, *Gantt-Pack* serves as your "work processor," rearranging tasks at the touch of a key.
- Print easy-to-understand charts that inform everyone on a project who is to do what tasks and when they should be done. Each person can get a copy of the schedule–not easily done without *Gantt-Pack*.
- Monitor a job's status at every stage and pinpoint when tasks are running late. Managers can then adjust schedules accordingly, or call up extra resources to keep the job on schedule.
- Arrange your database in many different ways! For example, tasks can be sorted according to a particular resource, making it possible to spot potential scarcities. A link to *Lotus 1-2-3* makes it possible to use schedule and resource data for financial analysis and productivity studies.

Company:
Human Edge

Product:
The Communication Edge

Category:
General Business Applications

Computer:
AT&T PC 6300

Media:
Diskette

Language:
Pascal

Requirements:
128 KB RAM
1 double-sided drive

Support:
Warranty
Must return warranty card in order to receive technical support (415) 493-3943
Training

Retail Price:
$195

Distributor:
Human Edge
2445 Faber Place
Palo Alto, CA 94303
Tel: (415) 493-1593

Description:

The Communication Edge is an expert system that prepares the user to conduct meetings and conversations effectively. It enables the user to emphasize communication strengths and avoid the pitfalls built into any conversation. The program presents the user with a series of surprise questions to assess his communication style and the approach of his counterpart. The software then generates a strategy detailing ideas for a better relationship and ways to communicate more effectively.

Company:
Human Edge

Product:
The Management Edge Version 2.0

Category:
General Business Applications

Computer:
AT&T PC 6300

Media:
Diskette

Language:
Pascal

Requirements:
128 KB RAM
1 double-sided drive

Support:
Warranty
Must receive warranty card in order to receive technical support (415) 493-3943
Training

Retail Price:
$250

Distributor:
Human Edge
2445 Faber Place
Palo Alto, CA 94303
Tel: (415) 493-1593

Description:

The Management Edge is an expert system designed to advise the user on improving management results with each subordinate. After the user completes the self-assessment portion of the program and provides information about the subordinate and the organization. The program generates a detailed management strategy on how best to work with the individual to get desired results. Topics covered include how to increase productivity, how to resolve on the job conflicts, and how to more effectively discipline or reward an employee.

Company:
Human Edge

Product:
The Negotiation Edge

Category:
General Business Applications

Computer:
AT&T PC 6300

Media:
Diskette

Language:
Pascal

Requirements:
128 KB RAM
1 double-sided drive

Support:
Warranty
Must return warranty card in order to receive technical support (415) 493-3943
Training

Retail Price:
$295

Distributor:
Human Edge
2445 Faber Place
Palo Alto, CA 94303
Tel: (415) 493-1593

Description:

The Negotiation Edge is an expert system designed to help the user prepare, work through, and successfully complete any negotiating or bargaining process. After completing a self-assessment, an assessment of the anticipated counterpart, and an assessment about the circumstances of the negotiation, the program generates a detailed negotiation plan with step-by-step suggestions for completing the process.

Company:
Human Edge

Product:
The Sales Edge

Category:
General Business Applications

Computer:
AT&T PC 6300

Media:
Diskette

Language:
Pascal

Requirements:
128 KB RAM
1 double-sided drive

Support:
Warranty
Must return warranty card in order to receive technical support (415) 493-3943
Training

Retail Price:
$250

Distributor:
Human Edge
2445 Faber Place
Palo Alto, CA 94303
Tel: (415) 493-1593

Description:

The Sales Edge is an expert system that provides the user with an individually tailored strategy on how to deal with specific customers. After the user completes a self-assessment and a customer assessment, the program generates a sales strategy report that advises the sales person on how to approach a sale given the users' and customers' personalities.

Company:
InFiSy Systems, Inc.

Product:
Accounts Payable

Category:
General Business Applications

Computer:	**Media:**
AT&T PC 6300	Diskette

Language:
COBOL

Requirements:
256 KB RAM

Support:
Software warranted for one year
End user software support—telephone & update 10 percent of list price per year
Education at InFiSy's Houston site $125 per half day session
Education at Dealer/Distributor or Customer site—Expenses $50 an hour-minimum of 10 hours

Retail Price:
$895

Distributor:
InFiSy Systems, Inc.
1416 E. North Belt, Suite 100
Houston, TX 77032
Tel: (713) 590-5241

InFiSy Systems, Inc. is an authorized Value Added Reseller for AT&T Computers.

Description:

Accounts Payable achieves accuracy by balancing batch and invoice, checking for duplicate invoices, audit trail, full General Ledger traceability, and checking negative invoices. The Accounts Payable system calculates discount, due date and stores normal General Ledger account. The system also processes payables in more than one month, performs a manual check, a manual check on automation, adjustments, prepayments, and debit memos. It also offers multiple methods of taking discounts, payment selectivity by due date, individual invoice, vendor and partial payment, multiple bank accounts, multiple lines of distribution, and description to General Ledger.

Company:
InFiSy Systems, Inc.

Product:
Bill-of-Material

Category:
General Business Applications

Computer: AT&T PC 6300

Media: Diskette

Language:
COBOL

Requirements:
256 KB RAM

Support:
Software warranted for one year
End user software support—telephone & update 10 percent of list price per year
Education at InFiSy's Houston site $125 per half-day session
Education at Dealer/Distributor or Customer site—Expenses $50 an hour-minimum of 10 hours

Retail Price:
$1,395

Distributor:
InFiSy Systems, Inc.
1416 E. North Belt, Suite 100
Houston, TX 77032
Tel: (713) 590-5241

InFiSy Systems, Inc. is an authorized Value Added Reseller for AT&T Computers.

Description:

This is a multilevel Bill-of-Material from which single-level, multilevel Bills-of-Material, and screens are generated. This system is integrated with Inventory, Routing, Scheduling, Job Cost and Order Entry. The Bill-of-Material application is used wherever possible to automate the movement of inventory by using a bill in lieu of individual component transaction.

Company:
InFiSy Systems, Inc.

Product:
Employee Performance Measurement System

Category:
General Business Applications

Computer:	**Media:**
AT&T PC 6300	Diskette

Language:
COBOL

Requirements:
256 KB RAM

Support:
Software warranted for one year
End user software support—telephone and update 10 percent of list price per year
Education at InFiSy's Houston site $125 per half-day session
Education at Dealer/Distributor or Customer site—Expenses $50 an hour-minimum of 10 hours

Retail Price:
$1,395

Distributor:
InFiSy Systems, Inc.
1416 E. North Belt, Suite 100
Houston, TX 77032
Tel: (713) 590-5241

InFiSy Systems, Inc. is an authorized Value Added Reseller for AT&T Computers.

Description:

This package provides the tools necessary to make employee productivity happen. Daily, weekly and monthly reports by employees list direct performance in detail and indirect labor hours by employee. Reports are summarized by department and by company. Direct labor performance can be increased and indirect labor hours decreased. Employee performance measurement helps to evaluate estimates. The system points out the need to examine estimating practices if the estimates are consistently out of line.

Company:
InFiSy Systems, Inc.

Product:
Estimating and Shop Order Routing Systems

Category:
General Business Applications

Computer:	**Media:**
AT&T PC 6300	Diskette

Language:
COBOL

Requirements:
256 KB RAM

Support:
Software warranted for one year
End user software support—telephone and update 10 percent of list price per year
Education at InFiSy's Houston site $125 per half day session
Education at Dealer/Distributor or Customer site—Expenses $50 an hour-minimum of 10 hours

Retail Price:
$1,395

Distributor:

InFiSy Systems, Inc.
1416 E. North Belt, Suite 100
Houston, TX 77032
Tel: (713) 590-5241

InFiSy Systems, Inc. is an authorized Value Added Reseller for AT&T Computers.

Description:

This application assists the manufacturing estimator in calculating cost and preparing quotes on four quantities and five mark-ups (one mark-up is usually cost). Mark-up can be different for material, outside, and labor. Quote is calculated after the input of standard router information. Standard Router is easy to input as it uses a standard operations file, work center file, inventory file, and material quantity discount file. Flexibility includes the option to estimate in pieces per hour or hours per piece, multiple set-ups and set-up frequency, scrap factor, sequence operations according to user specifications. The application also allows for multiple lines of description (up to 999). Standard Router is used to generate the shop floor router on receipt of order.

Company:
InFiSy Systems, Inc.

Product:
Fixed Asset System

Category:
General Business Applications

Computer:	**Media:**
AT&T PC 6300	Diskette

Language:
COBOL

Requirements:
256 KB RAM

Support:
Software warranted for one year
End user software support—telephone and update 10 percent of list price per year
Education at InFiSy's Houston site $125 per half-day session
Education at Dealer/Distributor or Customer site—Expenses $50 an hour-minimum of 10 hours

Retail Price:
$895

Distributor:

InFiSy Systems, Inc.
1416 E. North Belt, Suite 100
Houston, TX 77032
Tel: (713) 590-5241

InFiSy Systems, Inc. is an authorized Value Added Reseller for AT&T Computers.

Description:

Fixed Asset System tracks assets by asset number, serial number, and further by group, type, and class providing for monitoring of assets by department, building, division, type of equipment, or any method you choose. Tax and book depreciation are provided for with different start dates and depreciation methods. Fixed Asset System calculates depreciation on seven methods including ACRS. The application also includes easy start-up with cumulative depreciation being recalculated and automatic updating to General Ledger, including transfers. Preventive maintenance and fluid analysis help reduce repair costs and downtime.

Company:
InFiSy Systems, Inc.

Product:
General Ledger and Financial Statements

Category:
General Business Applications

Computer:	**Media:**
AT&T PC 6300	Diskette

Language:
COBOL

Requirements:
256 KB RAM

Support:
Software warranted for one year
End user software support—telephone and update 10 percent of list price per year
Education at InFiSy's Houston site $125 per half-day session
Education at Dealer/Distributor or Customer site—Expenses $50 an hour-minimum of 10 hours

Retail Price:
$895

Distributor:

InFiSy Systems, Inc.
1416 E. North Belt, Suite 100
Houston, TX 77032
Tel: (713) 590-5241

InFiSy Systems, Inc. is an authorized Value Added Reseller for AT&T Computers.

Description:

General Ledger and Financial Statements offers easy, accurate, input through full screen, on-line journal entries, full audit trail and reversing and recurring entries. This application will in the current year and prior year simultaneously adjust prior months then rerun ledger or statements as many times as desired. The automatic year-end close function transfers expenses and income to retained earnings. This application will also supply month and year-to-date detail General Ledger for the current year and the prior year, in addition to on-line inquiry of account detail. The user may employ his or her digit alphanumeric chart of accounts. The user can also design financial statements without regard to chart of account structure, balance sheet(s), cash flow or consolidated income statements, multiple company consolidation, profit center, cost center, budgets, and prior year. The system includes ratio analysis and use of nonfinancial data in financial statements, such as hours or pounds.

Company:
InFiSy Systems, Inc.

Product:
Inventory Control

Category:
General Business Applications

Computer:
AT&T PC 6300

Media:
Diskette

Language:
COBOL

Requirements:
256 KB RAM

Support:
Software warranted for one year
End user software support—telephone and update 10 percent of list price per year
Education at InFiSy's Houston site $125 per half-day session
Education at Dealer/Distributor or Customer site—Expenses $50 an hour-minimum of 10 hours

Retail Price:
$1,095

Distributor:
InFiSy Systems, Inc.
1416 E. North Belt, Suite 100
Houston, TX 77032
Tel: (713) 590-5241

InFiSy Systems, Inc. is an authorized Value Added Reseller for AT&T Computers.

Description:

This system helps improve customer service, lowers inventory investment, and improves purchasing discounts. Inventory Control provides up to the minute status of on-hand, on-order data from purchase orders, on-order data from work orders, customer and manufacturing requirements and last 24 months usage. Summary status is detailed by individual open order. Inventory Control is completely integrated with Order Entry, Job Cost, Purchasing, Estimating, Scheduling and Bill-of-Material. This application allows for a review of inventory on-screen or in reports. The File address feature allows quick access to inventory using many keys. Other features include assistance in physical inventory and average or standard cost.

Company:
InFiSy Systems, Inc.

Product:
Job Cost Accounting

Category:
General Business Applications

Computer:
AT&T PC 6300

Media:
Diskette

Language:
COBOL

Requirements:
256 KB RAM

Support:
Software warranted for one year
End user software support—telephone and update 10 percent of list price per year
Education at InFiSy's Houston site $125 per half-day session
Education at Dealer/Distributor or Customer site—Expenses $50 an hour-minimum of 10 hours

Retail Price:
$1,395

Distributor:
InFiSy Systems, Inc.
1416 E. North Belt, Suite 100
Houston, TX 77032
Tel: (713) 590-5241

InFiSy Systems, Inc. is an authorized Value Added Reseller for AT&T Computers.

Description:

This system provides up to date job costing information in summary and detail. Labor and overhead, material and outside manufacturing are tracked by operation in detail and summary. Inquiry can be made any time by job, part, customer, and customer purchase order showing actual costs versus estimated in hours and dollars and exact job status, i.e., operations/pieces completed. The report is printed in detail showing job, estimated costs versus actual costs by operation, and groupings of several jobs by subjob. Labor input uses payroll file and updates payroll. Material input to job costing from inventory, is available for accounts payable or direct in addition to cost/profit history by part, product line, customer, and operation. Full accounting for work in progress (WIP) is offered including partial shipments. The system is fully integrated with Inventory, Bill-of-Material, Payroll, Estimating, Shop Orders, Scheduling, and Employee Performance.

Company:
InFiSy Systems, Inc.

Product:
Order Entry, Invoicing and Product Sales Analysis

Category:
General Business Applications

Computer:	**Media:**
AT&T PC 6300	Diskette

Language:
COBOL

Requirements:
256 KB RAM

Support:
Software warranted for one year
End user software support—telephone and update 10 percent of list price per year
Education at InFiSy's Houston site $125 per half-day session
Education at Dealer/Distributor or Customer site—Expenses $50 an hour-minimum of 10 hours

Retail Price:
$1,095

Distributor:
InFiSy Systems, Inc.
1416 E. North Belt, Suite 100
Houston, TX 77032
Tel: (713) 590-5241

InFiSy Systems, Inc. is an authorized Value Added Reseller for AT&T Computers.

Description:

This system provides for easy on-line input of order with most data generated automatically from Accounts Receivable and Inventory files. It also provides automatic credit checking and credit hold. Order pricing is automatic using the list price adjusted for quantity discount, four alternate prices, custom price/class, customer product line discounts, contract pricing and/or order discounts. The packing list and invoice are printed as requested. Multiple lines of description can be used including a 90-character inventory item description. Line items can be shipped short or long, back ordered automatically or not back ordered, open order control is available by customer, due date, and other, in addition to full system integration with Inventory, Accounts Receivable, and General Ledger. Product Sales Analysis is available by customer, salesperson, and product in detail and summary on a date selective basis.

Company:
InFiSy Systems, Inc.

Product:
Payroll

Category:
General Business Applications

Computer:	**Media:**
AT&T PC 6300	Diskette

Language:
COBOL

Requirements:
256 KB RAM

Support:
Software warranted for one year
End user software support—telephone and update 10 percent of list price per year
Education at InFiSy's Houston site $125 per half-day session
Education at Dealer/Distributor or Customer site—Expenses $50 an hour-minimum of 10 hours

Retail Price:
$895

Distributor:

InFiSy Systems, Inc.
1416 E. North Belt, Suite 100
Houston, TX 77032
Tel: (713) 590-5241

InFiSy Systems, Inc. is an authorized Value Added Reseller for AT&T Computers.

Description:

The easy to input Payroll System includes automatic salary, automatic hourly from cost accounting, or prompted input by employee. Ten earnings categories with multiple pay rates, multiple checks per employee, ten deductions, one time override of deductions, taxes and pay rate, override of a deduction group, declining balance deduction, and deferred earnings are part of this flexible system. Payroll also features automatic distribution to General Ledger including appropriate accounting for overtime, double-time and the employee portion of FICA. The Payroll history file provides earnings, tax, and deduction history and analysis by employee and department for a specified time range. The system handles state and federal payroll taxes as well as calculating workman's compensation.

Company:
InFiSy Systems, Inc.

Product:
Production Planning and Measurement

Category:
General Business Applications

Computer: **AT&T PC 6300**

Media: Diskette

Language:
COBOL

Requirements:
256 KB RAM

Support:
Software warranted for one year
End user software support—telephone and update 10 percent of list price per year
Education at InFiSy's Houston site $125 per half-day session
Education at Dealer/Distributor or Customer site—Expenses $50 an hour-minimum of 10 hours

Retail Price:
$1,395

Distributor:

InFiSy Systems, Inc.
1416 E. North Belt, Suite 100
Houston, TX 77032
Tel: (713) 590-5241

InFiSy Systems, Inc. is an authorized Value Added Reseller for AT&T Computers.

Description:

Production Planning and Measurement provides manual or automatic scheduling and forward or backward scheduling. It also considers standard hours to order/receive, set-up time, runtime (pieces per hour or hours per piece), standard hours between operations, standard hours for outside operations, standard work week and holidays. The application provides material and outside schedules. In addition, material operations are automatically created, Bill-of-Material is used to produce router with each component part. The applications also provide override, delete, or insert operations. The reports available are Master Work Load Report, Master Work Order Schedule, Work Center Load Detail, and Work Center Schedule Detail which helps spot areas of underload and overload.

Company:
InFiSy Systems, Inc.

Product:
Purchasing

Category:
General Business Applications

Computer:
AT&T PC 6300

Media:
Diskette

Language:
COBOL

Requirements:
256 KB RAM

Support:
Software warranted for one year
End user software support—telephone and update 10 percent of list price per year
Education at InFiSy's Houston site $125 per half-day session
Education at Dealer/Distributor or Customer site—Expenses $50 an hour-minimum of 10 hours

Retail Price:
$1,095

Distributor:
InFiSy Systems, Inc.
1416 E. North Belt, Suite 100
Houston, TX 77032
Tel: (713) 590-5241

InFiSy Systems, Inc. is an authorized Value Added Reseller for AT&T Computers.

Description:

Purchasing requires minimum input for vendor information, automatically pulled from vendor master; name, address, terms, ship via, collect or prepaid freight and only input part number and quantity for each line item. Open purchase orders are by P.O., vendor, due date, part number, and buyer. Open purchase order status is immediately available. Purchasing provides a buying history in screen or report form along with vendor evaluation and control. Receiving system tracks receipts subject to inspection.

Company:

International Management Reporting Services, Inc.

Product:

MICRO CONTROL

Category:

General Business Applications

Computer: **AT&T PC 6300**

Media: Diskette

Language:
Compiled BASIC/Assembler

Requirements:
256 KB RAM

Support:
Installation
Training
Hotline (203) 359-9655

Retail Price:
$30,000 Plus Installation

Distributor:
International Management Reporting Services, Inc.
1 High Ridge Rd.
Stamford, CT 06905
Tel: (203) 359-9655

Description:

Developed by IMRS Inc., *MICRO CONTROL* is specifically designed for the multidivisional, multinational organization. Yet all data entry and processing is accomplished on AT&T, and other compatible personal computers at reporting locations and at corporate headquarters.

The comprehensive structure of *MICRO CONTROL* provides custom designed management reports at all levels of organization, without custom coding. It automatically consolidates data from local offices for regional, division, and corporate reports, converting local currencies as required.

The *MICRO CONTROL* program incorporates advanced modeling capabilities for preparation of budgets and forecasts, while the consolidation and reporting functions dramatically speed the management review cycle.

MICRO CONTROL is the new, cost-effective solution to the overwhelming tasks of financial control, planning and reporting.

Company:
KJ Software, Inc.

Product:
Achieving Financial Fitness

Category:
General Business Applications

Computer:	**Media:**
AT&T PC 6300	Diskette

Language:
TenCORE Language Authoring System

Requirements:
256 KB RAM
Color graphics adapter
Color monitor

Support:
Warranty
Hotline number

Retail Price:
$398

Distributor:
KJ Software, Inc.
3420 East Shea Blvd., Suite 161
Phoenix, AZ 85028
Tel: (602) 953-1544

Description:

Achieving Financial Fitness teaches useful and easy to understand methods for gaining practical knowledge of personal money management. The program helps users manage debt, improve credit standing and evaluate retirement and insurance needs. Due to the confidential nature of the data collected in this program, the user must enter his/her password to gain access to the course. Job Aids included are a Five Planner, Calendar, Date Reminder and a Calculator. Five Year Planner helps organize the future by allowing the user to store information about personal goals for the next five years. It also helps plan steps necessary to attain those goals. Calendar is a perpetual calendar. The on line system allows the user to mark important dates in red and reminds of those dates days in advance. The user may permanently store traditional dates, such as birthdays, so they will be noted for future use. At any time, the user can print any page of the calendar as well as the lists of reminder dates. Date Reminder is used in conjunction with the Calendar. It reminds the user days in advance of significant dates. Calculator is designed to help perform routine arithmetic operations (addition, subtraction, multiplication and division) necessary in handling financial affairs.

Company:
KJ Software, Inc.

Product:
Conquering Stress

Category:
General Business Applications

Computer:	**Media:**
AT&T PC 6300	Diskette

Language:
TenCORE Authoring Language

Requirements:
256 KB RAM
Graphics card
Color monitor is recommended, but not required

Support:
Warranty
Hotline number

Retail Price:
$398

Distributor:
KJ Software, Inc.
3420 East Shea Blvd., Suite 161
Phoenix, AZ 85028
Tel: (602) 953-1544

Description:

Conquering Stress, one of the programs in the *DAVID Noted Author Series*, guides users through the self-assessment and stress management techniques of stress expert, Dr. Ronald E. Barnes. The course includes a prescriptive test that identifies stressful situations at home, at work and during change; it then introduces techniques for managing these stressful situations. Job Aids included are a Five Year Planner and Calendar. The Five Year Planner helps to organize the user's future by storing information about personal goals for the next five years. It also presents techniques necessary to attain those goals. The Calendar provides a perpetual calendar for the next 20 years. The on-line system allows the marking of important upcoming dates in red and then reminds the user of those dates days in advance. The user may permanently store traditional dates, such as birthdays, so they will be noted for future years. At any time, any page of the calendar as well as the lists of reminder dates can be printed.

Company:
KJ Software, Inc.

Product:
Sharpening Your Executive Writing

Category:
General Business Applications

Computer:	**Media:**
AT&T PC 6300	Diskette

Language:
TenCORE Authoring Language

Requirements:
256 KB RAM
Graphics card
Color monitor is recommended, but not required

Support:
Warranty
Hotline number

Retail Price:
$398

Distributor:
KJ Software, Inc.
3420 East Shea Blvd., Suite 161
Phoenix, AZ 85028
Tel: (602) 953-1544

Description:

Sharpening Your Executive Writing, one of the programs in the *DAVID Noted Author Series*, is based on the works of Dianna Booher. This program helps executives learn and retain critical business writing skills. The program's goal is to make the executive an effective and convincing writer. The Writing Helper Job Aid which is included in this program can improve a writer's technique in such areas as outlining messages, developing and editing a first draft, and tailoring communications to specific audiences.

Company:
KJ Software, Inc.

Product:
Strengthening Your Leadership Savvy

Category:
General Business Applications

Computer:	**Media:**
AT&T PC 6300	Diskette

Language:
TenCORE Authoring Language

Requirements:
256 KB RAM
Graphics card
Color monitor is recommended, but not required

Support:
Warranty
Hotline number

Retail Price:
$398

Distributor:
KJ Software, Inc.
3420 East Shea Blvd., Suite 161
Phoenix, AZ 85028
Tel: (602) 953-1544

Description:

Strengthening Your Leadership Savvy, one of the programs in the *DAVID Noted Author Series*, is based on the works of Matthew Culligan, Suzanne Deakins and Arthur Young. This personalized program develops managers into more effective leaders. By interacting with the course material and answering the questions the program asks, users learn to assess and improve their management skills. A few of the topics covered in this program are creative listening, decision making, time management, delegation, goal setting and understanding body language. Job Aids included in this course are Calendar, Card File, Scheduling and Delegation. The Calendar provides a perpetual calendar for the next 20 years. The on-line system allows the marking of important upcoming dates in red and then reminds the user of those dates days in advance. Users may permanently store traditional dates, such as birthdays, so they will be noted for future years. At any time the user can print any page of the calendar as well as the lists of reminder dates. The Card File allows the creation of four files for business management including information on customer contacts, peer contacts or employees. The user can store this information, review it or edit it as needed. Scheduling provides a means of balancing the time available with personal tasks. This aid can analyze word load by storing weekly information and manipulating time demands. Delegation helps choose the right employee for a given task. It compares a list of personal characteristics to the requirements of the job and generates a list of the most qualified people.

Company:
Management Support Technology, Inc.

Product:
Expert Advisor

Category:
General Business Applications

Computer:
AT&T PC 6300

Media:
Diskette

Language:
PASCAL

Requirements:
128 KB RAM
2 disk drives or hard disk/one floppy

Support:
Customer service phone number (303) 860-1515

Retail Price:
$249

Distributor:
Management Support Technology, Inc.
1560 Broadway, Suite 755
Denver, CO 80202
Tel: (303) 860-1515

Description:

The *Expert Advisor* is a unique software program in the *MASTER WORKS* series designed for the microcomputer to assess the individual manager's work unit and alert him or her to potential problems. Updated regularly by the manager, it maps ongoing trends and provides suggestions for action which are relevant to the manager's specific situation.

Expert Advisor is tailored to the manager's organization. By initially "interviewing" the manager, the program gathers a large amount of information on the manager's organization and the issues confronting it. Information about the organization is modeled in a coherent, dynamic picture. This information is updated during short weekly sessions to identify changes in the organization and to help anticipate patterns which could be destructive or beneficial to the organization. *Expert Advisor* takes full advantage of the Total Model of organizations and puts the benefits into the individual manager's hands.

The *Expert Advisor* gathers information about changes in the organization as they occur. The *Expert Advisor* acts as a planner within the organization as it identifies trends and evaluates approaches to such trends while assessing how well the organization is functioning.

In addition, the *Expert Advisor* assists the manager in responding to destructive trends it has identified. The *Expert Advisor* provides guidelines to help the manager formulate realistic courses of action in view of anticipated trends, and simultaneously provides insight into the possible effects of such actions on the organization.

Company:
Management Support Technology, Inc.

Product:
Expert Manager

Category:
General Business Applications

Computer:	**Media:**
AT&T PC 6300	Diskette
6300 PLUS **AT&T PC 6300 PLUS**	

Language:
PASCAL

Requirements:
256 KB RAM
2 floppy disk drives or hard disk/floppy drive

Support:
Customer service support number (303) 860-1515

Retail Price:
$249

Distributor:
Management Support Technology, Inc.
1560 Broadway, Suite 755
Denver, CO 80202
Tel: (303) 860-1515

Description:

The *MASTER WORKS* series is a family of artificial intelligence software programs designed as "experts on a disk" for use by managers with their microcomputers. Like a consultant, these products interact with the user in a flexible, responsive way to provide the knowledge of an expert. *MASTER WORKS* is based on a revolutionary software technology that combines the latest in psychology and computer science.

The first product in the *MASTER WORKS* family is an expert in management skills, called *Expert Manager*. Topics covered by this product include: motivating, delegation, improving productivity, interviewing a prospective employee, monitoring and controlling performance, developing subordinates, coaching performance, constructive competition, establishing mission, counseling about performance problems, performance review, getting cooperation or collaboration, increasing job satisfaction, and getting new employees on board and up to speed.

As a computerized management consulting tool, *Expert Manager* is a source of information, an assistant to the manager, and an analysis device. *Expert Manager* guides the manager to sound decisions by helping him think through specific problems, especially in areas where he has little experience or knowledge.

Expert Manager provides the manager with a base of knowledge for solving problems, receiving guidance, and exploring courses of action on the job. It assists the manager in areas where he may lack knowledge and offers a patient, objective "expert" with whom the manager can work on management problems.

Company:
Micro-Tel, Inc.

Product:
MICROCALL-B Version 3.1

Category:
General Business Applications

Computer:	**Media:**
AT&T PC 6300 **AT&T PC 6300 PLUS**	Diskette

6300 PLUS

Language:
Compiled BASIC

Requirements:
256 KB RAM
Floppy disk
10 MB hard disk
RS-232 port
Printer

Support:
90-day warranty
Out-of-warranty repairs at $300 including a new 90-day warranty
Manual has tutorial section for user training

Retail Price:
$895–$3,295

Distributor:
Micro-Tel, Inc.
6075 The Corners Pkwy., Suite 109
Norcross, GA 30092
Tel: (404) 447-5408

Description:

MICROCALL is a call accounting software system that runs on the AT&T PC 6300 computer. It includes DDD, OUTWATS, INWATS, and INTERNATIONAL Rates Tables. The user may update these tables or purchase an update from MTI for $200.

Company:
MoneyCare, Inc.

Product:
***Financial Navigator* Version 1.0**

Category:
General Business Applications

Computer:	**Media:**
AT&T PC 6300	Diskette

Language:
Compiler Basic

Requirements:
128 KB RAM minimum

Support:
Free technical support via 800 numbers
90-day media warranty

Retail Price:
$295

Distributor:
MoneyCare, Inc.
253 Martens Ave.
Mountain View, CA 94040
Tel: (800) 824-9827 (National)
(800) 423-5248 (California)

Description:

The *Financial Navigator* is the first personal accounting system for people who are serious about their finances. Combining the financial integrity of a full double entry bookkeeping system with the flexibility of a database management system, the *Financial Navigator* offers comprehensive financial management capabilities. This system can be used to track all financial transactions or balances entered periodically to update the user's financial situation. Either way, the *Financial Navigator* will organize data so that the user may make better, more timely decisions and will provide professional caliber reports for use with advisors. Features include:

- On-line help screen and active function key displays
- Prepared or selected personal chart of accounts
- Additional accounts created on the fly
- Multiple distribution of transactions
- Automatic tracking of principal and interest on loans
- Automatic entries for payments or receipts
- Separate novice and expert modes of operation
- Detailed tracking of all investment types
- Over 40 reports including transaction registers, balance sheets, income statements, tax summaries investment analysis, and budget versus actual
- Creation of *DIF* files for use with spreadsheets and other programs
- Password protection of data
- Full budgeting and check printing capabilities
- Payee/payer organization, tracking, and reporting
- Demonstration data for fast and easy familiarization with the system
- Free Guide to Personal Finance

The *Financial Navigator* was designed by a team of financial professionals with many years of experience in accounting, financial planning, and investment advisory services.

Company:
Morgan Computing Company, Inc.

Product:
EasyGantt

Category:
General Business Applications

Computer:	**Media:**
AT&T PC 6300 **AT&T PC 6300 PLUS**	Diskette

6300 PLUS

Language:
Compiled BASIC

Requirements:
128 KB RAM

Support:
Technical support for registered users

Retail Price:
$49

Distributor:
Morgan Computing Company, Inc.
P.O. Box 112730
Carrollton, TX 75006
Tel: (214) 245-4763

Description:

An excellent tool for project planning using the well-known critical path method (CPM). Completely menu-driven, *EasyGantt* prompts the user in setting up projects with up to 3,000 activities while prioritizing the sequence of steps to be accomplished. The program has complete editing capabilities, which include renaming, changing time required, deleting old entries, and adding new ones. It even allows the user to update a project while it is under way and recalculate the schedule. *EasyGantt* will project the time to complete the project while charting the "critical path" and producing a time schedule (Gantt) chart.

Company:
Northwest Analytical, Inc.

Product:
NWA STATPAK

Category:
General Business Applications

Computer:
AT&T PC 6300

Media:
Diskette

Language:
MS-BASIC

Requirements:
64 KB RAM
Dual disk system

Support:
Warranty
Telephone support (503) 224-7727
Updates

Retail Price:
$495

Distributor:
Northwest Analytical, Inc.
520 N.W. Davis St.
Portland, OR 97209
Tel: (503) 224-7727

Description:

NWA STATPAK is a multifunction statistics package with extensive data management and manipulation capabilities. Interfaces with other software packages such as spreadsheets, databases, word processors, etc.

Company:
Online Financial

Product:
Platform Automation

Category:
General Business Applications

Computer:
AT&T PC 6300

Media:
Diskette

Language:
Assembler

Requirements:
64 KB RAM
132-column printer

Support:
Warranty
Training
One time set-up fee, $9,995—includes 5 day training, set up a user-site
8 percent maintenance fee

Retail Price:
$495 New Accounts
$495 Mortgage Payoff System
$450 Communication Emulator

Distributor:
Online Financial
400 Parameter Center Terrace,
Suite 500
Atlanta, GA 30346
Tel: (404) 396-1796

Online Financial is an authorized Value Added Reseller for AT&T Computers.

Description:

Online Financial has developed a new accounts processing system that is comprised of three steps:

- Inputting data required for new accounts
- Printing the appropriate forms
- Transmitting the required data to the host computer

SYSTEM ONE provides the customer with on-line Accounts Processing that is extremely user-friendly and requires minimal installation and training time.

NEW ACCOUNTS

When a customer wishes to open a new account, the system will display the information needed to set up the account. The system will prompt the new accounts counselor for the data required for the account type being opened.

After the new account information has been entered, any needed forms can then be printed before transmission occurs to the host computer.

After the applicable forms have been printed and the customer has verified name, address, and the customer signature has been obtained, the on-line set-up can begin.

EXISTING ACCOUNTS

Existing account information can be obtained from the host computer through the Inquiry and Maintenance functions.

Information may be extracted from existing accounts to aid in the set-up of new accounts.

For instance, if a customer wants to open a new CD account and already has a checking account at an institution, the use of the extract will, by inquiring to the host computer, display data fields such as name, address, social security number, and others. In addition to saving time, this function also helps to minimize errors. "Most used" menus for inquiry and maintenance are displayed.

TELLER FUNCTIONS

The systems also provides a start/end of day procedure to open a terminal and teller at the beginning of the day, and to close the terminal and teller at the end of the day. It also provides a totals function if applicable.

A Capture/Re-entry feature is provided to store information on a disk for future transmission to the host or to retain for recall later, if the user gets interrupted during account processing (i.e., if communications is not available).

A status line is provided, as the last line of the screen, displaying institution name, branch number, terminal number, teller number, date, and time of day.

Company:
Open Systems, Inc.

Product:
Accounts Payable Version 2.31

Category:
General Business Applications

Computer:	**Media:**
AT&T PC 6300 6300 PLUS **AT&T PC 6300 PLUS**	Diskette

Language:
Business BASIC

Requirements:
128 KB RAM
132-character printer
Hard disk recommended
MS-DOS 2.0 or above

Support:
Available from Open Systems Client Support Service
Hotline available to registered users for additional charge (800) 582-5000
Free hotline for registered dealers (800) 641-2000
Training seminars are held regionally on a regular basis

Retail Price:
$695

Distributor:
Open Systems, Inc.
6477 City West Pkwy.
Eden Prairie, MN 55344
Tel: (612) 829-0011

Description:

Open Systems Accounts Payable is an interactive application that handles prepayments, partial payments, installments, and returns; offers an automatic hold option on open invoices; and processes both automatic and manual checks. Accounts Payable offers parameter selection on reports by vendor, job, phase, and expense distribution. Reports generated include: purchases journal, open invoice report, cash-flow report, vendor analysis report, and more. Multiple level password protection ensures data security.

Company:
Open Systems, Inc.

Product:
Accounts Receivable Version 2.41

Category:
General Business Applications

Computer:	**Media:**
AT&T PC 6300 6300 PLUS **AT&T PC 6300 PLUS**	Diskette

Language:
Business BASIC

Requirements:
128 KB RAM
132-character printer
Hard disk recommended
MS-DOS 2.0 or above

Support:
Available from the Open Systems Client Support Service
Hotline available to registered users for additional charge (800) 582-5000
Hotline for registered dealers, free (800) 641-2000
Training seminars are held regionally on a regular basis

Retail Price:
$695

Distributor:
Open Systems, Inc.
6477 City West Parkway
Eden Prairie, MN 55344
Tel: (612) 829-0011

Description:

Open Systems Accounts Receivable is an interactive application that produces timely invoices and statements, as well as detailed aging reports. The program maintains both open item and balance forward customers, and calculates finance charges and discounts from user-defined parameters. Sales history reporting by customer, salesperson, inventory item, product category, or invoice date emphasizes profitability for rating the true performance of a company's sales. Gross profit analysis summarizes daily profits. Other reports generated include: sales journal, miscellaneous credits journal, cash receipts journal, open invoice report, aged trial balance report, customer analysis report, and more. Multiple level password protection ensures data security.

Company:
Open Systems, Inc.

Product:
Fixed Assets

Category:
General Business Applications

Computer: **AT&T PC 6300**

Media: Diskette

Language:
Business BASIC

Requirements:
128 KB RAM
132-character printer
Hard disk recommended
MS-DOS 2.0 or above

Support:
Available from Open Systems Client Support Service
Hotline available to registered users for additional charge (800) 582-5000
Hotline for registered dealers, free (800) 641-2000
Training seminars are held regionally on a regular basis

Retail Price:
$695

Distributor:
Open Systems, Inc.
6477 City West Parkway
Eden Prairie, MN 55344
Tel: (612) 829-0011

Description:

Open Systems Fixed Assets is an interactive application that delivers complete capital investment control and reporting. Fixed Assets also offers detailed lease versus buy analyses to help users make better business decisions. Fixed Assets processes new, changed, and retired assets; delivers all information needed for computing capital gains and tax liabilities; and allows calculation of depreciation by accelerated cost recovery system, sum-of-years digits, straight-line method, declining balance, and no depreciation. In addition, *Open Systems* Fixed Assets permits tracking on three different books for general ledger accounting, tax reporting, and other reporting.

Company:
Open Systems, Inc.

Product:
General Ledger Version 2.21

Category:
General Business Applications

Computer:	**Media:**
AT&T PC 6300 **AT&T PC 6300 PLUS**	Diskette

6300 PLUS

Language:
Business BASIC

Requirements:
128 KB RAM
132-character printer
Hard disk recommended
MS-DOS 2.0 or above

Support:
Available from Open Systems Client Support Service
Hotline available to registered users for additional charge (800) 582-5000
Hotline for registered dealers, free (800) 641-7000
Training seminars are held regionally on a regular basis

Retail Price:
$695

Distributor:
Open Systems, Inc.
6477 City West Parkway
Eden Prairie, MN 55344
Tel: (612) 829-0011

Description:

Open Systems General Ledger is an interactive application with the added flexibility of user-customized financial statements. General Ledger maintains activity balances for 13 accounting periods and maintains this-year, last-year, and year-to-date budget figures and historical comparison for each account. The system consolidates General Ledger files for hierarchical department/division/company structures.

The General Ledger system accommodates 12-character alphanumeric account numbers and provides an automatic balancing control during data entry to ensure debit/credit balance. General Ledger provides automatic general journal posting from Accounts Receivable, Accounts Payable, Job Cost, Fixed Assets, and Payroll. The program generates many valuable reports, including general ledger journal report, general ledger and activity report, trial balance, income statement and balance sheet, and more. Multiple level password protection ensures data security.

Company:
Open Systems, Inc.

Product:
Inventory

Category:
General Business Applications

Computer:
AT&T PC 6300

Media:
Diskette

Language:
Business BASIC

Requirements:
128 KB RAM
132-character printer
Hard disk recommended
MS-DOS 2.0 or above

Support:
Available from Open Systems Client Support Service
Hotline available to registered users for additional charge (800) 582-5000
Hotline for registered dealers, free (800) 641-2000
Training seminars are held regionally on a regular basis

Retail Price:
$695

Distributor:
Open Systems, Inc.
6477 City West Parkway
Eden Prairie, MN 55344
Tel: (612) 829-0011

Description:

Open Systems Inventory is an interactive application that delivers improved market response and stock control. Inventory offers the flexibility of valuation by FIFO, LIFO, and average cost. An automatic alert reporting feature prevents lost sales due to stock outages and automatically calculates reorder quantities and reorder costs. The system allows multiple pricing structures and maintains on-hand, on-order, and committed balances.

The system allows on-line updates of Inventory items via the Sales Order Processing, Accounts Receivable, and Accounts Payable modules. Inventory offers parameter selection on reports by item, product category, and activity level, and generates many valuable reports, including a status report, alert report, and more. Multiple level password protection ensures data security.

Company:
Open Systems, Inc.

Product:
Job Cost

Category:
General Business Applications

Computer:
AT&T PC 6300

Media:
Diskette

Language:
Business BASIC

Requirements:
128 KB RAM
132-character printer
Hard disk recommended
MS-DOS 2.0 or above

Support:
Available from Open Systems Client Support Service
Hotline available to registered users for additional charge (800) 582-5000
Hotline for registered dealers, free (800) 641-2000
Training seminars are held regionally on a regular basis

Retail Price:
$695

Distributor:
Open Systems, Inc.
6477 City West Parkway
Eden Prairie, MN 55344
Tel: (612) 829-0011

Description:

Open Systems Job Cost is an interactive, single- or multiuser application that automatically records costs and revenues as other data is processed, and produces complete variance analyses against estimates by cost center. Job Cost provides accounting of estimated and actual costs by job and by job phase. The system provides optional interfaces with Accounts Payable automatically posts material, labor, and equipment charges to jobs and phases from invoices and material requisitions; posts revenue to jobs and phases from Accounts Receivable; posts labor hours and labor costs to jobs and phases from payroll; and creates overhead, finished goods, and work-in-process entries for posting to General Ledger.

Job Cost automatically allocates overhead based on labor costs, labor dollars, or material costs and provides for warranty accounting as a separate phase of each job.

The system provides parameter selection on reports by job, phase, and manager and generates many valuable reports, including a jobs listing, a job detail report, job profitability report, billing summary report, and more.

Multiple level password protection ensures data security.

Company:
Open Systems, Inc.

Product:
Payroll

Category:
General Business Applications

Computer:	**Media:**
AT&T PC 6300	Diskette

Language:
Business BASIC

Requirements:
128 KB RAM
132-character printer
Hard disk recommended
MS-DOS 2.0 or above

Support:
Available from Open Systems Client Support Service
Hotline available to registered users for additional charge (800) 582-5000
Hotline for registered dealers, free (800) 641-2000
Training seminars are held regionally on a regular basis

Retail Price:
$695

Distributor:
Open Systems, Inc.
6477 City West Parkway
Eden Prairie, MN 55344
Tel: (612) 829-0011

Description:

Open Systems Payroll is an interactive, single- or multiuser application that delivers comprehensive paycheck and expense control. Payroll allows the user to easily meet all government reporting requirements.

Payroll offers processing of payroll for regular, overtime, and doubletime for hourly employees; salary pay for salaried employees; piecework; tips; sick days and vacation days; six standard and five miscellaneous deductions; five taxable and/or nontaxable other pays; option for fixed federal, state, and local withholding; multiple rates and states.

The system provides processing of payroll input and reports by multiple companies, divisions, or groups. Payroll provides a General Ledger interface for posting labor cost data and payday liabilities and a Job Cost interface with labor input by job, department, and expense class.

Open Systems Payroll generates many valuable reports, including withholding report, department report, quarterly unemployment report, quarterly withholding report, sick leave and vacation report, and more.

The program prints automatic and manual checks, W-2s, employee lists, and mailing labels.

Multiple level password protection ensures data security.

Company:
Open Systems, Inc.

Product:
Purchase Order Processing

Category:
General Business Applications

Computer:
AT&T PC 6300

Media:
Diskette

Language:
Business BASIC

Requirements:
128 KB RAM
132-character printer
Hard disk recommended
MS-DOS 2.0 or above

Support:
Available from Open Systems Client Support Service
Hotline available to registered users for additional charge (800) 582-5000
Hotline for registered dealers, free (800) 641-2000
Training seminars are held regionally on a regular basis

Retail Price:
$695

Distributor:

Open Systems, Inc.
6477 City West Parkway
Eden Prairie, MN 55344
Tel: (612) 829-0011

Description:

Open Systems Purchase Order Processing is an interactive, single- or multiuser application that automatically processes new orders, received orders, and invoiced orders and handles order changes, cancellations, and returns.

Purchase Order Processing provides an optional Inventory interface for on-line updates of on-order and on-hand quantities, as well as costing statistics.

The system provides an optional General Ledger interface for unlimited expense distribution and an interface for posting invoiced orders and processing payments to vendors, in addition to analyzing cash requirements and vendor activity. An interface to Job Cost permits automatic updates of material, equipment, labor, overhead, and other costs by job and phase.

Purchase Order Processing allows parameter selection on reports by vendor, inventory item, and expense distribution. Reports generated include an open order report, purchases journal, and miscellaneous debits journal. Multiple level password protection ensures data security.

Company:
Open Systems, Inc.

Product:
Report Writer

Category:
General Business Applications

Computer: AT&T PC 6300

Media: Diskette

Language:
Business BASIC

Requirements:
128 KB RAM
132-character printer
Hard disk recommended
MS-DOS 2.0 or above

Support:
Available from Open Systems Client Support Service
Hotline available to registered users for additional charge (800) 582-5000
Hotline for registered dealers, free (800) 641-2000
Training seminars are held regionally on a regular basis

Retail Price:
$695

Distributor:
Open Systems, Inc.
6477 City West Parkway
Eden Prairie, MN 55344
Tel: (612) 829-0011

Description:

Open Systems Report Writer allows the user to easily generate a virtually limitless number of custom-designed reports using data from any of the Open Systems accounting applications. A data dictionary of over 900 elements permits a broad range of reports, which can be printed to the terminal, screen, or printer. In addition to its sophisticated report-generation capabilities, *Open Systems* Report Writer is a versatile data formatter. Through a simple menu selection process, accounting data can be reformatted to DIF/SDI, SYLK, and ASCII formats for interfaces with the most popular word processing, spreadsheet, and productivity packages.

Company:
Open Systems, Inc.

Product:
Sales Order Processing

Category:
General Business Applications

Computer:	**Media:**
AT&T PC 6300	Diskette

Language:
Business BASIC

Requirements:
128 KB RAM
132-character printer
Hard disk recommended
MS-DOS 2.0 or above

Support:
Available from Open Systems Client Support Service
Hotline available to registered users for additional charge (800) 582-5000
Hotline for registered dealers, free (800) 641-2000
Training seminars are held regionally on a regular basis

Retail Price:
$695

Distributor:

Open Systems, Inc.
6477 City West Parkway
Eden Prairie, MN 55344
Tel: (612) 829-0011

Description:

Open Systems Sales Order Processing is an interactive, single- or multiuser application that automatically processes sales orders from entry through packing, verification, and invoicing–including back orders and returned goods. Sales Order Processing prints packing slips, invoices, and credit memos and includes the option to print an invoice at the time an order is shipped. Sales Order Processing interfaces with Accounts Receivable for posting and tracking invoiced orders and offers optional additional interfaces with General Ledger, Job Cost, and Inventory. The General Ledger interface permits automatic posting of sales, credit, and cash receipt totals. The Job Cost interface allows input by job and phase for customer billing. The Inventory interface provides on-line updates of on-hand and committed quantities.

Company:
P2/i, Inc.

Product:
Periodical Filing System

Category:
General Business Applications

Computer:	**Media:**
AT&T PC 6300	Diskette

Language:
MAI Business BASIC/Micro (BB/M)

Requirements:
128 KB RAM
Runtime version of BB/M included

Support:
Phone-in support for dealers only (505) 822-8585
Product updates available
Dealer training available

Retail Price:
$195

Distributor:
P2/i, Inc.
A Division of Arinco Computer System
1704 Moon N.E., #7
Albuquerque, NM 87112
Tel: (505) 822-8585

P2/i, Inc. is an authorized Value Added Reseller for AT&T Computers.

Description:

P2/i's Periodical Filing System is designed to provide easy access to abstracts of articles or journals. It is geared to the needs of physicians, attorneys, and anyone else who must keep track of large volumes of periodical data. The system not only provides title and author information, but also allows for the entry of comments to indicate where the article is filed.

Company:

Procom Leasing & Management Corp.

Product:

Business Accounting & Management Information System (BAMIS)

Category:

General Business Applications

Computer:	**Media:**
AT&T PC 6300	Diskette

Language:

RM/COBOL

Requirements:

16 or 32 bit hard disk (10 MB)
128 KB RAM

Support:

This product is fully supported by Procom Leasing & Management Corp. and carries a 90-day warranty on the media. Remote nationwide customer service hotline is provided Monday through Friday between the hours of 8:00 a.m. and 5:00 p.m. local time. Installations, additional hotline coverage and extended maintenance agreements are available.

Retail Price:

$795 per module, combo $4,595

Distributor:

Procom Leasing & Management Corp.
1250 Broadway, 19th Floor
New York, NY 10001
Tel: (212) 279-1717
(800) 626-9011

Procom Leasing & Management Corp. is an authorized Value Added Reseller for AT&T Computers.

Description:

BAMIS is a modular yet tightly integrated accounting system that provides accounts payable, accounts receivable, inventory control, payroll and sales order entry in a total real-time system integrated into a common general ledger system. It's hallmark is richness of function with total data and fiscal integrity.

New users are provided menu to field-level help facilities throughout the system with input options and consequences described in simple english language terms. All major files (customer, inventory, chart of accounts, employee, vendor) can be alphabetically queried avoiding transaction coding. Erroneous responses are acknowledged as "confusing" with "one moment please" type prompts also addressing the many human factors of system interaction. Learnability, usability and human factors in the system are exceptional. BAMIS can also be customized for nominal fees to address company unique processing or reporting requirements. Both cash receipts and disbursement processing provides for either open item, or balance forward transactions plus projections on cash flow in either module. Billing handles both merchandise and service transactions.

Multiple company capability with multiple departments within each provides extensive operations and fiscal report capabilities. Orders on hard goods automatically reserves relieves inventory plus posts to receivables on shipment. The payroll system is constantly maintained to reflect legislative and tax changes in any federal, state or local statute. Data set archive management is via traditional journals to avoid data file growth and the associated utility processing and data processing skills.

ACCOUNTS RECEIVABLE, INVOICING, and SALES ANALYSIS

The Accounts Receivable module is designed for small to medium sized business needing to automate their Accounts Receivable function. The system provides for billing and cash transaction entries, related file maintenance, transaction journals, and reports essential to managing this key business function.

PAYROLL

The Payroll System is designed to perform all payroll functions for small to medium sized companies. The system comes with built in withholding tax formulas for federal, state and all local municipalities that have withholding taxes. These formulas are kept up to date as part of the software subscription service.

(Continued on next page)

Description: ***(Continued)***

INVENTORY MANAGEMENT

The Inventory System is meant to keep track of high volume nonserialized goods or low volume serialized goods for small to medium sized businesses. Inventory back-order quantities, committed quantities, on-order quantities, and on-hand balances are maintained via a transaction entry routine. Commitments, back-order, and shipment quantities are updated automatically when the companion sales order/invoicing modules are employed.

ACCOUNTS PAYABLE

The Payable System enables maintenance of key vendor information, plus processing of new invoices, vendor and miscellaneous disbursement, with payables aging and projections capability. All disbursements are linked to disbursement accounts defined by users with income statement and balance sheet integration, when it is used with the General Ledger System.

GENERAL LEDGER

The General Ledger system is designed to function along with other accounting modules and maintain the General Ledger and General Journal for small to medium sized businesses. Posting from other modules is dones quickly and automatically within the system.

SALES ORDER

The Sales Order System is designed to work along with the Accounts Receivable and Inventory Management Systems to provide a comprehensive, fully integrated Sales Order processing system for small to medium sized businesses. Sales Order cannot be used without these other systems.

Company:
Quadratron Systems, Inc.

Product:
Q-DATE

Category:
General Business Applications

Computer:	**Media:**
AT&T PC 6300	Diskette

Language:
C

Requirements:
Any printer
Any terminal

Support:
User manuals
Reference guides
Demonstration guides
Quick reference cards
Installation guides
Hotline support (OEM's only)
Training (OEM's only)
On-line help (818) 789-8588

Retail Price:
$155

Distributor:
Essex Office Systems
333 North Fairfax St.
Alexandria, VA 22341
Tel: (703) 549-9240

Description:

Q-DATE is an electronic calendar/scheduler consisting of a monthly, weekly, and daily display. *Q-ONE* processor compatible function-keys allow the user to easily INSERT, MOVE, REPLACE, COPY, DELETE, and SEARCH for appointments. Calendars may be set up with private appointment passwords, and any appointment can issue an alarm.

Company:
RealWorld Corporation

Product:
***RealWorld* Accounts Payable**

Category:
General Business Applications

Computer:	**Media:**
AT&T PC 6300	Diskette

Language:
COBOL BINARY

Requirements:
128 KB RAM
256 KB RAM recommended
Hard disk recommended
132-column printer

Support:
Support subscriptions are available at all levels
Regional training seminars available
User's Manual included

Retail Price:
$695

Distributor:
RealWorld Corporation
Dover Rd.
Willow Hill Bldg.
Chichester, NH 03263
Tel: (603) 798-5700
(800) 255-1115

Description:

This is an accrual Accounts Payable system, designed for small businesses, which provides rapid access to and control of cash outflow data. It allows the user to define Accounts Payable aging periods and General Ledger accounts to which distributions can be made, as well as set the parameters of various reports to fit the specific individualized company needs.

Company:
RealWorld Corporation

Product:
***RealWorld* Accounts Receivable**

Category:
General Business Applications

Computer:	**Media:**
AT&T PC 6300	Diskette

Language:
COBOL BINARY

Requirements:
128 KB RAM
256 KB RAM recommended
Hard disk recommended
132-column printer

Support:
Support subscriptions are available at all levels
Regional training seminars available
User's Manual included

Retail Price:
$695

Distributor:

RealWorld Corporation
Dover Rd.
Willow Hill Bldg.
Chichester, NH 03263
Tel: (603) 798-5700
(800) 255-1115

Description:

This is an open item and balance forward Accounts Receivable system for small businesses. The liberal use of "user definable parameters" allows the system to be easily tailored to fit specific company needs.

Company:
RealWorld Corporation

Product:
***RealWorld* General Ledger**

Category:
General Business Applications

Computer:	**Media:**
AT&T PC 6300	Diskette

Language:
COBOL BINARY

Requirements:
128 KB RAM
256 KB RAM recommended
Hard disk recommended
132-column printer

Support:
Support subscriptions are available at all levels
Regional training seminars available
User's Manual included

Retail Price:
$695

Distributor:
RealWorld Corporation
Dover Rd.
Willow Hill Bldg.
Chichester, NH 03263
Tel: (603) 798-5700
(800) 255-1115

Description:

This is an extremely flexible General Ledger, designed for small businesses, which allows customer formatting of vital financial reports to assist in financial management.

Company:
RealWorld Corporation

Product:
***RealWorld* Inventory Control**

Category:
General Business Applications

Computer:
AT&T PC 6300

Media:
Diskette

Language:
COBOL BINARY

Requirements:
128 KB RAM
256 KB RAM recommended
Hard disk recommended
132-column printer

Support:
Support subscriptions are available at all levels
Regional training seminars available
User's Manual included

Retail Price:
$695

Distributor:
RealWorld Corporation
Dover Rd.
Willow Hill Bldg.
Chichester, NH 03263
Tel: (603) 798-5700
(800) 255-1115

Description:

This is a highly flexible multiwarehousing Inventory Control system, designed for small businesses, which provides efficient methods of tracking goods and products.

Company:
RealWorld Corporation

Product:
***RealWorld* Order Entry/Billing**

Category:
General Business Applications

Computer:
AT&T PC 6300

Media:
Diskette

Language:
COBOL BINARY

Requirements:
128 KB RAM
256 KB RAM recommended
Hard disk recommended
132-column printer

Support:
Support subscriptions are available at all levels
Regional training seminars available
User's Manual included

Retail Price:
$695

Distributor:
RealWorld Corporation
Dover Rd.
Willow Hill Bldg.
Chichester, NH 03263
Tel: (603) 798-5700
(800) 255-1115

Description:

This Order Entry system runs in conjunction with the *RealWorld* Accounts Receivable and Inventory Control systems. It provides both one-step and two-step billing procedures.

Company:
RealWorld Corporation

Product:
***RealWorld* Payroll**

Category:
General Business Applications

Computer:	**Media:**
AT&T PC 6300	Diskette

Language:
COBOL BINARY

Requirements:
128 KB RAM
256 KB RAM recommended
Hard disk recommended
132-column printer

Support:
Support subscriptions are available at all levels
Regional training seminars available
User's Manual included

Retail Price:
$695

Distributor:
RealWorld Corporation
Dover Rd.
Willow Hill Bldg.
Chichester, NH 03263
Tel: (603) 798-5700
(800) 255-1115

Description:

This is an hourly and salary payroll system, designed for small businesses, which allows complete payroll record maintenance and easy compliance with changing tax laws. It allows the user to set various system-wide parameters and determine and tailor the payroll to his particular business.

Company:
RealWorld Corporation

Product:
***RealWorld* Sales Analysis**

Category:
General Business Applications

Computer:	**Media:**
AT&T PC 6300	Diskette

Language:
COBOL BINARY

Requirements:
128 KB RAM
256 KB RAM recommended
Hard disk recommended
132-column printer
Accounts Receivable and Inventory Control Modules

Support:
Support subscriptions are available at all levels
Regional training seminars available
User's Manual included

Retail Price:
$695

Distributor:
RealWorld Corporation
Dover Rd.
Willow Hill Bldg.
Chichester, NH 03263
Tel: (603) 798-5700
(800) 255-1115

Description:

This Sales Analysis system locates specific areas of increasing or decreasing sales, and allows a close analysis of the various components vital to increase revenues. Data from this system assists in formulating marketing and sales strategies.

Company:
Red Wing Business Systems, Inc.

Product:
RW Accounts Payable System

Category:
General Business Applications

Computer:	**Media:**
AT&T PC 6300	Diskette

Language:
BASIC

Requirements:
Two disk drives
128 KB RAM
80-column printer (or a hard disk system)

Support:
A 30-day money-back guarantee is offered for all Red Wing Software. Free support is also offered to all licensed customers for the first year that they own the software package. Support is done through dealers and directly through Red Wing Business Systems. The documentation manual is complete and will help customers learn the package at their convenience.

Retail Price:
$250

Distributor:
Red Wing Business Systems, Inc.
610 Main St.
P.O. Box 19
Red Wing, MN 55066
Tel: (612) 388-1106

Description:

The Red Wing Accounts Payable System helps the user determine cash requirements. When the user knows the due date of all invoices, they can be paid on time to maintain a better credit rating. While any good system will track due dates, the Red Wing Accounts Payable system also lets the user track units, cost per unit, purchases from vendors and commodity history; it also checks and graphically displays past cost per unit by vendor or selected commodity. The system is easy to use and extremely flexible.

Company:
Red Wing Business Systems, Inc.

Product:
RW Accounts Receivable System

Category:
General Business Applications

Computer:	**Media:**
AT&T PC 6300	Diskette

Language:
BASIC

Requirements:
Two disk drives
128 KB RAM
80-column printer (or a hard disk system)

Support:
A 30-day money-back guarantee is offered for all Red Wing Software. Free support is also offered to all licensed customers for the first year that they own the software package. Support is done through dealers and directly through Red Wing Business Systems. The documentation manual is complete and will help customers learn the package at their convenience.

Retail Price:
$400

Distributor:
Red Wing Business Systems, Inc.
610 Main St.
P.O. Box 19
Red Wing, MN 55066
Tel: (612) 388-1106

Description:

The Red Wing Accounts Receivable System allows users to do invoicing and end-of-month processing, send overdue reminders, and more. It is easy to use, flexible, has error checking capabilities, and integrates with both the General Ledger and Business Inventory programs. It helps determine who is selling, what is selling, where it is selling, who is buying, who is buying what, and who is paying. It helps users sell more because they know what types of products are selling, thus, their inventory can be adjusted. Users will also know when money is coming in by printing a receivables report by due date or discount date.

Company:
Red Wing Business Systems, Inc.

Product:
RW Asset Depreciation System

Category:
General Business Applications

Computer:
AT&T PC 6300

Media:
Diskette

Language:
BASIC

Requirements:
Two disk drives
128 KB RAM
80-column printer (or a hard disk system)

Support:
A 30-day money-back guarantee is offered for all Red Wing Software. Free support is also offered to all licensed customers for the first year that they own the software package. Support is done through dealers and directly through Red Wing Business Systems. The documentation manual is complete and will help customers learn the package at their convenience.

Retail Price:
$495

Distributor:
Red Wing Business Systems, Inc.
610 Main St.
P.O. Box 19
Red Wing, MN 55066
Tel: (612) 388-1106

Description:

The Red Wing Asset Depreciation system provides a tremendous tool for planning depreciation deductions and after-tax cash flow. The system provides a complete list of all assets, including the book value, market value, depreciation method, purchase date, useful life, asset basis, depreciation taken and remaining, and investment tax credit. The system is easy to use and extremely flexible.

Company:
Red Wing Business Systems, Inc.

Product:
RW Business Inventory System

Category:
General Business Applications

Computer:	**Media:**
AT&T PC 6300	Diskette

Language:
BASIC

Requirements:
Two disk drives
128 KB RAM
80-column printer (or a hard disk system)

Support:
A 30-day money-back guarantee is offered for all Red Wing Software. Free support is also offered to all licensed customers for the first year that they own the software package. Support is done through dealers and directly through Red Wing Business Systems. The documentation manual is complete and will help customers learn the package at their convenience.

Retail Price:
$350

Distributor:

Red Wing Business Systems, Inc.
610 Main St.
P.O. Box 19
Red Wing, MN 55066
Tel: (612) 388-1106

Description:

The Red Wing Business Inventory System is designed to help the professional manager make sure there is adequate inventory to cover the reasonable needs of a business, yet not burden the business with the costs of maintaining an excessive inventory. The manager can select three options to value the inventory, use two forms of measurement, establish varying sales prices for a product, monitor inventory in multiple locations, select one of three methods for forecasting inventory needs, monitor purchase orders, track excess or obsolete inventory, and get sales history reports.

Company:
Red Wing Business Systems, Inc.

Product:
RW General Ledger

Category:
General Business Applications

Computer: AT&T PC 6300

Media: Diskette

Language:
BASIC

Requirements:
Two disk drives
128 KB RAM
80-column printer (or a hard disk system)

Support:
A 30-day money-back guarantee is offered for all Red Wing Software. Free support is also offered to all licensed customers for the first year that they own the software package. Support is done through dealers and directly through Red Wing Business Systems. The documentation manual is complete and will help customers learn the package at their convenience.

Retail Price:
$500

Distributor:
Red Wing Business Systems, Inc.
610 Main St.
P.O. Box 19
Red Wing, MN 55066
Tel: (612) 388-1106

Description:

The Red Wing General Ledger is an easy-to-use, flexible system. The program is designed for the experienced and novice computer user. The nonaccounting person is able to set up his or her own accounting system through the aid of extensive documentation and instructional aid. For the accounting person, the system allows the selection of various report styles, selection of account numbering system and naming flexibility, enterprise and partnership accounting, and it saves transactions for a year. With the Red Wing Financial Management System, the computer takes the boring, tedious work out of keeping accurate records. The Red Wing System provides the flexibility to produce the types of records the user needs.

Company:
Red Wing Business Systems, Inc.

Product:
RW Payroll System

Category:
General Business Applications

Computer:
AT&T PC 6300

Media:
Diskette

Language:
BASIC

Requirements:
2 disk drives (or a hard system)
128 KB RAM
80-column printer

Support:
A 30-day money-back guarantee is offered for all Red Wing Software. Free support is also offered to all licensed customers for the first year that they own the software package. Support is done through dealers and directly through Red Wing Business Systems. The documentation manual is complete and will help customers learn the package at their convenience.

Retail Price:
$300

Distributor:
Red Wing Business Systems, Inc.
610 Main St.
P.O. Box 19
Red Wing, MN 55066
Tel: (612) 388-1106

Description:

The Red Wing Payroll System helps users manage their most valuable assets...their people. Regardless of how employees are paid (piecework, hourly, salary, bonus, commission, tips), the Red Wing Payroll System calculates their pay quickly and efficiently. All the information needed to complete FICA, federal and state unemployment taxes, local taxes and Social Security taxes are available upon request. Red Wing's Payroll automatically calculates and completes W-2 forms. The Payroll system will automatically post to the Red Wing General Ledger system.

Company:
Softtran Corporation

Product:
***Software 16* Accounting (also sold as BAMIS)**

Category:
General Business Applications

Computer:	**Media:**
AT&T PC 6300	Diskette

Language:
RM/COBOL

Requirements:
20 MB disk
1 MB RAM
RM/COBOL Runtime

Support:
90-days free
Then $250 per year, per end-user
Hotline number 1-800-NEED-AID
Training and detailed sales support provided by BAMIS, an AT&T VAR

Retail Price:
$695

Distributor:

Procom Leasing and Management Corp.
1250 Broadway, 19th Floor
New York, NY 10001
Tel: (212) 279-1717
Tel: (800) 626-9011

Procom Leasing and Management Corp. is an authorized Value Added Reseller of AT&T Computers.

Description:

Software 16 is a high-end, fully integrated, multiuser accounting system suitable for small businesses and for small business units of large organizations. It consists of six modules: Accounts Receivable, Accounts Payable, Inventory, Sales Order, Payroll, and General Ledger. They may be purchased one at a time or all together.

The system is applicable as a general accounting system to both service and hard goods companies. The addition of the Sales Order module makes it into a vertical package for hard goods distribution companies.

Software 16 contains features that make it easy to learn and to use. These include:

- Function-specific help screens for everything a user has to do to run the system. Hitting the question-mark key, at any time, brings up a full screen of plain English help. Each help screen is indexed to the pages in the user manual where its particular topic is discussed. The help screens are removable and reloadable.
- Name queries for customers, vendors, inventory items, employees, and general ledger accounts. The need to remember codes and numbers is eliminated by this system.
- Entry screens resemble their real life counterparts. The invoice screen looks like an invoice, and the payroll entry screen looks like a payroll check stub. Windowing on entry screens makes error correction easy.
- Real time updates assure that each user has up to the minute information. Inventory items canceled from one sales order, for example, will instantly show up as available for other sales orders being entered at the same time.
- Record level locking allows multiple-users to perform the same functions at the same time. When a user tries to access a record which is locked, he is told not only which other user has the record, but which terminal the other user is on.
- All reports can be displayed on the screen as well as printed on the printer. Windowing allows users to view different portions of reports which are too wide or too long to be displayed in total. Headings remain fixed as the user uses the cursor keys and the mouse to move the screen around the report.

(Continued on next page)

Description: ***(Continued)***

Software 16 is feature-rich and flexible. Some examples:

- The inventory system can store up to four sets of quantity discounts for up to four classes of customers.
- The payroll module comes with built-in withholding tax formulas for Federal, state, and local taxes for every municipality that has a withholding tax in all 50 states. Updates are provided by Softtran as tax legislation changes.
- The accounts receivable aging report can be run for different aging periods defined by the user each time the report is run.
- The accounts payable system allows for unresolved expenses, which are resolved at the close of the month.
- The general journal system features a 140 character explanation for each journal entry. Up to 99 legged entries are permitted.

The system is available in source code as well as object code format. Customizations and enhancements are available from Softtran.

Company:
Software Models

Product:
Finance Projections

Category:
General Business Applications

Computer:
AT&T PC 6300

Media:
Diskette

Language:
ASCII Data Files

Requirements:
64 KB RAM
80/132-column printer
Spreadsheet programs: *VisiCalc*, *SuperCalc*, *Multiplan*, *Lotus 1-2-3*.

Support:
90-day warranty against defect
Telephone support (714) 338-5075

Retail Price:
$59.95

Distributor:
Software Models
23913 Bowl Rd.
P. O. Box 1029
Crestline, CA 92325
Tel: (714) 338-5075
A Division of Computer Associates International, Inc.

Description:

Finance Projections is a collection of spreadsheet templates designed for use by all businesses that need to submit some kind of cash budget projections for loans. It may also be used for periodic planning of a cash budget. The package will accomplish a Break-Even Sales Analysis, a Cash Budget, Pro-Forma Balance Sheet, Pro-Forma Income Statement, Depreciation tables ranging from 10 to 30 years, Financial Ratio Formulas, and Net Present Value. The templates may be printed to a line printer, creating forms which follow the S.B.A. requirements for submitting projections to potential lenders.

Company:
Software Models

Product:
Home Finance Management

Category:
General Business Applications

Computer:	**Media:**
AT&T PC 6300	Diskette

Language:
ASCII Data Files

Requirements:
64 KB RAM
80/132-column printer
Spreadsheet programs: *VisiCalc*, *SuperCalc*, *Multiplan*, *Lotus 1-2-3*

Support:
90-day warranty against defect
Telephone support (714) 338-5075

Retail Price:
$39.95

Distributor:
Software Models
23913 Bowl Rd.
P. O. Box 1029
Crestline, CA 92325
Tel: (714) 338-5075
A Division of Computer Associates International, Inc.

Description:

Home Finance Management is a collection of spreadsheet templates designed to aid in the managing of the family's budget. These templates help create a personal budget for the year, a shopping list, and determine what the monthly payments will be when purchasing a home. This package also helps to determine how much the family can save using an IRA savings account and create the totals needed on the IRS Schedule A form.

Company:
Summa Software Corporation

Product:
Trader's Accountant

Category:
General Business Applications

Computer:	**Media:**
AT&T PC 6300	Diskette

Language:
Compiled BASIC and Machine Code

Requirements:
192 KB RAM
Printer
Modem
Double-sided, double-density diskettes

Support:
Toll-free support line for registered owners
(800) 792-2211

Retail Price:
$249

Distributor:
Summa Software Corporation
7885 S.W. Cirrus Dr.
Beaverton, OR 97005
Tel: (503) 644-3212

Description:

The complete portfolio accounting system. Handles all types of transactions for all types of securities. Reports profit/loss, splits, margin/cash account balances, interest, fees, and tax data. Features a simulation mode. Updates prices manually, automatic download and from TDM.

Company:
Summa Software Corporation

Product:
Winning on Wall Street: The Complete System

Category:
General Business Applications

Computer:	**Media:**
AT&T PC 6300 6300 PLUS **AT&T PC 6300 PLUS**	Diskette

Language:
Compiled BASIC and Machine Code

Requirements:
192 KB RAM
Graphics printer
Modem
Double-sided, double density diskettes

Support:
Toll-free customer support line for registered owners (800) 792-2211

Retail Price:
$695

Distributor:
Summa Software Corporation
7885 S.W. Cirrus Dr.
Beaverton, OR 97005
Tel: (503) 644-3212

Description:

Fully integrated decision support software system for stock market investors and traders. Provides sophisticated data management, classical and proprietary technical analysis techniques, and complete portfolio accounting.

Company:
SuperSoft, Inc.

Product:
Investment Taxpac

Category:
General Business Applications

Computer:
AT&T PC 6300

Media:
Diskette

Language:
BASIC

Requirements:
128 KB RAM
One disk drive
Printer

Support:
Phone support
Update notification

Retail Price:
$200

Distributor:
SuperSoft, Inc.
P.O. Box 1628
Champaign, IL 61820
Tel: (217) 359-2112

Description:

Investment Taxpac provides a quick and easy way to organize your investments while maintaining pertinent tax information . You can enter your investment transactions, update market values, produce investment reports, and organize tax records. It is ideal for the private investor, and it's tax deductible.

Company:
SuperSoft, Inc.

Product:
Optimizer

Category:
General Business Applications

Computer:
AT&T PC 6300

Media:
Diskette

Language:
BASIC

Requirements:
128 KB RAM
One disk drive

Support:
Phone support
Update notification

Retail Price:
$200

Distributor:
SuperSoft, Inc.
P.O. Box 1628
Champaign, IL 61820
Tel: (217) 359-2112

Description:

Through the power of linear programming the Optimizer provides you with the "optimal" solution to those complex business problems. By inputting your business's objectives and constraints into this straightforward, menu-driven program, you will be giving the Optimizer all the information it needs to provide you with the most cost effective, revenue intensive way to run your business.

Wouldn't you like to know the optimal price for your products, how to maximize employee efficiency, or how to schedule production to increase profits? With the Optimizer you get accurate answers to the questions that mean the most to your bottom line.

Company:
Thoughtware, Inc.

Product:
Trigger

Category:
General Business Applications

Computer:	**Media:**
AT&T PC 6300	Diskette
6300 PLUS **AT&T PC 6300 PLUS**	

Language:
Thoughtware Proprietary Language derived from BASIC

Requirements:
128 KB RAM
Dual disk drives or one drive and a hard disk

Support:
Introduction, how-to, and reference manual; disk-based tutorial; help screens; case studies; and application recommendations.

A separate training program, Managing by Exception, is packaged with *Trigger* to provide background in the management principles on which the program is based.
Tel: 1-800-THT-WARE/305-854-2318

Retail Price:
$495

Distributor:
Thoughtware, Inc.
2699 South Bayshore Drive
Coconut Grove, FL 33133
Tel: (305) 854-2318

Description:

Trigger is business software to help managers focus on the areas of their operations that contribute the most to profitability. *Trigger* monitors key performance areas, identifies exceptions to performance guidelines, and then issues action memos, which identify the problem, its probable causes, and the action to be taken to remedy it.

Company:
Timberline Systems, Inc.

Product:
***MEDALLION*/Accounts Payable**

Category:
General Business Applications

Computer:	**Media:**
AT&T PC 6300	Diskette

Language:
C

Requirements:
512 KB RAM
Printer
MS-DOS 3.1 or greater
Fixed disk
Serial port

Support:
Telephone support is available from Timberline under a support agreement. This is a fee-based service that can be purchased per call or by annual subscription. Call Timberline for current rates.

Training classes are optional and are offered in six regional training centers. Call Timberline for a current class schedule.

Upgrades/enhancements are available to all end-users who send in their program registration cards. When new versions are available, registered users may purchase them for a nominal fee.

Retail Price:
$990

Distributor:

Timberline Systems, Inc.
7180 S.W. Fir Loop
Portland, OR 97223
Tel: (503) 644-8155

Timberline Systems, Inc. is an authorized Value Added Reseller for AT&T Computers.

Description:

The accounts payable software is a part of the *MEDALLION* Collection of accounting modules from Timberline Systems and can operate either as a stand-alone module or integrated with other *MEDALLION* accounting programs. The software is designed for the first-time user and is easy to install and use. A concept known as "layered functionality" enables *MEDALLION* Accounts Payable to grow along with the needs of the user by exposing greater power and functionality as it is required in each individual user environment. This feature provides for longer product life and makes it possible for the software to appeal to a broad number of users.

The accounts payable module brings a whole new level of control over cash flow and the management of payments to vendor. Some of the features of accounts payable include:

- The capture of invoices and direct payments in a quick and easy manner that begins a process of improved cash management
- The selection of invoices for payment by due date, vendor code, or several other choices
- Easy processing of common exceptions such as one-time-only vendors and manual checks
- The provision for processing of partial payments of selected invoices
- Automatic distribution of accounting entries for the general ledger
- Printing of checks with easy-to-read vouchers

Complete accounting control is provided through the use of audit trails and optional password security over files.

The software comes with easy-to-read documentation and a tutorial with sample problems to simplify learning and installation of the accounts payable.

Company:
Timberline Systems, Inc.

Product:
***MEDALLION*/Accounts Receivable**

Category:
General Business Applications

Computer:
AT&T PC 6300

Media:
Diskette

Language:
C

Requirements:
512 KB RAM
Printer
Fixed disk
Serial port
MS-DOS 3.1 or greater

Support:
Telephone support is available from Timberline under a support agreement. This is a fee-based service that can be purchased per call or by annual subscription. Call Timberline for current rates.

Training classes are optional and are offered in six regional training centers. Call Timberline for a current class schedule.

Upgrades/enhancements are available to all end users who send in their program registration cards. When new versions are available, registered users may purchase them for a nominal fee.

Retail Price:
$990

Distributor:

Timberline Systems, Inc.
7180 S.W. Fir Loop
Portland, OR 97223
Tel: (503) 644-8155

Timberline Systems, Inc. is an authorized Value Added Reseller for AT&T Computers.

Description:

The accounts receivable software is a part of the *MEDALLION* Collection of accounting modules from Timberline Systems and can operate either as a stand-alone module or integrated with other *MEDALLION* accounting programs. The software is designed for the first-time user and is easy to install and use. A concept known as "layered functionality" enables *MEDALLION*/Accounts Receivable to grow along with the needs of the user by exposing greater power and functionality as it is required in each individual user environment. This feature provides for longer product life and makes it possible for the software to appeal to a broad number of users.

The accounts receivable module makes it possible to record charges, credits, and payments with a minimum of effort so that all customer accounts can be easily kept up-to-date. Professional-looking statements are regularly prepared at the time chosen by the user. Comprehensive reporting makes it possible to tell at a glance which accounts are overdue and how long they have gone unpaid. Credit management is simplified and the provision to charge and account for finance charges allows for a more thorough and timely management of receivables. Some of the features of accounts receivable include:

- The capture of charges and payments in a quick and easy manner that begins a process of improved billing and cash management
- A provision for open item and balance forward processing
- Variable aging periods and credit profile information
- The provision for processing of partial payments and printing of "past due" notices
- Automatic distribution of accounting entries for the general ledger
- Printing of a variety of reports including a sales report and the necessary interface to inventory

Complete accounting control is provided through the use of audit trails and optional password security over files.

The software comes with easy-to-read documentation and a tutorial with sample problems to simplify learning and installation of the accounts receivable module.

Company:
Timberline Systems, Inc.

Product:
***MEDALLION*/General Ledger**

Category:
General Business Applications

Computer:	**Media:**
AT&T PC 6300	Diskette

Language:
C

Requirements:
512 KB RAM
Printer
Fixed disk
Serial port
MS-DOS 3.1 or greater

Support:
Telephone support is available from Timberline under a support agreement. This is a fee-based service that can be purchased per call or by annual subscription. Call Timberline for current rates.

Training classes are optional and are offered in six regional training centers. Call Timberline for a current class schedule.

Upgrades/enhancements are available to all end users who send in their program registration cards. When new versions are available, registered users may purchase them for a nominal fee.

Retail Price:
$990

Distributor:

Timberline Systems, Inc.
7180 S.W. Fir Loop
Portland, OR 97223
Tel: (503) 644-8155

Timberline Systems, Inc. is an authorized Value Added Reseller for AT&T Computers.

Description:

The general ledger is a part of the *MEDALLION* Collection of accounting modules from Timberline Systems and can operate either as a standalone module or integrated with other *MEDALLION* accounting programs. The software is designed for the first-time user and is easy to install and use. A concept known as "layered functionality" enables *MEDALLION*/General Ledger to grow along with the needs of the user by exposing greater power and functionality as it is required in each individual user environment. This feature provides for longer product life and makes it possible for the software to appeal to a broad number of users.

MEDALLION/General Ledger produces the appropriate accounting reports on demand and is able to support either 12- or 13- period accounting. Complete accounting control is provided through the use of audit trails and optional password security over files.

Both standard reports and user-defined reports can be created by the system. Some of the standard reports include: trial balance, working trial balance, year-to-date ledger, depreciation schedule, and current ledger. The income statement, statement of changes in financial position, and balance sheet can be user-adjusted to reflect the format and comparisons desired by the end user.

The software comes with easy-to-read documentation and a tutorial with sample problems to simplify learning and installation of the general ledger.

Company:
Timberline Systems, Inc.

Product:
***MEDALLION*/Inventory**

Category:
General Business Applications

Computer:	**Media:**
AT&T PC 6300	Diskette

Language:
C

Requirements:
512 KB RAM
Printer
MS-DOS 3.1 or greater
Fixed disk
Serial port

Support:
Telephone support is available from Timberline under a support agreement. This is a fee-based service that can be purchased per call or by annual subscription. Call Timberline for current rates.

Training classes are optional and are offered in six regional training centers. Call Timberline for a current class schedule.

Upgrades/enhancements are available to all end users who send in their program registration cards. When new versions are available, registered users may purchase them for a nominal fee.

Retail Price:
$990

Distributor:

Timberline Systems, Inc.
7180 S. W. Fir Loop
Portland, OR 97223
Tel: (503) 644-8155

Timberline Systems, Inc. is an authorized Value Added Reseller for AT&T Computers.

Description:

The inventory software is a part of the *MEDALLION* Collection of accounting modules from Timberline Systems and can operate either as a standalone module or integrated with other *MEDALLION* accounting programs. The software is designed for the first-time user and is easy to install and use. A concept known as "layered functionality" enables *MEDALLION*/Inventory to grow along with the needs of the user by exposing greater power and functionality as it is required in each individual user environment. This feature provides for longer product life and makes it possible for the software to appeal to a broad number of users.

The inventory module is specifically designed for the wholesale/retail and construction accounting environment. The software provides for five costing methods: average cost, last cost, LIFO, FIFO, and "pooled." Each stock item can have up to four prices which can be easily changed at any time. On-line stock inquiry is provided by: stock description, unit of measure, quantity on hand, reserve, back order, and prices. The inventory module provides for transfers, returns and adjustment of stock items. Alternate stock items may be assigned, and up to 100 locations can be defined.

A variety of built-in reports are provided to aid in efficient inventory management, and invoices may be printed on plain paper or preprinted forms.

Complete accounting control is provided through the use of audit trails and optional password security over files.

The software comes with easy-to-read documentation and a tutorial with sample problems to simplify learning and installation of the inventory module.

Company:
Timberline Systems, Inc.

Product:
***MEDALLION*/Payroll**

Category:
General Business Applications

Computer:	**Media:**
AT&T PC 6300	Diskette

Language:
C

Requirements:
512 KB RAM
Printer
MS-DOS 3.1 or greater
Fixed disk
Serial port

Support:
Telephone support is available from Timberline under a support agreement. This is a fee-based service that can be purchased per call or by annual subscription. Call Timberline for current rates.

Training classes are optional and are offered in six regional training centers. Call Timberline for a current class schedule.

Upgrades/enhancements are available to all end users who send in their program registration cards. When new versions are available, registered users may purchase them for a nominal fee.

Retail Price:
$990

Distributor:
Timberline Systems, Inc.
7180 S.W. Fir Loop
Portland, OR 97223
Tel: (503) 644-8155

Timberline Systems, Inc. is an authorized Value Added Reseller for AT&T Computers.

Description:

The payroll software is a part of the *MEDALLION* Collection of accounting modules from Timberline Systems and can operate either as a standalone module or integrated with other *MEDALLION* accounting programs. The software is designed for the first-time user and is easy to install and use. A concept known as "layered functionality" enables *MEDALLION*/Payroll to grow along with the needs of the user by exposing greater power and functionality as it is required in each individual user environment. This feature provides for longer product life and makes it possible for the software to appeal to a broad number of users.

The payroll module provides for a totally automated processing of checks, tax calculations, deductions, payroll and tax reporting, and generation of entries for the general ledger. Some of the features of the payroll include:

- The production of weekly, biweekly, semimonthly and monthly reports
- Processing of up to 40 types of miscellaneous deductions which are user-defined
- Calculation of up to 20 "other pays" including vacation, holiday, sick pay, and more
- Quick and easy calculation of gross and net pay for an employee in a highly visual form that makes operation easy for persons familiar with manual payroll processing
- Withholding of and accounting for federal, state, and other taxes
- Printing of 941a and W-2 forms

Complete accounting control is provided through the use of audit trails and optional password security over files.

The software comes with easy-to-read documentation and a tutorial with sample problems to simplify learning and installation of the payroll.

Company:
Timberline Systems, Inc.

Product:
***MEDALLION*/Starter Set**

Category:
General Business Applications

Computer: AT&T PC 6300

Media: Diskette

Language:
C

Requirements:
512 KB RAM
MS-DOS 3.1.or greater
Fixed disk
Serial port
Printer

Support:
Telephone support is available from Timberline under a support agreement. This is a fee-based service that can be purchased per call or by annual subscription. Call Timberline for current rates.

Training classes are optional and are offered in six regional training centers. Call Timberline for a current class schedule.

Upgrades/enhancements are available to all end users who send in their program registration cards. When new versions are available, registered users may purchase them for a nominal fee.

Retail Price:
$100

Distributor:
Timberline Systems, Inc.
7180 S. W. Fir Loop
Portland, OR 97223
Tel: (503) 644-8155

Timberline Systems, Inc. is an authorized Value Added Reseller for AT&T Computers.

Description:

The Starter Set is a foundation piece for the *MEDALLION* Collection of accounting modules from Timberline Systems. It includes the operations guide and tutorial designed to orient users to the hardware and software environment their *Timberline* software will operate within. The Operations Guide documentation contains easy-to-follow instructions for all standard procedures and functions common to all *Timberline* software.

Included in this module is a sample problem designed to acquaint users with the concepts of utilities, file processing, updates, reporting, and other standard concepts used throughout other modules of the *MEDALLION* Collection. The "teach" section of the software is interactive with the user and helps to create a comfort and confidence level with the software necessary for the user to proceed with the installation of other modules from the *MEDALLION* Collection.

A single Starter Set is required for the operation of any and all *Timberline* software products.

Company:
TLB, Inc.

Product:
***Solomon III* Version 3.12**

Category:
General Business Applications

Computer:	**Media:**
AT&T PC 6300 6300 PLUS **AT&T PC 6300 PLUS**	Diskette

Language:
C

Requirements:
256 KB RAM
132-column printer
10 MB hard disk
One floppy disk drive

Support:
Dealer Support–Toll Free
User Support–Fee
A tutorial system is available that includes one hour free support

Retail Price:
General Ledger–$695
Accounts Payable–$695
Accounts Receivable–$695
Payroll–$695
Fixed Assets–$695
Inventory–$695
Purchasing–$595
Order Entry–$595
Sales Analysis–$295
Job Costing–$995
Address & Mail List–$195
Database Reporter–$595
Tutorial & Support Plan–$149

Distributor:
TLB, Inc.
Great Valley Corporate Center
267 Great Valley Pkwy.
Malvern, PA 19355
Tel: (215) 644-3344

Description:

Solomon III is a full-featured general accounting and management information software application developed for 16- and 32-bit microcomputers.

Included in the 13-module *Solomon III* Series are General Ledger, Accounts Payable, Accounts Receivable, Payroll, Order Entry/Invoicing, Inventory, Purchasing, Job Costing, Fixed Assets, Sales Analysis, Address and Mail List Management, Database Reporter, and Tutorial and Support Plan.

Solomon III is designed around a true database management system. Information from all modules is stored in a single large and well-organized database ensuring quick and easy access to any data item, for any information you need to produce, whenever it is needed, in whatever form it is needed.

Accuracy of financial information is maintained through a number of integrity features designed into the system. Through "batch control," *Solomon III* ensures that all transactions are balanced before being posted. Password protection is available for all screens and reports. *Solomon III*'s "transaction logging" feature creates files which are used to recreate corrupted databases. *Solomon III* features complete audit trail reports and queries.

Solomon III's modular design makes it ideal for a broad spectrum of business types and sizes.

Company:
TOM Software, Inc.

Product:
Distributor Business Management System

Category:
General Business Applications

Computer:	**Media:**
AT&T PC 6300	Diskette

Language:
TOMBASIC

Requirements:
TOMBASIC
UNIX or *MS*-DOS (depending on model)
SPEED I Database Management Utility

Support:
Training and technical support provided by the local licensed consultant
Fees depend on the consultant and the type of service provided

Retail Price:
\$800–\$3,500 depending on the hardware

Distributor:
TOM Software, Inc.
127 S.W. 156th Ave.
P.O. Box 66596
Seattle, WA 98166
Tel: (206) 246-7022

TOM Software, Inc. is an authorized Value Added Reseller for AT&T Computers.

Description:

Because of its modular structure, the Distributor System adapts to the demands of almost any distribution operation. From routine daily operations to complex financial reporting, the system provides efficiency, control, and reliability. With the General Ledger modules as the system's center, a variety of other applications can be added as needed–Order Entry, Inventory, Accounts Receivable, Payroll, Commission Accounting, Accounts Payable, Equipment Accounting, and Fixed Asset Accounting. Some system features are:

- Provides multiwarehouse capability
- Tracks inflation trends
- Prints invoices, work orders, backorders and checks
- Handles backorders with an automatic function in the Order Entry module
- Allows multiple invoices per purchase order
- Maintains nonstock items/service in Inventory Control
- Provides "search" function to locate records by phone number or alpha code

Company:
TOM Software, Inc.

Product:
General Business Management System

Category:
General Business Applications

Computer:	**Media:**
AT&T PC 6300	Diskette

Language:
TOMBASIC

Requirements:
TOMBASIC
SPEED I Database Management Utility

Support:
Training and technical support available from local licensed consultant
Fees depend on consultant and type of services provided

Retail Price:
$800–$3,500 depending on hardware

Distributor:

TOM Software, Inc.
127 S.W. 156th Ave.
P.O. Box 66596
Seattle, WA 98166
Tel: (206) 246-7022

TOM Software, Inc. is an authorized Value Added Reseller for AT&T Computers.

Description:

The TOM General Business Management System provides instant access to the up-to-date information needed to make decisions–and it supports decisions with precise, relevant data. Like all TOM Accounting systems, the General Business Management System is flexible enough to meet the requirements of a wide range of operations. All modules can be purchased standalone or in an integrated system. And as business grows or accounting needs change, the system can be expanded to include modules from the TOM Distributor System. Some system features are:

- Allows direct entry of invoices and cash receipts
- Analyzes sales by various customer categories, such as sales division, type area
- Automatically calculates discounts and due dates based on vendor payment terms
- Handles four standard pay periods: weekly, biweekly, monthly, semimonthly

Company:
TOM Software, Inc.

Product:
Project Management Information System

Category:
General Business Applications

Computer:	**Media:**
AT&T PC 6300	Diskette

Language:
TOMBASIC

Requirements:
TOMBASIC
SPEED I Database Management Utility

Support:
Training and technical support provided by the local licensed consultant
Fees depend on the consultant and the type of service provided

Retail Price:
$800–$3,500 depending on the hardware

Distributor:

TOM Software, Inc.
127 S.W. 156th Ave.
P.O. Box 66596
Seattle, WA 98166
Tel: (206) 246-7022

TOM Software, Inc. is an authorized Value Added Reseller for AT&T Computers.

Description:

The Project Management Information System helps alleviate problems common to many project-oriented companies: inaccurate costing and estimating that distort profitability figures, misquotes based on competition rather than true costs, use of common labor burden rates for all operations regardless of true costs, inability to judge backlog, lack of labor analysis to make best use of employee skills, lack of historical information. Addressing the needs of architects, public relations and advertising agencies, and collection firms, the Project Management System accommodates user-defined reports and project data to meet the specific requirements of each user. Some system features are:

- Supports multiple burden rates
- Handles integrated project estimating
- Forecasts demand for labor, inventory, purchases, and equipment

Company:
TRAC LINE Software, Inc.

Product:
TRAC LINE INTEGRATED ACCOUNTING

Category:
General Business Applications

Computer:
AT&T PC 6300

Media:
Diskette

Language:
RM/COBOL

Requirements:
10 MB hard disk
128 KB per user

Support:
Full national customer support, hotline service
90-day warranty
Local dealer support available per dealership
System includes on-screen Help menus
Self-paced tutorials
Complete system documentation

Retail Price:
$1,695

Distributor:
TRAC LINE Software, Inc.
51 Alpha Plaza
Hicksville, NY 11801
Tel: (516) 935-7500
(800) TRACLIN

Description:

TRAC LINE INTEGRATED ACCOUNTING combines Accounts Receivable, Accounts Payable, General Ledger, Inventory Control, Sales Orders, Sales Analysis, Salesforce Management, Serial Number Tracking, List Management, Billing, Purchasing, and Self-paced Learning–all in ONE package. The software is totally interactive, providing accurate, up-to-the-minute reporting throughout the entire system. From order entry to receivables, from inventory control to payables, each transaction automatically posts and updates the necessary areas of the software system.

Written in *RM*/COBOL, *TRAC LINE INTEGRATED ACCOUNTING* is designed as a multiuser system, but can be used by a single user equally well. It runs on a variety of operating systems and hardware units and expands with add-on vertical modules for specific businesses such as retailing, wholesaling, service professions, and manufacturing.

Designed as a solution for small business, *TRAC LINE INTEGRATED ACCOUNTING* requires at least 10 MB of disk storage and 128 KB RAM per user. It can be used with standard peripherals (monochrome monitor, 132-column printer, etc.) as well as specific items such as RS-232 cash drawers (used in the *RETAILING* vertical module), other size printers such as 40- and 80-column, and bar code readers.

Self-paced tutorial, clear and concise documentation, and on-line Help screens are available throughout the system.

Company:
Tymon, Inc.

Product:
PCM–*PC MANAGER* SOFTWARE Revision 1.8

Category:
General Business Applications

Computer:	**Media:**
AT&T PC 6300 6300 PLUS **AT&T PC 6300 PLUS**	Diskette

Language:
C

Requirements:
192 KB RAM
One 5-1/4" disk drive

Support:
Three months warranty
Return capability
Telephone technical support (206) 828-9493

Retail Price:
$175

Distributor:
Tymon, Inc.
519 First St.
Kirkland, WA 98033
Tel: (206) 828-9493

Description:

The PCM–*PC MANAGER* is a task oriented management tool in a software package that gives feedback on performance. It is a manager's personal productivity assistant. It is designed using the techniques and philosophies of the best self-help management ideas available today.

The product's uniqueness is in the dialogue with its user. Once the computer is turned on with the PCM installed, the user will be praised, prodded, and urged to perform certain tasks that he or she has indicated as important to their management effectiveness. For example, depending on the user's performance, the PCM may say: "You are focusing on your goals very well. Super performance!" or maybe, "Let's try harder to get things done–you can do it!" The *PC MANAGER* will remind the user of:

- Appointments scheduled
- Goals due within the next month
- Employee objectives due soon
- New employees–to give them extra feedback at the start
- Past things to do–priority items on the list over five days
- Employee performance reviews due within 30-days

The *PC MANAGER* will give feedback on:

- Getting things done
- Focusing on goal-related priority activities
- Giving positive and negative feedback to employees as necessary
- Using the *PC MANAGER* program
- Reviewing goals

Company:
XTEND Communications Corporation

Product:
SMDR Software

Category:
General Business Applications

Computer:	**Media:**
AT&T PC 6300	Diskette

Language:
Compiled Basic and Assembler

Requirements:
PC 6300 with 10 MB fixed disk drive
256 KB Proprietary Buffer interface
Optional printer
Color monitor
Product requires installation by XTEND Communications Corporation

Support:
90-day warranty
Optional extended software support agreement with hotline service and remote diagnostics

Retail Price:
Systems start at $8,400 depending upon PBX Line size and optional features

Distributor:
XTEND Communications Corporation
171 Madison Ave.
New York, NY 10013
Tel: (212) 725-2010

Description:

The XTEND CDR System is an on-line, microcomputer based, menu-driven Call Detail Reporting (CDR) System. The system has two main features: (1) Immediate, on-line call processing, where calls are recorded, priced, and summarized as they are made (2) Flexible, on-demand ad hoc information retrieval and reporting of call data. Call detail information is displayed on the microcomputer's screen and gives the user an up-to-date view of a call as it is made. The CDR system can process calls from any telephone PBX switch capable of producing a digital call record.

The XTEND CDR System captures and generates accurate information about each outgoing call. Rates for calls dialed to any point in the world are stored in the system's database. The cost of each call is instantaneously computed, collected and reported in summary and/or detail as requested by the user. This capability avoids the delay and tedious manual costing of calls and equipment. It also eliminates the monthly expense and inconvenience of processing call records by a service bureau.

All the relevant information needed to manage communications effectively is available within the XTEND CDR System, including telephone usage by extension number, department, division, and any other hierarchical organization summarization requested by the user. Also included is account/authorization code information and facility usage. Information is available to the user on demand and reflects up-to-the-minute call activity. Rates used to determine cost are maintained at the area code and exchange level, accurately reflecting Bell System pricing. XTEND CDR rates also include true international pricing, based on the city from which the calls originated.

Available now for most PBX systems including Dimension, Oki, Siemens, Northern Telecom, Focus, Mitel, Rolm, IBX, etc.

Company:
AT&T and Digital Research Inc.

Product:
DR Draw*

Category:
Graphics

Computer:
AT&T PC 6300

Media:
Diskette

Language:
Pascal/MT+

Requirements:
128 KB RAM

Support:
This product is fully supported by AT&T Information Systems and carries a 90-day warranty on the media. Remote nationwide customer service hotline Monday through Friday between the hours of 8:00 a.m. and 5:00 p.m. local time. Installation, additional hotline coverage, and extended maintenance agreements are also available.

Retail Price:
$295

Distributor:
AT&T (800) 247-1212
or call your local AT&T authorized dealer or Account Executive.

***This product has been certified by AT&T.**

Description:

Digital Research Draw is designed for anyone in a business or professional setting who needs to create visual displays for use in formal presentations or office communications. It is an efficient, effective alternative to current cut-and-paste methods of preparation of visuals. With *DR Draw*, the user can create complex visuals on the screen, such as:

- Organization charts
- Project-flow diagrams
- Logos
- Area layouts
- Block diagrams
- Formal presentation slides

DR Draw operates with the Concurrent *MS*-DOS operating system and is based on *Digital Research*'s Graphics System Extensions (GSX). GSX allows powerful, device-independent graphics displays to be created using *DR Draw*, without concern for the resolution or other characteristics of the particular terminal, printer, or plotter used. GSX utilizes the maximum resolution of each device.

Benefits of *Digital Research Draw*:
Just as word processors freed the writer and the typist from the time-consuming process of writing and rewriting, typing and retyping, *DR Draw* frees the picture editor from the tedious cut-and-paste methods currently used in producing complex visual displays for oral and written reports. The result is a variety of complex visuals for organization charts, diagrams, logos, layouts, 35mm slides, and overhead transparencies.

DR Draw, used in conjunction with *Digital Research Graph*, can handle most business and professional needs for the quick preparation of dramatic visual aids to convey information to a particular audience.

Using *Digital Research Draw*:
Easy to use, the interactive *DR Draw* helps the user create and edit presentation-quality charts and diagrams. Menus prompt the user through creation and manipulation of the picture elements which are the basic building blocks for a diagram.

To build a picture, the user selects geometric or text elements from the available options, using the graphics cursor to place elements in the desired locations in the diagram. In addition to lines and text, available picture elements include marker characters, arcs, pie segments,

(Continued on next page)

Description: ***(Continued)***

filled rectangles and polygons, and circles. Once created, any element may be moved, copied, scaled, or deleted. Element characteristics, including color, line style, text font, and fill pattern, can also be changed.

When building a diagram, the user may also change his or her view of the current picture to aid in construction and layout. The user can zoom in on a specific section of the diagram to work on details, zoom back out to view the whole picture, and then pan to a different section of the diagram and repeat this detailed editing process.

Pictures may be saved on disk for further editing or later use and can be sent to a printer or plotter.

Company:
AT&T and Digital Research Inc.

Product:
DR Graph*

Category:
Graphics

Computer: AT&T PC 6300

Media: Diskette

Language:
FORTRAN

Requirements:
128 KB RAM

Support:
This product is fully supported by AT&T Information Systems and carries a 90-day warranty on the media. Remote nationwide customer service hotline Monday through Friday between the hours of 8:00 a.m. and 5:00 p.m. local time. Installation, additional hotline coverage, and extended maintenance agreements are also available.

Retail Price:
$195

Distributor:
AT&T (800) 247-1212
or call your local AT&T authorized dealer or Account Executive.

***This product has been certified by AT&T.**

Description:

DR Graph is a comprehensive graphics program for creating graphs and text-only charts, which produces presentation-quality graphics for the business professional. *DR Graph* makes it easy to turn complex business or scientific data into clear, effective color graphics. Using data entered manually or created with popular spreadsheet programs such as *SuperCalc*, *VisiCalc*, and *Lotus 1-2-3*, you can quickly design effective, professional-looking line, bar, scatter, and stick graphs, as well as pie and text-only charts.

Easy formatting:

There are no complicated commands to learn. To create a graph, you simply choose options from menus; when you've completed your menu selections, you've completed the graph.

Design flexibility:

Choose from three different type styles (in addition to your machine type) for titles, legends, and annotation copy. Choose from a number of different line styles, line and bar widths, and eight filled patterns to add clarity and emphasis. Add borders, colors, and labels wherever you want them.

More powerful features:

Bar charts can be stacked, clustered, or arranged in steps or "sticks." Pie charts can include exploded "slices." And annotation can be incorporated, modified, and moved anywhere you want it.

Different graph types–line and bar for example–can be combined within one chart, and as many as four different charts or graphs can be combined on a single page.

See, Store, and Print:

DR Graph lets you see exactly what you've designed on the screen then print it on paper or transparency, or store it on disk to be recalled, printed, or updated later.

Level of Difficulty:

DR Graph is suitable for use by anyone familiar with simple microcomputer operation.

Features Summary:

- Simple formatting by menu selection.
- Line, bar, combined bar and line, pie, and text-only graphs.
- Complete control of design elements, including labels, title, legends, color, type styles, and borders.
- Up to 4 graphs on one page.
- Variable line and bar widths.
- Interfaces with popular spreadsheet programs.
- Annotation.
- Store, plot, or print hard copy.

Company:
Benchmark/Metasoft, Inc.

Product:
***THE BENCHMARK* Graphics**

Category:
Graphics

Computer:
AT&T PC 6300

Media:
Diskette

Language:
Machine Code & C

Requirements:
320 KB RAM

Support:
Telephone support (800) 621-1908

Retail Price:
$295

Distributor:
Benchmark/Metasoft, Inc.
6509 W. Frye Rd., Suite 12
Chandler, AZ 85224
Tel: (602) 961-0003

Description:

Two new graphics packages, Business Graphics and Presentation Graphics, have been designed to meet business and personal graphics requirements. Both graphics packages interface with the Financial Planner to enable the user to generate dramatic displays of business data. Business Graphics is capable of displaying data in a range of formats: clustered bar chart, stacked bar chart, line graph, and x-y plot. Presentation Graphics offers all of these formats along with commands that allow you to draw freehand as well as generate arcs, rectangles, circles, and text strings.

Company:
BPS

Product:
Overhead Express*

Category:
Graphics

Computer:
AT&T PC 6300

Media:
Diskette

Language:
C

Requirements:
192 KB RAM
Two double-sided disk drives, (hard disk compatible)
Dot matrix printer

Support:
This product carries a 90-day warranty on the media
Contact BPS for additional service options, (800) DIAL-BPS

Retail Price:
$195

Distributor:
AT&T (800) 247-1212
or call your local AT&T authorized dealer or Account Executive.

***This product has been certified by AT&T.**

Description:

Overhead Express is a fast, flexible software tool for producing high-quality overhead transparencies at minimal cost. Presentations are prepared on the AT&T PC 6300, printed out on a standard dot matrix printer, and copied onto transparencies on common office copy machines. An Express Editor includes 12 preformatted fill-in-the-blank templates of standard presentation pages, including a bullet list and title page. Layouts can be previewed instantaneously during editing. Four handsome typefaces are available in up to five sizes, both Roman and italic. Special features include boxes, lines, and graphic symbols, as well as a built-in screen show for on-line presentations.

Company:
Decision Resources

Product:
***CHART-MASTER*—Version 6.1**

Category:
Graphics

Computer:	**Media:**
AT&T PC 6300	Diskette

Language:
BASIC

Requirements:
Minimum 192 KB RAM (256 KB required for printer graphics, or for the *Polaroid* Palette, 320 KB recommended for color printers).
Two DSDD floppy disk drives or one DSDD floppy drive and one hard-disk drive

Support:
90-day warranty period offered from date of purchase
National account training program available for trainers and end users
Product Maintenance plan covers update releases
All registered users receive Graphiti newsletter
Customer service at (203) 222-1974

Retail Price:
$375

Distributor:
Decision Resources
25 Sylvan Rd., South
Westport, CT 06880
Tel: (203) 222-1974

Description:

CHART-MASTER 6.1 is a powerful flexible, easy-to-use business graphics program for creating bar, pie, area, scatter and line charts. Menus, preprogrammed settings and context-sensitive help screens allow a business user to create professional charts immediately.

Data may be entered manually, or automatically with *DataGrabber*, which allows quick and easy access to any spreadsheet program, such as *Lotus 1-2-3*, which stores data in Print (ASCII), *DIF* or SYLK file formats. *DataGrabber* recreates the user's data on-screen in spreadsheet form. The user highlights or "grabs" the data to be graphed and, in as few as eight keystrokes, selects all the data and labels for the chart.

CHART-MASTER 6.1 offers over 40 options that include hatch and line patterns, exploding pies, 8 fonts, 16 font sizes, axis control, and floating legends. The Symbol font contains 94 symbols depicting items, such as arrows, geometric shapes, people, transportation vehicles, dramatic impact to business presentations. A new typeset style, Helvetica-like "Swiss" font was added in revision 6.1.

Charts and graphs may be produced on screen, on over 80 printers and plotters, including *Hewlett-Packard Laserjet* and *Epson* LQ-1500, or on 35mm slides (with the *Polaroid* Palette). *CHART-MASTER* can be run from a hard-disk drive without inserting floppy disks first.

Software Digest, Inc., an independent organization that rates personal computer software, has rated *CHART-MASTER* 6.1 as one of the top business graphics package in a field of 17 products tested.

Company:
Decision Resources

Product:
***SIGN-MASTER*—Version 5.1**

Category:
Graphics

Computer:
AT&T PC 6300

Media:
Diskette

Language:
BASIC

Requirements:
Minimum 192 KB RAM (256 KB required for printer graphics, or for the *Polaroid* Palette, 320 KB recommended for color printers).
Two DSDD floppy disk drives or one DSDD floppy drive and one hard-disk drive

Support:
90-day warranty period offered from date of purchase
National account training program available for trainers and end users
Product Maintenance plan covers update releases
All registered users receive Graphiti newsletter
Customer service at (203) 222-1974

Retail Price:
$245

Distributor:
Decision Resources
25 Sylvan Rd., South
Westport, CT 06880
Tel: (203) 222-1974

Description:

SIGN-MASTER 5.1 is a menu-driven word charting program that allows a business person to enter text and tables using word processing editing features for creating agendas, outlines, summaries, forms, title pages, announcements, proposals, reports, instructional materials, financial summaries, and presentations.

SIGN-MASTER features seven type faces, including two Helvetica-like Swiss fonts, and the Symbol font, containing 94 commonly used business symbols.

Text options controllable by the user include font, size, italics, justification, pen color and underline. The user can modify plot area, location on the page, pen speed, frame, footnote, page formatting, margins, and spacing between lines.

Signs and tables may be produced on over 80 printers and color plotters, or on 35mm slides (with the *Polaroid* Palette). Hard disk users can install *SIGN-MASTER* on their hard disk, eliminating the need to insert a floppy disk to use the program.

Companion products include *CHART-MASTER* 6.1, which creates bar, pie, line and scatter charts, and DIAGRAM-MASTER 5.0, which produces organization, gantt and flow charts, as well as, freehand graphics.

Company:
Graphic Communications, Inc.

Product:
***GRAPHWRITER* Combination Set**

Category:
Graphics

Computer:	**Media:**
AT&T PC 6300 6300 PLUS **AT&T PC 6300 PLUS**	Diskette

Language:
C

Requirements:
192 KB RAM (256 KB when used with the *Polaroid* Palette)

Support:
Telephone technical support available, 8:00 a.m. to 6:00 p.m. EST. (617) 890-8778

Retail Price:
$595

Distributor:
Graphic Communications, Inc.
200 Fifth Ave.
Waltham, MA 02254
Tel: (617) 890-8778

Description:

GRAPHWRITER is a business graphics software package that assists the user to produce presentation quality charts for paper, transparencies, or 35mm slides. In addition to the standard pie, bar, and line charts, *GRAPHWRITER* offers a wide variety of specialized graphic formats including Gantt charts, organization charts, scatter charts, bubble charts, and many other special purpose chart formats. Menus, Help options, and "fill in the blanks" chart data forms allow even novice users to produce professional quality charts. *GRAPHWRITER* is compatible with all major pen plotters, laser jet and dot matrix printers, as well as the *Polaroid* Palette and Matrix slide image recorders.

Company:
International Microcomputer Software, Inc.

Product:
4-POINT GRAPHICS

Category:
Graphics

Computer:	**Media:**
AT&T PC 6300	Diskette
6300 PLUS **AT&T PC 6300 PLUS**	

Language:
Compiled BASIC

Requirements:
192 KB RAM
Graphics adapter

Support:
IMSI has a technical support department to handle all questions relating to *4-POINT GRAPHICS* or any of its other software products.

Retail Price:
$195

Distributor:
International Microcomputer Software, Inc.
1299 Fourth St.
San Rafael, CA 94901
Tel: (415) 454-7101

Description:

4-POINT GRAPHICS is a full-color, creative graphics presentation program that offers animation capabilities. A demo mode creates self-running, fast-paced business presentations. Up to 99 demo frames can be linked together to produce professional, animated business and graphic presentations. *4-POINT GRAPHICS* includes *Frieze*, a high-RAM utility program that allows the application to interface with other graph and image generating programs. Through *Frieze*, *4-POINT's GRAPHICS* and quality presentations can be output to over 30 of the most popular printers and plotters.

Company:
International Microcomputer Software, Inc.

Product:
***PC Paintbrush* Version 2.80**

Category:
Graphics

Computer:	**Media:**
AT&T PC 6300	Diskette

Language:
C, Assembler

Requirements:
Input Device, for example:
Mouse
Digitizing tablets
Joysticks

Support:
Technical Staff–(415) 454-7101

Retail Price:
$139

Distributor:
International Microcomputer Software, Inc.
1299 Fourth St.
San Rafael, CA 94901
Tel: (415) 454-7101

Description:

PC Paintbrush is a full-color, high-resolution graphic design program. It allows free-form drawing and painting and provides complete image editing capabilities. Editing features include enlargements, reductions, rotations, inversions, copying, pasting, and moving images. *PC Paintbrush* includes *Frieze*, a high-memory utility program that allows *PC Paintbrush* to interface with and enhance other graph and image generating programs. Through *Frieze*, *PC Paintbrush* outputs to over 30 of the most popular printers and plotters. *PC Paintbrush* supports 15 display adapters in over 50 resolutions and offers 10 input devices including mice, digitizing tablets, and joystick options.

Company:
Quadratron Systems, Inc.

Product:
Q-CHART

Category:
Graphics

Computer:
AT&T PC 6300

Media:
Diskette

Language:
C

Requirements:
Hard disk

Support:
Training and hotline support provided by Essex Office Systems

Retail Price:
$325

Distributor:
Essex Office Systems
333 North Fairfax St.
Alexandria, VA 22314
Tel: (703) 549-9240

Description:

Q-CHART is a flexible chart drawing program that allows novice users to represent data in predefined graphic formats, such as bar charts, pie charts, and line graphs. *Q-CHART* is specifically written to accept data from various applications software, including *Q-PLAN*, and integrate with *Q-ONE* word processing documents.

Company:
STSC, Inc.

Product:
***STATGRAPHICS*, Version 1.0**

Category:
Graphics

Computer: AT&T PC 6300

Media: Diskette

Language:
APL

Requirements:
MS-DOS, version 2.0 or later
384 KB RAM
A graphics adapter and compatible monitor
2 floppy disk drives or a hard disk
It supports 8087 math coprocessor
Most popular graphics adapters and dot matrix printers
A variety of high-quality pen plotters

Support:
HELP line manned from 9:00 a.m. to 6:00 p.m. EST
Newsletter for registered users
Periodic software enhancements are available
Warranty is included with the package
Training is also available at an additional charge

Retail Price:
$695

Distributor:
STSC, Inc.
2115 East Jefferson St.
Rockville, MD 20852
Tel: (301) 984-5129
(800) 592-0050

Description:

STATGRAPHICS is an interactive data analysis and statistical graphics system that integrates comprehensive statistical analysis with high-resolution color graphics. It offers over 250 functions for interactive data analysis and data management, including analysis of variance, regression analysis, experimental design, quality control procedures, multivariate techniques, nonparametric techniques, and extensive forecasting and time series analysis.

It is designed for engineers, statisticians, researchers, business analysts, and other professionals with a need for comprehensive data analysis capabilities.

Unique features include:

- Extensive integration of graphics with the statistical and data analysis procedures which allows users to explore data fully and to gain broader insights from the graphical representation of analysis.
- Broadest range of statistical and data analysis routines available in the microenvironment.
- Supports high-resolution color as well as monochrome graphics on screen; choice of output via dot matrix printer, high quality pen plotter, or screen.
- Optional access to source language for writing customized procedures.
- Includes import/outport facilities for ASCII files, *DIF* files, *Lotus 1-2-3* worksheets, and *Symphony* files.
- Completely menu-driven with optional command structure for experienced users.
- Extensive use of function keys.
- Includes a tutorial and reference cards.
- Includes sample data sets and examples.

Company:
Abry & Associates

Product:
Geomapper

Category:
Industry/Vertical

Computer:
AT&T PC 6300

Media:
Diskette

Language:
FORTRAN 77

Requirements:

512 KB RAM
8087 -2 math chip
10 MB hard disk
HI *DMP 29* plotter
Epson FX-100 printer

Support:

Training and technical support provided by author
Fees depend upon type of services provided

Retail Price:
$2,000–$8,000

Distributor:
Cambrian Corporation
12622 Kingsride
Houston, TX 77024
Tel: (713) 932-7153

Cambrian Corporation is an authorized Value Added Reseller for AT&T Computers.

Description:

All major Geomapper programs access the same data file structure, which allows to store well name, API number, X-Y or lat-long, KB elevation, status, tops from wells and seismic, lithology tops, other mappable parameters, and fault cut data. This program has a printer and a plotter version. Top names and number of picks for each top in the data file can be listed. The program posts at any scale well symbols, formation top elevators, isopach values or other mappable parameters.

Company:

ACCI Business Systems, Inc.

Product:

A/E Integrated Project Management Version 3.2U

Category:

Industry/Vertical

Computer:	**Media:**
AT&T PC 6300	Diskette
6300 PLUS AT&T PC 6300 PLUS	

Language:

MS-BASIC

Requirements:

1 KB RAM
10 MB hard disk
132-column printer

Support:

20 hours on-site training
Post-sale telephone support

Retail Price:

$6,250

Distributor:

ACCI Business Systems, Inc.
12707 N. Freeway, Suite 140
Houston, TX 77060
Tel: (713) 872-4134

Description:

A/E Integrated Project Management is a computer program for architectural or engineering firms that is designed to post time sheet and expense data to all project files as well as all related accounting files such as Payroll, Accounts Payable, Accounts Receivable and General Ledger (Financial Statements).

The Project Management/Billing module helps the user to easily pinpoint the losing areas of each project. "Contribution to Profit" of each project is clearly shown after each pay period. Invoicing is discretionary–all or part of any labor or expenses charge can be held. All labor and expenses for a job are shown permanently, regardless of the amount billed.

The Payroll Management module provides complete multistate payroll management. Payroll Management prints payroll checks automatically. Employee time can be charged to various departments as well as to various jobs. Productivity reports are available on each employee. Payroll Management posts automatically to General Ledger at the month's end.

The Accounts Payable module posts all expenses to jobs as vendor invoices are entered. It also posts reimbursable expenses to the Billing module. It systematically manages payments and discounts, prints checks to vendors, and posts automatically to General Ledger at the month's end.

The General Ledger module comes with the standard AIA Chart of Accounts or the ACEC Chart of Accounts on the disk. A firm-wide Balance Sheet and Income/Expense Statement are produced monthly, as well as Departmental Income/Expense Statement, if desired.

Company:
ACCI Business Systems, Inc.

Product:
Facility Personnel & Space Requirements Projections Version 4.0

Category:
Industry/Vertical

Computer:
AT&T PC 6300

Media:
Diskette

Language:
C BASIC

Requirements:
128 KB RAM
Floppy disk
132-column printer

Support:
Post-sale telephone support

Retail Price:
$1,500

Distributor:
ACCI Business Systems, Inc.
12707 N. Freeway, Suite 140
Houston, TX 77060
Tel: (713) 872-4134

Description:

Facility Personnel and Space Requirements Projections is a microcomputer program that facilitates the collection, organization, and reporting of personnel and space requirements used in architectural programming. It allows the describing of a company's organizational structure down to four levels per major grouping, projects personnel and nonpeople space requirements, and develops and models corporate space standards to be used for design of office and open space. Once the space standards have been assigned, manipulation of space requirements can be done by changing the square footage of the space standard. Reports generated by the system include: Personnel and Space Requirements, Space Requirements by Space Standard, Departmental Data Report, and Adjacency Report.

Company:
Advanced Computer Systems, Inc.

Product:
***MEDACS* Version 2.0**

Category:
Industry/Vertical

Computer:
AT&T PC 6300

Media:
Diskette

Language:
RM/COBOL

Requirements:

512 KB RAM
10 MB hard disk

Support:

Complete employee training
Installation
90-day support
On-line support available through continued support agreements
Telephone and on-line modem support also included

Retail Price:
$5,500

Distributor:

Advanced Computer Systems, Inc.
3490 Far Hills Ave.
Dayton, OH 45429
Tel: (513) 294-4477

Description:

Greater productivity, increased cash flow, and the best patient care are the goals of any practice in today's rapid-changing health care field. *MEDACS* can help medical practices to reach those goals because *MEDACS* is one of the leaders in practice management systems for the health care professional. ACS has designed a system that will quickly lead to greater efficiency, faster turnaround on reimbursements, and better information to assist in providing the best patient care possible.

MEDACS offers the following features:

- Reduces workload and improves cash flow.
- Speeds up the turnaround time and increases reimbursements on the third-party billing.
- Minimizes lost charges with a unique 3-step automatic collection system.
- Eliminates the need and expense of an outside billing service.
- Allows the flexibility to set different coding structures with five levels of charge, diagnosis, and procedure.
- Generates over 28 reports, including financial, diagnostic, and analysis information at regular intervals or upon demand.
- Patient recall scheduling makes future appointments easier to arrange. Coordinates off-premises patient care by:

  – Organizing patient information by facility to make hospital and nursing home rounds more efficient.

  – Providing admitting diagnosis.

  – Recording insurance information on each patient admitted.

  – Referring physicians.
- Keeps track of who is referring whom to a practice by physician and patient.
- Completes claims and billing with a single entry.
- Simple to set up and use because no previous data processing experience is required.
- Purchase only what is needed to get started and expand the system as practice grows.
- Operates on AT&T PC 6300, *UNIX* PC and 3B2 hardware.
- Backed by complete coordination of hardware and software plus comprehensive staff training and ongoing support.

Company:
Alpine Datasystems, Inc.

Product:
Alpine Legal Management single-user version

Category:
Industry/Vertical

Computer:
AT&T PC 6300

Media:
Diskette

Language:
DIBOL/SOFTBOL

Requirements:
Hard disk
256 KB RAM
UNIBOL Runtime System

Support:
30-day software warranty
Self-instruction or classroom training (depending on user preference)
Alpine Helpline telephone support
On-site consultation

Retail Price:
$1,495–$2,495

Distributor:

Alpine Datasystems, Inc.
111 S.W. Fifth Ave., Suite 1950
Portland, OR 97204
Tel: (800) 547-1837

Description:

Alpine Legal Management's single-user version provides complete timekeeping, billing, and management-reporting functions for small to medium-size law firms. It features multiple billing rates, unlimited narrative, automatic rebills, trust/retainer accounting, variable client/matter coding, and more than 15 statements formats. With over 400 users nationwide and high level of user satisfaction, Alpine Legal Management emphasizes increased profitability, productivity, and controls for firms of all disciplines.

Company:
AT&T and Supply Tech, Inc.

Product:
AT&T *Supply Link* Software*

Category:
Industry/Vertical

Computer:	**Media:**
AT&T PC 6300	Diskette

Language:
COBOL

Requirements:
256 KB RAM
10 MB hard disk
Color monitor (optional)
AT&T Model 4000 autodial modem
AT&T Enhanced Network Services (optional)
Epson FX-100 printer

Support:
This product is fully supported by AT&T Information Systems and carries a 90-day warranty on the media. Remote nationwide customer service hotline is provided Monday through Friday between the hours of 8:00 a.m. and 5:00 p.m. local time. Installation, additional hotline coverage, and extended maintenance agreements are also available. User's/Administrator's Documentation is provided.

Retail Price:
$3,000

Distributor:
AT&T (800) 247-1212
or call your local AT&T authorized dealer or Account Executive.

***This product has been certified by AT&T.**

Description:

Supply Link system is a fully integrated system that an automotive production parts supplier can use to receive Material Releases and support data from the major automobile manufacturers and send Advance Shipping Notifications (ASNs) to them electronically using the PC 6300. Its features are as follows:

- Prints all auto company releases in standard formats.
- Provides access to Ford Motor's News, Shortage Information Network (SIN), and Transaction Register Information Program (TRIP) systems.
- Menu-driven operations.
- Supports dial-up connections directly to each auto company's computer, using 3780 binary synchronous contention (BSC) protocol at 2400 bits per second (asynchronous ASCII protocol at 1200 bits per second for sending Chrysler ASNs).
- Capable of using the AT&T network data communication network instead of direct-dial connections for sending and receiving all data.
- Allows the user to select the color scheme for screen displays.
- Allows the user to quickly change the company name, computer codes, and computer phone numbers as needed.
- Automatically updates the General Motors computer password (used only for direct connections) and transmission sequences.
- Allows the user to assign ASN parameters to be filled in automatically for each shipping location to save operator time and effort, and reduce errors.
- Allows the user to use shipping addresses of up to five lines of forty characters.
- Has built-in functions to support sending and receiving test data for testing the users system with the manufacturers' computers.

Company:
Berman Technologies

Product:
***CROSS-SELL MANAGER* (Banking Software)**

Category:
Industry/Vertical

Computer: **AT&T PC 6300**

Media: Diskette

Language:
MS PASCAL

Requirements:
320 KB RAM
80-column printer
Color monitor

Support:
(800) 3BANKER
Tutorial with multiple training levels with the "Training The Trainer" approach
Can provide on-site training

Retail Price:
$5,500 Base module
$950 Workstation options available

Distributor:
Berman Marketing
P.O. Box 5712
Charlottesville, VA 22905
Tel: (804) 971-5989

Description:

Banking Software is a microbased platform automation system with micro to mainframe communication capabilities. The application includes forms generation and document preparation. It is designed to be a sales tool for use on platform to provide for user designed, personalized presentations of bank services and products. Extensive use of color and graphics in Banking Software provides visual appeal during the sales cycle. The application includes standard "What if" computations in addition to a new module—computational authoring—which allows the system to be a full functioning loan processing package. Banking Software includes an extensive prospect and customer tracking system and sales management reporting. Specifically designed to provide cross-selling prompts, Banking Software increases sales on the platform. The communication feature permits on-line or store and forward entry of new account information to the mainframe. It also provides for CIS inquiry. The application operates in a "shell" environment to permit exits to other application programs without exit to DOS.

Company:
Bobby J. Hall & Associates

Product:
Commercial Swine Management

Category:
Industry/Vertical

Computer:
AT&T PC 6300

Media:
Diskette

Language:
Compiled BASIC

Requirements:
256 KB RAM
Printer
Dual diskette drive or one diskette drive and a fixed disk

Support:
Dealer support
Direct telephone support line, (601) 684-8394
90-day warranty with software
Detailed user manual including a step-by-step sample problem

Retail Price:
$1,000

Distributor:
Bobby J. Hall & Associates
P.O. Box 646
McComb, MS 39648
Tel: (601) 684-6402

Description:

This application provides the hog producer a means of maintaining a current record of farrowing and feeder pig operation. Along with the detailed weekly breeding and production report, reports such as sow breeding and production summary, rank of sow productivity index, and performance evaluation based on specific traits can be obtained. The system also maintains detailed record and movement information on the feeder pig operation. The feeder pig enterprise provides detailed feed consumed by each group of pigs, feed cost per pig and projected marketing dates. Additionally, it allows the hog producer to maintain a detailed listing of each sow and feeder group health records, including all treatments, vaccination, reproductive problems (sows only), and other health problems.

Company:
Bobby J. Hall & Associates

Product:
Computerized Dairy Feeder System

Category:
Industry/Vertical

Computer:
AT&T PC 6300

Media:
Diskette

Language:
Compiled BASIC

Requirements:
256 KB RAM
Printer
Dual diskette drives or one diskette drive and a fixed disk

Support:
Dealer support
Direct telephone support line, (601) 684-8394
90-day warranty with software
Detailed user manual including a step-by-step sample problem

Retail Price:
On request

Distributor:

Bobby J. Hall & Associates
P.O. Box 646
McComb, MS 39648
Tel: (601) 684-6402

Description:

The Computerized Dairy Feeder System allows the farmer a means of controlling a computerized feeding system from the host computer. The amount of additional feed allocated to each animal can be automatically computed by the system and is based on milk production, stage of lactation, age, etc. All of these values are read from files created by the Dairy Herd Management System. Of course the user has the option of changing, deleting, or even adding additional animals not recommended by the system. A function of the system is the inventory control. The amount in inventory and the average price can be adjusted by the user. Any input that can be made by the user at the feeder computer keyboard can be made by the host computer. All animals to receive additional feed can be determined by the host computer and transferred automatically to the feeder computer, thus saving the user the laborious job of determining the additional feed each cow is to receive and then entering her into the system.

Company:
Bobby J. Hall & Associates

Product:
Cow/Calf Beef Herd

Category:
Industry/Vertical

Computer:
AT&T PC 6300

Media:
Diskette

Language:
Compiled BASIC

Requirements:
256 KB memory
Printer
Dual diskette drives or one diskette drive and a fixed disk

Support:
Dealer support
Direct telephone support line, (601) 684-8394
90-day warranty with software
Detailed user manual including a step-by-step sample problem

Retail Price:
$1,000

Distributor:
Bobby J. Hall & Associates
P.O. Box 646
McComb, MS 39648
Tel: (601) 684-6402

Description:

The Cow/Calf Beef Herd package consists of complete beef management, heifer management, and herd health management. The system maintains the heifer's record from time of birth, including vaccinations. At calving, her record (including health record) is automatically transferred to the Beef Cow file, so that her entries only have to be made once. Additionally, it allows the rancher to maintain a detailed listing of each cow's health records, including all treatments, vaccinations, reproductive problems, and other health problems. Individual calving dates, weaning dates, breeding dates and many other important management records (such as number of services, service sires, cow weight, calving intervals) are kept and maintained by the system. Calculations can be made for weight ratios and adjusted weights, for birth, 205 days, 365 days, 452 days, and 550 days. Adjusted heights are also calculated. The Most Probable Producing Ability is calculated and is included on the Produce of Dam summaries.

Company:
Bobby J. Hall & Associates

Product:
Crop Management System

Category:
Industry/Vertical

Computer:	**Media:**
AT&T PC 6300	Diskette

Language:
Compiled BASIC

Requirements:
256 KB RAM
Printer
Dual diskette drives or one diskette drive and a fixed disk

Support:
Dealer support
Direct telephone support line, (601) 684-8394
90-day warranty with software
Detailed user manual including a step-by-step sample problem

Retail Price:
$1,000

Distributor:
Bobby J. Hall & Associates
P.O. Box 646
McComb, MS 39648
Tel: (601) 684-6402

Description:

The Crop Management System is designed to provide the producer with a tool that will track and calculate actual cost of production. The system will track all crop production activities and related costs on a per field basis or for the entire enterprise. On demand, the T system will calculate the breakeven price and yield for each field in production and/or for the entire crop. The system makes use of user-defined files for storing information such as landlord (owner) information; individual field information; produce codes (crops grown, chemicals, fertilizers used, etc.); activity codes (tillage, labor, harvest, etc.); weed codes (weeds that may be a problem); how-applied codes (helps to determine and record weed control success related to method of herbicide application); and company code (tailors the system to place owner's name on reports, etc.). Activities are updated and added to the Product Lists, Field Information List, Landlord Activity Report Files, Crop Harvest Files, Acreage Report Files, and Breakeven Report Files. All reports are optional and can be run at any time.

Company:
Bobby J. Hall & Associates

Product:
Dairy Herd Management System

Category:
Industry/Vertical

Computer:	**Media:**
AT&T PC 6300 6300 PLUS **AT&T PC 6300 PLUS**	Diskette

Language:
Compiled BASIC

Requirements:
256 KB RAM
Printer
Dual diskette drives or one diskette drive and a fixed disk

Support:
Dealer support
Direct telephone support line, (601) 684-8394
90-day warranty with software
Detailed user manual including a step-by-step sample problem

Retail Price:
$2,000

Distributor:
Bobby J. Hall & Associates
P.O. Box 646
McComb, MS 39648
Tel: (601) 684-6402

Description:

The Dairy Herd Management System provides an easy and accurate means of maintaining complete records. The system allows the user to enter records and inquire by barn number, ear tag number, and tattoo number. Along with detailed master information reports for cows, heifers, and bulls, reports such as breeding records and production records can be obtained. Additionally, it allows the user to maintain a detailed listing of each cow's health records. At calving, a heifer's record is automatically transferred to the Dairy Cow File. Her entries only have to be made once. Individual year-to-date milk, butterfat, protein, and solids-nonfat, ME milk and fat, actual 305 and 365 lactations, lifetime production, rolling herd averages, calving dates, dry-up dates, breeding records, and classification records are maintained by the system. Over 40 ways to categorize the animals in the user herd, daily worksheets, and daily management and summary reports are included to help manage a successful dairy herd operation. The system can accommodate two or three daily milkings. It maintains a summary file, including lactation, calving, and breeding.

Company:
Bobby J. Hall & Associates

Product:
Least Cost Nutrition

Category:
Industry/Vertical

Computer:
AT&T PC 6300

Media:
Diskette

Language:
Compiled BASIC

Requirements:
256 KB RAM
Printer
Dual diskette drives or one diskette drive and a fixed disk

Support:
Dealer support
Direct telephone support line, (601) 684-8394
90-day warranty with software
Detailed user manual including a step-by-step sample problem

Retail Price:
$1,000

Distributor:
Bobby J. Hall & Associates
P.O. Box 646
McComb, MS 39648
Tel: (601) 684-6402

Description:

This Least Cost Nutrition package is designed for small feed mills, farms which manufacture their own feeds, and subsystems of larger mills. The Least Cost Nutrition option provides you with a means of formulating a feed ration, using those ingredients available, to meet predetermined nutritional requirements at the least possible cost. The system minimizes the cost of mixed feed products. It insures a more uniform feed product by giving you the exact amounts of ingredients to be used so that your feed will be correctly balanced and maintained at a constant level. It maximizes the use of available ingredients by taking into consideration all the ingredients you have available in inventory and maximizing their use. It reduces ingredient inventory and waste by knowing exactly how much of each ingredient is needed for your feed product. It helps in obtaining ingredient purchasing information, not only in providing the exact amount of each ingredient needed for your ration, but also with the price the unused ingredients would have to be utilized in the ration, all other factors being equal. You can also run "What If" problems to aid in purchase of ingredients. The Least Cost Nutrition package can determine the specific allotment of ingredients necessary to produce a given ration at minimum cost, while meeting all the quality constraints you have determined and entered into the system for the product.

Company:
Bobby J. Hall & Associates

Product:
Registered Beef

Category:
Industry/Vertical

Computer:
AT&T PC 6300

Media:
Diskette

Language:
Compiled BASIC

Requirements:
256 KB RAM
Printer
Dual diskette drives or one diskette drive and a fixed disk

Support:
Dealer support
Direct telephone support line, (601) 684-8394
90-day warranty with software
Detailed user manual including a step-by-step sample problem

Retail Price:
$1,000

Distributor:
Bobby J. Hall & Associates
P.O. Box 646
McComb, MS 39648
Tel: (601) 684-6402

Description:

The Registered Beef package provides the purebred and commercial cattleman an easy, accurate means of maintaining a complete, correct record of his or her cow, heifer, and calf herd; bull stud; and semen inventory and interfaces with the Embryo Transfer and Pedigree systems. The system maintains the calf's record from time of birth, including vaccinations. The calf can then be transferred to the heifer herd that includes detailed heat checking and A.I. breeding information. At calving, her records (including health records) are automatically transferred to the cow file. When a cow calves, the calving information and calf's ID is transferred automatically to the calf file, so that any entry in the system only has to be made once. Additionally it allows the rancher to maintain a detailed listing of each cow's health records including vaccinations, reproductive problems, genital examinations, and other health problems. Detailed history records are kept including all breedings, calvings, and calf performance for each calving record on the cow file. Multiple births and foster mothers are also included in each calving record in the cow file. The performance as a calf is also kept on all cows, bulls, and heifers. The bull record also includes the bull gain test. The correct calf record includes detailed identifications, birth, weaning, yearling weights, heights, adjusted weights and heights, and weight and height ratios. The Most Probable Producing Ability (MPPA) is also calculated and is included on the Produce of Dam Summary. Over fifty listings, summaries, management worksheets and reports and daily reports are provided.

Company:
Charley Ostrander

Product:
PETRO PHYSICIST

Category:
Industry/Vertical

Computer: **AT&T PC 6300**

Media: Diskette

Language:
GW BASIC

Requirements:
256 KB RAM
10 MB hard disk
Color monitor
132-Column printer
Epson FX-100 or *LQ 1500* preferred
Digitizing tablet

Support:
Training and technical support provided by author
Fees depend upon type of services provided

Retail Price:
$1,000–$15,000

Distributor:
Cambrian Corporation
12622 Kingsride
Houston, TX 77024
Tel: (713) 932-7153

Cambrian Corporation is an authorized Value Added Reseller for AT&T Computers.

Description:

The PETRO PHYSICIST operates on units of information called "files." A "file" is defined as a continuous section of log data that does not exceed 150 feet or 50 meters of holes. This file will contain all of the data from all of the curves throughout the specified section of the hole. The curve data is entered through the use of a digitizing tablet. By tracing the desired curves with the hand held cursor, all of the data points are entered into the system. The system will at all times direct user efforts and ask the pertinent questions about the curve being entered. If, for example, the density curve is to be digitized, the system will need to know whether a density porosity or a bulk density curve is to be used. This is needed in order to ask the proper questions regarding the scaling factors.

The system is "formatting oriented." Since a specific formation in a limited geographic region will generally have reasonably consistent analytical parameters, the PETRO PHYSICIST will remember them in a file that the user creates.

Company:
Comspec

Product:
Tapetran

Category:
Industry/Vertical

Computer:	**Media:**
AT&T PC 6300	Diskette

Language:
FORTRAN

Requirements:
650 KB RAM
8087 -2 math chip
10 MB hard disk
Tapetran processor and modem

Support:
Training and technical support provided by author
Fees depend upon type of services provided

Retail Price:
$30,000 sending unit and
$30,000 receiving unit

Distributor:
Cambrian Corporation
12622 Kingsride
Houston, TX 77024
Tel: (713) 932-7153

Cambrian Corporation is an authorized Value Added Reseller for AT&T Computers.

Description:

Tapetran is an integrated two-way communications system, linking management to any remote site (drilling rig, ship, or district office). Tapetran transmits drilling reports, mud logs, wireline logs, facsimile documents and seismic data up to 300 percent faster than conventional methods. Tapetran is also secure from line intrusion through data encryption. Tapetran transmits digital data such as maps with ease and much faster than other computer systems.

Company:
Creative Solutions, Inc.

Product:
***The 1040 Solution* 1985 Version**

Category:
Industry/Vertical

Computer:	**Media:**
AT&T PC 6300	Diskette

Language:
Digital Research Pascal/MT+

Requirements:
MS-DOS 2.x or 3.x
256 KB RAM
Hard disk drive
132-column printer

Support:
30-day money-back guarantee
Written warranty of performance
Telephone support (313) 995-8811 by staff trained in computers and accounting
Annual users' conference
Optional hands-on training available at Creative Solutions, Inc. offices

Retail Price:
$1,295; 1986 renewal is $695

Distributor:

Creative Solutions, Inc.
230 Collingwood, Suite 250
Ann Arbor, MI 48103
Tel: (313) 995-8811

Description:

The 1040 Solution is a sophisticated 1040 tax preparation system for professional in-house tax return processing. The data entry screens coincide exactly with the input sheets provided for all tax forms processed. Schedules include A, B, C, D, E, F, G, R, RP, SE, and W. Forms include the 1040, 1040ES, 1115, 2106, 2119, 2210, 2441, 3468, 3903, 4136, 4255, 4562, 4797, 4835, 4972, 5695, 5884, 6251, 6252, invoices, and automatic transmittal letters.

The operator may enter data in any order, and data is easily recallable for editing. The system will automatically choose the lowest tax alternative and will automatically recalculate all amounts after data entry is completed. The system generates *Client Arranger* sheets for use as organizers and pro formas all carry-forward data to the new year. Depreciation displays are fully integrated. The system can process returns singly or in batches of up to 40 clients. In addition to printing returns on preprinted forms, computer-generated boilerplate forms, and overlay forms, the 1985 system supports laser printing. Integrated state tax software is available for several states.

Company:
Creative Solutions, Inc.

Product:
***The Depreciation Solution* Version 4**

Category:
Industry/Vertical

Computer:	**Media:**
AT&T PC 6300	Diskette
6300 PLUS **AT&T PC 6300 PLUS**	

Language:
Digital Research Pascal/MT+

Requirements:
MS-DOS 2.x or 3.x
256 KB RAM
Two disk drives (hard or floppy)
132-column printer

Support:
30-day money-back guarantee
Written warranty of performance
Telephone support (313) 995-8811 by staff trained in computers and accounting
Annual users' conference
Optional hands-on training available at Creative Solutions, Inc. offices

Retail Price:
$495

Distributor:
Creative Solutions, Inc.
230 Collingwood, Suite 250
Ann Arbor, MI 48103
Tel: (313) 995-8811

Description:

The Depreciation Solution is a fixed asset ACRS accounting system for the professional accountant or corporate controller. Each asset may be depreciated in three ways using the same asset data to accommodate different federal, book, and nonconforming state treatments. The program handles requirements of the 1984 Deficit Reduction Act, including automatic limitations for luxury autos and listed property. Asset data may be updated at any time, and the system will automatically calculate and display ITC and calculated or forced depreciation amounts.

Reporting features include reporting of federal, book, or state methods; projection reports; selective listing of assets by location, property tax listings by date of acquisition; and worksheets for Forms 4797, 3468, and 4562. ACRS methods include 3, 5, 10, 15, and 18-year class life. Traditional methods include straight line, declining balance, and sum-of-the-years'-digits. The system will handle up to 5,000 assets per client on a hard disk and 1,000 assets per client on a floppy disk.

Company:
Creative Solutions, Inc.

Product:
***The Write-Up Solution* Version 6**

Category:
Industry/Vertical

Computer:	**Media:**
AT&T PC 6300	Diskette
6300 PLUS **AT&T PC 6300 PLUS**	

Language:
Digital Research Pascal/MT+

Requirements:
MS-DOS 2.x or 3.x
256 KB RAM
Hard disk drive
132-column printer

Support:
30-day money-back guarantee
Written warranty of performance
Telephone support (313) 995-8811 by staff trained in computers and accounting
Annual users' conference
Optional hands-on training available at Creative Solutions, Inc. offices

Retail Price:
$1,695; spreadsheet interface option is $75

Distributor:
Creative Solutions, Inc.
230 Collingwood, Suite 250
Ann Arbor, MI 48103
Tel: (313) 995-8811

Description:

The Write-Up Solution is an extremely flexible client write-up system for professional accountants. Features include flexible comparative and budgetary statements independent of the chart of accounts, multi-departmentals, and an automatic statement of changes in financial position report. The system supports automatic tax, inventory, recurring, accountant-defined, reversing journal entries, and up to 5,000 accounts. Other important features include a cumulative general ledger, an integrated after-the-fact payroll with the ability to enter payroll and regular disbursements in check sequence, 941 worksheets, W-2s and 1099 forms.

Multiple data entry options allow the operator to skip various data fields, enter them manually, or use automatic default values for maximum data entry speed. The general ledger may be rerun as often as necessary for each posting period, and adjusting entries may be posted directly to a prior month without a prior period rerun. The accountant may print statements for any current or prior year without rerunning the general ledger.

An optional interface to *Lotus 1-2-3* and other spreadsheet programs permits transfer of all or selected general ledger balances. Client data is fully integrated with a separate corporate tax return program available from Creative Solutions, Inc.

Company:
Cyndek, Inc.

Product:
SPORTSLOG

Category:
Industry/Vertical

Computer:	**Media:**
AT&T PC 6300	Diskette
6300 PLUS **AT&T PC 6300 PLUS**	

Language:
C

Requirements:
MS-DOS
128 KB RAM

Support:
Hotline support (203) 226-8088
Tutorial and demonstration included with the package

Retail Price:
$950

Distributor:
Cyndek, Inc
1221 Post Rd., East
Westport, CT 06880
Tel: (203) 226-8088

Description:

SPORTSLOG is a comprehensive sports data management and reporting system. It is easy to work with and designed for the particular needs of the sports administrator.

With *SPORTSLOG* the user can do virtually every administrative chore, from player registration to scheduling the "ref." It is a computer program engineered to reduce the time needed for administration, improve accuracy, speed up reporting cycles, and generally make life easier.

Company:

Datamatic, Inc.

Product:

Route Star–Meter Reading with Hand-Held Computers

Category:

Industry/Vertical

Computer: AT&T PC 6300

Media: Diskette

Language:
Assembler, Turbo Pascal

Requirements:
320 KB RAM
10 MB disk
One asynchronous communications port
Modem and hand-held computer(s)
CRT
Printer optional
MS-DOS

Support:
One-year warranty and maintenance
Training manual
On-site training available
24-hour emergency hotline

Retail Price:
$10,000 Hand-Held computers at $2,500

Distributor:

Datamatic, Inc.
2121 N. Glenville
P.O. Box 850461
Richardson, TX 75081
Tel: (214) 234-4491

Description:

This is a complete system that captures data at each meter with a hand-held computer and transfers this file to a billing and report generating system. All software, including communication and applications, is provided.

Company:
Decision Data & Services, Inc.

Product:
Farm Decision Aids

Category:
Industry/Vertical

Computer:	**Media:**
AT&T PC 6300	Diskette

Language:
BASIC

Requirements:
128 KB RAM
Printer Optional (one disk drive)

Support:
30 Day Warranty
Full Customer Support
Telephone (515) 233-4873

Retail Price:
$195 complete set
$49.95 for each module

Distributor:
Beacon MicroCenter, Inc.
538 South Duff
Ames, IA 50010
Tel: (515) 233-4873

Beacon MicroCenter, Inc. is an authorized Value Added Reseller for AT&T Computers.

Description:

The Farm Decision Aids package consists of four disks which may be purchased separately or as a package:

Disk 1. Management Decisions

- Equipment Decision
- Grain Selling Decisions
- Annual Cost of Ownership
- Land Purchase Analysis
- Grain Interest Cost

Disk 2. Livestock Breakeven Analysis

- Feeder Cattle
- Swine

Disk 3. Farm Profitability Analysis

Disk 4. Crop Budget Analysis

The scope of the programs Equipment Decisions will help you evaluate fixed and variable costs for owning and operating various farm machinery. Grain Selling Decisions will help you make marketing decisions based on storage costs. Grain drying and interest costs are also factored in. Annual Cost of Ownership will help you evaluate ownership charges allocated to your investments in buildings, breeding stock, machinery and land. Land Purchase Analysis will help you figure out the necessary cash flow for buying farmland and your equity growth. Grain Interest Cost will help you determine the profit in feeding cattle with basic costs and a wide range of variables. Swine Breakeven Analysis will help you figure the profit in farrow to finish, farrow to 40 pound, and feeder pit to finish production systems. Farm Profitability Analysis will help you assess the profitability of your operation by reviewing various rations and indicators of financial growth. Crop Budget Analysis will help you determine the profit in producing corn, soybeans, corn silage, oats, wheat or hay.

Company:
Decision Data & Services, Inc.

Product:
Farm Management Guide

Category:
Industry/Vertical

Computer:	**Media:**
AT&T PC 6300	Diskette

Language:
BASIC

Requirements:
256 KB RAM
2 disk drives
Printer optional

Support:
30-day warranty
Full customer support
Telephone (515) 233-4873

Retail Price:
$139.95 for each package Crop, Livestock, and Finance.

Distributor:

Beacon MicroCenter, Inc.
538 South Duff
Ames, IA 50010
Tel: (515) 233-4873

Beacon MicroCenter, Inc. is an authorized Value Added Reseller for AT&T Computers.

Description:

Farm Management Guide helps you record and analyze your crops, livestock and finances.

CROP

You can record information about three separate enterprises on each data disk. For each crop you can enter information and print reports on the following categories:

- Beginning Inventory
- Harvesting Information
- Crop Sales
- Storage Costs
- Other Income/Sales
- Drying costs
- Expenses
- Miscellaneous Information

There's room for 410 different entries on the data disk provided but total storage is limited only by the number of disks you use.

FARM FINANCIAL

You can record your farm's financial figures and generate balance sheet, trend analysis, profit and loss, and cashflow reports.

- Balance Sheet–You can enter up to 150 accounts. We list account types and examples to help you set up your own current intermediate and long-term assets and liabilities.
- History Trend Analysis–You can enter and change data for up to nine years as well as eight different securities for those nine years.
- Profit & Loss Statement–You can produce P & L statements based on current and previous financial statements.
- Cashflow–This report will tell you when your income and expenses will occur on a monthly basis. You'll know your cash position for each month of the year, when your borrowing will peak, and when you might have excessive cash.

LIVESTOCK

You can record information on three separate enterprises on each data disk. For each enterprise you can enter the information and print reports on each of the following categories:

(Continued on next page)

Description: ***(Continued)***

- Beginning Inventories
- Purchases
- Sales
- Expenses
- Transfers
- Births
- Deaths
- Butchered
- Miscellaneous Information
- Livestock Monthly Inventory

There's room for 381 different entries on the data disk provided but total storage is limited only by the number of disks you use.

Company:
Dun & Bradstreet Plan Services

Product:
The Personal Connection–Disability Income

Category:
Industry/Vertical

Computer:
AT&T PC 6300

Media:
Diskette

Language:
Compiled BASIC

Requirements:
128 KB RAM

Support:
Full documentation is included in price
Toll-free telephone number available for support
Nationwide–(800) 447-0683
Illinois only–(800) 322-4578

Retail Price:
$175

Distributor:
Dun & Bradstreet Plan Services
4517 North Sterling Ave.
Peoria, IL 61615
Tel: (309) 688-4095

Description:

Disability Income does for disability what Survivor Income does for life insurance. The user answers a series of questions relating to the client's income, spouse's income, investment income, inflation, salary increases, and needed replacement income. DI then provides a year by year analysis (both before and after tax), showing the cash flow that would actually be available compared to this objective. DI pinpoints not only the amount of disability income that would be needed, but also the need for inflation riders. It is also very valuable when trying to "prove" the need for additional coverage. In just seconds a complete report is presented, either before or after income tax, showing:

- Client's age
- Total income had disability not occurred*
- Income lost as a result of disability*
- Income available from Social Security*
- Income provided from salary continuation*
- Income provided from group LTD benefits*
- Income provided from individual LTD policies*
- Total income after disability*

*Adjusted for inflation

A summary analysis calculates the future and discounted present value of income before and after disability as well as the replacement sources. DI also shows the unrecovered loss of income as a lump sum value as well as a stream of income. DI is a very powerful program, yet easy to use and easy for both you and the client to understand. Data is produced on the CRT screen as well as a three-page hard copy printout.

Company:
Dun & Bradstreet Plan Services

Product:
The Personal Connection–Estate Tax

Category:
Industry/Vertical

Computer:
AT&T PC 6300

Media:
Diskette

Language:
Compiled BASIC

Requirements:
128 KB RAM

Support:
Full documentation is included in price
Toll-free telephone number available for support
Nationwide–(800) 447-0683
Illinois only–(800) 322-4578

Retail Price:
$305

Distributor:
Dun & Bradstreet Plan Services
4517 North Sterling Ave.
Peoria, IL 61615
Tel: (309) 688-4095

Description:

Estate Tax is an excellent hypothetical probate program. It calculates the federal estate and state pick-up tax for your clients and their spouses and allows you to determine the optimal estate plan, given all the alternatives under ERTA. Estate Tax is used by many banks, law firms, and accounting firms. The program allows the user to pick any year of death for either spouse or it will calculate their life expectancy. Any type of marital deduction may be used or it will calculate a "zero tax" marital, using the maximum exemption equivalent. Estate taxes may be paid from either the marital or residual estate and after determining the taxes and distribution in each estate, Estate Tax then computes the present value of the future tax in each estate.

Company:
Dun & Bradstreet Plan Services

Product:
The Personal Connection–Policy Analysis

Category:
Industry/Vertical

Computer:
AT&T PC 6300

Media:
Diskette

Language:
Compiled BASIC

Requirements:
128 KB RAM

Support:
Full documentation is included in price
Toll-free telephone number available for support
Nationwide–(800) 447-0683
Illinois only–(800) 322-4578

Retail Price:
$235

Distributor:
Dun & Bradstreet Plan Services
4517 North Sterling Ave.
Peoria, IL 61615
Tel: (309) 688-4095

Description:

The Policy Analysis program provides a comprehensive analysis and permanent record of the life insurance policies on your client's life as well as his or her spouse and children. Each policy is listed individually showing the company, date of issue, amount of insurance, type of insurance, riders, premium, ownership, beneficiary arrangement, policy loans, plus the cash value and dividends projected for three years. The program then calculates the internal cash flow for each of the three years. Policy Analysis is valuable as a database as well as in determining the efficiency of the overall insurance program. It also provides an excellent source for additional premium dollars.

The program produces a seven-page printed report and maintains the complete file on a diskette. Data is easily reviewed on the CRT screen and changes can be completed in just a few minutes.

Company:
Dun & Bradstreet Plan Services

Product:
The Personal Connection–Retirement Income

Category:
Industry/Vertical

Computer:
AT&T PC 6300

Media:
Diskette

Language:
Compiled BASIC

Requirements:
128 KB RAM

Support:
Full documentation is included in price
Toll-free telephone number available for support
Nationwide–(800) 447-0683
Illinois only–(800) 322-4578

Retail Price:
$455

Distributor:
Dun & Bradstreet Plan Services
4517 North Sterling Ave.
Peoria, IL 61615
Tel: (309) 688-4095

Description:

Retirement Income is much more than a retirement income analysis program. It is a comprehensive interactive "system" to determine the amount of capital needed at retirement to provide financial independence, as well as the tax efficiency of capital accumulation programs. Again, a year by year cash flow analysis is computed showing earned and investment income, income tax, net spendable income, allocation of income to investments, capital accumulated to date, and additional annual investments needed, if any. By measuring the total taxes paid during your client's career against the amount of capital accumulated and allocation to investments, you can quickly determine the "efficiency" of any investment program.

Up to twenty separate capital accumulation programs may be used with each having its own individual investment characteristics such as the rate of return, taxation, amount of annual or lump sum investment, etc. Retirement Income integrates your client's employer-sponsored pension benefits, nonqualified plans and Social Security discount for inflation. Retirement Income includes its own tax and annuity tables. Each capital account is kept in a permanent file on the diskette for later recall and updating. Retirement Income is easy to use and easy for you and your client to understand.

Company:
Dun & Bradstreet Plan Services

Product:
The Personal Connection–Survivor Income

Category:
Industry/Vertical

Computer:
AT&T PC 6300

Media:
Diskette

Language:
Compiled BASIC

Requirements:
128 KB RAM

Support:
Full documentation is included in price
Toll-free telephone number available for support
Nationwide–(800) 447-0683
Illinois only–(800) 322-4578

Retail Price:
$185

Distributor:
Dun & Bradstreet Plan Services
4517 North Sterling Ave.
Peoria, IL 61615
Tel: (309) 688-4095

Description:

Survivor Income is an interactive program designed to calculate the exact amount of life insurance your client should own to provide for the income and expenses of his survivors in the event of premature death.

Answer just 31 questions relating to income, costs, liabilities, inflation, interest rates, expenses, and objectives, and in just seconds you will have a complete year by year analysis showing:

- Surviving spouse's age
- College costs*
- Income needed*
- Surviving spouse's earned income*
- Social Security*
- Investment income
- Investment account balance

*Adjusted for inflation

A summary of analysis then calculates the loss of future income, as a result of premature death (both future and discounted present value) and how much will be replaced from Social Security, investment income and spouse's earned income. Finally, Survivor Income calculates EXACTLY how much additional life insurance would be needed to meet the client's objectives. Output data is produced on the CRT screen as well as a three-page printed report.

Company:
Educational Software Systems, Inc.

Product:
RX Processing System

Category:
Industry/Vertical

Computer:	**Media:**
AT&T PC 6300 6300 PLUS **AT&T PC 6300 PLUS**	Diskette

Language:
Pascal

Requirements:
256 KB RAM
Printer storage
Minimum 10 MB hard disk

Support:
Warranty: 60 days
Training: 2 days
User guide
Telephone support
Program updates
Medi-Span price updates

Retail Price:
$4,950

Distributor:
Educational Software Systems, Inc.
1545 Osgood St.
North Andover, MA 01845
Tel: (617) 683-4699

Description:

The RX Processing System is a comprehensive prescription processing and pharmacy management system. Major features include: third party billing, price updates, inventory control, patient profiles, report generator, accounts receivable, and nursing home. New prescriptions and refills are easily and quickly generated with a minimum of keystrokes. A patient's transaction history or a prescription's refill history are accessible at the touch of a key. Patient, drug, doctor, or SIG information can be added to or edited without disrupting the filling process.

Company:
Endata, Inc.

Product:
Juris-pc

Category:
Industry/Vertical

Computer:
AT&T PC 6300

Media:
Diskette

Language:
RM/COBOL

Requirements:
256 KB RAM
Hard disk

Support:
One year warranty
One year hot line support
Three days of classroom training all included in price

Retail Price:
$3,500–$4,500

Distributor:
Endata, Inc.
421 Great Circle Rd.
Nashville, TN 37228
Tel: (615) 256-7600

Description:

Juris-pc is a legal time and billing package designed for small and medium size law firms. The package includes a complete set of management reports, user-defined billing formats, open item receivables, flexible attorney allocations, an easy-to-read preliminary bill, and an integrated general ledger.

Company:
Eris Medical Technology Inc.

Product:
Eris *Uro-Diagnostic System*

Category:
Industry/Vertical

Computer:	**Media:**
AT&T PC 6300	Diskette

Language:
MS-DOS Version 2.11 *dBASE III* Version 1.1

Requirements:
6300 PC with 10 MB hard disk
512 KB RAM
Data Acquisition Board and controls
EMG board, Pre-amp (optional)
Gould P23 ID statham transducer, maximum of three (optional)
Flow Sensor (optional)
Hewlett-Packard Graphics printer 22250
To maintain patient usage system must be supplied by Eris (FDA requirements)

Support:
The Eris *Uro-Diagnostic System* is factory installed and complete training is supplied for customer use. Approximately three days on installation. Software/hardware technical support available and field service contract with "hotline" number.

Retail Price:
$16,750–$24,500

Distributor:
Eris Medical Technology Inc.
1308 Springfield Ave.
New Providence, NJ 07974
Tel: (201) 665-9260

Description:

The product described is a complimentary software/hardware package developed as a computerized urodynamic measurement system, Federal Register docket number (78N1950). This package is specifically designed for use in the medical areas of Urology and Gynecology. The software is an integrated package of Eris Proprietary control software includes graphic drivers, graphic editors, Data record/store/retrieve programs designed specifically for urodynamic readings of pressures (cystometrogram), muscle activity (electromyography), and urinary flow rates. This application fully integrates a database management system, *dBASE III*, word processing *PeachText*, and spreadsheet *PeachCalc*. All runtime application programs for the above are also proprietary software developed by Eris. This package includes report generators, patient history, patient demographics, full urodynamic data storage, test, read and edit functions, and full patient medical file maintenance.(e.g., physical exam, diagnosis, treatment etc.)

The system includes full screen displays of urodynamic recordings up to six channels, hard copy plot, auto retrieval of customer defined parameters upon completion of the test, and "window" function for closer examination of channel displays in the replot section of stored tests.

Urodynamic data are recorded during the test procedures and stored directly to the patient files; all patient data input such as history, demographic, diagnosis etc. are user-defined, and input to the database is done by using a "mouse", which eliminates keystrokes. By using a well documented database management system, the user has the ability to define extra applications programs for his or her personal use, with the decided advantage of using a fully documented relational database system capable of storing one billion records.

Company:
Fifth Generation Technologies, Inc.

Product:
ACES

Category:
Industry/Vertical

Computer:
AT&T PC 6300

Media:
Diskette

Language:
BASIC

Requirements:
Monitor
Two floppy disk drives or one floppy disk
One *Winchester* disk drive (minimum of 10 MB)
Printer and card reader or card scanner which is optional

Support:
The *ACES* System is fully supported by Fifth Generation Technologies, Inc. A maintenance plan is available from *FGT* after the initial software warranty expires. The warranty includes a toll-free hotline number 1-800-FGT-2001 and any update as long as the user is under the *FGT* warranty or maintenance agreement.

Retail Price:
Floppy $1,095
Hard disk $1,595

Distributor:
Fifth Generation Technologies, Inc.
600 Meadowland Pkwy.
Secaucus, NJ 07094
Tel: (201) FGT-2001

Description:

ACES Attendance Computerized Evaluation System by Fifth Generation Technologies, Inc. is a user-friendly, menu-driven computerized attendance system that responds quickly to the administrator/teacher's daily requirements with computerized attendance. *ACES* is targeted toward schools, districts, and boards of education for school administrators and teachers.

ACES Attendance Computerized Evaluation System eliminates the time-consuming, necessary task of comprehensive attendance paperwork and increases time available to execute attendance improvement programs.

ACES Administrative Attendance Management System monitors students' attendance, class cutting, transfers, and dropout rate by grade, school, and district. *ACES* also generates reports on these and special programs, as well as letters to appropriate recipients when necessary.

Major features include:

- Screen-Driven Data Validation.
- Audio Trail Provided by the System.
- User-defined Organized Course, Student, Teacher Number Structure, etc.
- Attendance Cards.
- Screen Display.

ACES generates historical reports within specific time frames according to student, special program, class, school and district. Such information is useful in analyzing the funding of school programs. *ACES* is a tracking system that is easy to use. Screen inquiries and hard copy report include the following:

- Teacher Daily Class Report.
- Home Attendance Report.
- Attendance/AWOP Report.
- AWOP Report (Class Cutting/Letters).
- Calendar Report or Student.
- Calendar Report (CL, SC, Dist.).
- Homeroom Absent/Late Summary.
- Master File Listing.
- Updating/Correction Report.
- Teacher Calendar Bar Chart.

(Continued on next page)

Description: ***(Continued)***

- Label System.
- Homeroom Accounting Report.
- Class Accounting Report.
- District Wide Accounting Report.

ACES provides a complete instruction manual with step-by-step instructions on the use of the system and its many capabilities. The instruction manual includes complete instructions for data entry and report formats for schools, districts, and board of education levels.

Company:
Fifth Generation Technologies, Inc.

Product:
***CARES*/Computer Attendance Registration Evaluation System**

Category:
Industry/Vertical

Computer: **AT&T PC 6300**

Media: Diskette

Language:
BASIC

Requirements:
128 KB RAM
Monitor
Two floppy disk drives or one floppy disk
One *Winchester* disk drive (minimum of 10 MB)
Printer and card reader or card scanner which is optional

Support:
The *CARES* System is fully supported by Fifth Generation Technologies, Inc. A maintenance plan is available from *FGT* after the initial software warranty expires. The warranty includes a toll-free hotline number 1-800-FGT-2001 and any update as long as the user is under the *FGT* warranty or maintenance agreement.

Retail Price:
Floppy $995
Hard disk $1,495

Distributor:
Fifth Generation Technologies, Inc.
600 Meadowland Pkwy.
Secaucus, NJ 07094
Tel: (201) FGT-2001

Description:

CARES/Computerized Attendance Registration Evaluation System by Fifth Generation, Technologies, Inc., is a user-friendly, menu-driven computerized registration system that responds to the administrator/teacher's daily transaction requirements. *CARES* is targeted toward schools, districts, and boards of education for school administrators and teachers.

CARES/Computerized Attendance Registration Evaluation System maintains an accurate head count of current student enrollments and keeps track of available space for new students without subjecting teachers and administrators to tedious and time-consuming paperwork. *CARES* lets administrators keep registration information—including past, current, and potential enrollment figures–easily accessible and under control of the administrators or teachers.

Major features include:

- Registration cards
- Screen display/hard copy
- Screen-driven data validation
- Letter system
- Directories
- User-defined number structure

CARES System offers accurate head counts of students within a school,a district, and/or total school systems. The results are instant access data that can be used for government funding programs and the ability to more effectively distribute students within the schools and districts. *CARES* screen inquiries and hard copy reports may be selected from the following:

- School Seat Inventory
- Registration of Class
- Teacher Schedule Report
- Class Inventory
- Project Class Accounting
- Teacher Student Schedule
- Seat Available Inventory
- Student Grade Analyst
- Student Department Analyst
- Course Directory
- Teacher Directory

(Continued on next page)

Description: ***(Continued)***

- Student/Parent Directory/Label System
- Student Class Catalog Directory
- Registration Cards

CARES System helps administrators assign student placement within classes, schools, or districts for any given calendar year. The system provides screen or printed reports on school placement, enrollment, cuts, and attendance. Statistical reports for schools, districts, boards,and state or federal requirements are easily generated. *CARES* System is an easy-to-use, menu-driven system.

CARES provides a complete step-by-step instruction manual on how to use the many capabilities of the system. The instruction manual includes complete instructions for data entry and report formats for schools, districts, and board of education levels.

Company:
Fisher Business Systems

Product:
FBS Construction Management System

Category:
Industry/Vertical

Computer:
AT&T PC 6300

Media:
Diskette

Language:
MS-BASIC

Requirements:
256 KB RAM
Minimum 10 MB hard disk

Support:
Complete one-year warranty
On-site installation and training
Extended support plans, and direct support telephone line

Retail Price:
$5,000—G/L, A/P, A/R

Distributor:
Fisher Business Systems
1010 Huntcliff Trace #2215
Atlanta, GA 30338
Tel: (404) 587-1717

Description:

The Fisher Construction Management System is designed for both light commercial and residential companies in the construction industry. The system is fully integrated and features job cost, scheduling, estimating (keyboard assembly and digitizer), general ledger, accounts payable (checkwriting and overpayment control included), client billing and other capabilities.

Company:
Fisher Business Systems

Product:
FBS Dental Practice Management System

Category:
Industry/Vertical

Computer:
AT&T PC 6300

Media:
Diskette

Language:
Compiled BASIC

Requirements:
128 KB RAM
10 MB hard disk

Support:
Optional through FBS, (404) 587-1717

Retail Price:
$2,800, with integrated financials, $4,100.

Distributor:
Fisher Business Systems
1010 Huntcliff Trace #2215
Atlanta, GA 30338
Tel: (404) 587-1717

Description:

The FBS Dental Practice Management System is designed to assist in the management of the dentist's office. The system contains all of the applications necessary to increase the productivity of the staff, facilitate the processing of insurance forms, schedule patients, collect accounts receivable, and analyze the financial nature of the practice. The system is fully integrated, and may be used in conjunction with the FBS Business Management System applications of Payroll, Accounts Payable, and General Ledger.

Company:
Fisher Business Systems

Product:
FBS Funeral Director Management System

Category:
Industry/Vertical

Computer:
AT&T PC 6300

Media:
Diskette

Language:
Compiled BASIC

Requirements:
128 KB RAM
10 MB hard disk

Support:
Optional through FBS, (404) 587-1717

Retail Price:
Director Mgt. module $3,200.00
With G/L, A/P, A/R, $4,500.00

Distributor:
Fisher Business Systems
1010 Huntcliff Trace #2215
Atlanta, GA 30338
Tel: (404) 587-1717

Description:

The FBS Funeral Director Management System is designed to assist the Funeral Director in following the recent legislation for completing the National Funeral Director's Pre-Need Record Keeping Forms. The System also prints Death Certificates, Veteran forms, Social Security forms, Purchase agreements and Service Program forms. Salesman commissions and Payments/Refunds are handled. The Funeral Director System may be integrated with the FBS Financial applications of Accounts Receivable, Accounts Payable, and General Ledger.

Company:
Fisher Business Systems

Product:
FBS Legal Practice Management System

Category:
Industry/Vertical

Computer:
AT&T PC 6300

Media:
Diskette

Language:
COBOL

Requirements:
256 KB RAM
10 MB hard disk

Support:
Warranty included
Training & support available

Retail Price:
Time & Billing $1,800
With Trust Accounting $2,700
With all Financials $4,000

Distributor:
Fisher Business Systems
1010 Huntcliff Trace, #2215
Atlanta, GA 30338
Tel: (404) 587-1717

Description:

The Legal Practice Management System is designed to form a "total solution" for the attorney. The System contains five modules which may be integrated or used in a standalone environment. The Trust Accounting module provides the legal firm with effective control and complete audit trails of client trust accounts. The Time Accounting and Billing module performs accounting for billable time and expenses so that bills get out on time and in a flexible, professional manner. The system also includes complete financial applications.

Company:
Fisher Business Systems

Product:
FBS Medical Practice Management System

Category:
Industry/Vertical

Computer:
AT&T PC 6300

Media:
Diskette

Language:
Compiled BASIC

Requirements:
128 KB RAM
10 MB hard disk

Support:
Optional through FBS, (404) 587-1717

Retail Price:
$2,800; with integrated financials $4,100

Distributor:
Fisher Business Systems
1010 Huntcliff Trace #2215
Atlanta, GA 30338
Tel: (404) 587-1717

Description:

The FBS Medical Practice Management System is designed to assist in the management of the physician's office. The system contains all of the applications necessary to increase the productivity of the staff, facilitate the processing of insurance forms, schedule patients, collect accounts receivable, and analyze the financial nature of the practice. The system is fully integrated, and may be used in conjunction with the FBS Business Management System applications of Payroll, Accounts Payable, and General Ledger.

Company:
Fisher Business Systems

Product:
FBS Restaurant Management System

Category:
Industry/Vertical

Computer:
6300 PLUS
AT&T PC 6300
AT&T PC 6300 PLUS

Media:
Diskette

Language:
Compiled BASIC

Requirements:
128 KB RAM
10 MB hard disk

Support:
Optional through FBS, (404) 587-1717

Retail Price:
Food Cost and Inventory Control $2,800
With Restaurant Payroll, G/L, & A/P $4,60
With additional Restaurant A/R $5,000

Distributor:
Fisher Business Systems
1010 Huntcliff Trace #2215
Atlanta, GA 30338
Tel: (404) 587-1717

Description:

The FBS Restaurant Management System is an integrated set of programs which addresses the areas of Food Cost and Inventory Control for the restaurateur. Applicable for fast food, family dining, fine dining, institutional, and catering operations, the system tracks inventory items, subrecipes, and menu items. The Restaurant Payroll (Optional) includes provisions for tip credit, voluntary deductions, and the latest IRS reporting requirements. The financial applications of Accounts Receivable, Accounts Payable, and General Ledger, are available in the FBS Small Business Management System.

Company:
Fisher Business Systems

Product:
FBS Retail Merchandise Management System

Category:
Industry/Vertical

Computer:
AT&T PC 6300

Media:
Diskette

Language:
RM/COBOL

Requirements:
256 KB RAM
10 MB hard disk

Support:
Optional through FBS, (404) 587-1717

Retail Price:
$3,500, $4,400 with A/P and G/L, $4,800 with additional payroll.

Distributor:
Fisher Business Systems
1010 Huntcliff Trace #2215
Atlanta, GA 30338
Tel: (404) 587-1717

Description:

This system provides the functions required by most retailers. Merchandising applications including sales analysis, open to buy, and sales history are included. Best candidates are retailers selling apparel, sporting goods, farm and feed supplies, as well as furniture and department stores. Sales volume of between $300,000 and $2,000,000 makes justification extremely easy.

Company:
G & G Software, Inc.

Product:
***G&G 1040* 1984 Release**

Category:
Industry/Vertical

Computer:	**Media:**
AT&T PC 6300	Diskette

Language:
Machine Language

Requirements:
128 KB RAM, 16-bit
At least two floppies with 180 KB
80-column screen
80-column printer

Support:
Manual is included
Office number is available

Retail Price:
$600, updates $300

Distributor:
G & G Software, Inc.
610 Park Blvd.
Austin, TX 78751
Tel: (512) 458-5760

Description:

G&G 1040 is a tax preparation package for the professional. It was designed by an attorney-certified public accountant to make use of IRS-supplied forms selected by the professional, as input sheets and to leave calculations and printing for a microcomputer. It supports 35 IRS forms with multiple schedules for B, C, D, E, F, SE, 1116, 2106, 3903, 4137, 4562, 4684, and 6252.

All calculations are performed by the programs, with the results carried to other forms as appropriate. When computations are necessary to choose the least tax's consequences, such computations are performed and the option resulting in the least possible tax chosen. Computation and recomputation of the entire return is accomplished in 10 to 15 seconds.

The user inputs data to screens designed to match IRS forms. Data entry to the screens from worksheets prepared by the professional is easily learned by a terminal operator. No duplication of information is required between forms.

Printing and computing all of the return is as simple as pressing one key. Reprinting of selected schedules is allowed as well.

Company:
Geophysical Techniques, Inc.

Product:
SURFAS

Category:
Industry/Vertical

Computer: AT&T PC 6300

Media: Diskette

Language:
FORTRAN 77

Requirements:
640 KB RAM
8087/287 math processor
10 MB hard disk
Color monitor
HI *DMP 41* pen plotter
HP 7400 pen plotter
FX-MX Epson 80 or *FX-MX Epson 130*-column printer

Support:
Training and technical support provided by author
Fees depend upon type of services provided

Retail Price:
$6,000–$10,000

Distributor:
Cambrian Corporation
12622 Kingsride
Houston, TX 77024
Tel: (713) 932-7153

Cambrian Corporation is an authorized Value Added Reseller for AT&T Computers.

Description:

SURFAS is a highly integrated, wholly interactive package that can be used to easily create and display surfaces. These surfaces represent any single-valued function (such as gravity, magnetic, geologic formation, tops, seismic ISOCHPAC, depth to a horizon, water depth, etc.) of two independent variables, typically X and Y coordinates. These observed data points may be randomly arranged over this two-dimensional space, with as many as twenty different variables defined at each point. The data points may also be organized as connected lists, commonly called profiles, such as shot lines. Gridding techniques are used to interpolate these data onto a square grid mesh, which in turn is used to generate a variety of two and three-dimensional displays. These grids may also be saved and recalled for functions such as editing, filtering and fitting, as well as being used in arithmetic operations with other grids, such as removing trends or examining residuals.

SURFAS is very nearly format-independent regarding input data points, and does not require a separate pass through the data to rewrite it in a special format.

Company:
G.R.U.S. Associates, Inc.

Product:
BOND SWAP

Category:
Industry/Vertical

Computer:
AT&T PC 6300

Media:
Diskette

Language:
C, using *INFORMIX*

Requirements:
512 KB RAM
80-column printer

Support:
Hotline number

Retail Price:
$995–$1,865

Distributor:
G.R.U.S. Associates, Inc.
64 Stone Ridge Rd.
Summit, NJ 07901
Tel: (201) 464-8610

Description:

BOND SWAP is a member of the family of fixed income applications that comprise the FIXED INCOME ANALYSIS SYSTEM. As with many of the modules that G.R.U.S. ASSOCIATES has developed for FIAS, it is designed to operate independently. It is a screen oriented calculator which provides for the comparison of bonds which are to be sold to those which are to replace them. This supplies the user with analysis as to why the transaction should or should not be consummated.

Company:

Helmsman Systems, Inc.

Product:

***H-MRP* Manufacturing Resources Planning Version 2.11-02**

Category:

Industry/Vertical

Computer:
AT&T PC 6300

Media:
Diskette

Language:
RATFOR, C

Requirements:
512 KB RAM
10 MB hard disk

Support:
Maintenance
Training
Hotline support available

Retail Price:
$9,995

Distributor:

Helmsman Systems, Inc.
1030 S. Winchester Blvd. #205
San Jose, CA 95128-3787
Tel: (408) 246-8300

Description:

H-MRP is a material requirements planning package that incorporates classic MRP concepts. *H-MRP* is an on-line, dependent demand, transaction driven, net change system. Included in the *H-MRP* package are *H-CHAMP*–Applications Environment; *H-BOMM*–Bills of Material Manager; *H-BUY*–Purchasing and Receiving; *H-STORE*–Inventory Management and Stores; *H-MAKE*–Work-in-Process Management; *H-PLAN*–Master Schedule and Planner Controls, and *MRP*.

H-MRP interacts with other suppliers' application software packages to support the needs of manufacturing company users. For instance, the *H-CHAMP* tools can be used to integrate the various *H-MRP* modules with presently installed accounting or sales and forecasting packages.

Company:
Intrex

Product:
INTRENET

Category:
Industry/Vertical

Computer:
AT&T PC 6300

Media:
Diskette

Language:
FORTRAN 77

Requirements:
640 KB RAM
8087 math chip
10 MB hard disk
Color monitor
Calcomp plotter
Modem

Support:
Training and technical support provided by author
Fees depend upon type of services provided

Retail Price:
$4,000–$8,000

Distributor:
Cambrian Corporation
12622 Kingsride
Houston, TX 77024
Tel: (713) 932-7153

Cambrian Corporation is an authorized Value Added Reseller for AT&T Computers.

Description:

Contemporary microcomputer systems now provide explorationists with capabilities which were unheard of a few years ago. Their low price and ease of use also make them available to any exploration group that needs to expand their data storage and analysis capabilities. One drawback associated with small systems is their limited storage capacity and the impracticality of interfacing them to large digitizing and display equipment. This limits not only the type and amount of data which can be collected and processed but also the options available in generating large high resolution plots of maps, well logs or synthetic seismic data.

The INTRENET service is designed to help reduce some of these restrictions for users of personal computers in geological and geophysical applications. The basis of the service is the use of a conventional PC in terminal emulation mode with a large computer system. The full size computer supports a wide variety of exploration software. This interface permits well logs, basemaps and seismic data that have been collected to be copied to the PC and stored on mini floppy disks.

Company:
Intrex

Product:
LOGGER

Category:
Industry/Vertical

Computer:
AT&T PC 6300

Media:
Diskette

Language:
FORTRAN 77

Requirements:
640 KB RAM
8087 -2 math chip
10 MB hard disk
Color monitor
Calcomp plotter
Modem

Support:
Training and technical support provided by author
Fees depend upon type of services provided

Retail Price:
$4,000–$8,000

Distributor:

Cambrian Corporation
12622 Kingsride
Houston, TX 77024
Tel: (713) 932-7153

Cambrian Corporation is an authorized Value Added Reseller for AT&T Computers.

Description:

LOGGER is the name applied to a package of programs or software modules designed for the collection, processing and display of open-hole well log data. The program applications are primarily manipulation and processing tools designed with the geological and geophysical explorationist in mind, rather than analytical tools for reservoir studios. The entire applications package is built around a structured data file system which permits logs to be stored in large numbers and directly accessed singly or in groups by specifying a series of general or exclusive identifiers.

The package can be used as an effective database monitor for large or small volumes of detailed well log data. Facilities are unavailable to include well tops and production data based on specific customer requirements. The modular nature of the package also permits easy addition of new applications and custom processing facilities dictated by individual needs.

Company:
Intrex

Product:
MAPSYS

Category:
Industry/Vertical

Computer:
AT&T PC 6300

Media:
Diskette

Language:
FORTRAN 77

Requirements:
640 KB RAM
8087 math chip
10 MB hard disk
Color monitor
Calcomp plotter
Sumagraphics digitizing table

Support:
Training and technical support provided by author
Fees depend upon type of services provided

Retail Price:
$4,000–$8,000

Distributor:

Cambrian Corporation
12622 Kingsride
Houston, TX 77024
Tel: (713) 932-7153

Cambrian Corporation is an authorized Value Added Reseller for AT&T Computers.

Description:

A flexible software package for the construction and manipulation of maps and related map data is a necessary requirement in many fields of technology. The use of maps in exploration geology and geophysics is an accepted part of the business. Maps must be copied, revised, rescaled, converted and updated on a continuous basis. This constant use of maps has historically required the assistance of large groups of draftsmen and technicians and has been a slow and error-prone necessity.

Most of the problems of turnaround time and error reduction in map preparation can be solved by using contemporary computer systems. Once a database has been established on a computer system, it can be expanded, edited, transformed, and reproduced countless times in formats to suit most users. MAPSYS is a package of interactive program modules designed to handle these procedures. It will run on processors of all sizes from microsystems to mainframes without loss of numerical data resolution or capability.

Company:
Intrex

Product:
MODEL B

Category:
Industry/Vertical

Computer:
AT&T PC 6300

Media:
Diskette

Language:
FORTRAN 77

Requirements:
640 KB RAM
8087 -2 math chip
10 MB hard disk
Color monitor
Calcomp plotter

Support:
Training and technical support provided by author
Fees depend upon type of services provided

Retail Price:
$6,000–$10,000

Distributor:

Cambrian Corporation
12622 Kingsride
Houston, TX 77024
Tel: (713) 932-7153

Cambrian Corporation is an authorized Value Added Reseller for AT&T Computers.

Description:

MODEL B is an established software package designed to bring interactive seismic modeling facilities into the hands of the geophysical interpreter. The package is modular in nature with small functional software units which can be assembled to suit the current needs of most exploration groups. It is designed to operate on any computer system from micros to mainframes which supports the Fortran language and the necessary graphics peripheral devices.

The package has been designed to require a minimum of training for program users. All program modules are terminal controlled and present jobs in a friendly manner using terminology and specifications familiar to geological and geophysical staff data file construction, cataloging, editing and reporting are all performed interactively to reduce the mechanics of data handling to a minimum.

Model construction may be performed using one of several algorithms or program options from a growing inventory of capabilities. The user may choose different levels of approximation to simulate the seismic process.

Company:
Intrex

Product:
PROTEUS

Category:
Industry/Vertical

Computer:
AT&T PC 6300

Media:
Diskette

Language:
FORTRAN 77

Requirements:
640 KB RAM
8087 math chip
10 MB hard disk
Color monitor
Calcomp plotter
Modem

Support:
Training and technical support provided by author
Fees depend upon type of services provided

Retail Price:
$4,000–$8,000

Distributor:
Cambrian Corporation
12622 Kingsride
Houston, TX 77024
Tel: (713) 932-7153

Cambrian Corporation is an authorized Value Added Reseller for AT&T Computers.

Description:

In an effort to provide uniform data storage and retrieval facilities Intrex has developed the PROTEUS exploration data management system. Its purpose is to store the diverse information used in geological and geophysical exploration such as basemaps, geologic surfaces, velocity functions, interpreted seismic sections, model profiles, well logs, processed seismic records, and others. Each data file is classified using preset type codes and user-defined identifiers. Data is recovered by respecifying these identifiers to localize the data by project, geographical area or any user-defined variable.

The PROTEUS system has been designed with earth science applications in mind and is highly modularized to accept a wide range of data on most contemporary computer systems. It is functional on equipment as small as personal computers or as large is full size mainframes. Differences in computer size affect only the speed and capacity of the software rather than its capabilities.

Company:
KJ Software, Inc.

Product:
Opening Doors and Closing Sales

Category:
Industry/Vertical

Computer:	**Media:**
AT&T PC 6300	Diskette

Language:
TenCORE Authoring Language

Requirements:
256 KB RAM
Graphics card
Color monitor is recommended, but not required

Support:
Warranty
Hotline number

Retail Price:
$398

Distributor:
KJ Software, Inc.
3420 East Shea Blvd., Suite 161
Phoenix, AZ 85028
Tel: (602) 953-1544

Description:

Opening Doors and Closing Sales, one of the programs in the *DAVID Noted Author Series*, teaches the selling techniques of best-selling author and sales expert, Tom Hopkins. This self-paced program includes "how to's" on influencing people, overcoming fear, creating free time, and improving motivation. The program will help in every facet of selling from prospecting to closing the sale. Job Aids included in this program are Ratios, Rehearsal, Card File and Calendar. Ratios helps the users keep track of performance in certain key areas of selling. It will assist in monitoring progress toward goals that have been set and measuring present performance against previous activity. Rehearsal lets the user sets of questions for computerized drills on a variety of topics. The users can add or delete subjects or questions as needed. The Card File allows the user to create files, store information, review it or edit it as needed. The Calendar provides a perpetual calendar for the next 20 years. The on-line system allows the marking of important upcoming dates in red and then reminds the user those dates days in advance. The user may permanently store traditional dates, such as birthdays, so they will be noted for future years. At any time, any page of the calendar as well as the lists of reminder dates can be printed.

Company:
Mark Clements

Product:
Oil & Gas Economic Analyzer

Category:
Industry/Vertical

Computer:
AT&T PC 6300

Media:
Diskette

Language:
LOTUS 1-2-3

Requirements:
256 KB RAM
10 MB hard disk
Epson FX-100 or *Epson FX-80* printer

Support:
Training and technical support provided by author
Fees depend upon type of services provided

Retail Price:
$600

Distributor:
Cambrian Corporation
12622 Kingsride
Houston, TX 77024
Tel: (713) 932-7153

Cambrian Corporation is an authorized Value Added Reseller for AT&T Computers.

Description:

The Oil & Gas Economic Analyzer includes fifteen years economic analyses by year, oil production decline rates, oil sale prices, gas production decline rates, gas sales prices, BTU adjusted sales price, lease costs, tangible and intangible drilling costs, water production, general and administrative costs, predicted future performance of oil/gas, tax considerations, present value profile, and investment overviews.

Company:
MicroPride, Inc.

Product:
Collect

Category:
Industry/Vertical

Computer:
AT&T PC 6300

Media:
Diskette

Language:
dBASE II/dBASE III

Requirements:
1 MB RAM
32 MB hard disk

Support:
The vendor will provide training and start-up support in establishing customer files.

Retail Price:
$1,995

Distributor:
MicroPride, Inc.
24-26 White St.
Red Bank, NJ 07701
Tel: (201) 530-5700

MicroPride, Inc. is an authorized Value Added Reseller for AT&T Computers.

Description:

Collect is designed to provide the collection agent with information that can be of vital importance in efficiently organizing and managing the collection business. Up to 60,000 debtors and 60,000 clients can be accommodated simultaneously. The collection agent is provided with immediate on-screen access to the complete history of any debtor, giving a chronological summation of each call or transaction that has taken place. A status report on all claims of a particular client is available for use by the collection agent's sales representative in generating new referrals. A tickler file is maintained as a daily reminder to the collection agent of the action list of all claims needing immediate attention. Other reports include a collection agent's activity report with the ability to cut checks and a claim summary report.

In the *MS*-DOS version an interface to *WordStar* word processing is available for debtor and client mailings. A similar word processing interface will be available in the *UNIX* System V version.

Company:
National Planning & Consulting Corporation

Product:
HYDRASEL

Category:
Industry/Vertical

Computer:
AT&T PC 6300

Media:
Diskette

Language:
BASIC (Compiled)

Requirements:
128 KB RAM
One floppy disk drive
Printer
Disk drive 360 KB (DS/DD)

Support:
Telephone support
Updates
Training is not necessary

Retail Price:
$395

Distributor:
National Planning & Consulting Corporation
1711 West 38th Place
Bay 1101
Hialeah, FL 33012
Tel: (305) 442-1133

Description:

HYDRASEL is a collection of three related programs. The major areas covered are the following: Pumping Systems, Sizing of Control Valves, and Volume Calculations of Complex Vessels. Pumping Systems is enhanced by its ability to work with two major classifications of pumping units: centrifugal pumps and rotary pumps. The Control Valve program determines sizing coefficients for liquid, gas, and vapor services involving normal or choked flow, and laminar or transitional flow. Complex Vessels solves involved mathematical procedures when volume is needed as a function of liquid level (h). The HYDRASEL program dramatically improves productivity by providing easy-to-follow screens and "what happens if" capability.

Company:
National Planning & Consulting Corporation

Product:
SELECTRA

Category:
Industry/Vertical

Computer:	**Media:**
AT&T PC 6300 6300 PLUS **AT&T PC 6300 PLUS**	Diskette

Language:
BASIC (Compiled)

Requirements:
128 KB RAM
One floppy disk drive
Printer
Disk drive 360 KB (DS/DD)

Support:
Telephone support
Updates
Training is not necessary

Retail Price:
$295

Distributor:

National Planning & Consulting Corporation
1711 West 38th Place
Bay 1101
Hialeah, FL 33012
Tel: (305) 442-1133

Description:

The SELECTRA program, developed by the mechanical engineering staff of National Planning and Consulting Corporation, is a collection of three independent but closely related programs for Mechanical Power Transmission Component Selection. The following elements can be readily determined: shaft, roller chain and sprockets, V-belts, and sheaves. In the past, selection of the mechanical elements previously described was a tedious process requiring use of a variety of graphs, tabulations, and mathematical equations. Even for those fully familiar with this activity it was often difficult to properly examine all the potential solutions to a given problem, and the results of these calculations were always open to human error because of the many steps involved. The SELECTRA program resolves all of the above by reducing the user's task to two basic requirements: (1) Define the correct inputs (data that is entered), and (2) Press the corresponding keys. The computer will provide an answer (or series of answers) to the problem in a fast and reliable manner. Possibility of error is minimized and all possible solutions can be evaluated with a minimum of effort.

Company:
New Systems, Inc.

Product:
POSCOM

Category:
Industry/Vertical

Computer:
AT&T PC 6300

Media:
Diskette

Language:
MBASIC

Requirements:
1 MB RAM

Support:
Installation
Training
Warranty
24-hour hotline service (602) 955-2709

Retail Price:
$6,000+

Distributor:
New Systems, Inc.
2505 E. Thomas Rd.
Suite 9
Phoenix, AZ 85016
Tel: (602) 956-0990

New Systems, Inc. is an authorized Value Added Reseller for AT&T Computers.

Description:

POSCOM is a Restaurant Management/Point of Sale System. It handles order entry through video display of guest check, menu item, and pricing control; labor control through employee scheduling, sales, tips, and federal reporting; allows flexible use of guest check and kitchen printers; and directly interfaces to Front Office System for automatic posting to guest accounts.

Company:
New Systems, Inc.

Product:
SIMCOM

Category:
Industry/Vertical

Computer:
AT&T PC 6300

Media:
Diskette

Language:
MBASIC

Requirements:
1 MB RAM

Support:
Installation
Training
Warranty
24-hour hotline service (602) 955-2709

Retail Price:
$7,500–$20,000

Distributor:
New Systems, Inc.
2505 E. Thomas Rd.
Suite 9
Phoenix, AZ 85016
Tel: (602) 956-0990

New Systems, Inc. is an authorized Value Added Reseller for AT&T Computers.

Description:

SIMCOM is a property management system. It handles reservations, rooms inventory, housekeeping, guest accounting, night audit, guest history, group/convention handling, travel agent accounting, GL, AP, AR, revenue, and statistical reports.

Company:
New Systems, Inc.

Product:
TASCOM

Category:
Industry/Vertical

Computer:
AT&T PC 6300

Media:
Diskette

Language:
MBASIC

Requirements:
1 MB RAM

Support:
Installation
Training
Warranty
24-hour hotline service (602) 955-2709

Retail Price:
$3,500

Distributor:
New Systems, Inc.
2505 E. Thomas Rd.
Suite 9
Phoenix, AZ 85016
Tel: (602) 956-0990

New Systems, Inc. is an authorized Value Added Reseller for AT&T Computers.

Description:

TASCOM is a telephone call accounting module. It is integrated with NSI *SIMCOM* Front Office System and interfaces to electronic phone PABXs. Calls are captured and computed to preset management parameters. Calls may be rated by either V & H coordinates, WATS, or highest rate within an area code. Appropriate flat rate and percentage surcharges are added, and calls are automatically posted to hotel guest accounts.

Company:
North American Financial Services

Product:
Branch Manager

Category:
Industry/Vertical

Computer:
AT&T PC 6300

Media:
Diskette

Language:
BASIC

Requirements:
512 KB RAM
Hard disk
132-column printer

Support:
Hotline number

Retail Price:
$2,275

Distributor:
North American Financial Services
11800 31st Court North
St. Petersburg, FL 33702
Tel: (813) 576-3511

Description:

Branch Manager offers platform automation capabilities, cross-selling, on line access to customer database, new account and loan processing and office automation including word processing and spreadsheet.

Company:
North American Software, Inc.

Product:
***BROKER'S HELPER* (Portfolio Management)**

Category:
Industry/Vertical

Computer: AT&T PC 6300

Media: Diskette

Language:
PASCAL

Requirements:
384 KB RAM
132-column printer

Support:
$49.50/month for 36 months provides full support
Changes
Upgrades
Hotline

Retail Price:
$995

Distributor:

North American Software, Inc.
4154 Crossgate Square
Cincinnati, OH 45236
Tel (513) 793-2240

Description:

The *BROKER'S HELPER* is designed to support all of the activities of a broker and, therefore, to significantly increase his or her earnings. The *BROKER'S HELPER* is designed to:

- Be used interactively, in real time, with one's clients to provide the full range of information needed to enable the client to move logically, and comfortably, to a decision—now.
- Provide total account management perspective (including non-house-holdings) virtually instantly, to permit superior financial management for all of the users' accounts.
- Provide a complete analysis of all effects (tax, risk exposure, debt, etc.) prior to action.
- Be easy to use and maintain in completely current state.
- Provide the power to automatically search out all appropriate accounts and clients for placement of a particular investment, or idea.
- Provide the means to record a client's interest in an investment at a specified price and automatically prompt the user when that price is reached.
- Provide an easy means of building knowledge of prospects and clients' total financial position and investment objectives.
- Provide instant and complete tax information prior to a decision.
- Respond rapidly, particularly when the pace is most hectic.
- Permit easy, rapid, and frequent communication with all or any selected group(s) of the user's clients.
- Automatically update security prices without a time commitment on the user's part.
- Permit the user to easily evaluate a client's changing risk exposure versus his or her objectives, by account, on an ongoing basis.

The *BROKER'S HELPER* is a comprehensive data management and analysis system, designed to be used on-line during the broker's hectic day. It is designed to maintain all records for each client and account, and each security that they hold regardless of whether it is held in-house. In addition, the *BROKER'S HELPER* can

(Continued on next page)

Description: ***(Continued)***

be used to maintain information about prospective clients and securities that the user may wish to follow. The major analytical tools provided for individual accounts are:

The Portfolio Review—This is the primary tool of account management, kept current as to both quantities and prices for each account. The user can instantly review types of securities held; amounts, current and original prices and values, unrealized gains or losses—short or long term—yield on original investment and on current value; annual income, percentage of account equity, cash and debt position and its effect on total portfolio yield, risk exposure versus account objectives, portfolio performance comparison versus leading indicators, and more.

Transaction Summary—This feature provides a review of all completed transactions for any time period chosen, in Schedule D form, showing both long and short term gains and losses. The user can also instantly review all purchases for the time period specified.

"What-If" Analysis—The user can open a "window" during a portfolio review that allows him or her to determine the effect of a series of possible trades on all aspects of the portfolio (listed above), including the effect of commissions and interest, without affecting the permanent files. "What if" analysis can be done while the client is on the phone, or in the user's office; and the user may also provide a complete print out—showing the before and after position automatically.

Company:
PCI Professional Systems Inc.

Product:
pc I Pharmacy System Version 2.50

Category:
Industry/Vertical

Computer:
AT&T PC 6300

Media:
Diskette

Language:
C

Requirements:
512 KB RAM
10 MB or above

Support:
Complete training and ongoing support: $75/month
Including "800" hotline support

Retail Price:
$8,500

Distributor:
PCI Professional Systems, Inc.
300 N. Crockett
Granbury, TX 76048
Tel: (817) 573-7011

Description:

The pc I (DOS) Pharmacy System is a comprehensive, user-friendly and widely accepted in-store pharmacy system. The pc I Pharmacy System was designed by pharmacists with more than 10 years' experience with computerization and is offered by the fastest growing independent pharmacy computer company in the U.S. This system is currently installed in more than 500 pharmacies across the country.

The pc I (DOS) Pharmacy System is designed to alleviate the major problem faced in the pharmacy practice including third party prescription processing, inaccurate or outdated pricing, and inefficient manual operations, and to allow the pharmacist to maintain a high quality, productive, and profitable pharmacy business. Features of the system include:

- Complete prescription filling support including allergy flags, automatic drug interaction checking, and patient counseling information
- Automatic pricing based on up to three (3) separate cost bases, up to 94 pricing tables, multiple pricing formulas, as well as competitive pricing options, variable and percentage copays, and discounting options
- Comprehensive third-party billing capabilities which allow for eligibility checking of both the patient and drug prior to dispensing and complete forms requirements for Medicaid programs and all major third-party carriers
- Complete reports capabilities for all legally required logs as well as medical expense summaries, transaction reports, and "customized" parameter driven reports
- Completely integrated accounts receivables, accounts payables, general ledger, nursing home, and sales analysis packages also available with the pharmacy system
- Help functions for each field and screen, and even second level help functions which reproduce user manual documentation

The pc I (DOS) Pharmacy System also supports color monitors for the 6300.

Company:
Parker Computer Systems

Product:
P.A.R.I.S Release 2.8

Category:
Industry/Vertical

Computer:
AT&T PC 6300

Media:
Diskette

Language:
Compiled BASIC

Requirements:
256 KB RAM
10 MB hard disk
Monitor
80-column printer

Support:
90-day warranty
Annual maintenance $600
On-site training available at additional cost
Telephone support included with annual maintenance contract

Retail Price:
$2,995

Distributor:
Parker Computer Systems
2601 Ridgemar Plaza, Suite 1
Fort Worth, TX 76116
Tel: (817) 735-9515

Description:

P.A.R.I.S is a complete office management system designed for use in either a single practice or a group or clinic environment. Both medical and dental versions of the system are available.

Major components of the system include: patient billing on an individual or family practice basis; insurance claim processing with up to nine different claim formats; statements; aging of accounts with end-of-day, end-of-month, and year-to-date processing; scheduling; and practice and patient analysis reporting. The system also generates mailing labels and has the capability to store certain text for merging with a word processor.

An electronic claims processing module is now available on a state-by-state basis.

Company:
Potterstown Enterprises

Product:
The ESTIMATOR

Category:
Industry/Vertical

Computer:
AT&T PC 6300

Media:
Diskette

Language:
BASIC

Requirements:
128 KB RAM
1 disk drive
132-column printer

Support:
Customization
Installation
Training
Support (201) 236-9659

Retail Price:
$4,000 for first 5 operations/tasks, $400 for each additional.

Distributor:
Potterstown Enterprises
Box 265, R. D. #3
Lebanon, NJ 08833
Tel: (201) 236-9659

Description:

The ESTIMATOR was developed to assist companies involved in machining and steel fabricating operations. It enables the user to estimate and develop work instructions for machine and plate shop operations quickly, accurately, and consistently. Fourty-two machine groups and tasks are programmed. They include: milling, drilling, turning, gear hobbing, grinding, saw cutting, flame cutting, fitting, welding, boxing, etc.

The program is customized to suit the user's facilities. Parameters for each machine tool or work center are coded into the program in order to achieve realistic instructions and high accuracy. Some of the special features incorporated in the system are:

- Set-up and handling times are related to the size of the workpiece, number of handlings, and type of machine or task.
- Speeds and feeds are decreased with increasing material hardness.
- Cutting depth and speed are decreased with decreasing rigidity of the set-up.
- When the required power exceeds the available power, then the feed or the speed is reduced until the required power equals the available power.
- The developed manufacturing hours and work instructions are displayed on the screen for review and corrections before being printed.

Anyone who can read blueprints and knows the company's work center capabilities can quickly be trained to develop consistent and informative estimates.

Company:
ProfitKey International

Product:
PROFITKEY

Category:
Industry/Vertical

Computer:
AT&T PC 6300

Media:
Diskette

Language:
RM/COBOL

Requirements:
128 KB RAM
Hard disk
Modem

Support:
Hotline support (603) 898-3100
Applications Engineers
Classroom training
Warranty

Retail Price:
$8,000–$42,000

Distributor:
ProfitKey International
200 Prestige Park
Salem, NH 03079
Tel: (603) 898-9800

Description:

PROFITKEY is an integrated system directed at the specific needs of the Job Shop, Traditional Manufacturer or Custom Manufacturer.

PROFITKEY is designed to provide the chief executive officer and his staff the tools required to plan and control company efficiency, thus maximizing profits. It is an on-line interactive system which will assist a company in reducing inventory and overtime, plus increasing cash flow, customer service and direct labor output.

PROFITKEY provides the user the tools for order entry, estimating, material planning, capacity planning, scheduling, shop floor control, and purchasing, plus the supporting accounting and financial functions.

PROFITKEY is a modular, transaction-driven, user-oriented system which provides the following exclusive displays:

The *CUSTOMER INQUIRY WORKBENCH* allows the user to monitor the status of any order in the shop, providing data on costs, deliveries, status, shipments and accounts receivable.

The *ESTIMATOR'S WORKBENCH* allows the user to interactively develop estimates for five quantities at a time, in spreadsheet fashion, incorporating information from previous jobs or quotes to save effort and provide consistency.

The *ORDER ENTRY WORKBENCH* initiates internal jobs or shop orders. Customer information, quotes, and details from previous jobs may be included in an order. Quantities, prices and projected delivery dates may be viewed during order entry.

The *DISPATCHER'S WORKBENCH* provides the tools to inquire into and update operations, routings and work center loads.

The *SCHEDULER'S WORKBENCH* provides the user with the tools to manipulate future loads by rescheduling any actual, unreleased or "what-if" order.

The *MASTER SCHEDULER'S WORKBENCH* provides the tools to develop and change master schedules, forecasts and planning bills as required.

The *PLANNER'S WORKBENCH* provides the tools to firm, release and reschedule orders and to inquire into the status of any requirement, order, item, or bill of material.

The *ENGINEER'S WORKBENCH* provides interactive tools for creating and editing engineering data, including bills of material, routings, and product costs.

The *PURCHASING WORKBENCH* provides the tools to inquire into and update purchasing and vendor information.

PROFITKEY will run on any hard disk system using *RM/COBOL*, including microcomputers.

Company:
Real Estate Microcomputer Systems, Inc.

Product:
Real Estate Investor II

Category:
Industry/Vertical

Computer:	**Media:**
AT&T PC 6300 6300 PLUS **AT&T PC 6300 PLUS**	Diskette

Language:
C

Requirements:
192 KB RAM
Single 320 KB disk drive

Support:
Telephone support from Real Estate Microcomputer Systems, Inc.
Support included with purchase price

Retail Price:
$295

Distributor:
Real Estate Microcomputer Systems, Inc.
526 NW Second St.
Corvalis, OR 97330
Tel: (503) 757-8887

Description:

Real Estate Investor II projects before- and after-tax cash flows resulting from the ownership of income producing property. Other reports include internal rate of return, financial management rate of return, and numerous cash on cash returns. Real estate industry standards were followed to produce both the Annual Property Operating Data (APOD) and the Cash Flow Analysis report.

Input is accommodated through a series of well-organized screens which allow for easy error correction or changes. The program performs a 5- or 10-year analysis, with an additional "Detailed Sales Analysis" in any one of the specified years. Analysis of a partial first year is also permitted. Eleven different loan types are provided, including amortized with multiple and retiring balloons, variable interest rates, interest accrued, and variable payments. All of the loans may be started or refinanced at any time during the holding period. Additionally, each of the projection assumptions may be varied from year to year (e.g., 2% appreciation this year, 5% next, and 6% thereafter).

An additional feature provides for the storage of formatted output as ASCII text files. This allows for instant telecommunications of reports via modem and also for the customization of output using a standard word processor.

Company:
Red Wing Business Systems, Inc.

Product:
RW Cow/Calf Production System

Category:
Industry/Vertical

Computer:
AT&T PC 6300

Media:
Diskette

Language:
BASIC

Requirements:
Two disk drives
128 KB RAM
80-column printer (or a hard disk system)

Support:
A 30-day money-back guarantee is offered for all Red Wing Software. Free support is also offered to all licensed customers for the first year that they own the software package. Support is done through dealers and directly through Red Wing Business Systems. The documentation manual is complete and will help customers learn the package at their convenience.

Retail Price:
$595

Distributor:
Red Wing Business Systems, Inc.
610 Main St.
P.O. Box 19
Red Wing, MN 55066
Tel: (612) 388-1106

Description:

The Red Wing Cow/Calf Production system makes it easy to keep management information on cows, calves, and bulls. The user can make comparisons of cows, calves, or bulls against others in their groups or against others in the same herd. This system works equally well for purebred or commercial breeders. Program features include automatically adjusted weaning weights using the operator's formula, automatic update of cow and bull records when calf entry is made, calculation of the Most Probable Producing Ability of each cow and bull, indexing of cows to the group and herd, grouping of cows, and up to 10 years of history for each cow and bull.

Company:
Red Wing Business Systems, Inc.

Product:
RW Crop Decision Aids

Category:
Industry/Vertical

Computer: **AT&T PC 6300**

Media: Diskette

Language:
BASIC

Requirements:
One disk drive
64 KB RAM
80-column printer (or a hard disk system)

Support:
A 30-day money-back guarantee is offered for all Red Wing Software. Free support is also offered to all licensed customers for the first year that they own the software package. Support is done through dealers and directly through Red Wing Business Systems. The documentation manual is complete and will help customers learn the package at their convenience.

Retail Price:
$95

Distributor:
Red Wing Business Systems, Inc.
610 Main St.
P.O. Box 19
Red Wing, MN 55066
Tel: (612) 388-1106

Description:

The Red Wing Crop Decision Aids system is helpful in determining which market prices are profitable for the user. It gives the opportunity to lock in a profit. When the weather changes the yield projections, the expected yield figures may be quickly changed and the profit situation determined. This application allows for comparing profits at varying prices and various production costs, various yields, or any other combination.

Company:
Red Wing Business Systems, Inc.

Product:
RW Crop Model

Category:
Industry/Vertical

Computer:
AT&T PC 6300

Media:
Diskette

Language:
Compiled BASIC

Requirements:
Two disk drives
256 KB RAM
80-column printer (or a hard disk system)

Support:
A 30-day money-back guarantee is offered for all Red Wing Software. Free support is also offered to all licensed customers for the first year that they own the software package. Support is done through dealers and directly through Red Wing Business Systems. The documentation manual is complete and will help customers learn the package at their convenience.

Retail Price:
$495

Distributor:
Red Wing Business Systems, Inc.
610 Main St.
P.O. Box 19
Red Wing, MN 55066
Tel: (612) 388-1106

Description:

The Red Wing Crop Model allows the user to obtain a complete set of future financial records for the upcoming year for several different crops. It helps the user make better production, financial and marketing decisions. The user can see the effect any management change would have on his or her operation. The system is easy to use and extremely flexible.

Company:
Red Wing Business Systems, Inc.

Product:
RW Dairy Production

Category:
Industry/Vertical

Computer: **AT&T PC 6300**

Media: Diskette

Language:
BASIC

Requirements:
Two disk drives
128 KB RAM
80-column printer (or a hard disk system)

Support:
A 30-day money-back guarantee is offered for all Red Wing Software. Free support is also offered to all licensed customers for the first year that they own the software package. Support is done through dealers and directly through Red Wing Business Systems. The documentation manual is complete and will help customers learn the package at their convenience.

Retail Price:
$595

Distributor:
Red Wing Business Systems, Inc.
610 Main St.
P.O. Box 19
Red Wing, MN 55066
Tel: (612) 388-1106

Description:

The Red Wing Dairy Production system provides dairymen with an easy-to-use method of keeping good management records on their dairy cows. Information on which cows to cull will be available based on lifetime cow cost compared to lifetime revenue. This system allows milk production to be maintained at the most efficient levels, and the dairyman will have a complete health record, including costs, symptoms, and a treatment schedule. The system is easy to use and extremely flexible.

Company:
Red Wing Business Systems, Inc.

Product:
RW Farm Inventory

Category:
Industry/Vertical

Computer: AT&T PC 6300

Media: Diskette

Language:
BASIC

Requirements:
Two disk drives
128 KB RAM
80-column printer (or a hard disk system)

Support:
A 30-day money-back guarantee is offered for all Red Wing Software. Free support is also offered to all licensed customers for the first year that they own the software package. Support is done through dealers and directly through Red Wing Business Systems. The documentation manual is complete and will help customers learn the package at their convenience.

Retail Price:
$250

Distributor:
Red Wing Business Systems, Inc.
610 Main St.
P.O. Box 19
Red Wing, MN 55066
Tel: (612) 388-1106

Description:

Managing changing quantities, with widely fluctuating values, requires an inventory management system designed exclusively for agriculture. The Red Wing Farm Inventory provides the information to answer questions such as "how much do I have available, what did it cost, what is it worth, and how long will it last?" The user can easily reduce inventory by a fixed amount per unit of time, such as a feeding operation would encounter. The system will also graphically display projected inventory changes.

Company:
Red Wing Business Systems, Inc.

Product:
RW Feedlot Decision Aids

Category:
Industry/Vertical

Computer:
AT&T PC 6300

Media:
Diskette

Language:
BASIC

Requirements:
Two disk drives
64 KB RAM
80-column printer (or a hard disk system)

Support:
A 30-day money-back guarantee is offered for all Red Wing Software. Free support is also offered to all licensed customers for the first year that they own the software package. Support is done through dealers and directly through Red Wing Business Systems. The documentation manual is complete and will help customers learn the package at their convenience.

Retail Price:
$95

Distributor:
Red Wing Business Systems, Inc.
610 Main St.
P.O. Box 19
Red Wing, MN 55066
Tel: (612) 388-1106

Description:

Cattlemen have found the Red Wing Feedlot Decision Aids system to be a useful tool in determining the profitability of a lot of cattle. It offers the opportunity to monitor profitability as the market changes and hedge the cattle when the price is right. It's flexible to fit the user's operation. The user enters as much or as little information as desired. Information can be utilized from the user's records, projections, or averages. The application also calculates return on investment and prints its own input sheet.

Company:
Red Wing Business Systems, Inc.

Product:
RW Swine Decision Aids

Category:
Industry/Vertical

Computer:
AT&T PC 6300

Media:
Diskette

Language:
BASIC

Requirements:
One disk drive (or a hard disk system)
64 KB RAM
80-column printer

Support:
A 30-day money-back guarantee is offered for all Red Wing Software. Free support is also offered to all licensed customers for the first year that they own the software package. Support is done through dealers and directly through Red Wing Business Systems. The documentation manual is complete and will help customers learn the package at their convenience.

Retail Price:
$95

Distributor:
Red Wing Business Systems, Inc.
610 Main St.
P.O. Box 19
Red Wing, MN 55066
Tel: (612) 388-1106

Description:

Red Wing Swine Decision Aids offers three programs in one: farrow to 40 lbs., 40 lbs. to finish, or farrow to finish. The user can quickly analyze his or her operation including fixed costs of operation, medical costs, total production costs, net profit, and return on investments. The user will not only determine the expected profit for each hog, but also total profit, gross income, cost percent of gain, and total cost of production.

Company:
Red Wing Business Systems, Inc.

Product:
RW Total Farm Model

Category:
Industry/Vertical

Computer:
AT&T PC 6300

Media:
Diskette

Language:
Compiled BASIC

Requirements:
Two disk drives (for a hard disk system)
256 KB RAM
80-column printer

Support:
A 30-day money-back guarantee is offered for all Red Wing Software. Free support is also offered to all licensed customers for the first year that they own the software package. Support is done through dealers and directly through Red Wing Business Systems. The documentation manual is complete and will help customers learn the package at their convenience.

Retail Price:
$795

Distributor:
Red Wing Business Systems, Inc.
610 Main St.
P.O. Box 19
Red Wing, MN 55066
Tel: (612) 388-1106

Description:

The Red Wing Total Farm Model helps you get a complete set of future financial records for the upcoming year for 12 different crops. Some of the features of the Total Farm Model include: detailed itemization of Receivables and Payables which looks at each one separately; increase or decrease yield of all crops; and ratio analysis. It also includes a Balance Sheet that looks at short-, intermediate-, and long-term assets. The Red Wing Total Farm Model handles many more farms and crops than the Red Wing Crop Model.

Company:
Resource Control Systems Corporation

Product:
PLACEMENT POWER

Category:
Industry/Vertical

Computer:	**Media:**
AT&T PC 6300 **AT&T PC 6300 PLUS**	Diskette

Language:
C

Requirements:
192 KB RAM
MS-DOS 2.0 or later

Support:
RCS Corp. offers consulting and training for additional fees
Consulting fees: $75 per hour
Training fees: $50 per hour
Phone support: RCS Corp. offers 30 days of free phone support. After that time, phone support can be extended for a fee of $75 per 6 months
Warranty: *PLACEMENT POWER* is warranted for 90 days against any defects. An extended warranty can be purchased for $75 per 6 months

Retail Price:
$695

Distributor:
Resource Control Systems Corporation
305 Madison Ave.
New York, NY 10165
Tel: (212) 697-0735

Description:

PLACEMENT POWER is specifically designed to meet the needs of an employment recruiter: from a temporary firm, to an employment agency, to an executive recruiter, to a search firm, to a corporate personnel office. As a flexible, user-friendly system, *PLACEMENT POWER* requires no computer background to use, and is therefore very easy to learn.

PLACEMENT POWER was developed by a team of personnel recruiting professionals and systems analysts to serve the unique needs of the personnel and recruiting industry. *PLACEMENT POWER* stores and retrieves candidate resumes by any combination and number of important criteria. The *SUPER SEARCH* feature allows the user to search for any records with specific words or phrases in the freewrite notes field. *PLACEMENT POWER* keeps track of client, resume sendout, applicant interview, and job requisition activities. Other features include a custom report generator, a daily report, and a client billing module.

PLACEMENT POWER is written in C-source code and is available on the *UNIX* system and *MS*-DOS operating systems, and thus can be transferred from AT&T's PC to its larger multiuser 3B series of computers with no data corruption.

PLACEMENT POWER can be integrated with word processing software to send out standard letters to clients and applicants.

RCS Corp. recognizes that all recruiting firms operate differently; therefore *PLACEMENT POWER* can be customized to each firm's individual specifications.

Company:
Santiago Data Systems, Inc.

Product:
Dental Manager Version 5.03

Category:
Industry/Vertical

Computer:	**Media:**
AT&T PC 6300	Diskette
6300 PLUS **AT&T PC 6300 PLUS**	

Language:
CB86 for *MS*-DOS

Requirements:
128 KB RAM
10 MB Hard disk
10 chr/inch and 6 lines/inch capable of 132 columns

Support:
30-day warranty
Toll-free telephone hotline support with direct, unlimited modem support for diagnostics and repair
Plus annual custom form support for $75 per month, billed quarterly

Retail Price:
$3,500 basic package
$500 Contracts Payable Module
$500 Appointment Schedule Module

Distributor:
Santiago Data Systems, Inc.
1820 Orangewood Ave. #113
Orange, CA 92668
Tel: (714) 633-7807

Description:

Dental Manager is an in-office automated management system which performs all the necessary patient accounting and information processing, including private billing, insurance billing, contract management, appointment scheduling, and production statistics in addition to interfacing directly with word processing through the most user-oriented relational database feature of the package.

The package may be installed by anyone and is neither computer, printer, nor terminal dependent. Included with the dealer support package is Santiago's extensive utility package which provides diagnostic programs, record examiners, and a powerful screen-oriented editor specifically for the manipulation of the 60-file database.

Santiago provides a comprehensive reference manual with photos and cartoons, a 12-chapter training guide, and on-line Help documentation for support, training, and reeducation.

Company:
Santiago Data Systems, Inc.

Product:
Medical Manager Version 5.03

Category:
Industry/Vertical

Computer:
AT&T PC 6300

Media:
Diskette

Language:
CB86 for *MS*-DOS

Requirements:
128 KB RAM
10 MB Hard disk
10 chr/inch and 6 lines/inch capable of 132 columns

Support:
30-day warranty
Toll-free telephone hotline support with direct, unlimited modem support for diagnostics and repair
Annual custom form support for $75 per month, billed quarterly

Retail Price:
$3,500 basic package
$500 Appointment Schedule Module
$500 Contracts Payment Module

Distributor:

Santiago Data Systems, Inc.
1820 Orangewood Ave. #113
Orange, CA 92668
Tel: (714) 633-7807

Description:

Medical Manager is an in-office automated management system which performs all the necessary patient accounting and information processing, including private billing, insurance billing, contract management, appointment scheduling and production statistics in addition to interfacing directly with word processing through the most user-oriented relational database feature of the package.

The package may be installed by anyone and is neither computer, printer, nor terminal dependent. Included with the dealer support package is Santiago's extensive utility package, which provides diagnostic programs, record examiners, and a powerful screen-oriented editor specifically for the manipulation of the 60-file database.

Santiago provides a comprehensive reference manual with photos and cartoons, a 12-chapter training guide, and on-line help documentation for support, training and reeducation.

Company:
Seismic Micro-Technology

Product:
KINGDOM

Category:
Industry/Vertical

Computer:
AT&T PC 6300

Media:
Diskette

Language:
FORTRAN 77

Requirements:
640 KB RAM
8087/287 math chip
10 MB hard disk
Color monitor
DMP 41 pen plotter or *HP 7400* pen plotter

Support:
Training and technical support provided by author
Fees depend upon type of services provided
300 page user's manual
90-day service warranty—$375 per year

Retail Price:
$3,750

Distributor:
Cambrian Corporation
12622 Kingsride
Houston, TX 77024
Tel: (713) 932-7153

Cambrian Corporation is an authorized Value Added Reseller for AT&T Computers.

Description:

The *KINGDOM* program carries users into the fine details of their seismic section and helps firm up a picture of the subsurface without magically transporting them into the strata thousands of feet below.

KINGDOM put over 130 different geophysical functions at the user's fingertips.

KINGDOM commands analyze seismic traces and other geophysical data. User's select the commands and design the displays as they analyze the data. The program runs either interactively or unattended through a batch command file.

KINGDOM helps solve real problems, whether those problems lie in acquisition, processing or interpretation. The *KINGDOM* program is limited only by the user's ingenuity.

KINGDOM for Acquisition:

- Vibrator Sweep Design
- Well Tying
- Trial Data Processing in the Field
- Resolution Evaluation

KINGDOM for Processing:

- Trace Processing Parameters Bright Spot Analyses
- Wavelet Estimation & Processing
- Resolution/Coherency Filters
- Deconvolution and Other Wiener Filters

Company:
The Software Library

Product:
Church Management Package

Category:
Industry/Vertical

Computer:	**Media:**
AT&T PC 6300	Diskette

Language:
Compiled Pascal

Requirements:
256 KB RAM
10 MB or larger hard disk
Any printer

Support:
Telephone support available at all times
90-day free support after purchase
User seminars at various locations

Retail Price:
$595–$795

Distributor:

The Software Library
3300 County Rd. 10, Suite 304
Brooklyn Center, MN 55429
Tel: (612) 566-4212

Description:

DEACON–Membership Information/Census System–maintains household and personal data, including interests, talents, educational status, special needs, history, and activities. The user can choose what names and other data to include on the reports.

STEWARD–Pledge/Dues/Contribution Recordkeeping System–maintains financial records for each financial contributor in a congregation. The system produces contributor statements and various analysis reports pertaining to pledges (dues) and contributions.

TRUSTEE–Fund Accounting and Budgeting System–provides complete fund accounting information for up to nine individual financial entities in a congregation. This software also handles dedicated funds and uses three years of history, as well as current-period and annual-budget values (available from printed reports), to make budget projections.

Company:
Software Models

Product:
Construction Job Cost Estimating

Category:
Industry/Vertical

Computer:
AT&T PC 6300

Media:
Diskette

Language:
ASCII Data Files

Requirements:
64 KB RAM
80/132-column printer
Spreadsheet program: *VisiCalc*, *SuperCalc*, *Multiplan*, *Lotus 1-2-3*

Support:
90-day warranty against defect
Telephone Support (714) 338-5075

Retail Price:
$59.95

Distributor:
Software Models
23913 Bowl Rd.
P.O. Box 1029
Crestline, CA 92325
Tel: (714) 338-5075

Description:

Construction Job Cost Estimating is a collection of spreadsheet templates designed for use by general contractors and architects. This enables contractors and architects to estimate the cost of building a home from the building site to the roof, allowing for contingencies, overhead, and profit margin. Since our package is divided into 18 separate phases, a contractor could deal with cost individually and summarize the cost in our Form 100. As our templates run from your spreadsheet program, it retains the "what-if?" features. This package could also be used by loan institutions and C.P.A. firms to help verify costs by a determined contractor or potential home builder.

Company:
Software Models

Product:
Real Estate Investment Comparisons

Category:
Industry/Vertical

Computer:	**Media:**
AT&T PC 6300 6300 PLUS **AT&T PC 6300 PLUS**	Diskette

Language:
ASCII Data Files

Requirements:
64 KB RAM
80/132-column printer
Spreadsheet programs: *VisiCalc*, *SuperCalc*, *Multiplan*, *Lotus 1-2-3*

Support:
90-day warranty against defect
Telephone Support (714) 338-5075

Retail Price:
$59.95

Distributor:
Software Models
23913 Bowl Rd.
P. O. Box 1029
Crestline, CA 92325
Tel: (714) 338-5075

Description:

Real Estate Investment Comparisons are spreadsheet templates designed for realtors selling investments and commercial property. The package is designed after the NIREB (National Institute of Real Estate Brokers) Forms B, C, D, G, and I-A. Salespersons may analyze the owner's income under different financing options for single properties. The Comparative Investment Analysis template is then used to compare financial data of various alternative investments. Individual Tax Analysis then summarizes the tax consequences from various types of taxable income. Excess Depreciation determines the gain on sale subject to income tax. The Internal Rate of Return template then calculates the true rate of return on an investment. Professionals such as loan institutions, property appraisers, and C.P.A. firms will also find this package useful.

Company:
Spectra Computer Services Ltd.

Product:
Spectra Property Master (Includes A/P & G/L)

Category:
Industry/Vertical

Computer: AT&T PC 6300

Media: Diskette

Language:
BASIC

Requirements:
256 KB RAM
10 MB of disk
Printer

Support:
90-day warranty including telephone support (800 toll-free)
Two day structured training course (recommended)
Extended warranty available which gives user all software updates and enhancements
A.M.S. for ongoing support and service

Retail Price:
$1,995–$6,750

Distributor:
Spectra Computer Services Ltd.
1510-363 Broadway
Winnipeg, Man. Canada R3C 3N9
Tel: (800) 665-0241

Description:

PROPERTY MASTER is a fully integrated property management system. It is a comprehensive package that has been modularly designed to meet your specific property management requirements (residential, commercial and shopping center management). The one step data entry concept in PROPERTY MASTER updates information in all modules simultaneously, which increases efficiency and eliminates possibilities for errors. All updating and edition in the PROPERTY MASTER is done on-line; therefore all errors are caught as they are entered and all reports are as up-to-date as the last data entry step. PROPERTY MASTER produces a complete audit trail of all functions, whether they are file maintenance or transaction entry steps. Some of the reports produced by PROPERTY MASTER include: Master Rent Rolls, Vacancy Listings, Lease Expiration Reporting, Parking Control Report, Mailing Labels, Invoices and Statements, plus many more. PROPERTY MASTER also includes an Accounts Payable system and a General Ledger system. The Accounts Payable system includes the ability to enter manual checks as well as have the system produce the checks. Some of the reports produced by the Accounts Payable system include: Vendor Aged Analysis, Outstanding Invoice Listing, and Checks Listings. The Accounts Payable system can be integrated to the Energy & Unit Maintenance systems, which allows you to track energy costs by building and maintenance costs by units. The General Ledger system is a full-function system that allows you to enter budgets, set up recurring journal entries, and produce comparative financial statements. The PROPERTY MASTER system also allows you to keep extensive histories, whether Tenant History, Vendor History or General Ledger History. The General Ledger package and Accounts Payable package can also be purchased separately.

Company:
Summa Software Corporation

Product:
Trader's Data Manager

Category:
Industry/Vertical

Computer:	**Media:**
AT&T PC 6300	Diskette

Language:
Compiled BASIC and Machine Code

Requirements:
192 KB RAM
Monitor
Graphics printer
Modem
Double-sided, double-density disks

Support:
Toll-free customer support line for registered owners (800) 792-2211

Retail Price:
$249

Distributor:
Summa Software Corporation
7885 S.W. Cirrus Dr.
Beaverton, OR 97005
Tel: (503) 644-3212

Description:

The investor's complete database with graphics and communications. Tracks all types of securities, market indices, and price/volume statistics, as well as user-defined formulas. Manual data entry and automatic download. Features fully interactive graphics and reports.

Company:
Summa Software Corporation

Product:
Trader's Forecaster

Category:
Industry/Vertical

Computer:
AT&T PC 6300

Media:
Diskette

Language:
Compiled BASIC and Machine Code

Requirements:
192 KB RAM
Monitor
Graphics printer
Double-sided, double-density disks

Support:
Toll-free support line for registered owners (800) 792-2211

Retail Price:
$299

Distributor:
Summa Software Corporation
7885 S.W. Cirrus Dr.
Beaverton, OR 97005
Tel: (503) 644-3212

Description:

Uses data retrieved and stored by Trader's Data Manager for sophisticated technical analysis and forecasting. Includes point and figure charting, plus over 20 other analysis techniques. Allows user-defined formulas. Features fully interactive graphics, autorun, and reports.

Company:
Timberline Systems, Inc.

Product:
AEPEX

Category:
Industry/Vertical

Computer:
AT&T PC 6300

Media:
Diskette

Language:
C

Requirements:
512 KB RAM
MS-DOS 3.1.or greater
Fixed disk
Serial port

Support:
Telephone support is available from Timberline under a support agreement. This is a fee-based service that can be purchased per call or by annual subscription. Call Timberline for current rates.

Training classes are optional and are offered in six regional training centers. Call Timberline for a current class schedule.

Upgrades/enhancements are available to all end-users who send in their program registration cards. When new versions are available, registered users may purchase them for a nominal fee.

Retail Price:
$5,790

Distributor:

Timberline Systems, Inc.
7180 S. W. Fir Loop
Portland, OR 97223
Tel: (503) 644-8155

Timberline Systems, Inc. is an authorized Value Added Reseller for AT&T Computers.

Description:

AEPEX is a complete project management, billing, and accounting package for architects and consulting engineers. The system is designed for the small to medium size firm of 50 employees or less. The *AEPEX* package is fully integrated and consists of five modules:

- A/E (project management, billing, and receivables)
- Payroll
- Accounts Payable
- General Ledger and Financials
- Starter Set

The A/E module captures time sheet input and posts to projects by task and function. Very flexible billing capabilities are included in the system to handle the various billing requirements of the design professional such as hourly, hourly to a maximum, fixed fee, percentage of construction cost, phased fixed fee, square footage, and others. The software can track projects under a variety of status codes and is able to provide a variety of billing and management reports providing both summary and detail information. A powerful feature of the system is its ability to create invoices in a variety of formats based upon individual client contract requirements.

The A/E module automatically feeds the appropriate information to both payroll and accounts payable so that duplicate input processing is eliminated and errors avoided. Payroll handles all employee pay and reporting requirements, and Accounts Payable manages cash flow and makes payments to consultants and vendors.

General Ledger and Financials are easily prepared to provide the design professional with the information needed to have a clear financial picture of his or her practice.

Company:
Timberline Systems, Inc.

Product:
***MEDALLION*/Builder**

Category:
Industry/Vertical

Computer:	**Media:**
AT&T PC 6300	Diskette

Language:
C

Requirements:
512 KB RAM
Printer
Hard Disk
MS-DOS 3.1 or greater
Fixed disk
Serial port

Support:
Telephone support is available from Timberline under a support agreement. This is a fee-based service that can be purchased per call or by annual subscription. Call Timberline for current rates.

Training classes are optional and are offered in six regional training centers. Call Timberline for a current class schedule.

Upgrades/enhancements are available to all end users who send in their program registration cards. When new versions are available, registered users may purchase them for a nominal fee.

Retail Price:
$5,990

Distributor:
Timberline Systems, Inc.
7180 S. W. Fir Loop
Portland, OR 97223
Tel: (503) 644-8155

Timberline Systems, Inc. is an authorized Value Added Reseller for AT&T Computers.

Description:

MEDALLION/Builder combines an innovative job cost control program with estimating and comprehensive accounting modules to provide a fully integrated accounting package tailored to the unique needs of builders. The package is designed for the first-time user and is easy to install and use. A concept known as "layered functionality" enables the user to access further capabilities of the software as he or she becomes more sophisticated in using the computer system. This feature also makes the software useful for the more sophisticated buyer who may have previous computer experience and is more demanding of the software than the first-time user. Specifically, *MEDALLION*/Builder is comprised of six modules:

- Job Cost
- Estimating
- Accounts Payable
- Payroll
- General Ledger and Financials
- Starter Set

The *MEDALLION*/Builder Job Cost module allows the builder to better track and control costs on his or her jobs. The software supports the job accounting standards as established by the NAHB.

Flexibility within the software enables the user to provide reporting in as much or little detail as is desired. *MEDALLION*/Estimating automates the creation of job estimates and speeds the take-off process.

Accounts Payable, Payroll, and General Ledger modules operate based upon input from the job cost module and information provided directly to these individual accounting modules through simple-to-use input screens. The programs make use of extensive documentation and user tutorials.

Company:
Timberline Systems, Inc.

Product:
***MEDALLION*/General**

Category:
Industry/Vertical

Computer:
AT&T PC 6300

Media:
Diskette

Language:
C

Requirements:
512 KB RAM
Printer
Fixed Disk
MS-DOS 3.1 or greater
Serial port

Support:
Telephone support is available from Timberline under a support agreement. This is a fee-based service that can be purchased per call or by annual subscription. Call Timberline for current rates.

Training classes are optional and are offered in six regional training centers. Call Timberline for a current class schedule.

Upgrades/enhancements are available to all end-users who send in their program registration cards. When new versions are available, registered users may purchase them for a nominal fee.

Retail Price:
$5,990

Distributor:

Timberline Systems, Inc.
7180 S. W. Fir Loop
Portland, OR 97223
Tel: (503) 644-8155

Timberline Systems, Inc. is an authorized Value Added Reseller for AT&T Computers.

Description:

MEDALLION/General combines an innovative job cost control program with estimating and comprehensive accounting modules to provide a fully integrated accounting package tailored to the unique needs of general contractors and sub contractors. The package is designed for the first-time user and is easy to install and use. A concept known as "layered functionality" enables the user to access further capabilities of the software as he or she becomes more sophisticated in using the computer system. This feature also makes the software useful for the more sophisticated buyer who may have previous computer experience and is more demanding of the software than the first-time user. Specifically, *MEDALLION*/General is comprised of six modules:

- Job Cost
- Estimating
- Accounts Payable
- Payroll
- General Ledger and Financials
- Starter Set

The *MEDALLION*/General Job Cost module will allow the contractor to better track and control costs on his or her jobs. The software supports the job accounting standards set forth by various trade associations such as the Associated General Contractors. Flexibility within the software enables the user to provide reporting in as much or little detail as is desired.

MEDALLION/Estimating automates the creation of job estimates and speeds the take-off process.

Accounts Payable, Payroll, and General Ledger modules operate based upon input from the job cost module and information provided directly to these individual accounting modules through simple-to-use input screens. The programs make use of extensive documentation and user tutorials.

Company:
TOM Software, Inc.

Product:
A & M Manufacturing Business Management System

Category:
Industry/Vertical

Computer:	**Media:**
AT&T PC 6300	Diskette

Language:
TOMBASIC

Requirements:
TOMBASIC
SPEED I Database Management Utility

Support:
Training and technical support provided by the local licensed consultant
Fees depend upon the consultant and the type of services provided

Retail Price:
$800–$3,500 depending on the hardware

Distributor:
TOM Software, Inc.
127 S.W. 156th Ave.
P.O. Box 66596
Seattle, WA 98166
Tel: (206) 246-7022

TOM Software, Inc. is an authorized Value Added Reseller for AT&T Computers.

Description:

The A & M Manufacturing System addresses the needs of small- to medium-sized manufacturing firms. It handles the functions required by the front office, sales, and administrative departments as well as those of the manufacturing and distribution departments. The manufacturing package provides the user with a closed-loop manufacturing system. Single-entry transactions, flow-through of the data between modules, and extensive availability of information through screen inquiries and reports are provided. Some system features are:

- Multilevel bill of materials up to 25 levels.
- Bill of materials "global change" function to replace one component with another.
- Work order status maintained as planned, firmed, released, completed.
- The MRP modules use a manufacturing (M day) shop calendar that is user-defined.
- Supports ABC cycle counting for physical inventory.

Company:
TOM Software, Inc.

Product:
Attorney Business Management System

Category:
Industry/Vertical

Computer:
AT&T PC 6300

Media:
Diskette

Language:
TOMBASIC

Requirements:
TOMBASIC
SPEED I Database Management Utility

Support:
Training and technical support provided by the local licensed consultant
Fees depend on the consultant and the type of service provided

Retail Price:
$800–$3,500 depending on the hardware

Distributor:
TOM Software, Inc.
127 S.W. 156th Ave.
P.O. Box 66596
Seattle, WA 98166
Tel: (206) 246-7022

TOM Software, Inc. is an authorized Value Added Reseller for AT&T Computers.

Description:

The Attorney Business Management System specifically addresses the time-keeping, billing, and accounting needs of small- to medium-sized law firms. The system allows for the direct input of attorney time cards, expense billings, and cash receipts. The system maintains work-in-process detail and accounts receivable summary data for all clients by matter. The system supports full accounting control and financial statements reporting with integrated word processing, records management, and financial analysis programs. Some system features are:

- Maintains contingent and noncontingent matters separately
- Tracks fees and expenses separately
- Supports both case and general retainers
- Tracks nonbillable and firm time

Company:
TOM Software, Inc.

Product:
Contractor Business Management System

Category:
Industry/Vertical

Computer:
AT&T PC 6300

Media:
Diskette

Language:
TOMBASIC

Requirements:
TOMBASIC
SPEED I Database Management Utility

Support:
Training and technical support provided by the local licensed consultant
Fees depend on the consultant and the type of service provided

Retail Price:
$800–$3,500 depending on the hardware

Distributor:
TOM Software, Inc.
127 S.W. 156th Ave.
P.O. Box 66596
Seattle, WA 98166
Tel: (206) 246-7022

TOM Software, Inc. is an authorized Value Added Reseller for AT&T Computers.

Description:

The Contractor System meets the key information need of today's general and specialty contractors: reliable, timely, and complete data for cost control, and decision making for high-volume as well as smaller operations. The system helps improve labor productivity through daily monitoring of project progress and supply requirements. Lower inventories, purchase order control and delivery budgeting can maximize cash position. Immediate posting to the Job Cost module, generation of projected gross margins, and accurate project estimating will aid in monitoring project profitability. Some system features are:

- Maintains summary job cost data
- Monitors equipment utilization continuously and accurately
- Calculates effective charge-out costs and produces asset maintenance and insurance records

Company:

TOM Software, Inc.

Product:

Medical Group/Clinic Management Information System

Category:

Industry/Vertical

Computer:	**Media:**
AT&T PC 6300	Diskette

Language:

TOMBASIC

Requirements:

TOMBASIC
SPEED I Database Management Utility

Support:

Training and technical support provided by the local licensed consultant
Fees depend on the consultant and the type of service provided

Retail Price:

$800–$3,500 depending on the hardware

Distributor:

TOM Software, Inc.
127 S.W. 156th Ave.
P.O. Box 66596
Seattle, WA 98166
Tel: (206) 246-7022

TOM Software, Inc. is an authorized Value Added Reseller for AT&T Computers.

Description:

The Medical Management System provides unique record keeping capability for the professional manager of specialty group practices, clinics, and problem-oriented health care facilities. The system produces superbill statements, follow-up statements and insurance forms for patient charges. Practice production is tracked to provide financial statistics by physician, procedure type, revenue center, and insurance carrier. Some system features are:

- One-step set-up of new accounts
- Handles multiple insurance carriers per account
- Automatic generation of statements and insurance forms
- On-line access to patient history including charges, receipts, billings insurance submittals, and appointments
- Credit Management reports identify, monitor, and control problem accounts
- Cycle billing improves cash flow

Company:
TOM Software, Inc.

Product:
Not-For-Profit Operations Management System

Category:
Industry/Vertical

Computer:
AT&T PC 6300

Media:
Diskette

Language:
TOMBASIC

Requirements:
TOMBASIC
SPEED I Database Management Utility

Support:
Training and technical support provided by the local licensed consultant
Fees depend on the consultant and the type of service provided

Retail Price:
$800–$3,500 depending on the hardware

Distributor:
TOM Software, Inc.
127 S.W. 156th Ave.
P.O. Box 66596
Seattle, WA 98166
Tel: (206) 246-7022

TOM Software, Inc. is an authorized Value Added Reseller for AT&T Computers.

Description:

The Not-For-Profit System accommodates fundraising activities and accounting needs of foundations, religious organizations, civic groups, hospitals, educational institutions, political organizations, and charities. This easy-to-use system keeps current, accurate records and simplifies personalization of fundraising requests–freeing up staff time from such tasks as updating membership directories and contribution records to give them more time for personal attention to other aspects of the user's program. The Contribution Accounting modules can standalone or integrate with TOM General Business modules for complete operation accounting control. Some system features are:

- Accommodates user-defined prospect and contributor profile data.
- Prints end-of-year contributor statements.
- Interfaces with TOM word processing system for personal solicitation, contribution acknowledgment, and general correspondence.
- Prints contributor directories, labels, and *ROLODEX* cards.

Company:
TOM Software, Inc.

Product:
Property Management Business Information System

Category:
Industry/Vertical

Computer:
AT&T PC 6300

Media:
Diskette

Language:
TOMBASIC

Requirements:
TOMBASIC
SPEED I Database Management Utility

Support:
Training and technical support provided by the local licensed consultant
Fees depend on the consultant and the type of service provided

Retail Price:
$800–$3,500 depending on the hardware

Distributor:

TOM Software, Inc.
127 S.W. 156th Ave.
P.O. Box 66596
Seattle, WA 98166
Tel: (206) 246-7022

TOM Software, Inc. is an authorized Value Added Reseller for AT&T Computers.

Description:

The Property Management System meets the record-keeping needs of the professional manager of residential apartments, subsidized housing, condominiums, and commercial property. The system supports several properties in a common system, yet produces individual property reports. Daily monitoring of rent receipts and tenant movement helps improve cash flow. Some system features are:

- Handles accounting on cash or accrual basis
- Information is on-line and available for inquiry at any time
- Tracks utility rates and energy use
- Monitors maintenance requirements

Company:
TOM Software, Inc.

Product:
Residential Contractor Business Management System

Category:
Industry/Vertical

Computer:	**Media:**
AT&T PC 6300	Diskette

Language:
TOMBASIC

Requirements:
TOMBASIC
SPEED I Database Management Utility

Support:
Training and technical support provided by the local licensed consultant
Fees depend on the consultant and the type of service provided

Retail Price:
$800–$3,500 depending on the hardware

Distributor:
TOM Software, Inc.
127 S.W. 156th Ave.
P.O. Box 66596
Seattle, WA 98166
Tel: (206) 246-7022

TOM Software, Inc. is an authorized Value Added Reseller for AT&T Computers.

Description:

The Residential Contractor System is a tool for managing the construction of single- or multifamily projects, providing reliable, timely, accurate information for job costing, materials management, labor utilization, financial dealings and general accounting. The system helps to improve productivity through daily monitoring of project progress and supply requirements. Lower inventories, purchase order control, and delivery budgeting can maximize cash position. Daily posting to the Job Cost modules, generation of projected gross margins and accurate future project estimating aid in monitoring profitability. Some system features are:

- Tracks job progress, highlights production problems, measures staff productivity
- Generates work schedules
- Tracks committed, payable, and paid costs
- Generates estimate purchase orders that can be modified for comparison of variables

Company:
TOM Software, Inc.

Product:
Restaurant/Food Service Management Information System

Category:
Industry/Vertical

Computer:
AT&T PC 6300

Media:
Diskette

Language:
TOMBASIC

Requirements:
TOMBASIC
SPEED I Database Management Utility

Support:
Training and technical support provided by the local licensed consultant
Fees depend on the consultant and the type of service provided

Retail Price:
$800–$3,500 depending on the hardware

Distributor:
TOM Software, Inc.
127 S.W. 156th Ave.
P.O. Box 66596
Seattle, WA 98166
Tel: (206) 246-7022

TOM Software, Inc. is an authorized Value Added Reseller for AT&T Computers.

Description:

The Restaurant System provides the main ingredient for successful food service operation: control over food and labor cost, waste, and spoilage. System reports help identify inventory shortages and their causes. The system computes inventory required to serve daily menus, tracks daily sales, and produces a consumption variance report. A cost-per-serving figure can be calculated from current inventory costs. Recipes can be costed and compared to determine profitability. Designed in consultation with restaurant industry professionals, the system meets the accounting needs of fast food, institutional, and white linen operations. Some system features are:

- Produces inventory reorder information
- Provides store control system for users not requiring detailed inventory information
- Calculates how menu mix affects sales and profits
- Updates food costs from Accounts Payable

Company:
TOPIC Systems, Inc.

Product:
***TOPFILE* /Youth Agency**

Category:
Industry/Vertical

Computer:
AT&T PC 6300

Media:
Diskette

Language:
BASIC

Requirements:
256 KB RAM
10 MB minimum hard disk and minimum of one 5 1/4" floppy drive (DS/DD)
MS-DOS (2.11 or later)
GW-BASIC, BASICA (or similar)

Support:
Telephone (914) 471-1363
Descriptive Manual
Full warranty on software, 90 days on media

Retail Price:
$2,000

Distributor:
TOPIC Systems, Inc.
P.O. Box 5279
Poughkeepsie, NY 12602
Tel: (914) 471-1363

Description:

Designed for use by police department youth agencies and various social service agencies (public and private) dealing with youths to maintain archival records of incidents, contacts, services rendered, etc.

Company:
TOPIC Systems, Inc.

Product:
***TOPOIL* Release 2.0**

Category:
Industry/Vertical

Computer:
AT&T PC 6300

Media:
Diskette

Language:
BASIC

Requirements:
256 KB RAM with *MS*-DOS and user-furnished *GW*-BASIC or BASICA or similar (level 2.0 or later). While smaller users can operate with two DS/DD 5 1/4" drives, the preferred configuration is 10 MB or larger hard disk with one floppy disk.

Support:
Telephone (914) 471-1363 and optional installation and training (at additional fee)
Full descriptive manual
Full warranty on software, 90 days for media

Retail Price:
$2,000

Distributor:
TOPIC Systems, Inc.
P.O. Box 5279
Poughkeepsie, NY 12602
Tel: (914) 471-1363

Description:

Designed to manage fuel oil and gasoline accounts with automatic degree day delivery tickets and full accounts receivable for fuel oil dealers. Provides for multiple tax districts and various state-by-state tax and reporting requirements. Produces full transaction statements and full historic records for preceding 12 months. Provides end-of-heating-season budget adjustment and recalculation of budgets for next heating season. Ideal for dealers with five or fewer fuel oil delivery trucks. More information available on request. Demonstration version available.

Company:
TRAC LINE Software, Inc.

Product:
BRANCH STORE RETAILING

Category:
Industry/Vertical

Computer:
AT&T PC 6300

Media:
Diskette

Language:
RM/COBOL

Requirements:
10 MB hard disk
128 KB per user

Support:
Full national customer support, hotline service
90-day warranty
Local dealer support available per dealership
System includes on-screen help menus
Self-paced tutorials
Complete system documentation

Retail Price:
$595

Distributor:
TRAC LINE Software, Inc.
51 Alpha Plaza
Hicksville, NY 11801
Tel: (516) 935-7500
(800) TRACLIN

Description:

BRANCH STORE RETAILING is a full point-of-sale recording system which also operates computer terminals and electronic cash drawers as cash registers. It will run as many "registers" as the hardware system permits.

This module gathers information to be fed into the main accounting system–*TRAC LINE INTEGRATED ACCOUNTING* and *RETAILING*–the master point-of-sale software running at the chain's main location.

BRANCH STORE RETAILING, just like the *RETAILING* master module, handles many types of payments–cash, check, charge, gift certificate, coupons, layaways–while operating cash drawers at many locations throughout the store. Special and promotional pricing routines give the retailer total flexibility for price changes and running special sales, while maintaining accurate inventory counts, sales statistics, and exact cash control.

Daily point-of-sale summary reports categorize sales by product, by salesperson, and by register or department, if desired.

BRANCH STORE RETAILING requires the base package *TRAC LINE INTEGRATED ACCOUNTING* and the master point-of-sale module, *RETAILING.*

Whenever the information from *BRANCH STORES* is transferred into *RETAILING*, all point-of-sale data automatically updates relevant files in the main accounting system–inventory, salesforce, bank deposits, charge card company records in accounts receivable, customer information, and more–giving the retailer an accurate, up-to-the-minute picture of all the business activities and those at each location.

Updating via media or over phone modems can be done at will.

Company:
TRAC LINE Software, Inc.

Product:
DISTRIBUTING

Category:
Industry/Vertical

Computer: AT&T PC 6300

Media: Diskette

Language:
RM/COBOL

Requirements:
10 MB hard disk
128 KB per user

Support:
Full national customer support, hotline service
90-day warranty
Local dealer support available per dealership
System includes on-screen help menus
Self-paced tutorials
Complete system documentation

Retail Price:
$695

Distributor:
TRAC LINE Software, Inc.
51 Alpha Plaza
Hicksville, NY 11801
Tel: (516) 935-7500
(800) TRACLIN

Description:

DISTRIBUTING, a module from the *TRAC LINE VERTICAL SOFTWARE SERIES*, offers the wholesaler specialized tasks above basic integrated accounting. These activities include: ability to run more than one company on the same accounting software, tracking and maintaining inventory at more than one warehouse or internal location, and variable pricing to automatically assign customer pricing through some 250 different pricing routines. *DISTRIBUTING* also includes all distribution management activities special to the wholesaler.

DISTRIBUTING does not stand alone. It integrates with *TRAC LINE INTEGRATED ACCOUNTING*, a general accounting package that contains accounts payable, accounts receivable, general ledger, sales order entry, inventory control, purchasing, sales analysis, salesforce management, list management, billing, serial number tracking, and self-paced learning.

Company:
TRAC LINE Software, Inc.

Product:
RETAILING

Category:
Industry/Vertical

Computer:
AT&T PC 6300

Media:
Diskette

Language:
RM/COBOL

Requirements:
10 MB hard disk
128 KB per user

Support:
Full national customer support, hotline service
90-day warranty
Local dealer support available per dealership
System includes on-screen Help menus
Self-paced tutorials
Complete system documentation

Retail Price:
$695

Distributor:
TRAC LINE Software, Inc.
51 Alpha Plaza
Hicksville, NY 11801
Tel: (516) 935-7500
(800) TRACLIN

Description:

RETAILING is one of the *TRAC LINE VERTICAL SOFTWARE SERIES* modules designed for special small business areas such as retailing, wholesaling, service contracting, and manufacturing.

RETAILING is a full point-of-sale recording system which also operates a computer terminal and electronic cash drawer as a cash register. *RETAILING* handles many types of payment–cash, check, charge, gift certificate, coupons, layaways–while operating cash drawers at many locations throughout the store. Special and promotional pricing routines give the retailer total flexibility for price changes and running special sales, while maintaining accurate inventory counts, sales statistics, and exact cash control.

Daily point-of-sale summary reports categorize sales by product, by salesperson, and by register or department, if desired. Additional options can be added for rental invoicing of products out for temporary use such as in movie clubs, branch store point-of-sale for running cash drawers at other locations or outlets, and installment billing for major purchases.

RETAILING requires the base package *TRAC LINE INTEGRATED ACCOUNTING.* All point-of-sale data automatically updates relevant files in the main accounting system–inventory, salesforce, bank deposits, charge card company records in accounts receivable, customer information, and more–giving the retailer an accurate, up-to-the-minute picture of his or her business activities.

Company:

Arlington Software + Systems Corp.

Product:

Personal Computer Automated Telemarketing System Version 3.0h/3.0N (LAN) (*PCAT*)

Category:

Integrated

Computer:	**Media:**
AT&T PC 6300	Diskette

Language:

Assembler, Compiled BASIC

Requirements:

256 KB RAM minimum
Modem for autodialing (compatible with *Hayes* modem
Printer recommended
Hard disk recommended
3B2 as file server (LAN)

Support:

Training available at additional cost
Normal telephone support is offered during business hours

Retail Price:

$855 (Single user license)
$3,000 (LAN license for support of 6 PC's)

Distributor:

Arlington Software + Systems Corp.
400 Massachusetts Ave.
Arlington, MA 02174
Tel: (617) 641-0290

Description:

PCAT is a sales and marketing productivity tool which is especially useful in situations involving extensive or repetitive telephone contact. This includes all types of selling and customer service.

With *PCAT* the user can automate a wide range of daily tasks such as prospecting, lead qualification and pre/post sale surveys, as well as the ability to respond to inquiries by phone or mail.

PCAT combines in one multifunction software package the tools required to keep track of people and companies that the user is interested in selling or servicing. *PCAT*'s integrated functions include:

- Telephone Autodialer
- Preformatted Customer Database
- Call Scheduler (by date, time and priority)
- Word and Forms Processor
- Script or Data Prompter
- Mailing List Processor
- File Conversion Utilities

Once a Customer Data File is established the user can select the person or company desired in a manner most suitable to the user's business operations. For example the user may wish to make calls by geography i.e., city or state, or by zip/area code; the user may call by Customer type number, or some other market criteria. With *PCAT* users can target their selling effort and measure the results in increased sales.

A user can place as many customer records in the file as the capacity of the storage media allows, up to 8,000 records per 10 MB hard disk.

In addition to all of the standard features in *PCAT*, an option provides the capability to run other applications at the same time as *PCAT*.

The Window Partition Option (APXCore) is a powerful software integration tool. The user can load several programs into the computer at the same time and even move data between them. The user can record keystroke sequences and compact operations to a few keystrokes.

The WPO allows users run up to eight tasks and allows concurrent (foreground/background) operation of any two.

Arlington also offers LAN versions of *PCAT*, and supports: *PCnet*, 3 COM network and *Novell NetWare*, and PC Network currently, Network *PCAT* costs $3,000 per cluster of six pc's.

Company:
AT&T and THE SOFTWARE GROUP

Product:
ENABLE*

Category:
Integrated

Computer:
AT&T PC 6300

Media:
Diskette

Language:
Assembler

Requirements:
256 KB RAM
2 double-density disk drives
Graphics board for on-screen graphics

Support:
This product is fully supported by AT&T Information Systems and carries a 90-day warranty on the media. Remote nationwide customer service hotline is provided Monday through Friday between the hours of 8:00 a.m. and 5:00 p.m. local time. Installation additional hotline coverage, and extended maintenance agreements are also available There are also formalized training sessions which may be purchased.

Retail Price:
$695

Distributor:
AT&T (800) 247-1212 or call your local AT&T authorized dealer or Account Executive.

***This product has been certified by AT&T.**

Description:

ENABLE integrates word processing, spreadsheet, graphics, database management and telecommunications in one easy-to-learn and easy-to-use product. It is based on a system-wide Master Control module that contains all services and facilities, and handles functions common to all modules.

With *ENABLE*, users can create a spreadsheet from Database Management Systems data, draw graphs from either the spreadsheet or the database, and insert the spreadsheet data, DBMS records and graphs between text in a word processing document. *ENABLE* provides an electronic desktop with up to eight separate windows which can be moved, shaped or zoomed to full-screen size. It allows concurrent operation of one application plus printing plus telecommunications.

One consistent set of commands and menus is used in all applications to facilitate learning the program. *ENABLE* is compatible with other microcomputer programs such as *Lotus*, *1-2-3*, *MultiMate*, *dBASE II*, *WordStar*, *VisiCalc* and *EasyWriter*.

New features now available with *ENABLE* version 1.1 include the system-wide Menu Generator and a window to DOS. Also included are automatic table of contents and indexing, multicolumn copy and move in the word processing module; user-configurable worksheets and *1-2-3* macro support in the spreadsheet; and VERIFY, MERGE and UPDATE commands as well as greatly expanded record size in DBMS. *VT*-100 and *VT*-52 emulation have been added to the telecommunications module and the product now supports almost 50 leading printers and plotters.

Company:
Benchmark/Metasoft, Inc.

Product:
***THE BENCHMARK* Administrator**

Category:
Integrated

Computer:	**Media:**
AT&T PC 6300	Diskette

Language:
Assembly

Requirements:
256 KB RAM

Support:
Telephone support (800) 621-1908

Retail Price:
$195

Distributor:
Benchmark/Metasoft, Inc.
6509 W. Frye Rd., Suite 12
Chandler, AZ 85224
Tel: (602) 961-0003

Description:

The Administrator is a simple directory program that integrates *THE BENCHMARK* application programs: Word Processor, Mailing List, Spelling Checker, Telecom, Business Graphics, Merge, Financial Planner, and Data Manager. Through the Administrator, the user can access any of these programs with a single keystroke. The Administrator also guides the user through configuration, disk formatting, and copying procedures as well as interfacing with most other *MS*-DOS applications programs and utilities.

Company:
Chang Labs

Product:
GraphPlan

Category:
Integrated

Computer:
AT&T PC 6300

Media:
Diskette

Language:
CB86

Requirements:
128 KB RAM
1 disk drive

Support:
Toll-free line for dealer and end user support
Nationwide (800) 972-8800
For California (800) 831-8080

Retail Price:
$295

Distributor:
Chang Labs
5300 Stevens Creek Blvd.
San Jose, CA 95129
Tel: (408) 246-8020

Description:

GraphPlan is a financial planning spreadsheet with integrated graphics. Provides "presentation quality" graphs as part of your "what if" analysis. Allows you to see what you have at any time, so adjustments can be made to your liking before printing it out. Automatically updates graphs instantly whenever a single change is made to your spreadsheet results. Includes built-in formulas for percentages, summing, statistics, ranking (in ascending or descending order according to your specifications), and sorting. Gives full line of graphics options, including vertical and horizontal bars, pie charts, tick marks, scattergrams, time line series, and exploded pie segments. Asks you how you want to set up graphs by allowing you to specify colors for each section, explode a pie chart (and display it in different shades or sort by segment), establish limits, add tic marks, and flip a bar chart sideways on the page to print it larger. Allows you to have multiple graphs in a chart, stack them vertically or horizontally, and combine different types of graphs on one sheet. Provides printouts with words, numbers, and images complete with X and Y labeled axes, dollar signs, commas, percent signs, pagination, footnotes, underlining, and centered headings. Has on-screen menus with built-in commands for fast data entry. Integrates with the *MicroPlan* financial planning spreadsheet and the FilePlan database manager.

Company:

Clover Data Systems, Inc.

Product:

Real Estate Brokerage Office System Version 2.41

Category:

Integrated

Computer:	**Media:**
AT&T PC 6300	Diskette

Language:

Compiled *dBASE II*

Requirements:

Z80, 8080 and 8086 families of processors
64 KB RAM (8 bit)
128 KB RAM (16 bit)
Minimum one floppy disk drive and a hard disk
80-column printer
Video display -24 x 80 character cursor-addressable

Support:

Telephone support to dealers and end users, via 800 number

Retail Price:

$2,500

Distributor:

Clover Data Systems, Inc.
541 South Broad St.
Lansdale, PA 19446
Tel: (215) 362-9000

Description:

REBOS manages the day-to-day activities of a real estate office for the broker/owner, office manager or secretary/processor. *REBOS* performs list management and computes pending sales commissions, cash flow projections, franchise and referral fees and company dollars. Special features include a tickler file which tracks each listing process and comes with a special runtime version of *dBASE II* plus a customer database for client follow-up. *REBOS* is password protected.

Company:
Control Data Corporation/BIS

Product:
Visi-On V. 1.2

Category:
Integrated

Computer:
AT&T PC 6300
6300 PLUS AT&T PC 6300 PLUS

Media:
Diskette

Language:
C

Requirements:
512 KB RAM user memory
RS232 serial port
Three MB available on supported hard disks
Supported mouse
One floppy disk drive-DS/DD or 1.2 MB high capacity
MS-DOS 2.0, 2.1, or 3.0

Support:
90-day replacement warranty
Support services hotline at (408) 866-2866
Back-up software available at nominal charge
On-site training available for a fee
Complete documentation and *Quick-start* training included with product

Retail Price:
Visi-On Applications Manager (with *Visi-On Graph*) $150
Visi-On Word $150
Visi-On Plan $150
Visi-On Presentations $150

Distributor:
Corporate Distribution thru:
Control Data Corporation/BIS
500 W. Putnam Rd.
Greenwich, CT 95134
Tel: (203) 622-2463
Retail Distribution thru:
Paladin Software Corporation
2895 Zanker Rd.
San Jose, CA 95134
Tel: (408) 946-9000

Description:

The *Visi-On* System currently brings four powerful applications together—word processing, spreadsheet analysis, business plots, and presentation graphics—in a unique, easy-to-use, integrated operating environment. *Visi-On* includes:

- *Visi-On Applications Manager* (required)
- *Visi-On Word*
- *Visi-On Plan*
- *Visi-On Graph*
- *Visi-On Presentations*

Visi-On Applications Manager works with the computers operating system to provide and control windowing and mouse operations, consistent command interface, file maintenance, virtual memory, information transfer between applications, and a user HELP network.

Visi-On Word provides a full range of word processing functions to prepare and accelerate the revision of all types of documents from simple memos to letters to complex proposals and manuscripts.

Visi-On Plan provides versatile electronic spreadsheet capabilities that maximize the user's ability to analyze plan, forecast, budget, calculate, test alternatives and generally examine and solve numeric, financial and related problems.

Visi-On Graph supports the transformation of a user's numeric data into meaningful charts, plots and graphs—including bar, line, area, pie, X-4 and high-low-close types—with a broad array of user design options controlling grids, shading, framing, labels and more.

Visi-On Presentations enables users to create business-oriented pictures and formal presentation—quality materials, including organization charts, Gantt charts, graphs, maps, symbols, sketches and composites.

Company:
Emerging Technology Consultants, Inc.

Product:
OFFIX

Category:
Integrated

Computer:
AT&T PC 6300

Media:
Diskette

Language:
Pascal

Requirements:
192 KB RAM
2 double-sided disk drives
Or one disk drive and hard disk

Support:
Telephone Support: (800) 782-4896, Monday through Friday, 8:30 a.m. to 5:30 p.m. MST. Full warranty against defective disks.

Retail Price:
$149

Distributor:
Emerging Technology Consultants, Inc.
1877 Broadway
Boulder, CO 80302
Tel: (303) 447-9495

Description:

OFFIX is the world's easiest to use software package that integrates filing, forms design, word processing, and report generation. *OFFIX* is designed for the user who wants a basic, multifunction office package that is so easy to learn, it requires no printed manual. The information necessary to use *OFFIX* is included in the package itself in the form of help screens, menus, tutorials, and descriptive information. All aspects of using the software package involve following office procedures and using familiar office terminology, rather than following computer procedures and using computer jargon. This concept is reflected in visual displays which include a filing cabinet, file drawers, and file folders.

OFFIX can handle routine correspondence, memos, form letters, and documents up to 100 pages. Forms can be created for every aspect of an office information system from invoices to inventories, and all this information can be output in an infinite number of ways through report generation.

Company:
EXECUCOM Systems Corporation

Product:
IFPS/Personal

Category:
Integrated

Computer:	**Media:**
AT&T PC 6300 **AT&T PC 6300 PLUS**	Diskette

Language:
Pascal

Requirements:
2 KB RAM double-sided diskette drive and either second diskette drive or hard disk
To use the plotting option: Color/Graphics Adapter, Graphics Monitor
For link to mainframe IFPS: Asynchronous Communications Adapter
For Printed Plots: Personal Computer Graphics Printer, DOS 2.0
Recommended for performance enhancement: DOS 2.0, 8087 Coprocessor, hard disk drive

Support:
Complete documentation and tutorial
User hotline
New product releases
Consulting

Retail Price:
$895; Volume discounts available

Distributor:
EXECUCOM Systems Corporation
Marketing Information Office
P.O. Box 9758
Austin, TX 78766
Tel: (512) 346-4987

Description:

IFPS/Personal is a decision support system that combines sophisticated financial modeling, integrated graphics, and full-screen editing with ease of use. It has the capability of doing "What-ifs," goal-seeking, solving simultaneous relationships, simultaneous views of model logic, and spreadsheet solution. It communicates to IFPS on most mainframes.

Company:
HAI Software, Inc.

Product:
***HAI*LINE* System**
Runtime (Utilities) Version 2.04
Inventory Version B.06
Manufacturing (BOM) Version B.04

Category:
Integrated

Computer:	**Media:**
AT&T PC 6300	Diskette
6300 PLUS **AT&T PC 6300 PLUS**	

Language:
HAI*BASIC

Requirements:
128 KB RAM
Requires two disk drives or hard disk
132-column printer required

Support:
90 days free telephone support
After that telephone support contract is $250 per year and covers all modules purchased
Training available

Retail Price:
Run time–$50
Inventory–$495
Manufacturing–$495
Package price–$900

Distributor:
HAI Software, Inc.
17151 Newhope St.
Suite 110
Fountain Valley, CA 92708
Tel: (714) 641-2844

Description:

*HAI*LINE* INVENTORY is an inventory package for components and finished goods. It includes average, standard, or latest cost price; allocations; orders; issues; receipts; sales; and cost price changes and adjustments. Reports include valuation, low or slow-moving stock, profitability by item, reorder reports, and product group analyses. A full audit is provided. *HAI*LINE* MANUFACTURING integrates with *HAI*LINE* INVENTORY and provides up to 10 subassembly levels and automatic issue from inventory when items are picked for manufacturing. Subassembly and product costs may be updated from their constituent component costs. Reports include product cost, a where-used list, a production list, material requirements and shortage, and picking lists. A full audit is provided.

Company:
Innovative Software

Product:
The Smart Software System 2.0

Category:
Integrated

Computer:	**Media:**
AT&T PC 6300 6300 PLUS **AT&T PC 6300 PLUS**	Diskette

Language:
C

Requirements:
256 KB RAM
2 floppy or one floppy + hard disk
MS-DOS 2.0 or higher

Support:
Example files and on-screen tutorials
Quick key reference guide
Registered SMART owners
Support hotline
On-going updates

Retail Price:
$895

Distributor:
Innovative Software
9300 W. 110 St., Suite 380
Overland Park, KS 66204
Tel: (913) 383-1089

Description:

The Smart Software System runs on the AT&T PC 6300 with a modularly integrated design pioneered by *Innovative* Software. Each of the system's three programs—The Smart Word Processor, The Smart Data Manager and The Smart Spreadsheet with Graphics—is designed around its own data structure, maintaining the full-featured, uncompromising capabilities of each application. A Time Manager and Communications are built into each standalone program.

The three programs not only are integrated, allowing users to move effortlessly from one application to another, but are powerful enough to compete as standalones with any single-application software package in their respective categories. Each program requires only 256 KB of memory, allowing each module to run on a standard PC 6300 without the need for memory upgrade. The modular approach to integration is the only design that eliminates compromise in any of the integrated packages.

The Smart Software System has a proprietary open-ended design that allows users to transfer data from other vendors' programs or develop their own custom applications. In addition, three exclusive features set the system apart from any other integrated software package: "confidence levels," "project processing," and "The Smart Programming Language."

SMART SOFTWARE INDIVIDUAL MODULES

- The Smart Data Manager: data management, communications, time manager, formula calculator, and programming language.
- The Smart Word Processor: word processing, communications, time manager, formula calculator, programming language, and type style (font) designer.
- The Smart Spreadsheet with Graphics spreadsheet graphics, communications, time manager, formula calculator, programming language, and type style (font) designer.

GENERAL HIGHLIGHTS OF SMART SYSTEM

- Built-in communications program.
- Built-in time manager/appointment scheduler.
- Built-in programming applications language.
- Three user "Confidence Levels"; so beginners don't face intimidating options, yet experts have all the power they need.

(Continued on next page)

Description: ***(Continued)***

- Efficient data storage techniques to assure maximum capacity.
- "Virtual Memory": extends available data area by paging to disk or RAM disk.
- Extensive formula calculator.
- Full-screen formula editor.
- Operates from menus, quick menu by-pass keys, and the Smart Programming Language.
- Simple English language commands, screen structures, and operating methods common throughout all modules.
- Macro capabilities (key define).
- Supports Intel 8087 and 80287 math coprocessors.

INTEGRATION HIGHLIGHTS

- Complete integration of data and commands between all Smart Modules.
- 25 on-screen windows.
- Multiple files, or spreadsheets or documents in memory and on-screen at once.
- Relational information transfers within and between files, spreadsheets or documents.
- Automatic "remembering", recording and re-execution of any task sequence within and between modules (Project Processing).
- Custom application development with the Smart Programming language.
- Data interfaces to other manufacturers' software.

DISPLAY AND OUTPUT HIGHLIGHTS

- Report-generating functions.
- Eleven different type styles (fonts).
- Type style (font) designer.
- Supports full color and B/W graphics, lines and boxes.
- Supports a range of medium and high resolution monitors.
- Supports most popular printers, plotters and graphics cards.

Company:
Martek, Inc.

Product:
Advanced Integrated Manufacturing System (AIMS) Version 3.0

Category:
Integrated

Computer:
AT&T PC 6300

Media:
Diskette

Language:
Basic

Requirements:
128 KB RAM
Basic Runtime module
10 MB hard disk

Support:
90-day warranty
On-site installation & training
Toll free 800 line
Extended warranty available

Retail Price:
$8,000–$40,000

Distributor:
Martek, Inc.
825 N. Cass Ave., Suite 115
Westmont, IL 60559
Tel: (312) 850-7244

Description:

AIMS is an integrated set of programs making up a very sophisticated interactive software system that allows better management of any manufacturing facility.

AIMS was specially designed for manufacturers based on commercial and military specifications. Its modular design enables the user to either start off with the entire system or with just a few modules. Since the modular design of AIMS accesses the same data files, redundancy is eliminated when data is entered. This results in a significant savings in time and totally eliminates duplication of effort. State-of-the-art design also enables the user to update shop floor information on a real time basis using the shop floor terminals. AIMS—Advanced Integrated Manufacturing System Modules—offers the following modules:

- PPS—Production Planning System
- SMS—Sales Management System
- SAS—Special Application System
- MMS—Material Management System
- FMS—Financial Management System

Depending on the size of the manufacturing facility the user can choose between two configurations of AIMS software, single user AIMS and multiuser AIMS can easily be upgraded from the single to a multiuser system as the user's company grows.

Company:

Micro Data Base Systems, Inc.

Product:

KnowledgeMan
K-Paint
K-Graph
K-Text

Category:

Integrated

Computer:	**Media:**
AT&T PC 6300	Diskette

Language:

C, Assembler

Requirements:
192 KB RAM (500 K mass storage)

Support:
Toll-free telephone support provided to registered users
Priority support telephone line available for a fee
Training seminars available in major American cities
Discovering *KnowledgeMan* (book tutorial) $19.95

Retail Price:
KnowledgeMan $500
K-Graph $225
K-Report $225
K-Text $175
K-Paint $100
K-Mouse $100
LAN *KnowledgeMan* (10 users) $1,495
LAN *K-Graph* $450
LAN *K-Report* $450
LAN *K-Text* $350
LAN *K-Paint* $200
LAN *K-Mouse* $200

Distributor:

Micro Data Base Systems, Inc.
P.O. Box 248
Lafayette, IN 47902
Tel: (317) 463-2581

Description:

KnowledgeMan is a comprehensive and integrated information management system for creating powerful decision-support systems. The system handles data management, ad hoc inquiries, spreadsheet analysis, statistical analysis, screen management, report forms management, and structured programming. The system offers an unlimited number of open files, with a maximum of 255 fields per file and 65,535 characters per field. Eighty-four hundred lines of on-line Help text provide immediate assistance to the user. Security capabilities include password checking, data encryption, and control of file and field access for read and write. The system has the ability to execute DOS commands and other programs from within *KnowledgeMan*. Optional components are available for multicolor business graphics (*K-Graph*), full-screen text processing (*K-Text*), forms painting (*K-Paint*), and mouse implementation (*K-Mouse*) and are fully integrated so that any capability may be exercised within any *KnowledgeMan* session. A runtime version of the system is available for independent software developers.

Company:
Mosaic Software, Inc.

Product:
Integrated 7

Category:
Integrated

Computer:
AT&T PC 6300

Media:
Diskette

Language:
C

Requirements:
320 KB RAM
One drive
MS-DOS 2.X

Support:
(800) 446-4620
Dealer training
Free updates
Dealer newsletter

Retail Price:
$695

Distributor:
Mosaic Software, Inc.
1972 Massachusetts Ave.
Cambridge, MA 02140
Tel: (617) 491-2434

Description:

Seven business functions: Spreadsheet, Graphics, Word Processing, Data Base, Terminal Emulation, Communications, Data Mail, Macros.

Company:
Quadratron Systems, Inc.

Product:
Q-OFFICE+

Category:
Integrated

Computer:
AT&T PC 6300

Media:
Diskette

Language:
C

Requirements:
Hard disk

Support:
Training classes and hotline support provided by Essex Office Systems

Retail Price:
$1,520

Distributor:
Essex Office Systems
333 North Fairfax St.
Alexandria, VA 22314
Tel: (703) 549-9240

Description:

Q-OFFICE+ is an integrated office automation package designed for ease-of-use and hardware independence. It is comprised of eight software modules, including *Q-ONE*, word processing; *Q-MENU*, menu generator and manager; *Q-DATE*, calendar/scheduler; *Q-MAIL*, electronic mail; *Q-CALL*, phone directory; *Q-FORM*, forms designer and manager; *Q-MATH*, full function calculator; and *Q-NOTE*, notepad/index program.

Company:
Samna Corporation

Product:
Samna +

Category:
Integrated

Computer:
AT&T PC 6300

Media:
Diskette

Language:
C, Assembler

Requirements:
512 KB RAM

Support:
Extended Service Contracts are available
Samna has eight support hotline numbers
Comes with 30-day free support
Corporate training programs are available upon request

Retail Price:
$695

Distributor:
Samna Corporation
32 Cherry Lane
Floral Park, NY 11001
Tel: (516) 775-2800

Description:

Samna + is a combined spreadsheet and word processing software package. Samna + includes the Samna Word III word processing software, along with a spreadsheet application and *Word Base Manager*. Samna + offers powerful, productive, and easy-to-learn word processing features, plus the *Seamless Integration* of line drawing, five-function math, *Word Base Manager*, spelling checker, and spreadsheet applications. In addition, users can sort by rows in as many as five different fields, add a column or row of numbers, and display a directory of all spreadsheets within a Samna document.

Company:
Software Products International

Product:
Open Access

Category:
Integrated

Computer:
AT&T PC 6300

Media:
Diskette

Language:
Assembler

Requirements:
256 KB RAM minimum
MS-DOS 2.0 or later
2 floppies with 320 KB minimum each or 1 floppy (320 KB minimum) and hard disk

Support:
60 days toll free telephone support after purchase. Extended 1-year service may be purchased for $95. It includes telephone support, update and enhancements for the package and newsletter.

Retail Price:
$695

Distributor:
Software Products International
10240 Sorrento Valley Rd.
San Diego, CA 92121
Tel: (619) 450-1526

Description:

Open Access is an integrated software package consisting of six modules: Relational Database, Spreadsheet, Business Graphics (using 3-D capabilities), Word Processing, Time Management and Communications. The six modules operate completely independent of each other, but all of its modules may share data either by exporting/importing data files or by virtually "contexting" data directly from program to another.

Windowing technology is used to its full advantage with Global features such as on-line Calculator, Window Directory for ease of access to files and records and help windows featuring context specific help as well as Function Key addressing.

Company:
Sorcim/IUS

Product:
SuperCalc*3 Release 2.0

Category:
Integrated

Computer:	**Media:**
AT&T PC 6300	Diskette

Language:
Sorcim/IUS Proprietary Language

Requirements:
96 KB RAM required
Monochrome or color
Over 50 printers and plotters supported

Support:
This product is supported by Sorcim/IUS
Carries a 90-day media warranty
Sorcim/IUS can be reached at (408) 942-1727

Retail Price:
$395

Distributor:
AT&T (800) 247-1212
or call your local AT&T authorized dealer or Account Executive.

***This product has been certified by AT&T.**

Description:

*SuperCalc*3 is an integrated package combining data management, spreadsheet analysis and graphics. Its easy-to-use spreadsheet capabilities allow you to handle complex financial and numerical analyses. *SuperCalc*3 helps solve modeling and forecasting problems. It produces presentation quality graphics which help a user make better decisions faster.

Highlights:

- Graphically displayed Help menus.
- Operates on 128 KB machine.
- Intelligently uses up to 640 KB RAM.
- Fully integrated.
- Efficient memory management (usable cells vs. worksheet size).
- Disk is not copy protected, works without program disk on hard drive machines.
- Single keystroke plotting and printing.
- *Sideways* program is now shipped with *SuperCalc*3 allowing you to print reports sideways using a variety of fonts.
- Superdata interchange–Interchanges *DIF* files with other spreadsheet programs.

*SuperCalc*3–Spreadsheet:

- Spreadsheet size is 9,999 rows by 127 columns.
- Simple to learn–detailed and on-line Help commands.
- Easy to use–simple English commands (fewer keystrokes).
- Efficient data (number) entry–return moves cursor.
- Sophisticated consolidation capability–(= ,-,/,*).
- Advanced Replicate/copy functions–absolute reference built into command structure.
- Enhanced color usage–negative and protected numbers.
- Spreadsheet border controls–printing.
- Powerful and flexible Execute functions–transferable to other worksheets and simple to develop.
- Advanced financial functions–IRR, NPV, FV, payment.
- Zero width column formatting and hidden cells.

(Continued on next page)

Description: ***(Continued)***

- Natural order of calculations.

*SuperCalc*3–Letter Writing and Text Editing:

- Text can be centered within a cell.
- Text automatically spills over column width.
- Continuous word viewing when scrolling left to right and up and down.
- Superior editing–Insert and Delete options, fast and easy error correction (type over mistakes to correct).
- Word processing and spelling checker linkage when interfaced to *SuperWriter* word processing program.

*SuperCalc*3–Data Management:

- Size: 9,998 records with as many as 127 fields per record.
- Find: Displays records that meet criteria. Program continues to search for next matching record.
- Extract: Copies all records that meet criteria to the output (designated range).
- Select: Copies all records that meet criteria and that are approved by the user to the output range.
- Criterion: Defines range where the criteria for the Find, Select, and Extract commands are found.
- Sorting: Provides option to perform a dictionary sort by rows or columns in a database according to primary or secondary key selections (ascending or descending order). Cell references are adjustable, and wildcard characters are available.
- Remain: Following database manipulation, this command allows user to remain at location (cell) most recently worked on.

*SuperCalc*3–Graphics:

- Eight graph types–simple pie, bar, line, stackbar, X-Y, high-low, exploding pie, and area.
- Unrestricted font selection–headings and labels (8 per graph).
- Unlimited color options–data, labels, headings, (21 per graph).

(Continued on next page)

Description: ***(Continued)***

- Unlimited color options–data, labels, headings, (21 per graph).
- Single keystroke plotting and editing.
- Intelligent automatic and manual scaling (variable tick points).
- Ten data ranges and up to 254 data series.
- Graph library and descriptor directors.
- Building data ranges–block and variable assignment.
- Solid, crosshatched, and outline coloring.
- High-resolution black and white graphics.
- Variable ticks and axis options.
- Outstanding pie graphics–circular, full color, enhanced formatting options, exploding segments, and pie mode.
- Graph copy and consolidation capability.

Company:
Access Technology, Inc.

Product:
20/20

Category:
Spreadsheets

Computer:
AT&T PC 6300

Media:
Diskette

Language:
C

Requirements:
256 KB RAM
Graphics terminal for on-screen graphics

Support:
Product training available
Hotline assistance
On-line help
Technical support staff for telephone consultation

Retail Price:
$500

Distributor:
Access Technology, Inc.
6 Pleasant St.
South Natick, MA 01760
Tel: (617) 655-9191

Description:

20/20 is a full featured, high-end electronic spreadsheet and financial analysis package that combines superior modeling capabilities with graphics, database management and project modeling features. *20/20* includes virtually all the basic spreadsheet features and has strong advanced operations, such as depreciation calculations investment analysis and goal-seeking. In addition, *20/20* is able to link worksheets. The project modeling feature allows a user to manage time-bound projects by calculating various time allocations based on data that the user specifies.

Company:
AT&T and Microsoft Corporation

Product:
Multiplan*

Category:
Spreadsheets

Computer:
AT&T PC 6300

Media:
Diskette

Language:
Microsoft Proprietary Language

Requirements:
128 KB RAM

Support:
This product is fully supported by AT&T Information Systems and carries a 90-day warranty on the media. Remote nationwide customer service hotline is provided Monday through Friday between the hours of 8:00 a.m. and 5:00 p.m. local time. Installation, additional hotline coverage, and extended maintenance agreements are also available.

A one-volume user's manual is provided.

Retail Price:
$195

Distributor:
AT&T (800) 247-1212
or call your local AT&T authorized dealer or Account Executive.

***This product has been certified by AT&T.**

Description:

Multiplan is a second generation spreadsheet that allows the user to create an almost infinite variety of worksheets to organize topics, data, and formulas for specific business needs. These worksheets will not only keep records of profits and losses, but make projections, store information, plan budgets, and perform sophisticated financial analyses involving cash flows and internal rates of return.

More powerful and flexible than earlier spreadsheets, it allows the user to define categories and relationships, and then performs computations, calculates results, and makes projections.

By using the grid of spaces (cells) arranged in rows and columns, complicated worksheets can be set up in minutes. A cell pointer illuminates each cell as it is ready to receive data, and direction keys move the pointer from cell to cell. Time consuming calculations can be processed in seconds. Names can be assigned to individual cells, rows, columns, and whole sections of the worksheet, making easy reading.

Whatever the project, the user can design the worksheet to fit the business needs and then enter the data. *Multiplan* does all the calculations and adjusts the figures when the user updates the sheet with new data. To make projections or test options, *Multiplan*'s "what if" capability recalculates the entire spreadsheet and shows the results without losing the current data. With *Multiplan*, decisions are based on solid facts and accurate estimates.

Multiplan allows the user to present information in printed reports that are clear, persuasive, and elegant. Its special format, alignment, and printout options allow the user to design professional quality reports.

Multiplan offers many features that make it easy to use. Among these are:

ENGLISH STYLE COMMANDS that can be entered with a single keystroke. Commands include Go To, Copy, Edit, Format, Help, Lock, Name, Window, Options, and External.

PROMPT LINE and STATUS LINE that help keep the user informed. The prompt line beneath the command menu tells the user what to do next. The status line shows the location of the active cell and displays its contents.

HIGHLY ACCURATE CALCULATIONS that can be made with 14-digit accuracy.

SWITCHING CAPABILITY between a spreadsheet display of formulas and values that makes it easy to work with large multidivisional financial models.

REPORT GENERATION CAPABILITY that allows for customization of reports. Formulas can be printed instead of values, borders can be suppressed, and the user can specify page margins.

Company:
Benchmark/Metasoft, Inc.

Product:
***THE BENCHMARK* Financial Planner**

Category:
Spreadsheets

Computer:
AT&T PC 6300

Media:
Diskette

Language:
Assembly

Requirements:
256 KB RAM

Support:
Telephone support (800) 621-1908

Retail Price:
$295

Distributor:
Benchmark/Metasoft, Inc.
6509 W. Frye Rd., Suite 12
Chandler, AZ 85224
Tel: (602) 961-0003

Description:

In keeping with the tradition of *THE BENCHMARK* Family, the Financial Planner is one of the finest spreadsheet programs available on the market today.

THE BENCHMARK Financial Planner utilizes a three dimensional data cube that allows you to view and analyze data in the traditional single sheet method as well as "through" the cube. The cube permits you to work with pages stacked one behind the other to complement your habit patterns learned from the first time you picked up a book.

Using the program, you can be productive with only one day of self-training. Help is available at all points in the program. Logical, mnemonic commands are used to help you learn and remember them.

A powerful programming language allows the sophisticated user to generate personalized templates and programs for data entry by the less sophisticated user. For example, you can create your own amortization schedule that prompts for variable data. Even a novice will be able to enter the necessary data and receive the desired information.

Company:
Chang Labs

Product:
Consolidation Module

Category:
Spreadsheets

Computer:
AT&T PC 6300

Media:
Diskette

Language:
CB86

Requirements:
128 KB RAM
1 disk drive

Support:
Toll-free line for dealer and end user support
Nationwide (800) 972-8800
For California (800) 831-8080

Retail Price:
$295

Distributor:
Chang Labs
5300 Stevens Creek Blvd.
San Jose, CA 95129
Tel: (408) 246-8020

Description:

Consolidation Module is an add-on to the *MicroPlan* financial planning spreadsheet. The package allows you to add, subtract, multiply, or divide an entire spreadsheet by another with only one command, thus providing a simple solution for compiling a corporate budget. Enables you to consolidate selected rows or columns of figures for generating a new table with only one command. Programs all steps through *MicroPlan*, so you can recalculate a complex multispreadsheet model with only one command. Permits others to produce your reports by following prompts and plugging in new numbers. Creates summaries column-by-column, row-by-row, or page-by-page. Lets you easily perform variance analysis by consolidating your budget with accrual figures and then having *MicroPlan*'s built-in formulas automatically calculate differences and figure variance percentages for items you select.

Company:
Chang Labs

Product:
Link Module

Category:
Spreadsheets

Computer: **AT&T 6300**

Media: Diskette

Language:
CB86

Requirements:
128 KB RAM
1 disk drive

Support:
Toll-free line for dealer and end user support
Nationwide (800) 972-8800
For California (800) 831-8080

Retail Price:
$295

Distributor:
Chang Labs
5300 Stevens Creek Blvd.
San Jose, CA 95129
Tel: (408) 246-8020

Description:

The *Link Module* is an add-on to the *MicroPlan* financial planning spreadsheet. Gives you the power to take raw data your microcomputer has accessed on a mainframe–or any other outside source including database systems, time-sharing systems, "calc" files and other spreadsheets–and post it directly into your *MicroPlan* spreadsheet. Allows you to pull in data from other application packages without having to re-enter data. Contains built-in commands for posting and tabulating data, so you can analyze the data by matching specific criteria while it is being loaded into *MicroPlan*. Automates the entire process of loading and analyzing data when used in conjunction with *MicroPlan*'s programming mode. Uses the same screen format and command structure as *MicroPlan* and is menu-driven for easy use.

Company:
Chang Labs

Product:
MicroPlan

Category:
Spreadsheets

Computer:	**Media:**
AT&T PC 6300 6300 PLUS **AT&T PC 6300 PLUS**	Diskette

Language:
CB86

Requirements:
128 KB RAM
1 disk drive

Support:
Toll-free line for dealer and end user support
Nationwide (800) 972-8800
For California (800) 831-8080

Retail Price:
$495

Distributor:
Chang Labs
5300 Stevens Creek Blvd.
San Jose, CA 95129
Tel: (408) 246-8020

Description:

MicroPlan is a financial planning spreadsheet for financial planners who update reports daily, weekly, monthly, and/or quarterly. Contains built-in financial and statistical formulas, so you don't have to devise them yourself. Has built-in addition, subtraction, multiplication, division, summing, and ratio functions. Displays or prints spreadsheet logic, so you can see how one row or column interrelates with another and verify that the results are accurate—eliminating the need to move from cell to cell to cell to check formulas. Saves the sequence of commands for those special tables that are updated over and over. Generates new results instantly when any set of assumptions is changed. Has up to 200 rows and 60 columns in each worksheet or table but allows the size of the spreadsheet to vary. Has special commands for advanced financial analysis, including complex depreciation, loan analysis, internal rates of return, tax computation, balance forward operations, and rolling forecasts. Has a built-in "Help" command. Lets you tap keys on the keyboard's calculator pad to enter all commands, so you don't have to learn the typewriter keyboard. Handles cashflow planning, budget preparation, variance reporting, product pricing analysis, financial report preparation, manufacturing planning, private investment counseling, merger and acquisition pro formas, capital budgeting, and sales forecasting. Provides "presentation-quality" reports. By using the add-on *Link Module*, you can take raw data your microcomputer has accessed on a mainframe—or any other outside source including database systems, time-sharing systems, "calc" files, and other spreadsheets—and post it directly to *MicroPlan* spreadsheets. By using the add-on *Consolidation Module*, an entire spreadsheet can be added, subtracted, multiplied, or divided by another and selected rows or columns of figures can be consolidated to generate a new table. In addition, you can recalculate a complex multispreadsheet model; let others produce your reports by following prompts and plugging in new numbers; and perform variance analysis by consolidating budgets with accrual figures and having the built-in formulas automatically calculate differences and figure variance percentages for selected items. Integrates with the *GraphPlan* financial spreadsheet, with the integrated graphics package and the FilePlan database manager.

Company:
Datamension Corporation

Product:
***Report Manager* AV Version 2.25**

Category:
Spreadsheets

Computer:	**Media:**
AT&T PC 6300	Diskette
6300 PLUS **AT&T PC 6300 PLUS**	

Language:
Assembler

Requirements:
2 disk drives or 1 disk drive
A hard disk 256 KB RAM or more

Support:
Toll-free phone support
Newsletter
Training

Retail Price:
$495

Distributor:
Manufacturers Representative
Western Technology Brokers
104 West 74th St.
New York, NY 10023
Tel: (212) 580-1500

Description:

Report Manager: programmable 3-D spreadsheet. Supports 255 distinct spreadsheet pages in memory at one time, as if stacked one behind the other to form a DataCube with a 16,000-cell matrix. Consolidations are instant. Supports: slicing and rotating DataCube, pointing and sorting in three dimensions (three sort fields); keyword search; read/write DIF and ASCII; read/write ranges; definable margins on printouts; seven ways to address cells, including English words; four windows; numbers with dollar signs and commas; negative values with minus signs, parentheses or "CR"; report linking; top-of-column totals; first-page summaries (for rollups/bundles); color. Uses all available RAM. Addresses all PC graphics characters. On-line help. 82 preprogrammed functions (math, trig, log, conditional, statistical, financial). Includes numerous printer configuration tables. Has built-in programming language, EXEC, for creating executable files (application generation). This allows naive spreadsheet users to effectively use program without mastering it.

Company:
Innovative Software

Product:
The Smart Spreadsheet with Graphics 2.0

Category:
Spreadsheets

Computer:
AT&T PC 6300

Media:
Diskette

Language:
C

Requirements:
256 KB RAM
2 floppy or 1 floppy + hard disk
MS/DOS 2.0 or higher

Support:
Example files and on-screen tutorials
Quick key reference guide
Registered SMART owners
Support hotline
Ongoing updates

Retail Price:
$395

Distributor:
Innovative Software
9300 W. 110 St., Suite 380
Overland Park, KS 66204
Tel: (913) 383-1089

Description:

The Smart Spreadsheet with Graphics boasts one of the largest spreadsheets available in the market, accommodating 999 columns by 9,999 rows. Through special data storage techniques, it can hold spreadsheets with up to four times more data within the same amount of memory than typical electronic spreadsheets. The Smart Spreadsheet also can be relational—allowing changes in the contents of one to affect the contents of others, which greatly facilitates financial consolidations. It also has full calculation and decision support functions.

Its built-in graphics capabilities include one-, two- and even three-dimensional bar charts; high-low charts; pie and cake charts; line, point and scatter graphs; and histograms. It also has on-screen slide-show capabilities and can output to a large number of printers, plotters, and the *Polaroid* Palette for 35mm slide production.

SPREADSHEET HIGHLIGHTS

- One of the fastest spreadsheets available.
- One of the largest spreadsheet capacities available.
- Multiple spreadsheets in memory at once.
- View Only spreadsheet ability (uses less RAM).
- Relational spreadsheets for easy financial consolidations.
- Sorting and organizing data capabilities.
- Calculation capabilities: math, trigonometric, statistical, financial, date, time, matrix and regression analysis.
- Decision-making capabilities: select, lookup, case, if/then/else, and/or, boolean, choose.
- Text manipulation capabilities: repeat midstring, concatenate.
- Full screen-formula editor.
- Eleven different types styles (fonts) on screen and in output.
- Password protection of spreadsheets.
- Linked-window scrolling.
- Report format generator.
- Custom application development with Project Processing and the Smart Programming Language.

(Continued on next page)

Description: *(Continued)*

GRAPHICS HIGHLIGHTS

- Automatic or user-defined scaling.
- Supports up to 16 colors.
- Supports color and B/W graphics on screen and in output.
- Supports 14 different fill patterns.
- Supports over 40 medium and high resolution monitors and graphic devices.
- Full support of the most popular printers, plotters and graphics cards.
- Allows for 18 basic graph types with 78 different permutations including: 3-D bar-charts (horizontal and vertical) pie and cake charts, line, point and scatter graphs, high-low charts, histograms, layer/area charts, combination line/bar charts.
- Fits up to 4 graphs on one page.
- Custom on-screen slide show presentations.
- Device independent; automatically optimizes the maximum number of colors and resolution of the output device.
- Full user control of titling, size, color, fonts and borders.
- Merge graphs with text into word processing documents.
- Interfaces directly with medium and high resolution 35mm slide makers.
- Quick cursor pointing at data to be graphed.
- Eleven different type styles (fonts) on screen and in output.

SPECIFICATIONS

- 9999 rows x 999 columns.
- "Sparse Matrix" data storage.
- Virtual Memory paging to disk, or RAM disk.
- 80 characters per cell for values and text.
- 1000 characters per cell for formulas.
- 25 on-screen windows.
- Directly reads Smart and *Lotus 1-2-3* files and formulas.
- Writes Smart, *Lotus 1-2-3* and text file formats.
- Supports Intel 8087 and 80287 math co-processors.

Company:
Lotus Development Corporation

Product:
1-2-3*

Category:
Spreadsheets

Computer:	**Media:**
AT&T PC 6300	Diskette

Language:
Assembly

Requirements:
192 KB RAM
MS-DOS 2.11 (Required Patch available through AT&T)
1 double-sided floppy-disk drive

Support:
This product is supported by Lotus Development Corporation and carries a one-year warranty on the media. Lotus can be reached at 1-(800) 343-5414; in MA (617) 253-9150.

Retail Price:
$495

Distributor:
AT&T (800) 247-1212
or call your local AT&T authorized dealer or Account Executive.

***This product has been certified by AT&T.**

Description:

1-2-3 is the established standard in spreadsheet software for business and professional use. For those who need a powerful program for data manipulation and analysis, *1-2-3* integrates three essential functions—spreadsheet, graphics, and information management.

1-2-3's worksheet measures 2,048 rows by 256 columns and provides more than 50 built-in functions for developing complex models with speed and ease. Included are mathematical, logical, financial, database statistical, date, and special functions.

Information management capabilities permit the user to retrieve data using a wide range of criteria and to rapidly enter, query, and sort the data. Offset look-up tables allow quick storage and retrieval of data such as tax rates or depreciation schedules.

A variety of graph types, including bar, XY, line, and pie, can be quickly constructed from the spreadsheet or database for use as a virtually instantaneous analytical tool.

1-2-3's keyboard macros enable the user to create single keystroke alternatives to frequently used keystroke sequences and to develop custom menus and applications. *1-2-3* can read standard ASCII text files and quickly translates standard *DIF*, *VisiCalc*, and *dBASE II* files.

1-2-3 features self-documented English commands and a six-lesson interactive tutorial diskette. Over 200 on-line Help screens, cross-referenced to the manual, guide the user through all aspects of the program.

Company:

Master Computer Systems, Inc.

Product:

***FORMIX* Screen Management System Revision 1.05, Copyright 1983**

Category:

Spreadsheets

Computer:
AT&T PC 6300

Media:
Diskette

Language:
Macro Assembler

Requirements:
128 KB RAM
1 disk drive

Support:
Warranty
Training
Telephone support (612) 944-5220

Retail Price:
$495

Distributor:
Master Computer Systems, Inc.
9531 West 78th St.
Eden Prairie, MN 55344
Tel: (612) 944-5220

Description:

FORMIX is a complete panel-oriented screen management system that interfaces with the popular development languages in the *MS*-DOS environment. It is for use by serious developers who require the highest degree of screen performance with their application. *FORMIX* drastically reduces the application development effort by providing a "Paint the Screen" process and a powerful interactive field-by-field edit/validation process. Application screens are interactively created, tested, and modified completely independent from the programming process. *FORMIX* provides customized screen, panel, and field sensitive Help as well as full system messaging.

Aimed at providing the best performance base from which to build application software, *FORMIX* is written entirely in Assembly Language; employing a Run Time Executive to manage all data traffic between the end user and the application program together with a series of unusually flexible screen development tools. The Executive-based edit/validation functions of *FORMIX* are so powerful that application programs are much smaller and easier to maintain. They load much faster and drastically outperform applications using high level language editing and validation.

Software developers are finding in *FORMIX* the same kinds of capabilities present in their expensive mainframe system software. *FORMIX* is helping them provide solutions for:

- Distributed PC data entry and editing/validation.
- Mainframe-like transaction processing with PCs.
- Off-loading CICS type applications to PCs.
- PC user interfaces to fourth generation development systems.
- Improving the performance of existing PC applications.
- Mainframe program development and testing on PCs.

The power and flexibility of *FORMIX* are illuminated when the system builder is allowed to control keyboard configuration, individual video attributes (monochrome and color), and screen messaging, both at screen paint time and at run time, under program control. *FORMIX* is so flexible that it will mold to fit almost any screen sensitive application. Other advanced features of *FORMIX* include:

(Continued on next page)

Description: ***(Continued)***

- Ability to change field processing sequences.
- Hidden field processing for security control.
- Configurable interrupt vector for other hardware/software environments.
- Preemptive user exit keys for special field processing.
- Graphic drawing capability.
- Panels providing dynamic screen building at run time.
- Powerful word processing commands.

Company:
Paladin Software Corporation

Product:
***FlashCalc* Version 1.0**

Category:
Spreadsheets

Computer:	**Media:**
AT&T PC 6300 6300 PLUS **AT&T PC 6300 PLUS**	Diskette

Language:
Assembler

Requirements:
64 KB RAM
One disk drive

Support:
90-day warranty
Hotline support
Nominal charge for upgrades, backups, and replacement outside warranty

Retail Price:
$129

Distributor:
Paladin Software Corporation
2895 Zanker Rd.
San Jose, CA 95134
Tel: (408) 946-9000

Description:

FlashCalc is a fast spreadsheet program with power user features at an affordable price. Extensive formatting features include variable width columns, cell protection, and currency and percent symbols. Power features include financial function, support for up to 640 KB RAM, and hard disk support. Easy-to-use, pop-down menus simplify loading and saving files, hardware configuration, and printing.

Company:
Paladin Software Corporation

Product:
***Visi-On Plan* Version 1.2**

Category:
Spreadsheets

Computer:	**Media:**
AT&T PC 6300	Diskette
6300 PLUS **AT&T PC 6300 PLUS**	

Language:
C

Requirements:
512 KB RAM
High resolution monitor
Hard disk color graphics card
Serial port
Visi-On Mouse

Support:
90-day warranty
User hotline
Nominal charge for upgrades
Backups and replacements outside warranty

Retail Price:
$395

Distributor:
Paladin Software Corporation
2895 Zanker Rd.
San Jose, CA 95134
Tel: (408) 946-9000

Description:

Visi-On Plan is the spreadsheet program for the *Visi-On* system. 511 rows x 128 columns of virtual memory allow all 65,000 cells to be used. It consolidates spreadsheets sorting on two keys. Extensive formatting capabilities include variable decimal places, currency symbols, percent signs, upper/lower bound checking, and cell protection. The application allows naming of ranges. *Visi-On Plan* offers 5.2 functions including date and financial functions. In addition, it provides easy transfer of data to *Visi-On Graph* and *Visi-On Word*.

Company:
Quadratron Systems, Inc.

Product:
Q-PLAN

Category:
Spreadsheets

Computer:
AT&T PC 6300

Media:
Diskette

Language:
C

Requirements:
Hard disk

Support:
Training and hotline support provided by Essex Office Systems.

Retail Price:
$395

Distributor:
Essex Office Systems
333 North Fairfax St.
Alexandria, VA 22314
Tel: (703) 549-9240

Description:

Q-PLAN is an easy-to-use, menu-driven spreadsheet which supports a variety of video attributes and business graphics, as well as variable width columns and multi-windowing.

Q-PLAN allows for the import and export of data from external programs, such as the *Q-ONE* word processor and *Q-CHART* business graphics program.

Company:
SuperSoft, Inc.

Product:
ScratchPad Plus

Category:
Spreadsheets

Computer:
AT&T PC 6300

Media:
Diskette

Language:
C

Requirements:
128 KB RAM
1 disk drive

Support:
Phone support
Update notification

Retail Price:
$195

Distributor:
SuperSoft, Inc.
P.O. Box 1628
Champaign, IL 61820
Tel: (217) 359-2112

Description:

ScratchPad Plus is the advanced electronic spreadsheet designed for the business professional. This product does away with those disastrous "out of memory" error messages. It uses virtual memory so you cannot run out of memory in the middle of a project. It lets you use up to 25,000 cells simultaneously in any spreadsheet application. It also lets you create spreadsheets up to 9,999 columns wide or 9,999 rows deep; the dimensions are up to you. In addition, you never need more than 192 K of memory no matter what size your application is.

ScratchPad Plus also contains a wide array of additional advanced features for the serious spreadsheet user.

Company:
TOM Software, Inc.

Product:
***D-CALC* Financial Analysis System**

Category:
Spreadsheets

Computer:	**Media:**
AT&T PC 6300	Diskette

Language:
TOMBASIC

Requirements:
TOMBASIC

Support:
Training and technical support provided by the local licensed consultant.
Fees depend on the consultant and the type of service provided.

Retail Price:
$800–$3,500 depending on the hardware

Distributor:
TOM Software, Inc.
127 S.W. 156th Ave.
P.O. Box 66596
Seattle, WA 98166
Tel: (206) 246-7022

TOM Software, Inc. is an authorized Value Added Reseller for AT&T Computers.

Description:

The *D-CALC* system creates an on-screen spreadsheet for financial modeling, budgeting, and data analysis. Whether financial planning needs are simple or complex, the user can use *D-CALC* to calculate and display results instantly on the computer screen. *D-CALC* can stand alone or be integrated with TOM accounting systems. The interface with General Ledger means the user can transfer account balances and budget figures to *D-CALC*, make projections and calculations, and then transfer new budget figures back to the General Ledger. Each *D-CALC* spreadsheet has 26 columns and 232 rows, and a virtually unlimited number of columns and rows can be created by connecting spreadsheets. In addition, *D-CALC* offers the unique option of changing the width of a column at any time. The user defines the format options for each printed financial statement and report–specifying column breaks and headings, footers, decimals, indentations, tab settings, and single and double underscores. Data can be easily transferred from one spreadsheet to another, and any spreadsheet can be stored by the system for later use.

Company:
Addison-Wesley Publishing Co., Inc.

Product:
***True BASIC* Version 1.0**

Category:
Systems Programming

Computer:	**Media:**
AT&T PC 6300	Diskette
6300 PLUS **AT&T PC 6300 PLUS**	

Language:
True BASIC

Requirements:
192 KB RAM

Support:
90-day limited warranty
Support phone: (617) 944-6795

Retail Price:
$149.90

Distributor:
Addison-Wesley Publishing Co., Inc.
Jacob Way
Reading, MA 01867
Tel: (617) 944-6795

Description:

True BASIC is a microcomputer version of the world's most popular programming language developed by John Kemeny and Thomas Kurtz, who originated BASIC over 20 years ago. This package includes the software as well as two carefully edited and designed manuals. A user's guide details everything the user needs to know in order to run *True BASIC*, and a reference manual tells the user how to write programs in *True BASIC*. Designed to run on a number of different microcomputers, *True BASIC* is a micro BASIC "true" to the standards set forth by the American National Standards Institute (ANSI).

Features of *True BASIC* include easy-to-understand, English-like syntax; sophisticated error-handling; on-line help facilities; a full-screen editor; windows; mouse support; simple menus; and programmed function keys. This fully structured language encourages good program design by featuring multiline function definitions and sub-routines with local variables. While the novice programmer will appreciate the easy-to-use features, the experienced programmer will appreciate its power and flexibility. With *True BASIC* the user can utilize all the memory available in the computer.

Company:
AT&T and Digital Research Inc.

Product:
Dr. Logo*

Category:
Systems Programming

Computer:	**Media:**
AT&T PC 6300	Diskette

Language:
C and Assembly

Requirements:
192 KB RAM

Support:
This product is fully supported by AT&T Information Systems and carries a 90-day warranty on the media. Remote nationwide customer service hotline is provided Monday through Friday between the hours of 8:00 a.m. and 5:00 p.m. local time. Installation, additional hotline coverage, and extended maintenance agreements are also available.

Retail Price:
$150

Distributor:
AT&T (800) 247-1212
or call your local AT&T authorized dealer or Account Executive.

***This product has been certified by AT&T.**

Description:

The advanced version of *Dr. Logo* provides both new computer users and professionals with a powerful and versatile language to expand their programming creatively. It is based on the popular, interactive Logo language which helps programmers design an intuitive intelligence into the operation of their applications. It is an effective tool for the creation of solutions to a wide range of programming problems.

Dr. Logo includes turtle graphics, a visual programming package for the immediate and easy development of impressive graphics. The language's modular structure permits the creation, modification, storage, and subsequent combination of structures and procedures. This simplifies the development of solutions to complex programming problems.

Dr. Logo is a powerful language for the manipulation of lists of information. Structures can be efficiently handled in any manner you choose, either on a character-by-character, word-by-word, or list-by-list basis. A powerful Help facility and sophisticated debugging facilities, including split-screen editing, make programming easier and faster.

Professionals are using *Dr. Logo* to handle sophisticated tasks such as artificial intelligence and knowledge-based systems. Logo is earning high praise among educators for its simplicity and almost unlimited utility. Its ease of use makes it an ideal language to extend the creativity of programmers of all ages and abilities.

Dr. Logo Features:

- Turtle Graphics Primitives
- Informative Error Messages and Help Facility
- Workspace Management Primitives
- Split-Screen Debugging Facilities
- Floating Point Package
- List Processing Primitives
- Recursion Supported
- Comments and Indentation
- Game Programming Primitives
- *Apple* Logo Compatible

(Continued on next page)

Description: ***(Continued)***

Turtle Graphics Primitives:

Dr. Logo's Turtle Graphics support high resolution graphic displays. A computer controlled graphics cursor called a turtle appears on the screen and responds to commands that make it move FORWARD and BACK, as well as rotate RIGHT or LEFT. The turtle traces its path as it moves across the screen. *Dr. Logo* includes primitives to query and change the turtle's current status with a high degree of accuracy.

Informative Error Messages and Help Facilities:

Dr. Logo reports program errors with friendly, concise diagnostic messages. Each message indicates precisely what is wrong without complicated terminology. It can display a definition and required syntax for each *Dr. Logo* primitive, minimizing the need to refer to the manual.

Company:
AT&T and Microsoft Corporation

Product:
GW*-BASIC Compiler

Category:
Systems Programming

Computer:	**Media:**
AT&T PC 6300	Diskette

Language:
Assembler

Requirements:
MS-DOS 2.11
256 KB RAM
2 floppy drives recommended

Support:
This product is fully supported by AT&T Information Systems and carries a 90-day warranty on the media. Remote nationwide customer hotline is provided Monday through Friday between the hours of 8:00 a.m. and 5:00 p.m. local time. Installation, additional hotline coverage, and extended maintenance agreements are also available.

Retail Price:
$395

Distributor:
AT&T (800) 247-1212
or call your local authorized AT&T dealer or Account Executive.

***This product has been certified by AT&T.**

Description:

Microsoft GW-BASIC Compiler combines software support for graphics and other extended features with the extensive capabilities of standard *Microsoft* BASIC. *GW*-BASIC Compiler allows software developers to secure programming investment, execute programs quickly and take full advantage of the hardware capabilities of the system.

GW-BASIC Compiler offers all the performance features of the *MS*-BASIC Compiler in addition to the extended capabilities available to *GW*-BASIC. This not only makes *GW*-BASIC easy to learn, but allows many applications already running under *Microsoft* BASIC to be easily transported to *GW*-BASIC. Because *GW*-BASIC Compiler is an optimized compiler, execution of programs is fast and efficient. *GW*-BASIC Compiler is also compatible with the *GW*-BASIC Interpreter. When used together, the interpreter and compiler make a productive design and development system. The programmer can interactively write and debug a program with the interpreter and then compile the program for fast execution.

Graphics are an increasingly important tool for communicating complex information effectively with computers. *GW*-BASIC provides a full set of graphic capabilities including lines, circles, shapes and paint-fill. *GW*-BASIC's utility is further increased with the ability to produce musical tones with string sequences and thereby generate music. *GW*-BASIC also supports nonkeyboard input devices like joysticks and lightpens to enhance the user's interaction with the *GW*-BASIC application RS-232 asynchronous communication support has been added to increase *GW*-BASIC's flexibility in communicating with other computers and peripheral devices.

Company:
AT&T and Microsoft Corporation

Product:
GW*-BASIC INTERPRETER

Category:
Systems Programming

Computer: AT&T PC 6300

Media: Diskette

Language:
Assembler

Requirements:
128 KB RAM

Support:
This product is fully supported by AT&T Information Systems and carries a 90-day warranty on the media. Remote nationwide customer hotline is provided Monday through Friday between the hours of 8:00 a.m. and 5:00 p.m. local time. Installation, additional hotline coverage, and extended maintenance agreements are also available.

Retail Price:
$65 (included with *MS*-DOS)

Distributor:
AT&T (800) 247-1212
or call your local authorized AT&T dealer or Account Executive.

***This product has been certified by AT&T.**

Description:

Microsoft GW-BASIC Interpreter combines software support for graphics and other extended features with the already extensive capabilities of *Microsoft* BASIC. Like the other members of the *Microsoft* family of BASIC implementations, *GW*-BASIC provides all the flexibility of *Microsoft* BASIC. This not only makes *GW*-BASIC easy to learn, but allows many applications already running under *Microsoft* BASIC to be easily transported to *GW*-BASIC. Graphics are an increasingly important tool for communicating complex information effectively with computers. *GW*-BASIC provides a full set of graphic capabilities including lines, circles, shapes, and paint-fill. *GW*-BASIC's utility is further increased with the ability to produce musical tones with string sequences and thereby generate music. *GW*-BASIC also supports nonkeyboard input devices like joysticks and lightpens to enhance the user's interaction with the *GW*-BASIC application. RS-232 asynchronous communication support has been added to increase *GW*-BASIC's flexibility in communicating with other computers and peripheral devices. And, to make *GW*-BASIC programs easy to write, Microsoft has provided a full-screen text editor for easy input and editing of the *GW*-BASIC programs.

GW-BASIC provides all the sophisticated language support required for today's business and personal computing applications.

Features:

- Sophisticated graphics and music generation capabilities.
- As easy to use as Microsoft's industry standard *MS*-BASIC.
- Full-screen editor for easy program development.
- Supports user-defined "soft keys."
- RS-232 asynchronous communication support.
- Event trapping for lightpen, joystick, and keyboard input.

Company:
AT&T and Ryan-McFarland Corporation

Product:
RM/COBOL* Compiler

Category:
Systems Programming

Computer:	**Media:**
AT&T PC 6300	Diskette

Language:
Machine language and C

Requirements:
64 KB RAM
1 disk drive

Support:
This product is fully supported by AT&T Information Systems and carries a 90-day warranty on the media. Remote nationwide customer service hotline is provided Monday through Friday between the hours of 8:00 a.m. and 5:00 p.m. local time. Installation, additional hotline coverage, and extended maintenance agreements can be purchased.

Retail Price:
$950 For Full System (includes Runtime)

Distributor:
AT&T (800) 247-1212
or call your local AT&T authorized dealer or Account Executive.

***This product has been certified by AT&T.**

Description:

RM/COBOL is a GSA certified (error-free) ANSI-'74 COBOL implementation. It offers all the features needed for serious business programming including multikey index files, record-locking, high-level access methods, interactive screen handling, and interactive debugging during program execution.

With more than 250,000 installations since 1975, *RM/COBOL* is the recognized standard for 8 and 16-bit COBOL programming.

RM/COBOL is currently supported on more that 200 different computer systems, from mainframe to micros. It generates portable source and object code which can run on any system that supports the language, regardless of where the code was developed.

More than 2,500 *RM/COBOL*-based applications and development tools are now available from over 300 independent application developers world wide. These applications include 75+ different vertical software categories, state-of-the-art account packages and programmer productivity tools.

Company:
AT&T and Ryan-McFarland Corporation

Product:
RM/COBOL* Runtime

Category:
Systems Programming

Computer:	**Media:**
AT&T PC 6300	Diskette

Language:
Assembler Binary

Requirements:
256 KB RAM

Support:
This product is fully supported by AT&T Information Systems and carries a 90-day warranty on the media. Remote nationwide customer service hotline is provided Monday through Friday between the hours of 8:00 a.m. and 5:00 p.m. local time. Installation, additional hotline coverage, and extended maintenance agreements can be purchased.

Retail Price:
$250

Distributor:
AT&T (800) 247-1212
or call your local AT&T authorized dealer or Account Executive.

***This product has been certified by AT&T.**

Description:

The *RM/COBOL* Runtime software allows previously compiled *RM/COBOL* programs to run in the PC 6300 machine environment. The Runtime loads the object programs, allocates storage and file buffers and executes the programs. This feature is especially useful to transport *RM/COBOL* programs written for other machines.

Company:

AT&T and The Santa Cruz Operation, Inc.

Product:

XENIX* System V, Release 2.0

Category:

Systems Programming

Computer:	**Media:**
AT&T PC 6300	Diskette

Language:

C

Requirements:

256 KB RAM

Support:

This product is fully supported by AT&T Information Systems and carries a 90-day warranty on the media. Remote nationwide customer service hotline is provided Monday through Friday between the hours of 8:00 a.m. and 5:00 p.m. local time. Installation, additional hotline coverage, and extended maintenance agreements are also available.

Retail Price:

All $995
Runtime Operating System $350
Development System $495
Text Processing $150

Distributor:

AT&T (800) 247-1212
or call your local AT&T authorized dealer or Account Executive.

***This product has been certified by AT&T.**

Description:

XENIX is a multiuser, multitasking operating system which allows simultaneous file sharing between independent terminal operators, or between any application programs under control of one or more system operators.

It is a fully licensed, commercially enhanced version of AT&T's *UNIX* System V Operating System, which has become the standard for multiuser, multitasking environments.

The *XENIX* Operating System for the AT&T PC 6300 consists of the full set of *XENIX* utilities to run business applications, administer the system, edit files, and communicate with either users. Standard features include the *UNIX* System V shell (command interpreter), the popular "C shell," the "vi" full screen visual editor, system administration commands, electronic mail, support for *UNIX* System networking, and over 100 other *UNIX* System commands. Also included is "vsh," the visual shell, which provides a menu interface to *XENIX*. A PC 6300 with *XENIX* will run programs developed for other 8086 with *XENIX* systems and most 186 and 286 systems without modification. Programs with greater than 64 KB of instruction (medium model applications) are supported by *XENIX* on the PC 6300.

With *XENIX*'s *Multiscreen* feature, the user can instantly call up, with one keystroke, a screen display from any of up to ten simultaneously running application programs, virtually simulating ten independent parallel terminals within the 6300 console. The user can control both background and foreground color of a color monitor.

XENIX can support three simultaneous users on the PC 6300, one user on the console and two remote users on serial ports.

XENIX also supports the use of floating point instructions. If a system includes the 8087 floating point coprocessor, *XENIX* makes full use of it to improve performance. Floating point instructions are emulated, in a way that is transparent to the user, for systems which do not include an 8087.

The hard disk can be shared between *XENIX* and DOS, allowing the user to alternate between systems. *XENIX* also includes utilities for moving files between DOS and *XENIX*.

XENIX supports networking via two features, uucp and "Micnet." The uucp utility permits communication between *XENIX* systems, using either modem or RS-232 serial communication lines. The user can transfer files, send mail messages, or send remote commands to any other *XENIX* or *UNIX* system, regardless of location.

(Continued on next page)

Description: ***(Continued)***

The *XENIX* Micnet facility provides the user with local area networking capabilities. Micnet consists of *XENIX* systems connected via serial communications lines through which users can communicate without knowing the network configuration, or even the particular systems to which other users are connected. Remote sites can be accessed via uucp, which is used transparently to the user by Micnet.

The *XENIX* Text Processing Package contains tools for the preparation of large or complex documents. Included are nroff (document formatter), troff (phototypesetting formatter), formatting macro packages, special formatting tools (such as "eqn" for mathematical equations and "tbl" for tables), and support for a variety of specific fonts and printer types. Also included are tools to check spelling and style in written text, and an on-line dictionary.

The *XENIX* Software Development Package supplies all the tools needed to write C and assembly language programs, It features the C-merge compiler, which allows users to develop software for both DOS and *XENIX* from a single set of source code. Proven productivity and support tools such as "SCCS" (a source code control system), "adb" (an interactive debugger), "lint" (program checker), the "lex" and "yacc" language tools, and the "make" program are also included.

Company:
BASIS Incorporated

Product:
***Business Basic/Extended* (*BB*^{X})**

Category:
Systems Programming

Computer: AT&T PC 6300
Media: Diskette

Language:
C, Assembler

Requirements:
1 MB RAM recommended
20 MB disk recommended

Support:
One-year warranty
800 hotline number

Retail Price:
$295

Distributor:
BASIS Incorporated
5700 Harper Dr., NE, Suite 290
Albuquerque, NM 87409
Tel: (505) 821-4407

Description:

BB^X (*Business Basic/Extended*) is a version of *Business Basic* source code compatible with *MAI Basic Four* and *SMC Thoroughbred Business Basic BB*^{X} includes all features of the *Basic Four* standard plus major enhancements. It has been designed from the beginning to operate in a single or multiuser mode on *MS*-DOS Version 2.x or higher *XENIX* and *UNIX* System V and networks Supervised by *IBM*, *Microsoft* and *Novell* network software.

BB^X is above a sophisticated business oriented BASIC language with a powerful file system and a utility set to aid program development and system management.

BASIS's *BB*^{X} system software products bring several key advantages to potential users:

- It is one of the fastest, most powerful development tools available for business oriented program creation
- It is one of the industry's largest libraries of horizontal and vertical applications currently existing in derivatives of this language
- It coexists transparently within its operating environment

BB^X provides a variety of advanced features and functions not normally associated with microcomputers. These include:

MULTI-TASKING: *BB*^{X} provides the ability to control resources between multiple attached PCs in a network or all system devices when running in a true multiuser system such as *UNIX* System V.

TASK OVERLAY: *BB*^{X} allows rapid "overlay" from disc of the executing task without modification or loss of the task's in-memory data area or symbol table.

PUBLIC PROGRAMMING: *BB*^{X} public programming feature provides a reentrant structure that allows calls to memory resident programs. Access to these in-memory routines is at a speed rivaling a program-resident subroutine. Public programming not only provides enhanced performance but also allows sophisticated routines to be shared throughout an entire system.

BB^X's file system provides a variety of powerful file structures which support the demanding disc storage

(Continued on next page)

Description: ***(Continued)***

and retrieval requirements of business data processing applications. These file structures (in BB^X's terminology) include:

INDEX: BB^X INDEX file presents a traditional random (or direct) access file structure.

KEYED: Through BB^X's KEYED file structure, records are written and recalled with a user-defined key. Record retrieval may be accomplished by physical location (index), full or partial key, and logical sequence (forward or reverse). and retrieval requirements of business data processing applications. These file structures (in BB^X's terminology) include:

INDEX: BB^X INDEX file presents a traditional random (or direct) access file structure.

KEYED: Through BB^X's KEYED file structure, records are written and recalled with a user-defined key. Record retrieval may be accomplished by physical location (index), full or partial key, and logical sequence (forward or reverse).

STRING: A STRING file is BB^X's nomenclature for unstructured file format. BB^X provides the capability of reading and writing *MS*-DOS, or *UNIX* System V files with complete compatibility.

In addition, BB^X supports device-independent display management functions including: character attribute handling, windowing, function key loading and edit keys handling.

Company:
California Automation, Inc.

Product:
***ANDROMEDA* Version 1.0**

Category:
Systems Programming

Computer:	**Media:**
AT&T PC 6300	Diskette

Language:
C

Requirements:
The *LATTICE* C compiler is recommended
ANDROMEDA supports the console
Serial terminals and a parallel printer
64 KB RAM required

Support:
Updates supplied to customers for the cost of the media
No charge for customer questions

Retail Price:
$290

Distributor:
RAYTRONICS
7392 Trade St.
San Diego, CA 92121
Tel: (619) 566-7515

Description:

ANDROMEDA is a multitasking operating system which has been designed from the ground up for real-time automation, control, monitoring, and message switching applications.

It is a true event-driven operating system, in which context switching between tasks is accomplished when internal or external events happen, so that system response is independent of the clock tick interrupt frequency. *ANDROMEDA* uses the clock interrupt only for time-of-day, device timeouts, and time delays requested by tasks.

ANDROMEDA is written partially in the C language and partially in assembly language. A major design goal was to make the system as efficient and as small as possible, while providing the features and flexibility needed for a practical operating system. As a result, *ANDROMEDA* is extremely responsive and fits into only 12 KB RAM. While compatible with DOS, *ANDROMEDA* may also run independent of DOS and may be configured to run from ROM memory.

- System Calls: *ANDROMEDA* provides system calls for loading, running, stopping, suspending, resuming, scheduling, aborting, delaying, and terminating tasks. Tasks may be called to run with a specified period or to run once, and parameters may be passed in the call statement. Stack and data space sizes are specified at load time, and dynamic stack overflow checking is provided on all running tasks. Tasks may be loaded to share data space or to have independent data spaces.
- Intertask Communications: Extensive intertask communications are provided through user-defined, but system-managed, dynamic queues. The dynamic memory pool size is user-defined and can be as large as one megabyte. The user may declare either circular queues or linked list queues, which may be independent or attached to tasks. The queue buffer size, queue resource interlocking, task interlocking and maximum dynamic message count can be specified by runtime calls. Up to three priorities of queues may be attached to each task, allowing true message priority separation such as for critical alarms, noncritical alarms and normal messages. Once a queue is defined, it is managed automatically by the system.
- Terminal and Printer Support: *ANDROMEDA* provides extensive terminal support functions for the console, serial terminals, and printers. Separate input and output areas (WINDOWING) can be defined for CRT terminals, and any task

(Continued on next page)

Description: ***(Continued)***

can set up full duplex communications. The system automatically manages the input and output cursors for the console or serial terminals so that input may be echoed in the input area with no effect on realtime output appearing simultaneously in the output area. Sixty system calls are provided for terminal support alone.

- DOS Compatibility: *ANDROMEDA* is DOS compatible and allocates DOS as a single-user (one at a time) utility. Any task can therefore acquire DOS for realtime file I/O operations. All *ANDROMEDA* tasks are standard DOS type EXE executable files. DOS generated errors are handled by *ANDROMEDA* so that only the task causing the error is terminated, while all the rest remain running. When a task panics, or is terminated, a user-definable message appears on the bottom line of the console CRT. Further, if a task aborts, any resources allocated to the aborting task are automatically released by the system.
- Customization by the Application Programmer: The guiding rule in the design of *ANDROMEDA* was to give the application programmer as much flexibility as possible in customizing devices, adding devices, adding and integrating device drivers, declaring dynamic pool size, and adding custom executive calls. This is accomplished by modules which may be linked into the executive. The sources for the C language customizing module and the assembly language customizing module are provided on the distribution diskette.
- Size of *ANDROMEDA*:" *ANDROMEDA* fits in only 12 KB RAM and is Rommable. It can also be configured to run without DOS, as might be required in board level products and independent controllers.

Company:
Digital Research Inc.

Product:
***CBASIC* Compiler**

Category:
Systems Programming

Computer:	**Media:**
AT&T PC 6300	Diskette

Language:
PL/M and Assembly

Requirements:
128 KB RAM

Support:
Support through information available on Digital Research's special interest group on CompuServe. User's Guide provided.

Retail Price:
$600

Distributor:
Digital Research Inc.
P.O. Box 579
160 Central Ave.
Pacific Grove, CA 93950
Tel: (408) 649-3896

Description:

CBASIC Compiler, a native code compiler, is a direct enhancement of the industry standard *CBASIC* language. Designed specifically for commercial applications, *CBASIC* Compiler's easily maintainable code simplifies implementation and support of large business systems. *CBASIC* Compiler's program structuring allows separate modules to be written, tested, and then combined to create a complete program. This efficient, modular, top-down approach makes *CBASIC* Compiler programs faster to write and easier to maintain.

One of *CBASIC* Compiler's most significant features is speed. Arithmetic functions are as fast as double-precision binary while retaining 14 decimal digits of accuracy. Because *CBASIC* Compiler generates native code in relocatable format, separate *CBASIC* Compiler modules, as well as assembler routines, can be easily linked together. *CBASIC* Compiler's record lock and unlock functions are designed to support Digital Research's multiuser and concurrent operating systems.

CBASIC Compiler includes a linkage editor and librarian. The linkage editor combines output generated by the compiler with required routines from the runtime library to create a composite program. It also produces overlay modules for use with *CBASIC* Compiler's CHAIN statement. The librarian combines many relocatable modules into an indexed library for rapid access by the linkage editor.

CBASIC Compiler Features:

- Extended Precision Decimal Arithmetic
- Support for Digital Research's Operating Systems, as *MS*-DOS and PC-DOS
- 32 KB Dynamically Allocated Strings
- Optional Declaration Statements
- Multiple Line Functions with Parameters
- Error Trapping
- Call Statements with Parameter Passing
- Reduced Software Development Time
- Expanded File Processing
- Chaining with Common Variables
- Graphics extensions via GSX

(Continued on next page)

Description: ***(Continued)***

Extended Precision Decimal Arithmetic

CBASIC Compiler maintains real numbers in a binary coded decimal (BCD) floating point format, retaining at least 14 significant digits. *CBASIC* Compiler supports integer arithmetic. Integer arithmetic is inherently faster on all microcomputers. By using integer variables whenever possible, program speed and throughput are increased tremendously.

Operating Systems Support

CBASIC Compiler operates with all of Digital Research's operating systems including multiuser *MP/M-86, CP/M-86*, and Concurrent *MS*-DOS. Files can be opened as LOCKED, UNLOCKED, or READ ONLY. When a file is opened UNLOCKED, individual records can be locked and unlocked to support shared access to the database. *CBASIC* Compiler supports multiple printers with the ATTACH function. The ATTACH function attaches a selected printer while the DETACH statement releases an attached printer.

With *CBASIC* Compiler's comprehensive graphics extensions, you can now write versatile graphics programs for a multitude of applications. The *CBASIC* Compiler graphic extensions are additional statements and functions recognized as reserved words by the compiler and implemented in a runtime library. The graphic extensions are not available for *MP/M-86*.

Company:
Digital Research Inc.

Product:
Digital Research C

Category:
Systems Programming

Computer: AT&T PC 6300

Media: Diskette

Language:
C

Requirements:
192 KB RAM

Support:
Support through information available on Digital Research's special interest group on CompuServe. User's Guide provided.

Retail Price:
$350

Distributor:
Digital Research Inc.
P.O. Box 579
160 Central Ave.
Pacific Grove, CA 93950
Tel: (408) 649-3896

Description:

C is the best language for systems implementation. C is an advanced, elegant programming language built for coding power and execution speed with a minimum of constraints. C gives skilled software developers the ability to take full advantage of the inherent structure of the computer, including large model support on the 8086. C is ideal for performance-critical applications and systems-level programming.

The *Digital Research C* programming development system includes a feature-packed compiler, linker, and a comprehensive runtime library which contains a wide range of utilities.

Digital Research C is a complete implementation of the C language, fully compatible with the *UNIX* operating system standard C language. The runtime support library handles everything from transcendental functions to input-output. Altogether, *Digital Research C* is an integrated answer to all your programming needs.

C is not for everyone, but for the experienced software developer, it is one of the most powerful programming tools available.

Features Summary:

- Full C language implementation compatible with *UNIX* System V
- Version 7
- Single and double-precision floating point
- 8087 numeric processor support
- Enhanced programming/debugging tools
- Comprehensive utility package included
- Multiple 8086 memory model support

Company:
Digital Research Inc.

Product:
Pascal/MT+

Category:
Systems Programming

Computer:	**Media:**
AT&T PC 6300	Diskette

Language:
Pascal/MT+

Requirements:
128 KB RAM

Support:
Support through information available on Digital Research's special interest group on CompuServe. User's Guide provided.

Retail Price:
$600

Distributor:
Digital Research Inc.
P.O. Box 579
160 Central Ave.
Pacific Grove, CA 93950
Tel: (408) 649-3896

Description:

Pascal is a highly structured language originally designed for teaching programming. Data types are extensive and matched to your programming needs. These qualities, plus compactness and execution speed, have made Pascal highly regarded as a microcomputer development language.

Benefits of *Pascal/MT+*

Digital Research's *Pascal/MT+* is a direct-compiling dialect of the full ISO standard Pascal–greatly enhanced and extended to maximize the inherent versatility and portability of Pascal. The *Pascal/MT+* native code compiler executes much faster than traditional p-code Pascal compilers.

Pascal/MT+ supports floating point real numbers for scientific applications and decimal numbers for arithmetic precision in business applications. ROM-able code can be generated for industrial applications. And in educational environments, *Pascal/MT+* is easily learned and never outgrown.

Pascal/MT+ is the best software development tool available today. The *Pascal/MT+* programming system includes a compiler, a linker, a runtime support library, a disassembler, and a symbolic program debugger. And Digital Research has developed a unique Speed Programming Package that locates syntax errors, a major timesaver in program development.

Features Summary:

- Superset of ISO standard Pascal
- Separate modular compilation
- Efficient native code
- ROM-able machine code
- Complete development tools
- Enhanced arithmetic functions
- Extended data types
- Powerful overlay capabilities
- Compatible with Display Manager and Access Manager
- Compatible with GSX Graphics
- 8087 numeric processor support

Company:
Digital Research Inc.

Product:
PL/1

Category:
Systems Programming

Computer:	**Media:**
AT&T PC 6300	Diskette

Language:
PL/M and Assembly

Requirements:
192 KB RAM

Support:
Support through information available on Digital Research's special interest group on CompuServe. User's Guide provided.

Retail Price:
$750

Distributor:
Digital Research Inc.
P.O. Box 579
160 Central Ave.
Pacific Grove, CA 93950
Tel: (408) 649-3896

Description:

PL/1 is a high-performance professional programming language. *PL/1* is a powerful, easy-to-learn, all-purpose language that rivals both FORTRAN for scientific applications and COBOL for commercial applications. This makes *PL/1* the best language to meet all the needs of a professional programmer.

Digital Research has created the first implementation of *PL/1* for microcomputers.

Based on the widely used ANSI Standard Subset G, *Digital Research PL/1* programs are easily ported from micro to mini to mainframe. And, by following a few simple rules, your programs are also portable from mainframe to mini to micro!

The *Digital Research PL/1* program development system includes an optimizing native code compiler, a relocatable assembler, a relocating linker, a library manager, a cross-reference generator, and a comprehensive library of useful built-in functions. Together, these tools provide a fast, integrated system for developing your own scientific, commercial, and system software.

Best of all, the programs you create with *PL/1* are extremely efficient. That's the result of the state-of-the-art optimization and decades of compiler experience behind *Digital Research's PL/1* for microcomputers.

Features Summary:

- Structured control statements
- Fixed binary integers
- Single and double precision floating point
- 15-digit arithmetic
- Bit string operations
- Character string operations
- Full control of compiler storage allocation
- User controlled error handling
- Supports Display Manager and Access Manager
- Supports Graphics via GSX

Company:
EZ-PC, Inc.

Product:
E-Z PC

Category:
Systems Programming

Computer:	**Media:**
AT&T PC 6300	Diskette
6300 PLUS **AT&T PC 6300 PLUS**	

Language:
Assembler, BASIC

Requirements:
96 KB RAM
Hard disk
MS-DOS 2.0+

Support:
90-day media warranty
User hotline: (404) 979-5867

Retail Price:
$89.95

Distributor:
EZ-PC, Inc.
4131 Wrexham Drive
Lithonia, GA 30058
Tel: (404) 979-5867

Description:

E-Z PC is basically two programs in one package combining a menu of DOS commands to provide an easy alternative to memorizing the DOS manual with another menu which provides immediate and painless access for 20 programs and batch jobs.

From the DOS command menu, the user may execute or request help for any command after positioning the cursor over the particular selection. The DOS command screen provides detailed, step-by-step instructions to create or build the DOS command.

The program menu may be set up by answering just a few simple questions. There are no batch jobs to create or special programs to write. Once *E-Z PC* knows about the user's application it may be simply selected from the program menu. When the application is done, the user will return to *E-Z PC* automatically. There are also user-definable Help screens available from the program execution menu.

Company:
Liberty Bell Publishing

Product:
dWINDOW

Category:
Systems Programming

Computer:
AT&T PC 6300

Media:
Diskette

Language:
Assembler

Requirements:
9 KB RAM
Monochrome or color
Bit map graphics or mouse not required
DOS version 2.0, 3.0, 3.1
dBASE version 2.40, 2.41, 2.43 and higher

Support:
Warranty; 30-day refund policy
User support: 503-221-1806

Retail Price:
$165
dBASE II $99
dBASE III $99–$149 1.1

Distributor:
Liberty Bell Publishing
618 NW Glisan, Suite 203
Portland, OR 97209
Tel: (503) 221-1806

Description:

dWINDOW.EXE is an assembly language program, around 9 KB, which adds 25 new SYNTAX statements to *dBASE II*. Assembly language is as close to the machine instructions as a program can get. Programming in assembly language results in fast-operating software while minimizing the amount of computer memory necessary to run it.

dWINDOW addresses the need of *dBASE* programmers to quickly and easily design screen input/output for their database programs. Further, it increases the methods available for programmers to create user-friendly software systems with menu-driven or selectable program features.

dWINDOW is a programmers' tool kit of new syntax. *dWINDOW* syntax adds program "STATEMENTS" which allow windowing techniques. Without the use of windowing, programmers have been limited to 2000 characters of information on the screen. By using overlaying windows of information, similar to the pages in a book, programmers will not be limited by screen size or number of characters.

dWINDOW allows for the creation of databases of windows. By addressing windows of information, rather than files or pages of information which are usually retrieved character by character, programmers will have faster response times in data retrieval.

dWINDOW reduces the programming time required to format input/ output data. Productivity increases while programming costs decrease. *dWINDOWs* concise and simple instructions eliminate numerous lines of *dBASE* II code previously required to perform similar operations, if they could be done at all. It makes menus and screen generation routines easy and fast.

dWINDOW users can prepare financial or company reports, including bar charts or other character set pictures, and transmit them easily over available networking systems. Character graphics are defined as the ASCII set of characters supplied with the standard monochrome version of the personal computer. Most windowing packages require the use of bit-mapped graphics, which involves purchasing a color monitor and a color-graphics board. Both are additional expenses to the user. *dWINDOW* works with character graphics and is easily transmitted via modem lines. Character graphics reduce the number of transmissions necessary to transmit similar bit-mapped information. Overall, the reduction in transmissions reduces the user's "Phone Bill"!

(Continued on next page)

Description: ***(Continued)***

READ BAR is a method of selecting items from screen menus. Because of its popularity and ease of use, we have provided a READ WINDOW ROW statement in *dWINDOW*.

User-friendly is the keyword in automated processing. *dWINDOW* addresses user friendliness, providing programmers the tools necessary to create user-friendly software. Applications programs are provided to teach users how to use *dWINDOW* effectively in their own software.

dWINDOW provides a DOS command statement allowing users to execute any operating system command–including the running of other programs while under *dBASE II* program control. A virtual database operating system with the full power of *dBASE II*'s instruction set for operating control and functioning–plus having the database always at hand, *dWINDOW* opens the way for effective integrated software.

dWINDOW provides an INKEY statement to input from keyboard any one of the 255 keyboard characters available without echoing to the screen. The full character set is testable.

The printing of full screens of information is simply accomplished with a PRINT SCREEN statement provided by *dWINDOW*.

For the user who has purchased a color monitor and board, *dWINDOW* provides full color capabilities. All characters and attributes are selectables for both monochrome and color systems.

Company:
Mainstay Software Corporation

Product:
MAINSTAY

Category:
Systems Programming

Computer:	**Media:**
AT&T PC 6300	Diskette

Language:
Microsoft Pascal and assembly language

Requirements:
512 KB RAM minimum
640 KB RAM recommended
Internal or external hard disk with minimum of 1.5 MB of available storage

Support:
Hotline
Demo diskette
Reference manual
User guide
Application Development Guide with sample applications on diskette
Quick Reference Guide are available at extra cost
Training and consulting are also available for an additional fee

Retail Price:
$1,495

Distributor:
Mainstay Software Corporation
1745 Stout St., Suite 201
Denver, CO 80202
Tel: (303) 298-8961

Description:

MAINSTAY is a microcomputer software package that allows the rapid development of custom applications by combining an analytical database management system with a full programming language and a user interface toolkit.

MAINSTAY also provides users with an effective environment for database management, information analysis, and modeling.

Key *MAINSTAY* features are:

- Comprehensive analytics including full modeling and forecasting
- A powerful procedural application development language
- User interface toolkit enabling easy and rapid customization of menus and forms for individual applications and the ability to customize logos, prompts, error messages, and help messages
- Functions and options for end user ad hoc inquiry, data analysis, and reporting
- A multidimensional, unstructured data model that allows many data structures, such as relational, hierarchical, network, and time series, in the same database. The user can dynamically add, modify, or delete data elements
- Virtual memory technology for handling very large databases
- The ability to issue DOS commands through a host function
- Full-screen editor with multiple buffers
- Ability to enter, store, and edit textual information of unlimited length
- Access to up to nine databases at one time

Company:
Microsoft Corporation

Product:
Microsoft* COBOL Version 2.0

Category:
Systems Programming

Computer:	**Media:**
AT&T PC 6300	Diskette

Language:
Assembler

Requirements:
128 KB RAM
Two disk drives

Support:
This product is supported by Microsoft. The media is warranted for 90 days from date of purchase. The Microsoft customer hotline (206) 828-8089 is available to answer technical questions about the product and how it works.

Retail Price:
$700

Distributor:
AT&T (800) 247-1212
or call your local authorized AT&T dealer or Account Executive.

***This product has been certified by AT&T.**

Description:

COBOL 2.0 is Microsoft's most advanced version of the COBOL language. It is based on the Level 2 language specifications set forth in the ANSI 74 standard (ANSI 3.23-1974). Generally COBOL implementations based on the full set definition are only found on mainframe computers. *Microsoft* COBOL 2.0 will provide a comparable programming environment that, because of the rigid standardization of this popular business applications language, will allow software developers on mainframes and minicomputers to port their applications to micro-based systems.

The Federal Software Testing Center (GSA) certifies COBOL compilers for compliance with the standard. In doing so they set up four validation levels: low, low-intermediate, high-intermediate, and high. Each level is based on a specified set of requirements for the COBOL language nucleus and other 11 modules (table-handling, sequential I-O, relative I-O, indexed I-O, sort-merge, report writer, segmentation, library, debug, inter-program communication, and communication). The report writer module is optional. *Microsoft* COBOL 1.x was validated at the low-intermediate level. *Microsoft* COBOL 2.0 will be validated at the high level.

Microsoft COBOL 2.0 will include the following features:

- Multikey ISAM
- Built-in sort/merge
- Interactive screen handling extensions
- Record and file locking support facilities (for those environments that support multiple users)
- Indexed file recovery utility
- Interactive symbolic debug facility

Company:
Microsoft Corporation

Product:
Microsoft* FORTRAN

Category:
Systems Programming

Computer:	**Media:**
AT&T PC 6300	Diskette

Language:
Pascal

Requirements:
256 KB RAM
Two disk drives are recommended for easier operation

Support:
This product is supported by Microsoft. The media is warranted for 90 days from date of product purchase. The Microsoft customer hotline (206) 828-8089 is available to answer technical questions about the product and how it works.

Retail Price:
$350

Distributor:
AT&T (800) 247-1212
or call your local authorized AT&T dealer or Account Executive.

***This product has been certified by AT&T.**

Description:

FORTRAN is the language of choice for many scientific and technological applications. It has an enormous number of existing applications programs and subroutines written for mainframes and minicomputers, many of which can be adapted for microcomputers. *Microsoft* FORTRAN has many features of the ANSI X3.9-1978 standard for FORTRAN at the subset level, and has many features of the full standard, plus extensions to take advantage of the microcomputer environment. This makes *MS*-FORTRAN extremely versatile in meeting the program needs of most engineers and scientists who are moving from larger computers to micros.

The design approach of getting the highest possible utility from a microcomputer carries over from one *Microsoft* language to the next, and *MS*-FORTRAN is no exception. *MS*-FORTRAN shares the same assembler, editor, linker, and user-interface characteristics with *MS*-Pascal and *Microsoft's* other compilers. *MS*-Pascal and *MS*-FORTRAN also share code generators and even have similar error messages. This means you can easily combine the structured capabilities of Pascal with the mathematics capabilities of FORTRAN and get maximum flexibility in your program design.

MS-FORTRAN has an extensive subroutine library, including useful subroutines for 16- and 32-bit integer arithmetic and 32- and 64-bit floating point arithmetic. Addition, subtraction, and conversion to 16-bit integers are all done on-line. Multiplication and division are performed by optimized assembly routines. Because of this, programs execute up to ten times faster in *MS*-FORTRAN than in other microcomputer implementations of the language.

For flexible I/O formatting, *MS*-FORTRAN includes some features of both list-directed and generalized I/O. It is also possible to write nonstandard I/O drivers for each peripheral interface, making it easier to interface FORTRAN programs with the nonstandard peripherals common to scientific and engineering work.

Company:
Microsoft Corporation

Product:
Microsoft* Macro Assembler

Category:
Systems Programming

Computer: **AT&T PC 6300**

Media: Diskette

Language:
Pascal

Requirements:
128 KB RAM
Two disk drives are recommended although one disk drive is adequate if output is sent to the same physical disk from which the input was taken.

Support:
This product is supported by Microsoft. The media is warranted for 90 days from date of product purchase. The Microsoft customer hotline (206) 828-8089 is available to answer technical questions about the product and how it works.

Retail Price:
$100

Distributor:
AT&T (800) 247-1212
or call your local authorized AT&T dealer or Account Executive.

***This product has been certified by AT&T.**

Description:

Microsoft Macro Assembler is a powerful assembler for 8086/8088-based microcomputers employing the *MS*-DOS operating system. *MS*-Macro Assembler incorporates many features usually found only in large computer assemblers. Macro assembly, conditional assembly and a variety of assembler directives provide all the tools necessary to derive full use and full power of the microprocessor. And even though *Microsoft's* Macro Assembler offers more sophisticated features than other microcomputer assemblers, it is still easy to use.

The *MS*-Macro Assembler can be used to develop subroutines for functions not easily accommodated in high level languages. *MS*-Macro Assembler can also be used on a standalone basis to develop complete assembly language programs. *MS*-Macro Assembler is especially useful for coding I/O driver routines, distributed network applications, and handling virtual memory requirements. And, because *MS*-Macro Assembler produces relocatable object code and uses the standard *MS*-DOS *MS*-LINK facility, routines can be linked with programs written in any of Microsoft's high-level languages running under *MS*-DOS.

MS-Macro Assembler's relocatable code has the added advantage of being loaded anywhere in memory so the program can execute where it is most efficient, instead of in some fixed range of memory addresses. And, relocatable code means that programs can be created in modules, each of which can be assembled, tested, and perfected individually. This saves development time because testing and assembly are performed on smaller pieces of code before being linked together into the whole program.

All the *MS*-Macro Assembler's features are accomplished without sacrificing speed or memory requirements. The program resides in approximately 70 KB of memory and has an assembly rate of over 500 lines per minute. Typical of *Microsoft*, *MS*-Macro Assembler has been developed with all the features required to get the best performance out of both the software and the microcomputer.

Company:
Microsoft Corporation

Product:
Microsoft* Pascal

Category:
Systems Programming

Computer: AT&T PC 6300

Media: Diskette

Language:
Pascal

Requirements:
256 KB RAM
Two disk drives are recommended for easier operation

Support:
This product is supported by Microsoft Corp. The media is warranted for 90 days from date of product purchase. The Microsoft customer hotline (206) 828-8089 is available to answer technical questions about the product and how it works.

Retail Price:
$300

Distributor:
AT&T (800) 247-1212
or call your local authorized AT&T dealer or Account Executive.

***This product has been certified by AT&T.**

Description:

MS-Pascal provides a powerful system development language that allows programmers to create highly readable, modular and transportable code. *MS*-Pascal is well-suited for most system software programming tasks, such as building operating system extensions and database managers. In addition, Pascal's clean block structure and procedure orientation make system programming more efficient than with assembly language. As a result, program development time is reduced significantly and products are more reliable.

MS-Pascal offers more extensions to the ISO standard and the related ANSI standard than most other versions of Pascal. All of Microsoft's enhancements to Pascal are logical extensions to the standards. The enhancements have been carefully engineered to maintain the structured nature of the language while assimilating powerful new capabilities. Enhancements including low-level escapes and addressing modes and the use of a common linker with *MS*-BASIC, *MS*-FORTRAN, and assembly language programs makes *MS*-Pascal especially adaptable for diverse and complex applications.

MS-Pascal generates native machine code, which ensures that compiled application programs execute quickly. Because low-level escapes to machine level allow programs to access assembler routines and memory locations directly, *MS*-Pascal programs can achieve speeds comparable to those written in machine language. In addition, *MS*-Pascal's optimizing code generator produces compact code. These features make *MS*-Pascal superior in power, speed, and versatility for a wide range of commercial applications.

Company:
Morgan Computing Company, Inc.

Product:
***Advanced Trace86* V.1.2**

Category:
Systems Programming

Computer:	**Media:**
AT&T PC 6300 6300 PLUS **AT&T PC 6300 PLUS**	Diskette

Language:
Assembler

Requirements:
128 KB RAM

Support:
Telephone support

Retail Price:
$175

Distributor:
Morgan Computing Company, Inc.
P.O. Box 112730
Carrollton, Texas 75006
Tel: (214) 245-4763

Description:

Advanced Trace86 is a sophisticated debugger that allows the assembly language enthusiast to trace, step-by-step, the execution of a compiled program. A diversity of tracing options are available to switch from full native speed execution of code to single stepping. There is even a facility to program specific conditions for breakpoints that is more flexible and powerful than any other system on the market today. Additionally, it has incorporated the capability of directly editing in Assembler and then directly saving the edited code as a .COM or .EXE file. No recompiling and relinking is necessary! *Advanced Trace86* runs programs at slow speed while displaying, all on one screen, an assembler version of a compiled program, the machine registers, and data in memory. Also, a program can be loaded and run from *Advanced Trace86*. Then at any time while the program is executing normally, it is possible to break out and begin tracing from that point forward. The users can write labels and comments in code and save these on disk. Polish Hex/Decimal Calculator as well as hex to decimal and decimal to hex conversion are provided. *Advanced Trace86* also has the ability to toggle between the tracing screen and the program's output screen (or set up two monitors!).

Company:
Morgan Computing Company, Inc.

Product:
Professional BASIC

Category:
Systems Programming

Computer:	**Media:**
AT&T PC 6300 **AT&T PC 6300 PLUS**	Diskette

Language:
Assembler

Requirements:
320 KB RAM

Support:
Telephone support

Retail Price:
$99

Distributor:
Morgan Computing Company, Inc.
P.O. Box 112730
Carrollton, TX 75006
Tel: (214) 245-4763

Description:

Professional BASIC is a new version of the BASIC language that can access the full memory the AT&T PC 6300. *Professional BASIC* dynamically allocates memory to allow 640 KB or more to be used for programs, data, or a combination of each. It's now possible to create, for example, a 250 x 250 array with BASIC! The most extraordinary new feature is the window-oriented system of more than a dozen trace screens (full/half window) allowing the user to view program flow, changes in variables or array elements, the progress of FOR/NEXT loops or GOSUBs, and more as the program executes. *Professional BASIC* utilizes "process visualization" to enable anyone, from the professional to the student, to see on the screen exactly how a program is working. *Professional BASIC* also extends normal BASIC by allowing labeled GOSUBs and GOTOs, cross referencing, setting breakpoints, extended line renumbering options, as well as large integers (2 billion plus), large reals (10^{+-} 308), a maximum file size of more than 4 billion bytes, and more. Since the user can run most of the PC BASIC programs with little or no modification, it is an excellent tool for both application development and education.

Company:
Red Wing Business Systems, Inc.

Product:
RW Master Menu System

Category:
Systems Programming

Computer:	**Media:**
AT&T PC 6300	Diskette

Language:
BASIC

Requirements:
This system requires a hard disk unit

Support:
A 30-day money-back guarantee is offered for all Red Wing Software. Free support is also offered to all licensed customers for the first year that they own the software package. Support is done through dealers and directly through Red Wing Business Systems. The documentation manual is complete and will help customers learn the package at their convenience.

Retail Price:
$25

Distributor:

Red Wing Business Systems, Inc.
610 Main St.
P.O. Box 19
Red Wing, MN 55066
Tel: (612) 388-1106

Description:

Red Wing Business Systems' Master Menu lets the user switch from one system to another just by pushing a key. Rebooting the computer is no longer necessary every time the user wants to switch systems. The Red Wing Master Menu also handles other systems. From word processing to spreadsheets to production systems, all can be handled quickly and efficiently. The Master Menu is easy to install using the manual that comes with the software. The Red Wing Master Menu makes the hard disk drive faster and easier to use. In addition, the user can operate all of his or her software from one Master Menu.

Company:
Red Wing Business Systems, Inc.

Product:
RW Multi-Client System

Category:
Systems Programming

Computer:	**Media:**
AT&T PC 6300	Diskette

Language:
BASIC

Requirements:
This system requires a hard disk unit

Support:
A 30-day money-back guarantee is offered for all Red Wing Software. Free support is also offered to all licensed customers for the first year that they own the software package. Support is done through dealers and directly through Red Wing Business Systems. The documentation manual is complete and will help customers learn the package at their convenience.

Retail Price:
$25

Distributor:
Red Wing Business Systems, Inc.
610 Main St.
P.O. Box 19
Red Wing, MN 55066
Tel: (612) 388-1106

Description:

Many times a user will want to use Red Wing to keep financial records for many clients. Until now, the user had to load the client data from the floppy disk onto the hard disk every time the records were updated. Then when the user wanted to switch to another client, data had to be copied from the hard disk to the floppy disk, the other client's data disk placed in the computer and the information copied from the floppy to the hard disk. The Red Wing Multi-Client System eliminates these problems. The user simply enters a three-character code and switches from one set of records to another.

Company:
Relational Database Systems, Inc.

Product:
C-ISAM*

Category:
Systems Programming

Computer:
AT&T PC 6300

Media:
Diskette

Language:
C

Requirements:
24 KB RAM
C language compiler

Support:
Contact RDS for support and maintenance policies
Technical support number (415) 424-0151

Retail Price:
$225

Distributor:
Relational Database Systems, Inc.
4100 Bohannon Drive
Menlo Park, CA 94025
Tel: (415) 322-4100

***This product has been certified by AT&T.**

Description:

C-ISAM is a B+ Tree access method that allows programmers to create, manipulate, and retrieve data using indexed files.

C-ISAM's flexible indexing structure eases program development and increases file access speeds. Index keys can be composed of up to eight discontiguous record segments of differing data types. An unlimited number of fields can be indexed within a file, and duplicate values can be allowed or disallowed for each index created.

C-ISAM's index value compression reduces required disk storage. A programmer can specify that leading duplicate characters, trailing blanks, and duplicate values be suppressed within the stored index value.

With *C-ISAM*, a programmer does not have to define file sizes in advance, or periodically run recompaction utilities. All *C-ISAM* files grow dynamically and reuse space left by deleted records. The index files are automatically updated and their respective index structures balanced when a data file modification occurs.

Single file and record locking procedures, performed automatically by *C-ISAM*, ensure data integrity in active multiuser environments. Optionally, the programmer can specify that record locking be controlled by an application.

C-ISAM is ideal for the full spectrum of software applications and is used in many operating systems and languages.

Company:
STSC, Inc.

Product:
***APL*PLUS* PC System**

Category:
Systems Programming

Computer:	**Media:**
AT&T PC 6300	Diskette

Language:
APL

Requirements:
256 KB RAM
Version 2.0 or greater
1 disk drive
Both monochrome and graphic display monitors are supported for most popular display adapters.
Any printer compatible with the personal computer being used will work with the *APL*PLUS* PC System, but not all printers can produce the traditional APL symbols. An *IBM* or *Epson* graphic printer or compatible, or other printers that support the APL character set, are recommended.

Support:
Telephone Help-line manned from 10:00 A.M. to 6:00 P.M. Monday through Friday
Training available by calling a sales representative at (301) 984-5123
Newsletter for registered users
Periodic software enhancements
Warranty included with package

Retail Price:
$595

Distributor:
STSC, Inc.
2115 East Jefferson St.
Rockville, MD 20852
Tel: (301) 984-5129
(800) 592-0050

Description:

The *APL*PLUS* PC System is an advanced application development system based on the APL language. It gives problem-solvers the power to deliver totally integrated, highly efficient solutions to problems that conventional software simply can not handle.

Most languages require the programmer to go through an enormous number of steps before an idea becomes reality. But with the the *APL*PLUS* PC System, those same programs can be developed four to ten times faster using APL's concise and intuitive symbolic notation.

Features include online Help facility, built-in full-screen editing, APL and native file systems, built-in terminal emulator, high-resolution graphics, report formatting facility, screen management, interfaces to other languages and software packages, and extensive documentation.

Company:
SuperSoft, Inc.

Product:
Disk-Edit

Category:
Systems Programming

Computer:
AT&T PC 6300

Media:
Diskette

Language:
C

Requirements:
128 KB RAM

Support:
Phone support
Update notification

Retail Price:
$100

Distributor:
SuperSoft, Inc.
P.O. Box 1628
Champaign, IL 61820
Tel: (217) 359-2112

Description:

Disk-Edit is an invaluable disk utility useful in saving accidentally erased files, recovering information from crashed databases, and a wide variety of programming situations. It provides access to all the raw information on your disk in both HEX and ASCII. You can scroll through it, alter it using a set of text editing commands, move back and forth between the HEX and ASCII windows, and perform string searches to find specific data.

Once you are in Disk-Edit you have a full range of text editing commands at your control, including forward space, back space, next line, previous line, view next screen, view previous screen, beginning of file, end of file, string searching, write to disk, and several others.

A uniquely powerful disk data manipulation tool, Disk-Edit is invaluable for every programmer or computer user.

Company:
SuperSoft, Inc.

Product:
SuperSoft Basic Compiler Version 2.4

Category:
Systems Programming

Computer:	**Media:**
AT&T PC 6300	Diskette

Language:
C

Requirements:
128 KB RAM required

Support:
SuperSoft hotline number: 217-359-2691

Retail Price:
$300

Distributor:

SuperSoft, Inc.
P. O. Box 1628
Champaign, IL 61820
Tel: (800) 762-6629

Description:

The SuperSoft BASIC compiler is fast, produces small code, compiles large programs, and is highly compatible with the *Microsoft* BASIC interpreter. It comes complete with:

- Full 8087 support–making math operations lightning fast
- IEEE floating point–for fast, precise scientific calculations
- BCD math–for exact decimal numbers in business applications
- Fully implemented double precision–increasing the accuracy of math operations
- Precise error messages–codes and subcodes
- Easy interface to C and assembly code
- ROMable code
- Allowance for 32,767 bytes per record
- Allowance for 2 gigabyte random file
- No runtime license fee required

Company:
SuperSoft, Inc.

Product:
SuperSoft FORTRAN Version 2.04 ANSI X3.9-1966 with Extensions

Category:
Systems Programming

Computer: AT&T PC 6300

Media: Diskette

Language:
Assembly code and FORTRAN

Requirements:
128 KB RAM required

Support:
SuperSoft hotline number: 217-359-2691

Retail Price:
$325

Distributor:
SuperSoft, Inc.
P. O. Box 1628
Champaign, IL 61820
Tel: (800) 762-6629

Description:

SuperSoft answers the need for a high quality FORTRAN compiler under *MS*-DOS. Some of the major advantages it offers over other FORTRAN compilers include:

- Extended code and data space under *MS*-DOS–for compiling extremely large programs.
- Optional 8087 support–for faster math operations.
- Full IEEE floating point.
- Full ANSI '66 FORTRAN–plus several useful extensions.
- Double precision and complex numbers.
- Optional RATFOR preprocessor–allowing the use of loop structures and structured programming techniques.
- Capability to produce fast, compact code.
- Runs in only 128 KB RAM.

Company:

TOM Software, Inc.

Product:

***SPEED* I Software Application Development Utility**

Category:

Systems Programming

Computer:	**Media:**
AT&T PC 6300	Diskette

Language:

TOMBASIC

Requirements:

TOMBASIC

Support:

Training and technical support provided by the local licensed consultant

Fees depend on the consultant and the type of service provided

Retail Price:

$800–$3,500 depending on the hardware

Distributor:

TOM Software, Inc.
127 S.W. 156th Ave.
P.O. Box 66596
Seattle, WA 98166
Tel: (206) 246-7022

TOM Software, Inc. is an authorized Value Added Reseller for AT&T Computers.

Description:

Time and money are the major system development concerns of both the data processing professional and the system user. The *SPEED* I system development and database management utility has been saving time and cutting costs at all stages of system development, including design, coding, debugging, documentation, and maintenance since 1978. Some features are:

- Simplifies system design.
- Reduces application development time–some users say by as much as 80 percent.
- Assists even relatively inexperienced programmers to become immediately productive.
- Makes system debugging time very short.
- Generates complete documentation.
- Makes program modification easy.
- Virtually eliminates system maintenance problems.

Company:
TOM Software, Inc.

Product:
TOMBASIC

Category:
Systems Programming

Computer:
AT&T PC 6300

Media:
Diskette

Language:
C

Requirements:
UNIX or *MS*-DOS (depends on model)

Support:
Training and technical support provided by the local licensed consultant
Fees depend on the consultant and the type of service provided

Retail Price:
$800–$3,500 depending on the hardware

Distributor:
TOM Software, Inc.
127 S.W. 156th Ave.
P.O. Box 66596
Seattle, WA 98166
Tel: (206) 246-7022

TOM Software, Inc. is an authorized Value Added Reseller for AT&T Computers.

Description:

TOMBASIC is an interpretive BASIC language that operates on several computers that support the *UNIX* operating system or a C compiler. *TOMBASIC* is a subset of BASIC-2, developed by Wang Laboratories, Inc. With few exceptions, programs written in BASIC-2 can also run under *TOMBASIC*. Programs written in *TOMBASIC* are completely portable across all computers that run *TOMBASIC*. *TOMBASIC* is "customized" for each computer's operating system implementation. Once installed, *TOMBASIC* looks and operates the same on all machines. Applications written in *TOMBASIC* can be transferred from one installation to another without modification, regardless of the original computer implementation.

Company:
Addison-Wesley Publishing Company, Inc.

Product:
MicroTEX

Category:
Word Processors

Computer:	**Media:**
AT&T PC 6300	Diskette

Language:
C

Requirements:
512 KB RAM
1.5 MB hard disk spaces for some fonts
4 MB for all fonts

Support:
Limited 90-day warranty

Retail Price:
$495

Distributor:
Addison-Wesley Publishing Company, Inc.
Jacob Way
Reading, MA 01867
Tel: (617) 944-3700

Description:

MicroTEX is a full microcomputer implementation of Donald Knuth's computer typesetting system, *TEX*, developed by David Fuchs for most *MS*-DOS machines. It offers writers in academic, professional, and business environments the opportunity to produce technical text, in an attractive form, on a personal computer. *MicroTEX* is particularly valuable where the document to be produced contains extensive mathematics, or where the user is concerned about typographical quality.

MicroTEX contains the power of *TEX* implementations on larger machines. Both input and output files from *MicroTEX* are fully compatible with all implementations of the most current versions of *TEX* on mainframe and minicomputers. The software includes plain *TEX* macros and plain *TEX* fonts. The complete package also contains a driver for several popular dot matrix printers and a copy of Knuth's *TEX* user's manual, The TEXbook. Since *MicroTEX* is compatible with other *TEX* systems, output on laser printers and phototypesetters is also possible.

MicroTEX includes the following features:

- Justification
- Hyphenation
- Pagination
- Kerning
- Ligatures
- Accents
- Tabular alignment
- Running heads
- Numbering and placement of footnotes
- Floating figure insertions Widow control
- Index and table of contents preparation

MicroTEX's state-of-the-art technical typesetting capabilities enable writers to incorporate mathematical expressions like these into their text:

$$\mathbf{S}^{-1}\mathbf{TS} = \mathbf{dg}(\omega_1, \ldots, \omega_n) = \mathbf{\Lambda}, \sum_{i=1}^{\infty} \frac{1}{2^i} = 1, \quad \underbrace{\{\overbrace{a, \ldots, a}^{k\ a\text{'s}}, \overbrace{b, \ldots, b}^{l\ b\text{'s}}\}}_{k+1 \text{ elements}}, \quad \sqrt{1+\sqrt{1+\sqrt{1+x}}},$$

(Continued on next page)

Description: ***(Continued)***

David Fuchs has worked with Donald Knuth on the *TEX* project at Stanford University for more than six years. Addison-Wesley is the publisher of several books related to *TEX*, including The TEXbook and TEX: The Program, by Knuth, and the forthcoming LATEX: A Document Preparation System, by Leslie Lamport. Other books are planned, as well as software to provide *MicroTEX* users with added capabilities.

Company:
AT&T and MicroPro International Corp.

Product:
WordStar* 2000

Category:
Word Processors

Computer: AT&T PC 6300 | **Media:** Diskette

Computer:
AT&T PC 6300

Media:
Diskette

Language:
MicroPro Proprietary Language

Requirements:
256 KB RAM

Support:
This product is fully supported by AT&T Information Systems and carries a 90-day warranty on the media. Remote nationwide customer service hotline is provided Monday through Friday between the hours of 8:00 a.m. and 5:00 p.m. local time. Installation, additional hotline coverage, and extended maintenance agreements are also available.

Retail Price:
$495

Distributor:
AT&T (800) 247-1212
or call your local AT&T authorized dealer or Account Executive.

***This product has been certified by AT&T.**

Description:

WordStar 2000 redefines state-of-the-art by offering advanced word processing technology with a human touch. The user can experience the power of a dedicated word processor with a product that is simple to learn and use.

WordStar 2000 features mnemonic commands, programmable function keys, "undo," on-screen tutorials and help, windows, ready-made formats, key glossary, and math. In addition, the package includes on-screen boldfacing and underlining, typewriter mode proportional spacing, footnotes, spelling correction, and mail merging.

Company:
AT&T and MicroPro International Corp.

Product:
WordStar* Professional

Category:
Word Processors

Computer:	**Media:**
AT&T PC 6300	Diskette

Language:
Assembler

Requirements:
192 KB RAM for *CorrectStar*

Support:
This product is fully supported by AT&T Information Systems and carries a 90-day warranty on the media. Remote nationwide customer service hotline is provided Monday through Friday between the hours of 8:00 a.m. and 5:00 p.m. local time. Installation, additional hotline coverage, and extended maintenance agreements are also available.

Retail Price:
$495

Distributor:
AT&T (800) 247-1212
or call your local AT&T authorized dealer or Account Executive.

***This product has been certified by AT&T.**

Description:

WordStar Professional is a full-featured word processing package.

WordStar Professional Key Features:

WordStar Professional offers a wide range of word processing capabilities–from creating, editing, and proof reading documents to merging data and producing tables of contents and indexes. *WordStar* Professional includes these powerful, integrated applications:

- *Wordstar*, the world's best-selling word processing program for microcomputers.
- *WordStar* Tutor, the on-disk tutorial that helps you master *WordStar* in eight quick, entertaining lessons.
- *CorrectStar*, the fastest, most accurate spelling corrector for personal computers.
- *MailMerge*, the versatile text- and data-merging program for *WordStar*.
- *StarIndex*, for automated production of tables of contents, indexes, and more.

WordStar Key Features:

- Whether you're writing a business report or a novel, *WordStar* has everything you need to edit, insert, delete, and rearrange text.
- Offers simultaneous editing and printing; dynamic page-break display on screen; flexible formatting; automatic search and replace, word wrap, and right-margin justification are shown on-screen.
- Special print effects (boldface, underline, strikeout, subscripts, superscripts) lend a professional look to documents.
- The newest version features a new, easy-to-understand manual; new, user-friendly installation program; color selection for color video displays; and function keys you can define yourself.
- *WordStar* Tutor enables the complete novice to become a proficient *WordStar* user with guided lessons that offer hands-on practice.

CorrectStar Key Features:

- Locates and corrects typos and misspellings in *WordStar* documents–with the touch of a key.

(Continued on next page)

Description: ***(Continued)***

- Based on Houghton-Mifflin's highly respected *American Heritage Dictionary.*
- Deadly accurate, because its 65,000 word dictionary represents 99 percent of today's most frequently used words.
- Automatically loads the 9000 most common words into memory (88 percent of today's most frequently used words), resulting in lightning-fast response.
- Allows users to create a personal dictionary of special terms and names.
- Lets you make a correction with a single key or bypass the word (like a special abbreviation) throughout the document.
- Automatically reforms the paragraphs to keep margins aligned once a correction is made.
- Optional hyphen help feature divides words into proper syllables.
- Can be accessed directly through *WordStar.*

MailMerge Key Features:

- Merges data and form letters for customized mailings.
- Saves time by building new documents from shorter sections of text.
- Creates mailing labels and invoices from data files.
- Enhances the power and versatility of *WordStar.*

StarIndex Key Features:

- Numbers paragraphs, sections and chapters.
- Automatically builds tables of contents and alphabetized indexes for major reports, proposals, and books.
- Offers personalized and conventional format guidelines.

Company:
AT&T and Microsoft Corporation

Product:
Microsoft* Word

Category:
Word Processors

Computer:	**Media:**
AT&T PC 6300	Diskette

Language:
Microsoft proprietary language

Requirements:
256 KB RAM
2 double-sided disk drives

Support:
This product is fully supported by AT&T Information Systems and carries a 90-day warranty on the media. Remote nationwide customer service hotline is provided Monday through Friday between the hours of 8:00 a.m. and 5:00 p.m. local time. Installation, additional hotline coverage, and extended maintenance agreements are also available.

A one-volume User's Manual is provided.

Microsoft Word is very easy to learn. Self instruction is aided by the on-line help facility.

Retail Price:
$375

Distributor:
AT&T (800) 247-1212
or call your local AT&T authorized dealer or Account Executive.

***This product has been certified by AT&T.**

Description:

Microsoft Word is a well-known word processing package which can create, edit, and format all types of documents, from a one-page memo to a book-length manuscript. Whatever the business or type of writing, *Microsoft* Word is applicable.

Microsoft Word allows the user to enter documents in much the same way as on a typewriter, but documents can be revised quickly and easily. Commands for Word are easy to learn and use, so that editing a document is just as easy as creating it. Commands can usually be executed by pressing only one or two keys.

Word has several characteristics that distinguish it from other, less powerful word processing packages:

WINDOWS allows simultaneous viewing and editing of different parts of one or several documents. In addition, text can be moved between windows. Word can have up to eight windows at a time.

GLOSSARY stores often-used text (such as addresses, mathematical equations, or standard parts of a contract) in special files and inserts the files into the document, saving retyping of text.

GALLERY stores models for often-used formats (such as memo, letter, invoice, or report) in style sheets. It also stores specifications for page length and width, margins, line and paragraph spacing, and indentations. In this way, a standard format can be invoked by simply attaching a style sheet to the document. Up to 124 style sheets can be created.

UNDO allows the user to get back to the previous version of the document, reversing the effect of the last editing change. The UNDO works with an unlimited amount of text and can even "undo" itself, so that a user isn't stuck with a change.

HELP, which is on-line, explains other commands. Word is one of the few packages with a dynamic HELP capability, which suggests the command best suited to the current situation. The user simply presses a key to get the HELP screen.

JUMP and SCROLL commands allow the user to access different parts of the document in two ways. The JUMP command moves to specific location instantly. SCROLLING can be done vertically or horizontally with four cursor movement keys. Horizontal scrolling allows a look at the text that is wider than 80 or 132 columns, up to 255 characters.

Microsoft Word has many applications, such as the usual letter writing memo and report preparation, all in a multiuser environment. Such applications include contracts, corporate phone directories, employee handbooks, time sheets, and customer lists.

Company:
Benchmark/Metasoft, Inc.

Product:
***THE BENCHMARK* Spelling Checker**

Category:
Word Processors

Computer:
AT&T PC 6300

Media:
Diskette

Language:
Assembly

Requirements:
256 KB RAM

Support:
Telephone support (800) 621-1908

Retail Price:
$125

Distributor:
Benchmark/Metasoft, Inc.
6509 W. Frye Rd., Suite 12
Chandler, AZ 85224
Tel: (602) 961-0003

Description:

THE BENCHMARK Spelling Checker was designed to run with and complement *THE BENCHMARK* Word Processor. There is complete compatibility and integration between the two programs. The Spelling Checker maintains menu and directory similarity to all other members of *THE BENCHMARK* family. The user may add or delete words from the 27,000 word main dictionary or create his or her own specialized dictionary. You can queue up to 99 files for spelling check and refer to dictionaries simultaneously. The Spelling Checker is menu-driven.

Company:
Benchmark/Metasoft, Inc.

Product:
***THE BENCHMARK* Word Processor**

Category:
Word Processors

Computer:
AT&T PC 6300

Media:
Diskette

Language:
Assembly

Requirements:
256 KB RAM

Support:
Telephone support (800) 621-1908

Retail Price:
$395

Distributor:
Benchmark/Metasoft, Inc.
6509 W. Frye Rd., Suite 12
Chandler, AZ 85224
Tel: (602) 961-0003

Description:

THE BENCHMARK Word Processor set the standards for performance, ease of use, and functionality in the microcomputer industry. A beginning operator can learn to use *THE BENCHMARK* Word Processor with only a few hours of self-training. It is self-promoting throughout. There are no cumbersome control codes that must be memorized. Commands are in plain English, and they require only logical single keystrokes. Help is available at any point that it is needed. No other word processor can match the variable information fill-in or standard document generation capabilities of this package.

Company:
Bruce & James, Program Publishers, Inc.

Product:
***Wordvision* Writing Tool**

Category:
Word Processors

Computer:	**Media:**
AT&T PC 6300	Diskette

Language:
8086 Macro-assembler

Requirements:
96 KB RAM
1 disk drive

Support:
Third-party telephone support available
One free call, $15/15 minutes for additional calls

Retail Price:
$49.95

Distributor:
Bruce & James, Program Publishers, Inc.
2355 Leavenworth St., Suite 103
San Francisco, CA 94133
Tel: (415) 775-8400

Description:

Wordvision Writing Tool is a powerful, yet easy-to-use word processing program designed primarily for personal writing and editing. Text size is limited by available memory. The cursor moves forward and backward. Erasing and excerpt marking can all be done by character, word, line, sentence, or paragraph. The cursor can also be moved by both "screen" and "printed" pages. The "window" allows simultaneous viewing of two separated portions of text. Page format is set by graphic display. Text format and emphasis appear on screen as they will be printed. Program controls may be customized to the user's preference.

Company:
Chang Labs

Product:
MemoPlan

Category:
Word Processors

Computer:	**Media:**
AT&T PC 6300 6300 PLUS **AT&T PC 6300 PLUS**	Diskette

Language:
C

Requirements:
128 KB RAM
One disk drive

Support:
Toll-free line for dealer and end user support
Nationwide (800) 972-8800
California (800) 831-8080

Retail Price:
$195

Distributor:
Chang Labs
5300 Stevens Creek Blvd.
San Jose, CA 95129
Tel: (408) 246-8020

Description:

MemoPlan is a word processor for memos, letters, reports, and short documents. Allows you to work on two documents simultaneously on a split screen, perhaps one an outline and the other a final document. Lets you scroll each window individually and copy blocks of text from one window to another. Permits you to keep five documents active at the same time, so you can move from one to another with a single keystroke. Lets you display each document on your screen in succession without having to go through a lengthy saving and retrieving process. Protects you from inadvertently deleting something by allowing you to "undelete" (recover) the last text deleted–with a single keystroke. Automatically saves your work thereby protecting you from losing work due to a power failure or by mistakenly shutting off your computer before saving it. Has three menus available as you work. These are arranged according to how frequently you need them. Has additional built-in "Help" descriptions for every command. Supports true proportional spacing between letters and words, thus eliminating unsightly gaps for a more professionally printed document.

Company:
Innovative Software

Product:
The Smart Word Processor 2.0

Category:
Word Processors

Computer:	**Media:**
AT&T PC 6300	Diskette

Language:
C

Requirements:
256 KB RAM
Two floppy or one floppy and hard disk
MS/DOS 2.0 or higher

Support:
Example files and on-screen tutorials
Quick key reference guide
Registered SMART owners
Support hotline
Ongoing updates

Retail Price:
$295

Distributor:
Innovative Software
9300 W. 110 St., Suite 380
Overland Park, KS 66204
Tel: (913) 383-1089

Description:

The Smart Word Processor features accurate on-screen text representation, such as multiple type styles for instant visual feedback; custom definable fonts; "flying reform" for automatic, continual formatting; on-screen page breaks; and graphic character sets for drawing lines or boxes around important information.

It also features multiple windows that let users view or reference different documents simultaneously; a stet ("undo") function that reinstates deleted material; math and decision functions; footnoting capability; and "cut-and-paste" in and between documents. When integrated with The Smart Data Manager and The Smart Spreadsheet with Graphics, text, tables of numbers, graphs and charts all can be included in the same document, even on the same page within a document.

Highlights:

- Unlimited document size capacity
- On-screen calculation and decision-making capabilities
- Multiple documents in memory at once
- On-screen "cut and paste", moving, copying, and other editing within and between documents
- Automatic "flying reform" reformatting of text after editing
- Visible margin and tab markers
- Temporary Margins
- Undelete; "second thought" editing
- Cursor "pointing" for easy text moving
- Search and replace: global, partial, and conditional
- Sort blocks of document alphabetically
- Markers, areas marked with in document for quick reference scrolling and viewing
- User controlled scrolling rates
- Automatic footnoting at end of page or document
- Draw custom design documents with boxes, grids, and lines
- Built-in mail merge facility

(Continued on next page)

Description: ***(Continued)***

- Merging of graphs, spreadsheets and data manager information into documents
- Wraps text around inserted graphs
- Type style (font) designer
- Advanced custom formatting functions
- Custom application development with "Project Processing" and the Smart Programming Language

Specifications:

- "Virtual Memory" paging to disk or RAM disk
- 25 on-screen windows
- Eleven different type styles (fonts) on screen and in output
- Reads and writes Smart and ASCII text file formats
- Converts *WordStar* files to Smart files
- Text Editor; editing of any text file

Company:
Leading Edge Products, Inc.

Product:
***Leading Edge* Word Processing Version 1.3**

Category:
Word Processors

Computer:	**Media:**
AT&T PC 6300	Diskette

Language:
Proprietary

Requirements:
2 floppy disk drives
Monochrome or color monitor
256 KB RAM

Support:
Toll free technical hotline (800) 523-HELP

Retail Price:
$100-$250

Distributor:
Leading Edge Products, Inc.
225 Turnpike St.
Canyon, MA 02021
Tel: (617) 828-8150

Description:

The *Leading Edge* Word Processing Package contains all the features found in most professional word processors plus the following unique features:

- Menu-drive text processing and menu by pass features.
- Easy file handling (drawers, folders).
- Unlimited page and document size, unlimited pages per document, instantaneous Go To Page as well as convenient forward and backward scrolling between pages.
- U.S. and foreign decimal tabs, dot leader tabs, right flush and column center tabs.
- Automatic backup and pagination (orphan and widow).
- Multiple document window capability.
- Glossaries (text and keystroke macro capability).
- Recall overtype, recall delete, archive delete, recall archive delete.
- Reverse indent and end indent.

Features using forward and backward highlighting include cut and paste, search and replace, named cut and named paste and hot print. Additional versions containing merge print and spelling correction are available.

Company:
Lexisoft, Inc.

Product:
***Spellbinder* Version 5.3**

Category:
Word Processors

Computer:	**Media:**
AT&T PC 6300 6300 PLUS **AT&T PC 6300 PLUS**	Diskette

Language:
Assembler

Requirements:
96 KB RAM
1 disk drive (two preferred; hard disk OK)

Support:
Can recommend trainers across country
Support through dealer network
Phone support

Retail Price:
$495, Scientific $295 extra

Distributor:
Lexisoft, Inc.
P.O. Box 1378
Davis, CA 95617
Tel: (916) 758-3630

Description:

Spellbinder is both a full-feature word processing and an office management system. Its basic features are easy to learn, yet it also provides such powerful capabilities as Electric Webster spelling and grammar checkers, automatic hyphenation, footnoting, and forms-handling. *Spellbinder* also interfaces with many database managers, spreadsheets, and accounting software produced by other manufacturers. Other features include on-screen indents for outline creation, footnoting, horizontal scrolling, one-stroke function keys, and extremely flexible print formatting. The integrated print formatter allows bidirectional printing, true proportional spacing, print to and from screen, and two-column printing. Besides forms handling, office management capabilities include mail merge, mail labels, cue sorting, alphanumerical selection and sorting, boilerplating, column manipulations, an on-screen calculator, plus the ability to add features to suit the unique requirements of each user. *Spellbinder Scientific* adds scientific characters and multiline formulas and chemical structures.

Company:
Lifetree Software, Inc.

Product:
***Volkswriter Deluxe* Version 2.0**

Category:
Word Processors

Computer:	**Media:**
AT&T PC 6300 **AT&T PC 6300 PLUS**	Diskette

6300 PLUS

Language:
Pascal

Requirements:
128 KB RAM
Two disk drives
80-column monitor

Support:
Direct from manufacturer at no charge, (408) 373-4904

Retail Price:
$295

Distributor:
Lifetree Software, Inc.
411 Pacific St.
Monterey, CA 93940
Tel: (408) 373-4718

Description:

Volkswriter Deluxe with *TextMerge* is the most complete word processing package available for the AT&T PC 6300 and compatible machines.

Volkswriter Deluxe combines the clear and concise qualities of the original *Volkswriter* with many new features to meet all the needs of the demanding word processing professional.

Volkswriter Deluxe Features:

- *TextMerge* for generating form letters and labels.
- Horizontal scrolling to 250 characters.
- Document size up to 1,000,000 characters (1 MB).
- Underline, boldface, and special effects shown on-screen.
- Multiple fonts and colors.
- Multilingual and scientific character support.
- Chapter end footnotes.
- NotePad.
- True proportional spacing.
- DOS 2.X directory support.
- Cursor movement by character, word, line, screen and page.
- Unlimited block moves, copies, deletes, saves and appends.
- Unlimited column moves, copies, deletes, saves and appends.
- Automatic pagination on-screen.
- Newly revised documentation: a new manual and a quick reference card.
- Recently recompiled for a more compact code that makes the program even faster at loading and operating.
- Enhanced communication support with a new file filter.

Company:
Lifetree Software, Inc.

Product:
***Volkswriter Scientific* Version 1.0**

Category:
Word Processors

Computer:	**Media:**
AT&T PC 6300	Diskette
6300 PLUS **AT&T PC 6300 PLUS**	

Language:
Basic/Assembly

Requirements:
256 KB RAM
PC-DOS 2.0 or higher
Two double-sided disk drives or a hard disk
80-column display
Color graphics adapter

Support:
Direct from manufacturer at no charge, (408) 373-4904

Retail Price:
$495

Distributor:
Lifetree Software, Inc.
411 Pacific St.
Monterey, CA 93940
Tel: (408) 373-4718

Description:

Volkswriter Scientific is an innovative scientific word processor for the AT&T PC 6300 and compatibles. Designed to meet the needs of chemists, physicists, engineers, and others, this program lets the user compose text and create elaborate scientific formulas in which multiple type sizes, symbols, and styles appear on-screen as they will be printed. On-screen tutorials and nine help menus assure that complex technical composition can be done with ease and accuracy. On-screen features include:

- Tutorials and nine help menus.
- Over 400 bit-mapped characters, each made with a maximum of two key strokes, including the Greek alphabet, two sizes of Roman letters, subscript and superscript numerals, and scientific and engineering symbols.
- Boldface, italics, microproportional spacing, and microjustification.
- Up to five text levels per line.

As type sizes, symbols, and styles can be mixed at will, the user can create headlines, bylines, formulas, and character patterns (such as the benzene rings of organic chemistry) without the limitation of fixed pitch horizontal boundaries. Elaborate structural compositions are facilitated by micropositioning control, which allows the position of each character on a line to be adjusted one pixel at a time.

Compatible with any ASCII-formatted word processor, *Volkswriter Scientific* is especially well-suited for use in conjunction with Lifetree's standard word processor, *Volkswriter Deluxe*.

With a desk-top PC, a graphics card, and a simple dot matrix printer, *Volkswriter Scientific* gives you capabilities that formerly required a mainframe and a complicated typesetting program.

Company:
MARC Software International, Inc.

Product:
***WordMARC*—Word Processor**

Category:
Word Processors

Computer: AT&T PC 6300

Media: Diskette

Language:
FORTRAN

Requirements:
256 KB RAM

Support:
On-site training available
Self-teaching guide delivered
"800" hotline available

Retail Price:
$495

Distributor:
MARC Software International, Inc.
260 Sheridan Ave., Suite 200
Palo Alto, CA 94306
Tel: (415) 326-1971

Description:

WordMARC offers the functionality and ease of use of dedicated word processors. There are no codes or commands to memorize. Documents are printed as they are displayed on the screen.

WordMARC word processing gives the user a standardized package across computers, operating systems, and users. *WordMARC* is designed for preparing, editing, and printing complex documents.

Although *WordMARC* provides the power for dedicated word processing, it is still easy for the casual user. Function keys, menus, and prompts make *WordMARC* as suitable for memo and letter preparation as its power makes it suitable for report generation.

WordMARC's powerful formatting capabilities provide instantaneous reformatting and repagination after such editing functions as cut and paste, insert, margin changes, hyphenation, search and replace, and spelling correction. All reformatting occurs in the background without additional user input. This means increased speed and productivity especially when working with long documents. *WordMARC* is particularly suited to environments in which intensive report generation or documentation preparation is necessary.

WordMARC has independent format lines which may be inserted or changed anywhere in the document. The user may have an unlimited number of format lines in each document and any number of format lines per page, all of which are stored with the document.

Movement through *WordMARC* documents is easy with the quick-skip cursor function. The cursor can move forward or reverse by letter, word, space, sentence, screen, page or designated character.

The *WordMARC* system includes a spelling checker accessing four levels of dictionaries, a merging facility for customized correspondence and reports, automatic headers and footers, and integrated, advanced scientific typing including Greek and math characters and 13 levels of super and subscripts.

All menus, prompts, error messages, and standing formats may be customized by the user to provide individual styles and to standardize document generation in a multiuser environment.

For environments in which personal computers are part of the office automation system MARC's communication program, *LinkMARC*, transfers fully compatible *WordMARC* documents between personal computers running *WordMARC*, and *UNIX* System V computers running *WordMARC*.

Company:
Morgan Computing Company, Inc.

Product:
***TED* Version 2.0**

Category:
Word Processors

Computer:	**Media:**
AT&T PC 6300	Diskette
6300 PLUS **AT&T PC 6300 PLUS**	

Language:
Assembler

Requirements:
128 KB RAM
One disk drive
Single-sided

Support:
Technical support for registered users

Retail Price:
$95

Distributor:
Morgan Computing Company, Inc.
P.O. Box 112730
Carrollton, TX 75006
Tel: (214) 245-4763

Description:

TED is a programmer's full-screen text editor that is ultra-fast and powerful (works like TSO/SPF). The application was designed by programmers for programmers, with speed (program and up to 7,000 lines of text are completely RAM resident) and ease of use as primary goals. There are features such as: optional automatic version, date, and time updating; the option to display and print text with line numbers; programmable function keys with powerful macro capabilities; and *EASY REFERENCE*–the ability to instantly refer to text other than the section you are currently editing. *TED* also allows manipulation of lines and blocks of lines (copy, move, delete), file merge, search and replace operations, and more. Requires 128 KB RAM, written in Assembler,

Company:
Oasis Systems

Product:
***Punctuation* + *Style* Version 1.21**

Category:
Word Processors

Computer:	**Media:**
AT&T PC 6300 6300 PLUS **AT&T PC 6300 PLUS**	Diskette

Language:
Assembler

Requirements:
32 KB RAM

Support:
Telephone hotline support offered:
(619) 279-5711

Retail Price:
$125

Distributor:

Oasis Systems
7907 Ostrow St., Suite F
San Diego, CA 92111
Tel: (619) 279-5711

Description:

Punctuation + *Style* finds, marks, and documents over two dozen types of punctuation errors in a text file, including unpaired format commands. Checking for specific errors can be turned off, and all checking can be turned off and on again within a text file. *Punctuation* + *Style* provides a critique of the user's writing, suggesting alternatives for misused or overworked phrases. It also shows where active voice can replace passive voice to add clarity and precision. It works with most *MS*-DOS and CP/M 80 86 compatible word processors.

Company:
Oasis Systems

Product:
***THE WORD PLUS* Version 2.1**

Category:
Word Processors

Computer:	**Media:**
AT&T PC 6300	Diskette

Language:
Assembler

Requirements:
32 KB RAM

Support:
Telephone hotline support offered:
(619) 279-5711

Retail Price:
$150

Distributor:
Oasis Systems
7907 Ostrow St., Suite F
San Diego, CA 92111
Tel: (619) 279-5711

Description:

THE WORD PLUS is a complete spelling check package. Using a 45,000 word dictionary, it allows users to view misspelled words in context, look up correct spellings, make corrections, and add words to the dictionary, all with the press of a button. It hyphenates words automatically and helps users solve and create crosswords, anagrams, and other word puzzles. Word-count and word-frequency functions are also included. This package works with almost any *MS*-DOS and CP/M-80 word processor.

Company:

Office Solutions, Inc.

Product:

***OfficeWriter* Release 3.5**
***OfficeSpeller* Release 3.5**
***OfficeLink/Wang* PC Release 3.5**

Category:

Word Processors

Computer:	**Media:**
AT&T PC 6300	Diskette
6300 PLUS **AT&T PC 6300 PLUS**	

Language:

PASCAL, C

Requirements:

192 KB RAM minimum
256 KB RAM recommended
2 disk drives (one must be DS) or hard disk

Support:

Toll-free telephone support for licensed customers available directly from OSI at (608) 274-5047 or (800) 228-0747.

Centralized training and support program materials available from OSI.

Upgrades to new product releases available directly from OSI for $50.

Warranty provisions as outlined on the Program License Agreement.

Retail Price:

OfficeWriter with
OfficeSpeller $445
OfficeWriter $325
OfficeLink/Wang PC $195
OfficeSpeller $165

Distributor:

Office Solutions, Inc.
2802 Coho St.
Madison, WI 53713
Tel: (608) 274-5047

Description:

OfficeWriter is a powerful word processor for the AT&T PC 6300 that is extremely easy to learn and use. When *OfficeWriter* was designed, a great deal of attention was paid to the details of keyboard layout and user prompting, making it one of the easiest to learn and most natural to use word processors on the market.

A complete selection of sophisticated editing features is included with *OfficeWriter*. For example, a powerful document merge (mail merge) capability exists, as well as database and spreadsheet interfaces. Other features include footnoting and endnoting, proportional spacing, right justification, document to ASCII conversion, document to RFTDCA format conversion, *MultiMate* document to *OfficeWriter* document conversion, horizontal scrolling, decimal tabbing, column move/copy, automatic pagination, document libraries, print spooling, boilerplating, scientific and foreign language support, multiple column print, selectable colors and soft hyphenation. Over 40 different printers as well as cut sheet feeders are supported. Additional custom printer support is available directly from OSI.

Features include automatic screen formatting, so the user needs to reformat the text. Very little memorization is needed when learning *OfficeWriter*, because most functions are initiated by pressing a single labeled key. Twenty of *OfficeWriter* 's functions are labeled on the molded plastic function key.

Advanced features use the "Alt" key, and all Alt key sequences are logically designed and labeled on the Keyboard Reference Ruler. There are no "Ctrl" or "Esc" key sequences in *OfficeWriter* that require extensive memorization on the part of the user. The on-screen tutorial makes customers productive with *OfficeWriter* in 30 minutes.

The *OfficeSpeller* Module is a fully integrated spelling corrector based on the Proximity/Merriam-Webster Linibase. The dictionary contains over 80,000 words and allows the user to check and correct the spelling of a single word or the entire document without leaving the edit session. *OfficeSpeller* checks for phonetic and typographical misspellings of individual words.

OfficeSpeller also allows the user to create an additional custom dictionary of familiar names, abbreviations, acronyms and other user-specific terminology that is limited in size only by available disk space. The user later add, edit and delete words contained in the custom dictionary.

OfficeSpeller will give the user suggested phonetic alternatives for misspelled words when requested, allow

(Continued on next page)

Description: ***(Continued)***

for typing in the correct spelling of the word or bypassing the word altogether and search for the next incorrect spelling.

At a time when compatibility between systems in the corporate environment becomes critical, Office Solutions offers *OfficeLink*/DCA. This new module allows document transfer between the AT&T PC 6300 using *OfficeWriter* and larger *IBM* systems using *IBM*'s strategic document format called DCA (Document Content Architecture). *OfficeLink*/DCA is the third in a series of products which allows *OfficeWriter* documents to be easily transferred to and from other popular dedicated word processing systems. This announcement is complemented by the expectation of *IBM*'s related software products which facilities document transfer between the PC 6300 and other systems. *OfficeLink*/DCA is designed to work with these new products and take advantage of the added functionality.

OfficeLink/DCA is included with *OfficeWriter* Release 3.5. *OfficeWriter* requires at least 192 KB of memory. Documents larger than approximately sixteen pages will require 256 K of memory.

OfficeLink/DCA which can be accessed via an *OfficeWriter* menu item, converts *OfficeWriter* documents into *IBM*'s Revisable Form Text (RFT). The resulting documents can them be transferred to a mainframe running *IBM*'s DISOSS (Distributed Office Support System), which features document storage, retrieval and electronic mail capabilities. Document transfer can be facilitated using *IBM*'s Personal Services/PC, Personal Services/370, Personal Services/36, or other DIA (Document Interchange Architecture) communications methods. Once in DISOSS, documents can subsequently be down-loaded into a number of *IBM* dedicated word processors, including the Displaywriter, 5520, 8100, or another *IBM* PC running *OfficeWriter*, Displaywriter or any other DCA compatible software. *OfficeLink*/DCA is included free of charge when the user purchases *OfficeWriter* Release 3.5.

The *OfficeLink*/*Wang* PC option allows the user to transfer documents between an AT&T PC 6300 using *OfficeWriter* and a *Wang* PC. Documents passed between the two systems maintain complete document integrity and are fully revisable. Using an *OfficeWriter* menu item, the user can convert *OfficeWriter* or *Wang* PC documents in either direction. Once the user has converted the document, the transfer from one machine to the other is done by using a diskette. This is possible due to the fact that the 5-1/4" diskettes can be read by either computer.

(Continued on next page)

Description: ***(Continued)***

OfficeLink/Wang PC can be purchased with *OfficeWriter* Release 3.0, or can be purchased separately at a later time. *OfficeWriter* requires 192 KB of memory.

The *Wang* PC must have at least 256 KB RAM, and be capable of running *Wang* Word Processing Release 2.0. If the user wishes to transfer documents between the *Wang* PC and the *Wang* OIS or VS system, the user will also need the *Wang* 928 Emulation Board and the *Wang* Document Filing Utilities. When doing this, the *Wang* PC diskette must have been formatted on the *Wang* PC. Failure to do so will result in the message "Cannot Determine Type" when using the Document Filing Utilities. A copy of *OfficeLink/Wang* PC must be purchased for every copy of *OfficeWriter* using this feature.

Company:
Quadratron Systems, Inc.

Product:
Q-ONE

Category:
Word Processors

Computer:
AT&T PC 6300

Media:
Diskette

Language:
C

Requirements:
Hard disk

Support:
Training and hotline support provided by Essex Office Systems.

Retail Price:
$495

Distributor:

Essex Office Systems
333 North Fairfax St.
Alexandria, VA 22341
Tel: (703) 549-9240
Tel: (818) 789-8588

Description:

Q-ONE is a, menu-driven word processor that contains all the functionality of a dedicated word processor at a fraction of the cost. Special features include windowing, mail merge, list processing, multicolumn text, footnoting, internal math, automatic numbering, outlining, and a 90,000 word spelling dictionary that suggests alternate spellings, and a *Wang* to *Q-ONE* conversion utility.

Q-ONE is ideal for both word processing professionals and unsophisticated executives. Each user can set their own skill level, thereby establishing the amount of menu help they need while creating or editing a document.

Q-ONE also provides shortcut commands that allow the sophisticated user to bypass menus and perform operations more quickly and efficiently.

Company:
Samna Corporation

Product:
Samna Word III

Category:
Word Processors

Computer:
AT&T PC 6300

Media:
Diskette

Language:
C, Assembler

Requirements:
DOS 2.0 or 2.1
312 KB RAM required for PCs and compatibles using DOS 3.0 or higher

Support:
Extended Service Contracts are available
Samna has eight support hotline numbers
Corporate training programs are available upon request

Retail Price:
$550

Distributor:
Samna Corporation
32 Cherry Lane
Floral Park, NY 11001
Tel: (516) 775-2800

Description:

Samna Word III is a full function word processing software package for the AT&T PC 6300. Word III features many enhancements beyond basic word processing, including faster operating speed, support for 11 different keyboards, selectable output to any desired printer port, and an enhanced document directory. The package also includes support for *MS*-DOS, "Hot Key" support, soft hyphenation, enhanced footnoting default pages, Samna/ASCII translation, and proportional spacing and justification to support the *Hewlett-Packard* LaserJet printer. Word III includes all the capabilities of Word II and Word I, such as *MailMerge*, Zoom, Fold, and math functions.

Company:
Sorcim/IUS

Product:
SuperWriter*

Category:
Word Processors

Computer:
AT&T PC 6300

Media:
Diskette

Language:
Sorcim/IUS Proprietary Language

Requirements:
Memory size 48 KB RAM
Over 40 printers supported

Support:
This product is supported by Sorcim/IUS and carries a 90-day media warranty. Sorcim/IUS can be reached at (404) 451-7216.

Retail Price:
$295

Distributor:
AT&T (800) 247-1212
or call your local AT&T authorized dealer or Account Executive.

***This product has been certified by AT&T**

Description:

SuperWriter is a full function word processing system with an integrated spelling checker.

Highlights:

- Menu-driven commands
- On-Screen help
- Document history summaries
- 10 Minutes to SuperWriter tutorial
- 20,000 word spelling checker
- Interface to *SuperCalc*3
- Integrated Mail Merge

Features:

- Automatic centering
- Automatic underlining
- Move, copy or delete blocks of text
- Proportional spacing
- Bold face print
- Super-/subscripts
- Variable pitch
- Automatic page numbering
- Headers and footers
- Form letter generation
- Justification: flush right, flush left or both
- Move by character, word or paragraph

Company:
TOM Software, Inc.

Product:
***D.A.T.A.* 3500 Word Processing System**

Category:
Word Processors

Computer:
AT&T PC 6300

Media:
Diskette

Language:
TOMBASIC

Requirements:
TOMBASIC

Support:
Training and technical support provided by the local licensed consultant.
Fees depend on the consultant and the type of service provided.

Retail Price:
$800–$3,500 depending on the hardware

Distributor:
TOM Software, Inc.
127 S.W. 156th Ave.
P.O. Box 66596
Seattle, WA 98166
Tel: (206) 246-7022

TOM Software, Inc. is an authorized Value Added Reseller for AT&T Computers.

Description:

D.A.T.A. 3500 brings word processing capabilities to the same computer that operates accounting, scientific, and engineering applications. It interfaces with TOM business systems, using data from any accounting file to produce all types of documents–from short memos, letters and contracts to specifications and manuals containing hundreds of pages. *D.A.T.A.* 3500 can stand on its own as a sophisticated word processor. The system is easy to use–can initiate functions using a single keystroke, detailed operator prompts, and error messages to guide; the text appears on the screen as it is printed out; and the built-in dictionary checks spelling and hyphenation. *D.A.T.A.* 3500 is complete–it provides all the features of a dedicated word processor.

Company:
Triad Computing, Inc.

Product:
***T3* Scientific Word Processing System**

Category:
Word Processors

Computer:
AT&T PC 6300
6300 PLUS **AT&T PC 6300 PLUS**

Media:
Diskette

Language:
MS PASCAL

Requirements:
512 KB RAM
Color monitor/monochrome monitor
Color/graphics monitor adapter or graphics card

Support:
Interrupt
Training sessions can be arranged

Retail Price:
$595

Distributor:
Triad Computing, Inc.
1190 B Foster Rd.
Las Cruces, NM 88001
Tel: (505) 522-4600
(800) 874-2383

Description:

The *T3* Scientific Word Processing System was designed by mathematicians for other mathematicians, scientists, and their support staffs. It allows the use and definition of many fonts and accepts superscripts, subscripts, and complex expressions in a simple and straightforward manner.

Subscripts and superscripts appear on the screen in correct half-line positions. Up to 12 levels of subscripts and 12 levels of superscripts allow for easy typing of complex expressions, matrices, etc. as individual units. For example, when a tab is inserted before a matrix, the entire matrix moves as a unit.

There is no limit to the number of fonts allowed in a system, and up to eight fonts (128 characters each) can be used in a document. The user can add other fonts or modify existing ones using the built-in font editors.

To use these fonts, the user builds objects called keyboards. A keyboard is built by assigning any characters from any fonts to the keys of the PC keyboard. Keyboards supplied with the system include standard, mathematics, italics, scripts, and chemistry. Sequences of keystrokes can be saved and recalled to simplify entering of complex expressions such as integrals, summation signs, and benzene rings.

The user controls the operation of *T3* with menus and forms. Powerful operations for cursor movement and selection make the use of these forms and menus easy.

APPENDIX
HARDWARE ADJUNCTS

Company:
AT&T and LOGITECH, Inc.

Product:
MOUSE 6300 with Custom Software*

Computer:
AT&T PC 6300

Media:
Diskette

Language:
Modula-2

Requirements:
256 KB RAM for mouse driver, Setmouse, Draw/Writer
128 KB RAM for mouse driver alone
AT&T 473 printer and compatibles

Support:
This product is fully supported by AT&T Information Systems and carries a 90-day warranty on the media. Remost nationwide customer service hotline is provided Monday through Friday between the hours of 8:00 a.m. and 5:00 p.m. local time. Installation, additional hotline coverage, and extended maintenance agreements are also available.

MOUSE 6300 is supported through the AT&T Services Group. The hotline number is 1-(800) 247-1212.

Retail Price:
$150

Distributor:
AT&T (800) 247-1212 or call your local AT&T authorized dealer or Account Executive.

***This product has been certified by AT&T.**

Description:

MOUSE 6300 is an opto-mechanical mouse with a keyboard interface designed for use with the AT&T PC 6300. MOUSE 6300 is ideal for graphics, and both mousebased and keyboard based application software. A Mouse Diskette, standard with every unit, contains the following programs: "Mouse," a Microsoft compatible driver, "Setmouse," an easy to use menu system, and "Draw/Writer," a text and graphics editor. Through Setmouse the user can create and save a specific mouse setting for each of the application programs, or can use the standard default setting. Draw/Writer is ideal for creating memos, charts and simple schematics that combine text and graphics.

Company:

MetraByte Corporation

Product:

50,000 S/S Data Acquisition and Control Board DASH16

Computer:	**Media:**
AT&T PC 6300	Diskette

Language:

BASIC, ASSEMBLER, FORTRAN, PASCAL, C The source code to the ASSEMBLY language driver is available for 25,00 so the PC 6300 user may adapt the software to any language that supports a CALL.

Requirements:

128 KB RAM
1 floppy disk

Support:

Telephone support direct from factory

Retail Price:

$945

Distributor:

MetraByte Corporation
254 Tosca Drive
Stoughton, MA 02072
Tel: (617) 344-1990

Description:

DASH16 plug-in board for the PC 6300 provides sixteen channels of of Analog to Digital and two channels of Digital to Analog conversion, both at 12 bits of resolution. A counter timer and eight lines of digital input/output complete the system to allow real monitoring and control of Laboratory and Industrial processes. On-board DMA hardware and software drivers allow transfer of converted data directly into memory and up to 50,000 samples per second. Switch selectable gains allow the direct connection of low level sensors.

A complete SOFTWARE LIBRARY is included with the board. An easy-to-use BASIC CALL makes simple the task of acquiring data from the sensors. Programs for calibration and test, graphing, data logging, and linearization support all on-board functions. Source code is included on the disk so the PC 6300 user may customize the software. The DASH16 is supported by other commercially available software packages for FFT analysis and laboratory control.

Applications include:

- Voltage and current measurement
- Voltage and current control
- Sense detection and control switches
- FFT and audio applications
- Control laboratory equipment and log experimental data
- Build product test stations and log quality parameters
- Control industrial processes

Company:
MetraByte Corporation

Product:
Data Acquisition and Control Board DASCON1

Computer:
AT&T PC 6300

Media:
Diskette

Language:
BASIC and ASSEMBLER

Requirements:
128 KB RAM
1 floppy disk

Support:
Telephone support direct from factory

Retail Price:
$495

Distributor:
MetraByte Corporation
254 Tosca Drive
Stoughton, MA 02072
Tel: (617) 344-1990

Description:

DASCON1 plug-in board for the PC 6300 provides 4 channels of integrating dual slope Analog to Digital (30 Samples/Sec) and two channels of Digital to Analog conversion, both at 12 bits of resolution. A real time clock with battery backup and 12 lines of digital input/output complete the system to allow monitoring and control of Laboratory and Industrial processes. On-board instrumentation amplifiers and switch selectable gains allow the direct connection of sensors such as Resistive Temperature Devices and Strain Gauges. External screw terminal solid state I/0 and electromechanical relay boards are available for the DASCON1.

A complete SOFTWARE LIBRARY is included with the board. An easy-to-use BASIC CALL simplifies the task of acquiring data from the sensors. Programs for calibration and test, graphing, data logging, and linearization support all on-board functions. Source code is included on the disk so the PC 6300 user may customize the software.

Applications include:

- Voltage and current measurement
- Voltage and current control
- Sense and control switches
- Sense temperature
- Control laboratory equipment and log experimental data
- Build product test stations and log quality parameters
- Control industrial processes

Company:
MetraByte Corporation

Product:
Data Acquisition and Control Board DASH8

Computer:
AT&T PC 6300

Media:
Diskette

Language:
BASIC and ASSEMBLER

Requirements:
128 KB RAM
1 floppy disk

Support:
Telephone support direct from factory

Retail Price:
$395

Distributor:
MetraByte Corporation
254 Tosca Drive
Stoughton, MA 02072
Tel: (617) 344-1990

Description:

DASH8 plug-in board for the PC 6300 provides eight channels of of Analog to Digital conversion at 12 bits of resolution. Three 16 bit counter timers and seven lines of digital input/output complete the system to allow monitoring and control of Laboratory and Industrial processes. Expansion boards allow up to 128 channels of differential input or 112 thermocouples with cold junction compensation and open thermocouple detect. Switch selectable gains on the expansion board allow the direct connection of low level sensors, strain gauges, and others.

A complete SOFTWARE LIBRARY is included with the board. An easy-to-use BASIC CALL makes simple the task of acquiring data from the sensors. Programs for calibration and test, graphing, data logging, and linearization support all on-board functions. Source code is included on the disk so the PC 6300 user may customize the software. The DASH8 is supported by other commercially available software packages for analysis and control. An interrupt driven mode allows up to 4,000 samples/second with the DASH8.

Applications include:

- Voltage and current measurement
- Sense and control switches
- Sense temperature
- Log experimental data
- Build product test stations and log quality parameters
- Monitor industrial processes

Company:

MetraByte Corporation

Product:

IEEE-488 interface bus control Board IE-488

Computer:
AT&T PC 6300

Media:
Diskette

Language:

BASIC and ASSEMBLER FORTRAN, PASCAL, C, TURBO PASCAL

Requirements:
128 KB RAM
1 floppy disk

Support:
Telephone support direct from factory

Retail Price:
$275

Distributor:

MetraByte Corporation
254 Tosca Drive
Stoughton, MA 02072
Tel: (617) 344-1990

Description:

The IE-488 interface board for the PC 6300 converts the PC 6300 into a complete IEEE-488 bus controller. The system will handle up to 14 other talker/listener devices, any one of which may also be transferred to or from. The IE-488 interpreter includes a group of subroutines which may be used to condition data before the data transfer when using assembly language subroutines. Programmable Interrupt, DMA and normal transfer modes allow data transfer at up to 450K bytes/second.

A complete SOFTWARE LIBRARY is included with the board. An easy-to-use BASIC CALL makes simple the task of controlling the IEEE-488 bus. The board and software handle all of the system timing for TALKING and LISTING and CONTROLLING the IEEE-488/GBIB/HPIB and complies 100% with the IEEE-488 Standard of November 1978.

Applications include:

- Laboratory automation
- Automated manufacturing and test
- Interface to plotters and printers
- Instrumentation interface

Company:
Microsoft Corporation

Product:
***Microsoft* Mouse**

Computer: AT&T PC 6300

Media: Diskette

Language:
Assembler for Mouse driver

Requirements:
Microsoft Mouse (bus version), 64 KB RAM, DOS, one disk drive
Microsoft Mouse (serial version), 64 KB RAM, DOS, one disk drive, RS-232C serial port

Support:
90-day warranty for both mouse hardware and software
Customer hotline for registered owner of product

Retail Price:
Bus Mouse—$175
Serial Mouse—$195

Distributor:
Microsoft Corporation
10700 Northup Way
Box 97200
Bellevue, WA 98009
Tel: (206) 828-0180

Description:

The *Microsoft* Mouse is a hand-held editing and pointing device. It provides a faster, more natural way of moving around the screen than using direction keys. Just slide the mouse around on a hard surface and the cursor makes corresponding moves on the screen.

Microsoft Mouse is designed for the user to take full advantage of next-generation, graphics-oriented software. The mouse system provides everything needed to get started; the mouse, computer interface, a practice application and programs can be used right away.

Microsoft Mouse Menu is a program that allows the user to use the mouse with applications such as *Microsoft Multiplan*, *Microsoft* Project or *WordStar*. The user may also use it to create menus for editing and formatting existing application programs.

Microsoft Notepad, a screen-oriented text editor, offers the capability to edit any document that requires a straightforward format.

Writing anything becomes easier when *Microsoft* Mouse teams up with *Microsoft* Word. With the mouse, selecting commands or editing text is a simple matter of pointing and pushing a button.

Company Index

Product Index

Category Index

Communications

Database Management Systems

Education/Training

General Business Applications

Graphics

Industry/Vertical

Integrated

Spreadsheets

Systems Programming

Word Processors

Hardware Adjuncts

SOFTWARE PRODUCT DATA SHEET

☐ New Form
☐ Updated Information

COMPANY: ______________________________

Address: ______________________________

____

Phone: (   ) ______________________________

Area Code

PRODUCT: ______________________________

DESCRIPTION: (500 words or less, attach separate sheet.)

LANGUAGE: ______________________________

REQUIREMENTS (i.e. Memory Size, Compilers, Peripherals, etc.):

____

SUPPORT (i.e. Warranty, Training, Hot Line Number, etc.):

____

____

COMPUTER: ______________ **UNIX SYSTEM V RELEASE NO.** (if applicable): ______________

MEDIA (i.e. Diskette, 9-track tape, etc.): ______________________________

AVAILABILITY (Now? When?): ______________ **RETAIL PRICE:** ______________

DISTRIBUTOR: ______________________________

Address: ______________________________

____

Phone: (   ) ______________________________

Area Code

COMPANY/PRODUCT TRADEMARK SPECIFICATIONS (if not applicable, specify "None Required"):
NOTE: It is important that spelling, capitalization, and trademark designation be accurate.

____

____

SIGNATURE: ______________________________

NAME/TITLE (Please print): ______________________________

DATE: ______________

For submission of Software mail to:

Vendor Involvement Program
AT&T Information Systems, Inc.
One Speedwell Avenue
Room 744W
Morristown, NJ 07960

SOFTWARE PRODUCT DATA SHEET

☐ New Form
☐ Updated Information

COMPANY: ______________________________

Address: ______________________________

____

Phone: (   ) ______________________________

Area Code

PRODUCT: ______________________________

DESCRIPTION: (500 words or less, attach separate sheet.)

LANGUAGE: ______________________________

REQUIREMENTS (i.e. Memory Size, Compilers, Peripherals, etc.):

____

SUPPORT (i.e. Warranty, Training, Hot Line Number, etc.):

____

____

COMPUTER: ______________ **UNIX SYSTEM V RELEASE NO.** (if applicable): ______________

MEDIA (i.e. Diskette, 9-track tape, etc.): ______________________________

AVAILABILITY (Now? When?): ______________ **RETAIL PRICE:** ______________

DISTRIBUTOR: ______________________________

Address: ______________________________

____

Phone: (   ) ______________________________

Area Code

COMPANY/PRODUCT TRADEMARK SPECIFICATIONS (if not applicable, specify "None Required"):
NOTE: It is important that spelling, capitalization, and trademark designation be accurate.

____

____

SIGNATURE: ______________________________

NAME/TITLE (Please print): ______________________________

DATE: ______________

For submission of Software mail to:

Vendor Involvement Program
AT&T Information Systems, Inc.
One Speedwell Avenue
Room 744W
Morristown, NJ 07960